Desktop Publishing with WordPerfect® 5.1

Dennis P. Curtin

Prentice Hall
Englewood Cliffs, New Jersey 07632

Library of Congress Cataloguing-in-Publication Data

Curtin, Dennis P.
    Desktop publishing with WordPerfect 5.1 / Dennis P. Curtin.
        p.   cm.
    Includes bibliographical references (p.   ) and index.
    ISBN 0-13-204751-9 (3 1/2" disk : pbk.).—ISBN 0-13-204710-1 (5 1/4" disk : pbk.)
    1. Desktop publishing—Computer programs. 2. WordPerfect (Computer program) I. Title.
Z286.D47C87 1992
686.2' 2544536—dc20

91-31360
CIP

WordPerfect® is a registered trademark of WordPerfect Corporation.

Acquisition editor: Liz Kendall
Editorial/production supervision: Nancy Benjamin
Copy editor: Beth Morel
Designer and chapter-opening illustrator: Janis Owens
Cover designer: Thomas Nery
Cover art: Type collage by Sheldon Rose
Interior art production: Suzanne Dougherty
Desktop publishing: Cathleen Morin
Prepress buyer: Ilene Levy
Manufacturing buyer: Ed O'Dougherty
Supplements editor: Lisamarie Brassini
Editorial assistant: Jane Baumann

Printed in the United States of America
10 9 8 7 6 5 4 3 2 1

ISBN 0-13-204751-9 {3 1/2" DISK}
ISBN 0-13-204710-1 {5 1/4" DISK}

Prentice-Hall International (UK) Limited, *London*
Prentice-Hall of Australia Pty. Limited, *Sydney*
Prentice-Hall Canada Inc., *Toronto*
Prentice-Hall Hispanoamericana, S.A., *Mexico*
Prentice-Hall of India Private Limited, *New Delhi*
Prentice-Hall of Japan, Inc., *Tokyo*
Simon & Schuster Asia Pte. Ltd., *Singapore*
Editora Prentice-Hall do Brasil, Ltda., *Rio de Janeiro*

CONTENTS

CONTENTS

In the early days of computing, word processing was a two-step process. To enter and edit text, users loaded a text editing program. When the document was finished, they then loaded a text formatting program to set margins, boldface key words, and so on. Only later were editing and formatting functions merged into the single-step programs we use today.

Until recently, these one-step word processing programs were much better at editing documents than they were at formatting them. As a result of expanded formatting possibilities created by the introduction of the laser printer, a new category of programs, called desktop publishing programs, was introduced. The first of these new programs was PageMaker®, followed in short order first by Ventura® Publisher and then by many others. To use these programs, you must again enter and edit your document in one step on a word processing program and then in a second step retrieve it with the desktop publishing program for formatting. If the document needs extensive revision, it's usually much easier to do with your word processing program because the editing features of desktop publishing programs are so limited (although they are improving).

Recently, some word processing programs such as WordPerfect have begun to merge the two steps by incorporating the most frequently used desktop publishing features. This makes it possible for you to create, edit, format, and lay out sophisticated documents using your word processing program only. Now, you don't have to learn two entirely different programs to desktop publish documents.

The desktop publishing features that have been added to WordPerfect and other word processing programs include advanced text-handling and graphics-handling features. For example:

- You can choose from a wide selection of type (called fonts).
- You can precisely control character and line spacing.
- You can print documents in multiple columns.
- You can add horizontal or vertical rules of varying widths, place boxes around graphics or paragraphs, or use shades of gray to highlight different elements.
- You can print graphics, such as line drawings and photographs, side by side with text.
- You can automatically generate tables of contents, indexes, and other such lists.
- You can save formats and add them to a menu so you can quickly apply them to other elements in a document.

Knowledge of these features and how to use them does not a desktop publisher make. The goal of desktop publishing is to produce documents that get results. Just as in traditional publishing, good taste and a sense of design make documents more inviting and readable. To improve the design of your documents, you need to read further and, above all, experiment. Programs such as WordPerfect make it easy to change formats and immediately see the results in printouts. To improve your documents, take advantage of this ability to explore the world of graphic design.

BACKGROUND REQUIRED

This text is not for beginners, because it focuses on WordPerfect's desktop publishing features. To make this emphasis possible, the book assumes that you know basic word processing procedures, such as entering, editing, saving, and printing. If you need help recalling any of WordPerfect's basic word processing procedures, you can refer to the *WordPerfect 5.1 Quick Reference Guide* by the author of this text. This concise book guides you step by step through all of WordPerfect's procedures (including many of those discussed in this text).

CONCEPTS AND PROCEDURES

This text is organized into thirteen chapters. Each chapter is organized into topics that focus on a single area of desktop publishing. Each topic discusses both concepts and procedures.

Desktop Publishing Concepts

The concepts of desktop publishing are emphasized because they provide the background for procedures, not only for WordPerfect but for all desktop publishing programs. This text also emphasizes publishing concepts. Understanding the terms and procedures used in the publishing and printing fields is essential if you are to communicate with other professionals. Also, when you understand concepts, procedures are easier to learn because they fit into a framework. Understanding concepts also makes it much easier to transfer your understanding to other programs and other computers.

WordPerfect Procedures

Procedures are the specific skills you have to acquire to use a program. Throughout this text, all procedures are first discussed in detail and then summarized step by step in KEY/Strokes boxes. You can refer to these boxes when working on the activities in this text or when working on your own documents. Their format makes it easy to find the step-by-step procedures when you need them.

HANDS-ON ACTIVITIES

Concepts and procedures tell you why to do something and how to do it, but to fully understand desktop publishing, you have to put concepts and procedures to work at the keyboard. To provide this experience, over 130 tutorials, exercises, and projects have been integrated throughout this text.

Tutorials

A hands-on tutorial opens each topic. The purpose of these tutorials is to demonstrate each procedure, so you gain experience in performing it and you can see the impact that it can have on your documents. After you complete each tutorial, the discussion of concepts and procedures that follows is easier to understand because you already have an idea of how the procedure works in practice.

Exercises

Exercises at the end of each topic provide additional opportunities to practice and gain experience with the concepts and procedures discussed in the topic. For step-by-step instructions, you are referred to the appropriate KEY/Strokes boxes, giving you experience in looking up the information you need. These exercises have been selected so they are relevant to desktop publishing and should prove challenging.

Projects

Projects at the end of each chapter introduce problem-solving applications. Background material is provided for each project, but no specific procedures are given. To complete the projects, you must have already mastered the appropriate topics. One project, a newsletter, appears in many chapters, evolving into an illustrated, four-page document by the end of Chapter 10. This project allows you to take a single document through each of the most frequently used desktop publishing steps.

TIPS

Tips in most topics suggest shortcuts and discuss advanced procedures. It is not intended that you master the contents of these tips the first time through the text. However, they should prove useful as your mastery of the program increases.

QUESTIONS

Questions at the end of each chapter test your understanding of the concepts and procedures you have studied. There are four types of questions: true/false, fill in the blank, match the columns, and write out the answers.

DISKS

Since this text is not a keyboarding text, all of the documents used in tutorials, exercises, and projects are available on the *Student Resource Disk* to accompany *Desktop Publishing with WordPerfect 5.1* that can be found at the back of this text (5¼- and 3½-inch editions are available). To complete an activity, you retrieve and format the appropriate document as described in the activity's instructions. The availability of these disk files eliminates typing time, allowing you to focus on developing your design, formatting, and page layout skills.

> ### NOTE ON DISK FILES
>
> The files on the disks that accompany this text were all formatted on a LaserJet printer with Postscript. After retrieving a file, press **Shift-F7** to display the Print menu. If the listed printer is "*HP LaserJet III Postscript,*" then you need to change a default setting so documents are automatically formatted for your printer. To do so, press **Shift-F1** to display the Setup menu, then press **I** for *Initial Settings.* Press **F** for *Format Retrieved Documents for Default Printer,* then press **Y** for *Yes.* Press **F7** to return to the Edit screen.

To help you plan and organize your courses, the publisher has developed a variety of supplements. Contact your local Regents–Prentice Hall representative to order any of these items.

- The *Instructor's Manual with Tests*, developed by Donna Matherly of Tallahasscc Community College, contains suggested course outlines, teaching tips for each topic, answers to end of chapter quizzes, production tests, and much, much more.
- The *Instructor's Resource Disk* to accompany *Desktop Publishing with WordPerfect 5.1* contains the same files as the student disk, but all of the documents are formatted as they would be at the end of an activity. In addition, files for extra exercises and production tests have been added to the disks. These disks are available in both 5¼- and 3½-inch formats. *Instructor's Resource Disks* are packaged with copies of the *Instructor's Manual with Tests*.
- A keyboard template for WordPerfect 5.1 is available free for each copy of the text adopted for use in your classes. These templates are available for regular or enhanced keyboards. (Regular keyboards have the function keys grouped together at the left end of the keyboard while enhanced keyboards have them in a single row at the top of the keyboard.)
- Prentice Hall and Bitstream have joined forces to offer instructors a special discount on FaceLift for WordPerfect, Version 1.5. This type tool for WordPerfect 5.1/5.0 comes with 16 attractive, scalable fonts for dot-matrix, inkjet, and Hewlett-Packard DeskJet and LaserJet (and compatible) printers. One FaceLift package and a special discount offer is available to instructors adopting this text. Contact your local Regents–Prentice Hall representative for details.

When using this text in the classroom, you can tailor its length to your course by the selective assignment of topics and activities. The more you cover, the longer and more detailed the course will be. Each topic has been designed as an independent unit, so it is easy to skip topics or change their sequence.

This text can be used with any system that already runs the WordPerfect program. For example, a dot-matrix printer can be used to print out documents with various fonts and graphics. The process may be slower and the printed quality of documents may not be as good as that produced on more sophisticated systems, but students will learn the concepts and procedures just as well.

This text has a traditional emphasis. It introduces students to the terms they will encounter in desktop publishing that are universally understood among publishing and printing professionals. It will come as no surprise to you that many people like to avoid learning new technical terms. It does not help, however, to substitute simpler terms when students will work with designers and service bureau people who use the accepted terminology only. (WordPerfect Corporation does not make this easy, because it does not always use accepted terminology. For instance, WordPerfect assumes that users are not willing to learn about font measurements, so it often refers to them as fine, small, large, extra large, and so on. It also misuses the conventional terms for leading. Pointing out these aberrations in terminology to students is a good thing, because software companies have the tendency to invent their own idiosyncratic terms for processes and procedures that already have established names.)

THANKS

This book was a joy to do, because everyone involved in producing it tried their hardest to make it the best possible book. This doesn't always happen—professionals work on too many books to take a special interest in each. In this case, however, everyone outdid themselves. Although I accept responsibility for the final results and any shortcomings that you find, I want to express my appreciation to the following people.

During the early stages of this text's development, a small group of talented and dedicated people gathered at Liz Kendall's request to critique the author's progress and make suggestions for improvements. This text is brimming with their ideas and the author is grateful to them for taking the time and trouble to share these with him. A number of other teachers helped refine ideas further as the book was developed. Thanks again to the following teachers:

- Joan Dennis of Anne Arundel Community College
- Sandra Devall of College of the Mainland
- Lois Elliot of Prince George's Community College
- Lois Fischer of Chubb Institute
- Janet E. Giglia of Berkeley College
- Katherine Hartman of Northern Virginia Community College
- Dolores Hofmann of Bryant & Stratton
- Toni M. Hutto of Wake Technical Community College
- Kim Kohlmeyer of Elgin Community College
- Suzanne Lambert of Broward Community College
- Donna Matherly of Tallahassee Community College
- Lynda Money of Weber State College
- Margaret Vota of City College of San Francisco
- Mary Walthall of St. Petersburg Junior College

Alice Barr took the author to visit a number of college teachers and helped him realize the need for a text in this area. Donald Lavange and Durk Merrell of WordPerfect Corporation supplied the author with early versions of WordPerfect 5.1 for testing. Peggy Curtin handled all communications with computer companies and coordinated the art program for the series. Nancy Benjamin oversaw all production aspects and orchestrated schedules and assignments. Janis Owens designed the book and developed some of the design-related art. Cecil Yarbrough helped solve many technical problems and was helpful to the author on several content issues. Sarah J. MacArthur of Hartwick College was kind enough to test all of the tutorials, exercises, and projects and make many suggestions for improvements. Kathy Famulari tested an early draft of the manuscript and suggested corrections and improvements. Cathy Morin not only tested all of the activities and made many other helpful suggestions to the author, she also desktop published the text. Suzanne Dougherty prepared all of the line art used throughout the text with Corel Systems Corporation's CorelDRAW program.

Also, thanks to Elizabeth Mancuso and Jim Welch at Bitstream, Inc. for their help is making Bitstream fonts available to college students and instructors. Finally, clip art images used in the text and supplements have been provided from the PicturePak™ clip art libraries by Islandview/MGI. You can contact Islandview/MGI at P.O. Box 11087, Richmond, VA 23230-1087, or 1-800-368-3773 for information on these and other libraries of ready-to-use art.

Dennis P. Curtin
Marblehead, Massachusetts

CONVENTIONS

This text uses the conventions for keys, commands, and prompts found in the table "Key Conventions" below.

KEY CONVENTIONS

Name	IBM Keyboard	This Text
Enter or Return	↵Enter	**Enter**
Caps Lock	Caps Lock	**Caps Lock**
Control	Ctrl	**Ctrl**
Escape	Esc	**Esc**
Function keys	F1 through F10	**F1** through **F10**
Home	Home	**Home**
End	End	**End**
Page up	PgUp	**PgUp**
Page down	PgDn	**PgDn**
Delete	Del	**Del**
Backspace	←Backspace	**Backspace**
Insert	Ins	**Ins**
Print screen	PrtSc	**PrtSc**
Shift	⇧Shift	**Shift**
Space bar	None	**Spacebar**
Alternate	Alt	**Alt**
Left arrow	←	←
Right arrow	→	→
Down arrow	↓	↓
Up arrow	↑	↑
Tab	Tab	**Tab**
Backtab	⇧Shift - Tab	**Shift-Tab**
Hyphen or minus sign	-	**Hyphen**
Underscore	_	**Underscore**

Commands

■ Keys you press sequentially are separated by commas. For example, if you are to press **F8**, release it, and then press **Enter**, the instructions read **F8**, **Enter**.

■ Keys you press simultaneously are separated by hyphens. For example, if you are to hold down the **Ctrl** key while you press **F8**, the instructions read **Ctrl**-**F8**.

Prompts

All prompts that appear on the screen are shown in *italic*. When a prompt appears, you type a response and then press **Enter**. All answers you type in response to prompts are shown in **BOLDFACE**.

Summary
Now that you have read about how keys and commands are presented,
see if you can understand the following instructions.

To delete a word
1. Move the cursor anywhere in the word to be deleted.
2. Press **Ctrl**-**Del**.

To delete a word, you first move the cursor under any character in the
word you want to delete. You then hold down the **Ctrl** key while you
press the **Del** key.

To save the document
1. Press **F10** and the prompt reads *Document to be saved:*
2. Type **MEMO.WP5** and then press **Enter**.

To save the document, you press **F10**. A prompt appears asking you for
the name of the file you want to save. You type the filename (in this case,
MEMO.WP5) and then press **Enter**.

Introduction

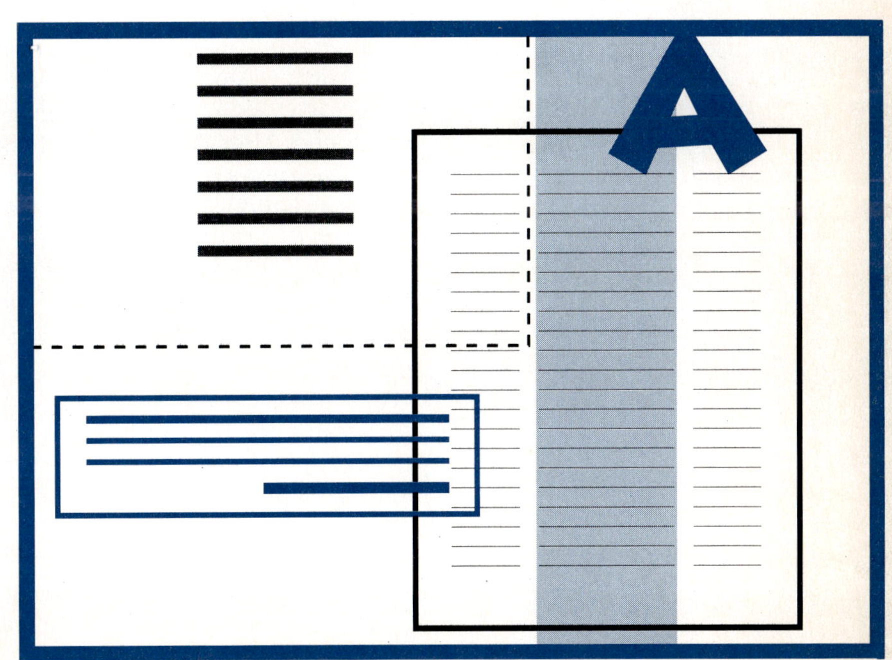

Desktop Publishing Processes

After completing this overview, you should be able to:
- Describe the three stages of publishing: creation, production, and manufacturing
- Describe the role that desktop publishing plays in the publishing process
- Describe the tasks best done with traditional publishing methods and those done best with desktop publishing

▷ DESKTOP PUBLISHING CONCEPTS

In the days when typewriters were the only widely available word processing device, professional-looking documents could be created only by commercial printing firms. This situation remained unchanged during the early days of microcomputing. Even though documents could be prepared faster on microcomputers, their printed quality was no better than those prepared on a typewriter. This situation has changed only recently with the introduction of laser printers and new applications programs designed to take advantage of them. With the introduction of these two new elements, the field of **desktop publishing** became possible. You can now prepare professional-looking documents right on your desktop. Desktop publishing really began when Apple Computer introduced the Macintosh computer and a laser printer in 1985. Shortly thereafter, the PageMaker program was introduced. This was the first desktop publishing program that would run on a microcomputer, although similar programs, like Interleaf, already existed but ran only on larger and more powerful computers. Increasingly, desktop publishing features are being added to all computer programs, including spreadsheets and databases. It is now possible to desktop publish with these programs as well as the more powerful and expensive programs that are dedicated solely to desktop publishing.

The publication of documents using traditional procedures takes a great deal of time, money, and experience. The popularity of desktop publishing stems from the fact that it reduces the time and money required to do a professional-looking job. However, desktop publishing still requires skill, and a lot of it. In traditional publishing, the tasks involved in publishing a document are handled by many separate specialists. For example, one person will design a publication, another will indicate on the manuscript how each element is to be treated, a third will set the type, and a fourth will print it. When a document is

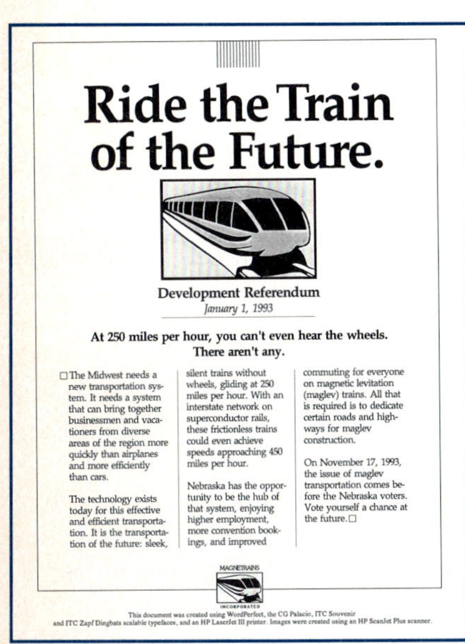

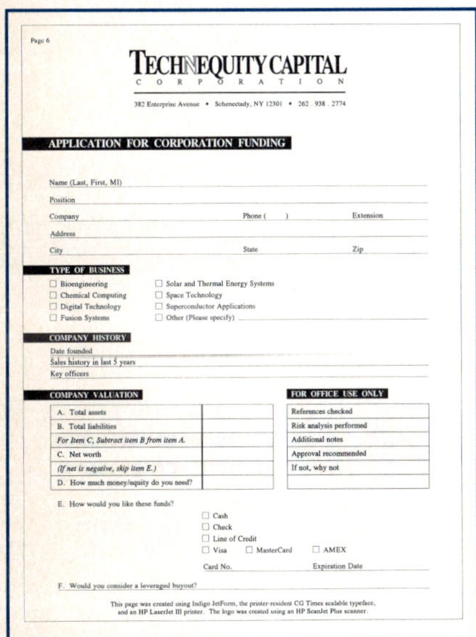

Desktop Published Documents
When done skillfully, desktop published
documents look as if they were prepared using
traditional publishing methods.
(Courtesy of Hewlett-Packard Company)

desktop published, one person only is frequently responsible for all these tasks and any others in the process.

Publishing, whether done traditionally or on the desktop, is not a single task but rather a process involving many steps that must be completed in sequence. Understanding the entire process helps you to understand how and where desktop publishing fits into the publishing picture.

The publishing process starts with a writer and ends with a printed document that is sold or otherwise distributed. Let's look at the entire process, comparing traditional publishing with desktop publishing. As you will see, the two approaches have a great deal in common. While reading about this process, keep in mind that if a job is small and relatively unimportant, some of the following steps will be skipped. Also, be aware that the traditional process and the desktop process work well together. It is common for projects to begin on the desktop where the document is designed and created and end up at a commercial printer for printing and binding.

The Creation Phase

When we think about publishing, we most frequently think about newspapers, magazines, and books. However, these types of publications actually comprise a small portion of all published materials. The vast majority of published materials are generated by business, industry, and education, and include reports, newsletters, proposals, and manuals.

To publish any of these documents, the content must first be created. Generally, the ***creation phase*** begins when a need is established for a new document. In this first phase, the fact that the publication will be traditionally published or desktop published is irrelevant. All of the steps in creating the document are completed even if the final document is to be typed on a typewriter.

Once the need for a publication is established, someone begins writing it. In some cases, a single author writes a document and it is ready to be produced. He or she is the sole judge of its acceptability. With more complex or important documents, however, more than one person is usually involved. The person who actually writes the document may not be the same person who needs it prepared. In the case of magazines or books, publishing companies have editors who decide what types of articles or books should be written and who should write them. In advertising, the copywriter writes to meet the needs of the account manager. In business, a staff member prepares a report for an executive. In all of these situations, the writer prepares a draft and obtains feedback from the person in charge of the project. The manuscript is then revised based on this feedback and a more polished version is produced. This review and rewrite process may require several cycles until everyone in the process is satisfied.

A few years ago, manuscripts were neatly typed doublespaced during this stage, but today they are frequently created on a computer so that both a printout and an electronic disk file are available for subsequent processing steps. Usually, printouts are circulated for comments and editing. However, this is increasingly being done using the electronic files. This process, called ***on-line editing***, allows various people to comment on or change the file. All changes are recorded so they are obvious to others whose advice might be desired or whose approval might be required.

The Production Phase

A completed manuscript is not the end of the publishing process, but the beginning. Once the manuscript is completed, it is ready for the ***production phase*** where it is prepared for the printer. In this phase, a ***production editor*** performs all of the production tasks or oversees and coordinates other specialists who perform them. Again, all of the steps are completed regardless of the publishing process that will be used to produce the final document.

Design

One of the first things prepared when a manuscript is finished is a ***design*** that specifies how the finished publication will look. The person who prepares this design is called a ***designer***. The designer's job is to provide samples and a detailed list of specifications for each element in the document. These materials are used as a guide by those who set the job into type and lay it out the way it will appear in the final publication.

In the publishing industry, design is a highly skilled profession. In desktop publishing, however, this is one area that presents the greatest difficulties, because most documents are not designed by professionals. Since it takes a great deal of experience to create good designs, many desktop published documents are not well designed. The only way to avoid this pitfall is to keep your designs as simple as possible and experiment frequently. Over time, your designs should improve so they are not only more attractive but also more functional. Also, years of experience have been compiled into readily available reference books such as *The Chicago Manual of Style* and *Words into Type*. Following the guidelines suggested in these books will have a dramatic effect on the look and functionality of your publications.

Copyediting

While a design is being prepared, the manuscript (or electronic file if on-line editing is being used) is copyedited to correct errors in spelling, grammar, and punctuation. Suggestions are also made to the writer on ways to make the document clearer to the reader.

Typemarking

When the design is complete, the manuscript is then ***typemarked***. Typemarking a manuscript annotates it so a commercial typesetter or a desktop publisher knows how to treat each element, based on the specifications supplied by the designer. Typemarking specifies such formats as the margins, placement of page numbers, the size and kind of type to be used, and the spacing to be left between various elements.

Art Preparation

If a publication is to be illustrated, charts, graphs, line drawings, and photographs are prepared. In some cases, this art is prepared specifically for a single publication. Many programs have been developed to assist in the preparation of this art, and these are frequently used in desktop publishing. In other cases, picture research is used to locate existing art. If the art is owned by someone else, written permission is obtained to use it. It is important to be aware that almost all art prepared since the turn of the century is still protected by copyright. Using such art without written permission is illegal and can cause serious problems for you or the firm that you work for.

The Manufacturing Phase
Once the production phase is completed, the manufacturing phase begins. In this stage, the document is printed for final distribution. It is in this ***manufacturing phase*** that there is the greatest difference between traditional and desktop publishing processes.

Typesetting
If you look carefully at this or any other book, you'll notice that the type is much more attractive than what you would see in a typed document. One thing that makes it different is that it uses different sizes and styles of type.

In traditional publishing, the manuscript (called the ***copy***) is ***set*** into type by a ***typesetter*** (also called a *compositor* or *typographer*). Not too many years ago type was set by hand, one character at a time. Today it is set using phototypesetting equipment that works much like a sophisticated desktop publishing program. The person setting the type knows what to do because he or she follows the typemarked specifications on the manuscript.

In desktop publishing, it may be you who performs this task because the phrase *desktop publishing* really refers to this stage (along with pasteup). As you will soon discover, some copy is easier to set than other copy. Typesetters refer to copy that is free of tables and other complex elements as ***straight copy***. They refer to the most difficult copy as ***penalty copy*** and charge extra for setting it.

Proofreading
After the document has been set in type, ***galley proofs*** are printed. These proofs show how each element is formatted but the text has not yet been broken into final pages. These galley proofs are proofread by the typesetter and the production editor to ensure that no errors were introduced during typesetting. The writer also reviews the proofs and uses this last opportunity to make final changes and corrections. If any changes are to be made to the copy, they are indicated with ***proofreader's marks***. The proofread galley proofs are returned to the typesetter, and any indicated corrections are made.

In desktop publishing, proofreading is done after the document is formatted but before final page layout is begun. It is important to make the copy as accurate as possible before laying out pages because changes become more and more difficult to make. Any changes that affect the length of a single page can ripple through the document, requiring changes on many of the following pages.

Pasteup
For a document to be printed, it must first be laid out or ***pasted up*** so all of the elements are arranged on the page. This process is called ***makeup*** or ***page makeup***. If a publication is heavily illustrated, or if the design is complicated, a ***dummy*** may first be prepared. To prepare a dummy, a copy of the galley proofs is cut up and pasted onto grids to show where page breaks fall and where illustrations and other

Proofreader's Marks

All corrections are indicated on manuscripts and typeset copy using proofreader's marks.

Mark	Meaning	Mark	Meaning
⊙	Insert period	*rom.*	Roman type
⋏	Insert comma	*caps.*	Caps—used in margin
:	Insert colon	≡	Caps—used in text
;	Insert semicolon	*c+sc*	Caps & small caps—used in margin
?	Insert question mark	≡	Caps & small caps—used in text
!	Insert exclamation mark	*l.c.*	Lowercase—used in margin
=/	Insert hyphen	/	Used in text to show deletion or substitution
V	Insert apostrophe		
ᵛᵛ	Insert quotation marks	ℓ	Delete
⊥ₙ	Insert 1-en dash	ℐ	Delete and close up
⊥ₘ	Insert 1-em dash	*w.f.*	Wrong font
#	Insert space	⌒	Close up
ld>	Insert ( ) points of space	⌐	Move right
shill	Insert shilling	⌐	Move left
V	Superior	⌐	Move up
Λ	Inferior	⌐	Move down
(/)	Parentheses	‖	Align vertically
[/]	Brackets	=	Align horizontal
⊡	Indent 1 em	⊐⊏	Center horizontally
⊞	Indent 2 ems	⊔⊓	Center vertically
⁊	Paragraph	*eq.#*	Equalize space—used in margin
no ⁊	No paragraph	⌵⌵⌵	Equalize space—used in text
tr	Transpose[1]—used in margin	....	Let it stand—used in text
∼	Transpose[2]—used in text	*stet.*	Let it stand—used in margin
sp	Spell out	⊗	Letter(s) not clear
ital	Italic—used in margin	*run over*	Carry over to next line
___	Italic—used in text	*run back*	Carry back to preceding line
b.f.	Boldface—used in margin	*out, see copy*	Something omitted—see copy
∼∼∼	Boldface—used in text	*9/?*	Question to author to delete[3]
s.c.	Small caps—used in margin	∧	Caret—General indicator used to mark position of error.
≡	Small caps—used in text		

elements should be positioned. This dummy acts as a guide for the typesetter when he or she is laying out the pages.

In traditional publishing, one way to prepare the pasteup is for the typesetter to print a set of the galleys on special high-quality paper that provides a very sharp image. These **reproduction proofs** (called *repros*) are then used in pasting up very accurately laid out pages, with all illustrations in place and page numbers added. The various elements are cut from the repro proofs and pasted into place on boards. With newer equipment, this can be done electronically using computers and display screens.

The final pasted-up document is called a **mechanical**, **board**, or **camera-ready copy**. A camera is used to photograph this mechanical to create the negatives used in the plate-making process. If electronic page makeup is used, the typesetter can bypass hand assembling the galleys. Instead, the negatives, called **film**, used to make the printing plates are generated directly. This process is referred to as "going directly to film."

In desktop publishing, you can do much pasteup electronically by arranging text and illustrations on the screen. This is why some people call desktop publishing *page layout*. When you make your final printout, you have camera-ready copy that you can distribute as is, copy on a copy machine, or send to a printer if a higher-quality publication is required. However, if the document is complex, some handwork may be required to insert illustrations or other elements.

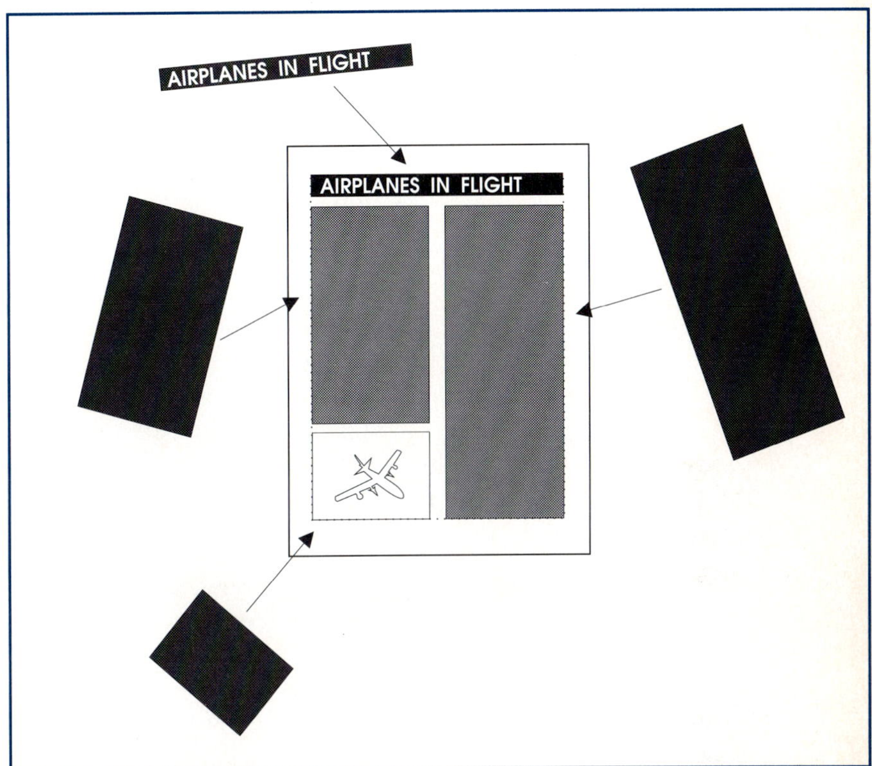

Pasteup
Pasting up a document is the process of assembling headings, text, and graphics in their proper place.

Printing and Binding
In traditional publishing, a publication is almost always printed by a commercial printer on an **offset press**. If the document has been desktop published, it may be printed on a laser printer. However, offset printing is still the least expensive way of producing hundreds or thousands of copies. Commercial printers can also take any illustrations you provide and integrate them into the publication for you in spaces that you have indicated. The resulting quality will be much higher than if you printed the illustrations on a laser printer.

The commercial printer can also print in color at a much higher quality than color printers and copiers can produce, so the publication need not be just a single color throughout. A second color can make section openers and subheads stand out. Even if color is used nowhere else, this makes the publication more attractive.

Once the document is printed, it may have to be bound. If so, it can be bound in a wide variety of styles that range from ring binders to the binding used for a book like this one.

Formatting Basics

When you load a word processing program and open a new document, any text you enter is automatically formatted using the default settings. For example, margins may be 1 inch on all sides, and text may be aligned with the left margin and single spaced. If you want to set different margins or center or double-space some or all of the text, you must override the default settings at the appropriate place in the document. You can format a document before, while, or after entering it. For example, before entering text, you might change the margins or page length. While entering text, you might boldface and underline keywords and titles. After entering text, you might change the position of page numbers on the page.

You can easily experiment with formats until you find the ones you like. Formatting and text entry are separate operations, so if you want to change margins after you have entered text, you simply use the margin commands, and all of the text realigns to the new margins. You do not have to reenter the text each time you change the format, as you do in a typed document.

Whether or not you see them on the screen, many formats are created by entering codes at selected points in the document. For example, common settings, such as hard carriage returns, spaces, tabs, alignment between margins, and emphasized characters, are controlled by codes. When you print the document, these codes are sent to the printer to instruct it how to print the document. A code might tell the printer to advance to the top of the next page after printing 54 lines, print a page number at the bottom of the page, or indent a paragraph 5 spaces from the left margin. Usually, these codes are hidden unless you use the program's command that displays them.

There are two types of codes, open and paired. Only WordPerfect calls them this, but the analogy works for all programs.

Open codes, like those used to change tabs or margins, affect all text either from the code to the end of the document or to the next code of the same type. Other open codes, like those that indent text, affect all text until the next hard carriage return.

Some programs group several related open codes together and display them as a format line, sometimes called an embedded ruler line. You can insert these format lines throughout the document wherever you want to change one or more of the settings it controls. Typical format line settings are for left and right margins, tab stops, text alignment, headers and footers, and page numbers.

Paired codes must be entered in pairs, one code to begin a format and another to end it; for example, one code starts boldfacing, and one code ends it.

You can enter paired codes in two ways, depending on whether you are formatting new or existing text. To format new text, you enter a beginning code, type text, and then enter an ending code. To format existing text, you select a block of existing text, and then execute the format command that automatically inserts codes at the beginning and end of the selected block.

If you insert text into a document containing paired codes, the position of the cursor determines the format of the text that you insert. If the cursor is between the codes, the text is formatted just like the other text between the code. If the cursor is outside of the codes, the text is not formatted.

Using a Mouse

A Mouse

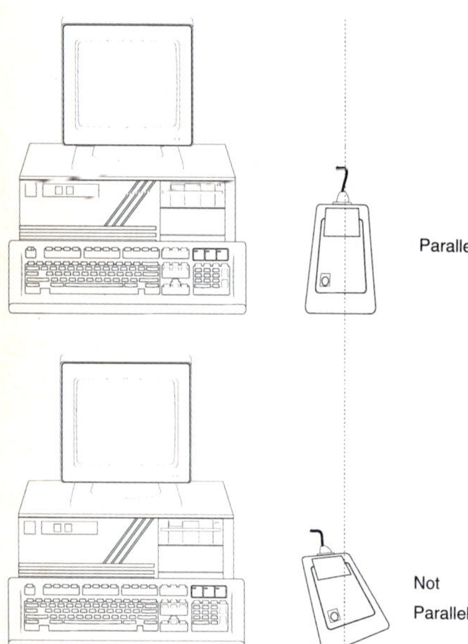

Holding and Dragging a Mouse
Hold the mouse parallel to the center line of the screen.

WordPerfect 5.1 added support for a **mouse**. As you move the mouse around on a flat, smooth surface, it feeds electrical signals to the computer that move a **mouse pointer** on the screen so you can point to items. You can use a mouse for several procedures, including the following:

- Making menu choices from pull-down menus
- Moving the cursor through the document
- Selecting (blocking) text so that it can be copied, moved, deleted, or formatted

When you use a mouse for the first time, you will experience some frustration. It seems hard to point to just the right place, and to click or hold the button at the right time. Don't let these frustrations get you down; everyone experiences them. In a few days, you'll wonder how you ever got along without it. However, once you have mastered it, you have to decide when to put it down. Many operations can be performed faster from the keyboard. Users who continually switch back and forth between the keyboard and a mouse actually work slower than those who think through the fastest approach to a task.

Holding and Dragging the Mouse

When you use a mouse, you roll it across the surface of the desk. This motion tells the mouse which way to move the mouse pointer on the screen. To make the mouse pointer move in a predictable direction, it is important that you hold the mouse so that it is oriented parallel to the middle line of the screen. This way, when you move the mouse up, down, or sideways, the mouse pointer moves in the expected direction. If you hold the mouse at an angle, your hand motion and the motion of the mouse pointer will not be coordinated.

Basic Mouse Commands

When you use a mouse, here are some of the basic commands to remember.

- The **mouse pointer** appears when you move the mouse and disappears when you press a key.
- **Point** means to position the mouse pointer over or on some items on the screen.
- **Clicking** refers to pressing one of the buttons on the mouse.
- **Drag** means to hold down one of the mouse buttons while you move the mouse. You do this frequently when you want to highlight a block of text so you can format it. In other situations, this action drags the highlighted item to a new position on the screen.

- *Cancel* (same as pressing **F1**) by pressing the middle button on a three-button mouse or holding down either button and clicking the other on a two-button mouse.
- *Double clicking* refers to pressing one of the buttons on the mouse twice in rapid succession. Double clicking the left button is the same as clicking the left button and then pressing **Enter**. The first click highlights an item, and the second click selects it. For example, if a prompt such as *Document to be saved: FILENAME* is displayed, double clicking on the filename following the prompt with the left button displays the prompt *Replace FILENAME? No (Yes).*

Clicking the Right Button

Clicking the right button performs one of three procedures:

- If a menu is displayed, it is the same as pressing **F7**. The menu is exited.
- If no menu is displayed, it displays the pull-down menu bar. Pressing it again removes the menu bar.
- Holding down the button and dragging the mouse scrolls the document on the screen.

Clicking the Left Button

Clicking the left button performs several procedures:

- It moves the cursor to the same position as the mouse pointer.
- It highlights a menu item pointed to with the mouse pointer.
- It cancels a menu if the mouse pointer is not positioned on a menu choice.

Using the Mouse with Pull-Down Menus

You can use a mouse to execute commands listed on the pull-down menus (see the table "Mouse Commands and the Menu"). To display the pull-down menu bar, click the right mouse button (click it again to remove the menu).

To pull down a menu from the menu bar, point to the menu name, then click the left button. You can also point to any menu name, hold down the left button, and drag the mouse pointer along the menu bar to pull down other menus.

To select a command from a pulled-down menu (or any other menu), point to the command with the mouse pointer and click the left button. You can also point to any command, hold down the left button, and then drag the mouse pointer to highlight any other command. Once the desired command is highlighted, release the left button.

To exit the menus without making a choice, point anywhere but to a command and click the left button. If you are holding the left button down to drag between choices, release it when not pointing to a command.

MOUSE COMMANDS AND THE MENU

Action	Button to Click
Activate the menu	Right
Remove the menu	Right
Pull down a menu	Left
Make a menu choice	Left

REVIEW

- Publishing has three distinct phases: creation, production, and manufacturing.
- In the creation phase, the document is written.
- In the production phase, the completed manuscript is edited and typemarked for the typesetter or desktop publisher, the document is designed, and all art is prepared.
- In the manufacturing phase, the manuscript is set into type by a typesetter or desktop publisher, and then printed. If the document is being printed by a commercial printer, plates are first made for use in the printing process. The document is then bound (if desired) and distributed.

QUESTIONS

TRUE/FALSE

T   F

1. Desktop publishing requires less skill than traditional publishing methods.
2. Desktop publishing and traditional publishing methods differ the most at the manufacturing stage.
3. In the production phase, multiple copies of the document are produced.
4. Design is the simplest aspect of desktop publishing.
5. Typemarking specifies how elements are to be set into type.
6. A dummy can be used as a guide during the pasteup process.

FILL IN THE BLANK

1. The person who oversees the process of turning a manuscript into a published document is called a(n) ___________ editor.
2. The manuscript used to set type from is called the ___________ .
3. When electronic files are used for editing, the method is called ___________ editing.
4. Traditional publishing and desktop publishing are most dissimilar at the ___________ stage.

1. Design
2. Proofreader's marks
3. Production editor
4. Typemarking
5. Typesetter
6. Galley proofs
7. Pasteup
8. Dummy
9. Reproduction proofs
10. Mechanical
11. Page makeup
12. Film
13. Offset press

___ Assembling the pieces so they can be used to print the document
___ Proofs that are not yet paginated
___ The final copy used to make negatives
___ A mock-up of what a publication will look like
___ The process of assembling repros
___ A printing press
___ The person who sets type for documents
___ The stage of the document when printing plates are made
___ The process of specifying how a document should look when finished
___ The person who guides a publication through to publication
___ Transferring specs to the manuscript to guide the person setting the type
___ The marks that indicate where corrections are to be made in the copy or proofs
___ The stage when negatives for printing are made

WRITE OUT THE ANSWERS

1. List and briefly describe the three phases in the creation of a publication.
2. Describe the job of the typesetter.
3. Explain briefly how a document is pasted up using traditional publishing methods.

PROJECTS

PROJECT 1

EXPLORING LIBRARY RESOURCES

Visit your campus or local library and look up *The Chicago Manual of Style* and *Words into Type* in the card catalog. Locate the books and skim through them to see the kind of information they contain. Also check in the card catalog under the subjects "publishing," "printing," or "typography" to see if any other titles are listed. List any below that you want to thumb through.

____

____

____

____

____

____

____

PROJECT 2

THE DESKTOP PUBLISHING ADVISOR NEWSLETTER

Throughout this text, you will be formatting a newsletter on desktop publishing. In a project at the end of most chapters, you will be adding formats until you have a completely formatted and illustrated newsletter. In this project, you print out the unformatted version of this document to use as a reference as you proceed.

1. Retrieve the ADVISOR.WP5 document.
2. Press **Shift-F7** to display the Print menu, then press **F** for *Full Document.*
3. Clear the document from the screen without saving it.

Typefaces, Typestyles, & Type Sizes

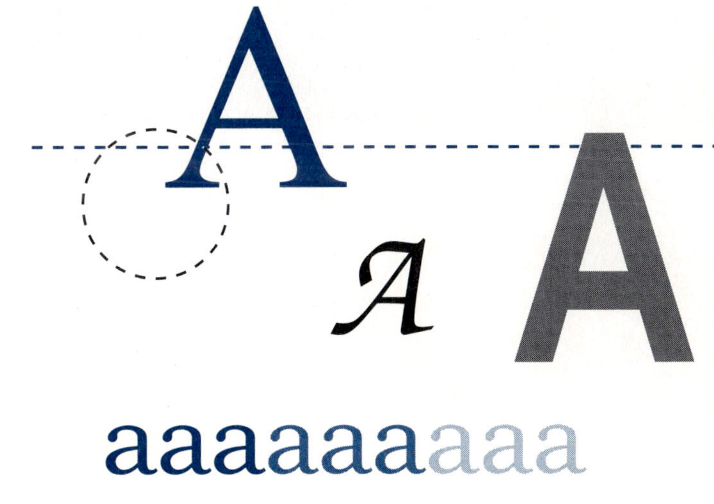

Points and Picas: How Publishers Measure

After completing this topic, you should be able to:
- Define points and picas and explain what they measure
- Define ems and ens and explain what they are used for
- Change WordPerfect's units of measurement, and enter settings in inches, centimeters, or points

▶ TUTORIAL

In this tutorial, you change WordPerfect's units of measurements to points.

GETTING STARTED

1. Retrieve the MEASURE.WP5 document.

CHANGING THE UNITS OF MEASUREMENT

2. Press **Shift-F1** to display the Setup menu.
3. Press **E** for *Environment*.
4. Press **U** for *Units of Measure*.
5. Press **D** for *Display and Entry of Numbers for Margins, Tabs, etc.* and the cursor jumps up to that line.
6. Type **p** (for points).
7. Press **S** for *Status Line Display* and the cursor jumps up to that line.
8. Type **p** (for points).
9. Press **F7** to return to the Edit screen.

EXPLORING THE STATUS LINE

10. Move the cursor through the document, watching the status line as you do so.
11. Position the cursor under each of the Xs (*[X1]*, *[X2]*, and so on) that follow the subheads and the last paragraph. Refer to the status line indicators and list the position of each *X* in points in the table below.

Item	Ln	Pos
X1		
X2		
X3		
X4		

12. Ask your instructor what units he or she prefers for you to use. If they are inches or centimeters, repeat Steps 2 through 9 but enter **i** (for inches) or **c** (for centimeters) instead of **p** (for points).

13. Clear the screen without saving the document.

▶ DESKTOP PUBLISHING CONCEPTS

6 points

8 points

10 points

12 points

14 points

18 points

24 points

Font Sizes

Hairline

.5 point

1 point

2 points

4 points

8 points

12 points

Rules

Desktop publishing uses the computer to set type and lay out pages, tasks that have been performed for hundreds of years using more traditional publishing methods. As you can imagine, a field as established as publishing has its own special expressions, called *terms of the trade*. Here we concentrate on the most basic new terms, the ones that publishing and printing professionals use to describe measurements. In these fields, the familiar units of inches and centimeters are used only to specify paper sizes and occasionally margins. All other measurements are given in units called *points* and *picas*, and *ems* and *ens*. Understanding these units of measurement is essential to working together successfully with other professionals in the publishing field.

Points and Picas

For the first few hundred years of publishing, there were no standard measurements in printing, so type (usually made of wood or metal) varied widely depending on which foundry produced it. In 1878 the ***point system***, developed by a French typographer, was adopted as a standard system for measuring type and has been in use ever since. This standardization allows type from different foundries to be used in the same document.

The point system has two basic units, the point and the pica.

Points

Points (abbreviated *pt*) are used to specify measurements that relate to type. A point is equal to 0.013837 inches (about 1/72 inch) so a 72-point type would be almost, but not quite, 1 inch high. Points can specify the following:

- **Type**. The size of the type used to print documents is specified in point sizes. For example, you can specify a 12-point or an 18-point type.
- **Rules**. Many documents contain rules that separate elements or add a decorative touch. The thickness of these rules is specified in points. For example, you can specify a ½-, 1-, or 2-point rule.
- **Line spacing**. The terms *single spacing*, *double spacing*, and so on, refer to line spacing measurements that are not accurate or flexible enough for published documents. Therefore, line spacing in publishing (called *leading* and rhymes with *heading*) is specified in points.

Picas

Picas (abbreviated *pi*) are used to specify layout measurements such

Leading

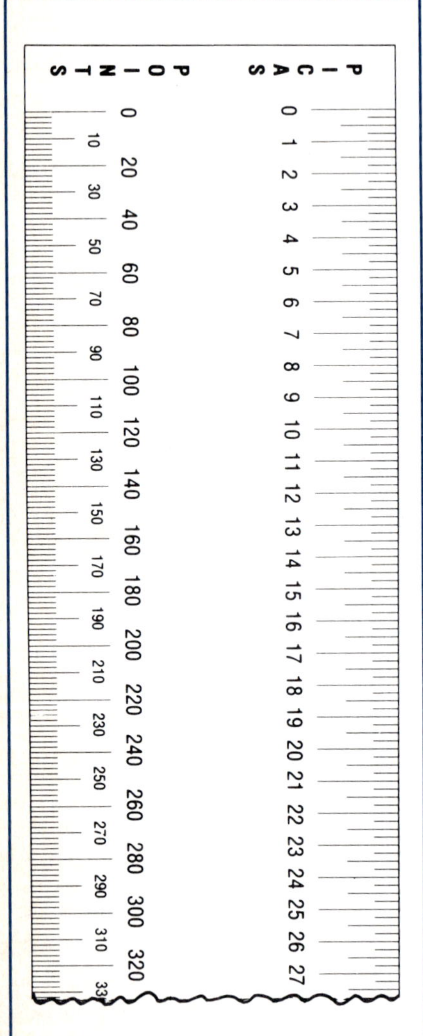

The Pica Rule

as the width and depth of type pages or columns. For example, you might say that the type block on a page is to be 20 picas wide by 36 picas deep. A pica contains exactly 12 points and there are approximately 6 picas to the inch.

Pica Rules
It takes a little experience to become comfortable working with points and picas, but it's really quite easy. To help, you should have a **pica rule** (also called a *pica stick* or *line gauge*). This ruler gives measurements in inches, picas, and points. Using a pica rule, you can easily measure printouts to be sure that elements are spaced as they should be. A pica ruler is bound in at the back of this book.

Ems and Ens
Most units of measurement in desktop publishing are absolute. For example, a point, pica, or inch is always the same length, regardless of when or where it is used. When setting type, however, some measurements are best when they are proportional to the size of the type being used. For example, paragraph indents look better when they are larger for a larger type than for a smaller one. To allow for measurements that are proportional to the type size, publishers use *ems* and *ens* and design specifications frequently call for em or en bullets, indents, spaces, or dashes.

Ems
An **em** is simply a square area that is as tall and wide as the type size being used. The em's name comes from the fact that it is approximately the size of an uppercase letter *M*. For example, if the type size is 12 points, it has an em of 12 points. If the type is 18 points, it has an em of 18 points. If an em bullet is called for in either of these font sizes, it would be 12 by 12 points or 18 by 18 points. If an em dash or space is called for, it would be 12 or 18 points long. (A special type of em is the **pica em**, which is always 12 points square.) Ems are used for the following items:

- **Indents**. Paragraph indents (called *indention* and not *indentation*) should be proportional to the size of the type used. For this reason paragraphs are frequently indented 1 em. In copy, em indents are specified by a square box

- **Spaces**. Em spaces are often used, for example, after numbers in lists and in illustrations to separate a figure title from any preceding number and following caption. In copy, em spaces are specified by a square box just as indents are.

- **Dashes**. The em dash can be a substitute for the comma, parentheses, the colon, or even the period. It can also indicate zero amounts on financial statements. In copy, an em dash is specified by a dash with a number 1 above it and a letter *M* below. For comparison's sake, a hyphen is specified by a short equal sign (=).

- **Bullets**. Many lists are set off using bullets or dingbats. These special characters should be proportional to the type size being used, so they are frequently specified in ems.

Ens
An **en** is approximately one-half the width of an em, or the size of an uppercase letter *N* in the font you are using. Ens are used for the following:

- **Spaces**. En spaces are used in places where you want more space than a normal space but less than an em space. In copy, an en space is specified with a box with the letter *N* in it, or a box with a diagonal slash in it.

- **Dashes**. The en dash is shorter than the em dash and is used to join ranges of numbers such as 1–2, or words to phrases that contain two or more words such as "New York–London." In copy en dashes are specified by a dash with the number 1 above and the letter *N* below.

- **Bullets**. When lists are set off using bullets, the bullets are sometimes specified in ens instead of ems.

Em Squares and Dashes

- ■ 8 point em square
- — 8 point em dash
- ■ 12 point em square
- — 12 point em dash

Em and En Proofreader's Marks

Em space	□
En space	⊠
Em dash	$\frac{1}{M}$
En dash	$\frac{1}{N}$

En Squares and Dashes

- ▪ 8 point en square
- - 8 point en dash
- ▪ 12 point en square
- — 12 point en dash

When you enter a number to change margins, set tabs, and so on, WordPerfect assumes that the number is in the default unit of measurement (which is originally set to inches). If you want to enter a measurement in any other unit, you can do so by following the number with one of the codes described in the table "Units of Measurement Codes." When you do so, the number that you enter is automatically converted into the default unit of measure and displayed in those units on any menus. For example, if you enter **72p** (72 points) when the default unit is inches, it is automatically converted and displayed on the screen as 1 inch. WordPerfect can accept numbers with up to six digits, although all of them are not displayed on the screen.

UNITS OF MEASUREMENT CODES

c	*Centimeters.* For example, **5c** specifies five centimeters.
p	*Points.* For example, **5p** specifies five points.
w	*1200ths of an inch.* For example, **300w** specifies ¼ inch.
i or "	*Inches.* For example, **5i** or **5"** specifies five inches.

If you work in one unit more frequently than in other units, you should display the Setup menu (**Shift-F1**) and then use the Environment choice to change the default unit of measurement. For example, when desktop publishing, you may occasionally want to change the default units of measurement to points so you don't have to enter the code letter **p** all the time. When you change the default unit of measurement, you can also specify that the cursor's position on the status line is indicated in the same units.

➔ **K E Y / S t r o k e s**

Changing the Units of Measurement

1. Either: Press **Shift-F1** to display the Setup menu.
   Or: Pull down the File menu and select *Setup.*
2. Press **E** for *Environment.*
3. Press **U** for *Units of Measure.*
4. Press **D** for *Display and Entry of Numbers for Margins, Tabs, etc.*
5. Type **p** for *points* (or any other unit of measurement code described in the table "Units of Measurement Codes").
6. Press **S** for *Status Line Display.*
7. Type **p** for *points* (or any other unit of measurement code described in the table "Units of Measurement Codes").
8. Press **F7** to return to the Edit screen.

EXERCISE 1

MEASURING BOOKS

Using a pica rule, measure the size of the type page in three different books. Be sure to include any headers or footers in the measurement. Indicate the type page's width and depth (the height) in the spaces below.

Book	Width	Depth
Book 1		
Book 2		
Book 3		

Look through the books for em spaces and em dashes. If you find some, indicate how they were used.

✔ TYPE MEASUREMENT TIPS

- When entering measurements for such things as margins and tab stops, you can enter fractions and WordPerfect automatically converts them to the default unit of measure. For example, you can enter one and one-half as **1 1/2** rather than **1.5**. This is especially useful when entering measurements like one-third that do not have an exact decimal equivalent.
- Whereas 72 points are normally slightly less than an inch, WordPerfect rounds them off so they are exactly one inch. Each point in WordPerfect is therefore exactly 1/72 inch.

Typefaces

▶ T U T O R I A L

In this tutorial, you change the typefaces used to print sections of a document. When you are finished, your printed document should look similar to the figure "Typical Typefaces."

GETTING STARTED

1. Retrieve the TYPEFAC1.WP5 document and enter your name following the heading "*Name:*" on the first line.

ENTERING A BASE FONT CODE

2. Position the cursor under the "*F*" in the line that reads "*Font Two.*"
3. Press **Ctrl-F8** to display the Font menu.
4. Press **F** to select *Base Font* and display a list of the fonts available on your system. The current base font is marked with an asterisk.
5. Highlight *Courier* if it is listed, otherwise highlight any font not already marked with the asterisk. If the list is longer than the screen, you can use the cursor movement keys to scroll it.
6. Press **S** to select **S**elect (on some printers, the prompt reads *Point size: 12*. If this prompt appears, press **Enter** to confirm the size.)

ENTERING MORE BASE FONT CODES

7. Position the cursor under the "*F*" in the lines that read "*Font Three*" and "*Font Four*" and repeat Steps 2 through 6 to select a new base font for each line. Avoid selecting fonts that you have already selected or that are listed as bold or italic. If your screen does not list four fonts, quit after selecting each of those that are listed.

FINISHING UP

8. Save and print the document. Your results will depend on the system you are using but, ideally, each line is printed in a different typeface.

Font One

Font Two

Font Three

Font Four

Typical Typefaces

9. Reveal codes in the document (**Alt-F3** or **F11**) and look for the font codes. Each lists the base font that you entered for the line. Write the names on the printout on the same line as the line they formatted.

▶ DESKTOP PUBLISHING CONCEPTS

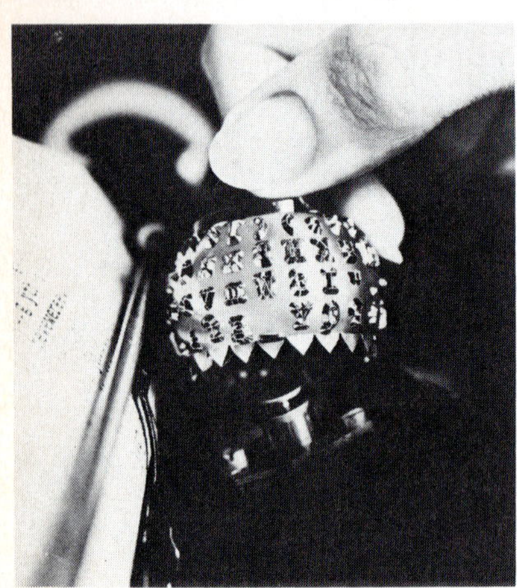

A Typeball Font
(Courtesy of International Business Machines Corporation)

Avant Garde Gothic
Bookman
Courier
Helvetica
New Century Schoolbook
Palatino
Times Roman
Zapf Chancery

Typefaces

One of the hallmarks of professionally prepared documents is the tasteful use of different kinds of type. This textbook, for example, uses one type for headings and another for the text itself.

To increase a document's visual impact in this way, you must have a basic understanding of fonts. A font is simply a complete set of the characters that you need to print a document in one typeface, typestyle, and type size. It includes uppercase (capital) letters, lowercase letters, numbers, punctuation marks, and other special characters. Pick up a typeball from a typewriter, and you are holding a font.

Fonts are available in many designs, called typefaces; each typeface has several typestyles; and each typestyle comes in various sizes. In this topic we explore the basic design, the typeface.

CASE

The terms *uppercase* and *lowercase*, like many other publishing terms, come from the typesetting field. When type was set by hand, all the characters were stored in typecases. The typesetter selected individual characters from the case and assembled them by hand into words, sentences, paragraphs, and pages. The capital letters were stored in the upper part of the typecase, and the other letters in the lower part, hence the terms *uppercase* and *lowercase*.

Courtesy of the Bettmann Archive, Inc.

Typeface refers to a type's particular design. Typical typefaces include Helvetica, Times Roman, Bookman, New Century Schoolbook, and Palatino. The characters in each typeface have distinctive proportions and thicknesses of lines that make them unique. However, typefaces fall into two major categories, serif and sans serif.

■ **Serif typefaces** have smaller lines, called *serifs*, that finish off the main strokes of a letter. The most common serif typeface is

Fonts

Fonts come in many typefaces. Each typeface has several variations, called typestyles, and each typestyle comes in several sizes.

Typeface	Typestyle	Type Size
Times Roman	Normal	8 point
Helvetica	**Bold**	**10 point**
Courier	*Italic*	*12 point*
Palatino	*Bold italic*	*14 point*

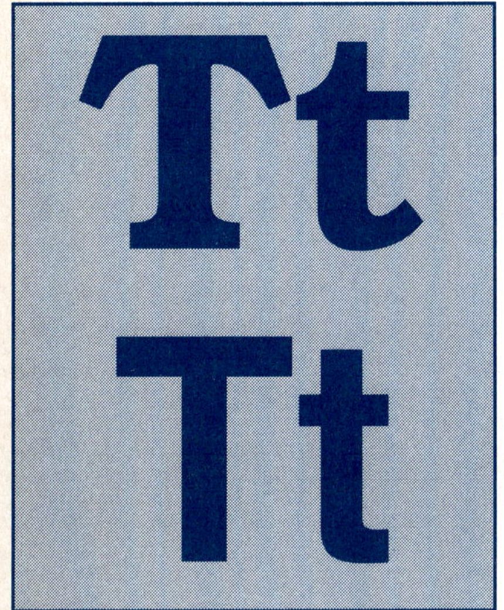

Serif and Sans Serif Fonts
A serif font (top) is more decorative than a sans serif font (bottom)

Times Roman and Helvetica Fonts
The most common serif typeface is Times Roman. The most common sans serif typeface is Helvetica.

Times Roman, also called Dutch in some variations.

- ***Sans serif typefaces*** do not have the decorative cross marks at the end of main strokes (*sans* is French for *without*). The most common sans serif typeface is Helvetica, called Swiss or Univers in some versions.

The design of fonts is subjective and there are slight variations from one manufacturer to another even when the fonts have the same name. You will see this if you print the same document on two different printers, each of which has a typeface called Times Roman or Helvetica.

In many cases, typeface designs are almost identical but their names are different. This is because the design itself cannot be protected by copyright but the name can be. Companies that want to issue a font without permission can do so, as long as they use a different name for their version. This is why some fonts are called Dutch or Swiss when they resemble Times Roman or Helvetica as closely as they possibly can.

Selecting Typefaces

When choosing the typefaces to use in a document, there are several things to consider. For example, many people believe that serif typefaces are more readable because the serifs at the bottom of the characters guide your eye along the line. However, this is subjective and depends partly on the application, the audience, and other elements of the design. Many publications combine the two types, using a sans serif type for headlines and a serif type for the body of the text. Although opinions vary, in reading through books on type, you frequently find the following adjectives associated with serif and sans serif typefaces:

Serif	Sans Serif
Traditional	Clean
Easy to read	Modern
Distinctive	Contemporary
Decorative	Uncluttered

When choosing typefaces for a document, try to limit your choice to no more than two. Too many typefaces can make a publication look amateurish and cluttered unless handled by someone with a superb sense of design. If you use only two,

abcdefghijklmnopqrstuvwxyz & ? ! 1 2 3 4 5 6 7 8 9 0

Times Roman

abcdefghijklmnopqrstuvwxyz &?!1234567890

Helvetica

you can then add impact by changing their sizes and styles (like bold and italic) where needed. The typeface should also be related to the type of document you are creating. Occasionally, one typeface matches up better than others for a specific type of document.

Bitstream Font Recommendations
This illustration shows the fonts recommended for specific document types by Bitstream, a major electronic font foundry.
(Courtesy of Bitstream Inc.)

NEWSLETTERS/BROCHURES	ADVERTISEMENTS	OFFICE MATERIAL	FLYERS
Bitstream Charter	ITC Avant Garde Gothic	Prestige	Futura Medium
Swiss Light	**Windsor**	Swiss Monospaced	**Hobo**
Broadway	**ITC Bolt Bold**	Bitstream Charter	**Clarendon**
Century Schoolbook	**Bitstream Cooper**	Zapf Calligraphic	ITC Korinna
Provence	ITC Korinna	**ITC Souvenir**	**Franklin Gothic**
Zapf Elliptical	ITC Benguiat	ITC Bookman	ITC Garamond Condensed

PRESENTATIONS	REPORTS / PROPOSALS	MANUALS / CATALOGS	INVITATIONS
ITC Lubalin Graph	Bitstream Amerigo	Baskerville	University Roman
Swiss Condensed	Activa	ITC Garamond	ITC Zapf Chancery
Swiss Compressed	ITC Clearface	Goudy Old Style	ITC Galliard
Handel Gothic	Zapf Humanist	**Swiss Bold**	Bernhard Modern
Bitstream Amerigo	Zurich Light	Serifa	Bodoni Book
ITC American Typewriter	Hammersmith	Zurich	ITC Tiffany
		Zurich Condensed	

▷ W O R D P E R F E C T   P R O C E D U R E S

With WordPerfect, you change typefaces by changing the base font. The *initial base font* is the default font for your documents. If your documents automatically print in 12-point Times Roman, then your base font is 12-point Times Roman. You can specify a new initial base font for all documents, or just for the current document.

→ KEY/Strokes

Specifying the Initial Base Font for All Documents

1. Either: Press **Shift-F7** to display the Print menu.
   Or: Pull down the File menu and select *Print*.
2. Press **S** for *Select Printer*. (The printer you are using is highlighted and marked with an asterisk.)
3. Press **E** for *Edit*.
4. Press **F** for *Initial Base Font* to display a list of fonts available for your printer.
5. Press the cursor movement keys to highlight the initial base font that you want to use. (The current initial base font is marked with an asterisk.)
6. Press **S** for *Select* to change the initial base font. (If you select a scalable font, the prompt reads *Point size:* followed by the current size. Press **Enter**, or type a new size and then press **Enter**.)
7. Press **F7** repeatedly to return to the Edit screen.

```
Document: Initial Font

  Helvetica Oblique
  ITC Avant Garde Gothic Book
  ITC Avant Garde Gothic Book Oblique
  ITC Avant Garde Gothic Demi
  ITC Avant Garde Gothic Demi Oblique
  ITC Bookman Demi
  ITC Bookman Demi Italic
  ITC Bookman Light
  ITC Bookman Light Italic
  ITC Zapf Chancery Medium Italic
  ITC Zapf Dingbats
  New Century Schoolbook
  New Century Schoolbook Bold
  New Century Schoolbook Bold Italic
  New Century Schoolbook Italic
  Palatino
  Palatino Bold
  Palatino Bold Italic
  Palatino Italic
  Symbol
* Times Roman

1 Select; N Name search: 1
```

→ KEY/Strokes

Specifying the Initial Base Font for the Current Document

1. Either: Press **Shift-F8** and then **D** for *Document*.

   Or: Pull down the Layout menu and select *Document*.

2. Press **F** for *Initial Base Font* to display a list of fonts available for your printer.

3. Press the cursor movement keys to highlight the initial base font you want to use. (The current initial base font is marked with an asterisk.)

4. Press **S** for *Select* to change the initial font. (If you select a scalable font, the prompt reads *Point size:* followed by the current size. Press **Enter**, or type a new size and then press **Enter**.)

5. Press **F7** to return to the Edit screen.

After selecting an initial base font you can enter a new base font code anywhere in the document to change it. The font specified in the code affects all text from where you insert the code to the next base font code or the end of the document. For example, if you insert a base font code midway down page 1 of your document, the top half of the page is formatted with the initial base font and the lower half with the new base font.

Changing the Base Font within a Document

1. Move the cursor to where you want to change the base font.
2. Either: Press **Ctrl-F8** and then **F** for *Base Font*.
   Or: Pull down the Font menu and select *Base Font*.
   A list of fonts available for your printer is displayed.
3. Press the cursor movement keys to highlight the base font you want to use. (The current base font is marked with an asterisk.)
4. Press **S** for **S**elect to change the base font and return to the Edit screen. (If you select a scalable font, the prompt reads *Point size:* followed by the current size. Press **Enter**, or type a new size and then press **Enter**.)

✔ **TYPEFACE TIPS**

- If your system uses downloadable soft fonts, you may have to use WordPerfect's Initialize Printer command on the Print menu (**Shift-F7**) to download the fonts to the printer. You have to do this only once, at the beginning of a session. The fonts will remain in the printer until you shut it off.
- To use fonts, they must be available to your printer. The appendix "Cartridges and Fonts" describes how you obtain and install fonts.

▶ **EXERCISES**

EXERCISE 1

CHANGING THE BASE FONT FOR ALL DOCUMENTS

In this exercise, you check the initial base font being used for all documents and, if you choose to, change it.

1. Follow the instructions in the KEY/Strokes box "Specifying the Initial Base Font for All Documents" to see which font is the current initial base font for all documents. If you prefer a different font for all documents, select the one that you want to use. If you prefer to leave the setting unchanged, press **F7** to return to the Edit screen.

EXERCISE 2

CHANGING THE BASE FONT FOR THE CURRENT DOCUMENT

In this exercise, you change the initial base font in a letter and make printouts until you find the typeface that you like best.

1. Retrieve the TYPEFAC2.WP5 document.
2. Reveal codes (press **Alt**-**F3** or **F11**), and enter your name in place of the text "*Your Name*" that is already there. (Be careful not to delete any of the existing codes.)
3. Follow the instructions in the KEY/Strokes box "Specifying the Initial Base Font for the Current Document" to change the initial base font for the document. When finished, make a printout.
4. Change the initial base font again, and then make another printout.
5. Continue changing initial base fonts and making printouts until you find the one you like best, and then save the document.

EXERCISE 3

PRINTING THE PRINTER TEST DOCUMENT

WordPerfect supplies a file named PRINTER.TST that you can print to see what features your printer supports. In this exercise, you print this file. To begin, retrieve the file onto the screen.

- On a hard disk system, this file is in the same directory as your WordPerfect program files.
- On a floppy disk system it is on the *WordPerfect 1* or the Install/Learn/Utilities disk.

Make a printout and examine it carefully to see what works and what doesn't. Different printers produce different results. Experiment by following the instructions in the KEY/Strokes box "Specifying the Initial Font for the Current Document" to change the base font for the document. When finished, make another printout and compare it with the first.

Typestyles

After completing this topic, you should be able to:

- Explain that typefaces are usually available in a variety of styles
- Describe how WordPerfect uses the phrase "font appearance" instead of the word "typestyle"
- Change typestyles in your own documents

► T U T O R I A L

In this tutorial, you change the typestyles used to print several terms in a document. When you are finished, your printed document should look similar to the figure "WordPerfect's Font Appearances."

GETTING STARTED

1. Retrieve the TYPESTY1.WP5 document and enter your name.

ASSIGNING A TYPESTYLE

2. Position the cursor under the "B" in "*Bold.*"
3. Press **Alt**-**F4** or **F12** to turn on *Block On* and then press **End** to block the word "*Bold.*"
4. Press **Ctrl**-**F8** to display the Font menu.
5. Press **A** to select *Appearance.*
6. Press **B** to select *Bold.*

ASSIGNING OTHER TYPESTYLES

7. Repeat Steps 2 through 6 for each phrase and change their appearance to the one specified. For example, underline the word "*Underline,*" double underline the term "*Double Underline,*" and so on.

FINISHING UP

8. Save and print the document. Your results will depend on the system you are using.
9. Change the base font for the document and make another printout. Compare the two printouts to see how all font appearances apply to the underlying base font specified for the document.

Normal
Bold
<u>Underline</u>
<u>Double Underline</u>
Italic
Outline
Shadow
SMALL CAPS

WordPerfect's Font Appearances

All typefaces come in several **typestyles**, or variations, based on their case, slant, thickness, or width.

Just as typefaces are categorized as serif or sans serif, typestyles are categorized as italic or roman. **Roman** is upright and italic is slanted.

Typestyles

Typefaces come in a variety of styles including bold, italic, and bold italic. This figure illustrates the different styles available with the eleven type families supplied with Adobe's PostScript. Adobe is one of the major suppliers of fonts used in desktop publishing.

Normal
Bold
Italic
Bold Italic
SMALL CAPS

The Helvetica Typeface Family

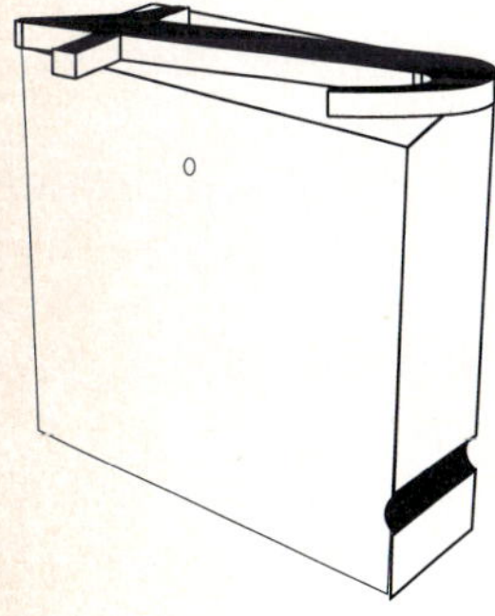

Italic Type

ITC Avant Garde Gothic Book
ITC Avant Garde Gothic Demi
ITC Avant Garde Gothic Book Oblique
ITC Avant Garde Gothic Demi Oblique
ITC Bookman Light
ITC Bookman Demi
ITC Bookman Light Italic
ITC Bookman Demi Italic
Courier
Courier Bold
Courier Oblique
Courier Bold Oblique
Helvetica
Helvetica Bold
Helvetica Oblique
Helvetica Bold Oblique
Helvetica Narrow
Helvetica Narrow Bold
Helvetica Narrow Oblique
Helvetica Narrow Bold Oblique
New Century Schoolbook Roman
New Century Schoolbook Bold
New Century Schoolbook Italic
New Century Schoolbook Bold Italic
Palatino
Palatino Bold
Palatino Italic
Palatino Bold Italic
Symbol Σψμβολ
Times Roman
Times Bold
Times Italic
Times Bold Italic
ITC Zapf Chancery Medium Italic
ITC Zapf Dingbats ■ ✄ ▲ ▼ ● ✪ ✳

All of the styles related to a specific typeface are called a **typeface family** or type family. The typical typeface family includes the following typestyles:

■ The basic font in any type family is a typestyle called normal or **lightface**.

■ Bold often includes varying degrees of boldness. For example, in ascending order of boldness, typefaces can be extra light, light, book, medium, demibold, semibold, heavy, bold, extrabold, black, and ultrabold. Bold is used to make words or phrases "jump out" at the reader.

Helvetica
Helvetica (Narrow)

Type Widths

- Italic typefaces are slightly slanted. (in some variations, these are called **oblique**.) Italic type is frequently used for quotations, introductions, and captions.
- Bold italic typefaces combine the features of both bold and italic type.
- Small capital letters, called **small caps**, are uppercase letters that are approximately the size of the lowercase letters in the font that they accompany. For example, the phrase "Small Caps" set with small caps appears as "SMALL CAPS." Small caps are frequently used in titles and subheads.
- Many typefaces also come in varying widths, for example, extra condensed, condensed, elongated, narrow, compressed, expanded, extended, and wide.

These variations are important, especially since printers used for desktop publishing must have access to a normal version of the selected typeface to print regular text and a bold or italic version to print boldfaced or italicized text. If the printer has access only to Times Roman normal and Times Roman bold, it cannot print text in Times Roman italic. Most printers used in desktop publishing have fonts for at least normal, bold, italic, and bold italic styles for their built-in typefaces.

When using typestyles other than normal, do so sparingly. Large blocks of text in italic or bold type are hard to read. If you do use them for a block of text, any words that would normally be bold or italic should be set in normal type so they still stand out.

➤ WORDPERFECT PROCEDURES

In WordPerfect, the term **font appearance** refers to what others call typestyle. The appearance choices from which you can choose are listed in the table "Appearance Styles."

When changing typestyles (or sizes) in WordPerfect, you should understand the terms *current font* and *font attribute*.

The current font is the typeface in effect at the cursor's position. If you have not entered a new base font code in the document, the current font is the initial base font. If you have entered a base font code anywhere in the document, when the cursor is below that font code, the current font is the one specified in the base font code.

Font appearances (and sizes) are applied to the current font. For example, if the current font is 12-point Times Roman, and you select bold, the text is printed in 12-point Times Roman bold. Your printer must support the font appearance that you select, and your program must be installed for your printer to print out the correct results. Otherwise, your results may not be exactly what you expect. For example, if you specify italic type and your printer does not have an italic font in the size you specified, it may be printed in either normal type or underlined.

Changing Font Appearance

1. Move the cursor to where you want the new font appearance to begin. (If formatting existing text, block the text that you want to format.)
2. Either: Press **Ctrl-F8** and then press **A** for *Appearance*.

   Or: Pull down the Font menu and select *Appearance*.
3. Select any of the styles described in the table "Appearance Styles."
4. If entering new text, type it in, and then use one of the following procedures to turn the format off:
   - Press → to move the cursor to the right of the off code, or
   - Press **Ctrl-F8** and then press **N** for *Normal*, or
   - Pull down the Font menu and select *Normal*.

APPEARANCE STYLES

1. *Bold* prints text darker than normal.
2. *Undrln* prints text underlined.
3. *Dbl Und* prints text with a double underline.
4. *Italc* prints text in an italic typeface.
5. *Outln* prints outline characters.
6. *Shadw* prints characters with a shadow effect.
7. *Sm Cap* prints lowercase letters as small uppercase ones.
8. *Redln* highlights text being considered for insertion, and is an editing format, not a desktop publishing format.
9. *Stkout* highlights text being considered for deletion, and is an editing format, not a desktop publishing format.

- To insert new text at the beginning or the end of formatted text, use the Reveal Codes command (**Alt-F3** or **F11**) to position the cursor. If the new text is to have the same format, position the cursor between the codes. If the new text is to have a different format, position the cursor outside the codes.
- If you block a section of formatted text between codes used to change its appearance (or size) and then copy or move the block, the copied or moved block will have the same format as the original even if you do not copy the codes.
- You can set the way typestyles are displayed on your screen by changing the Color/Fonts/Attributes settings on the Display menu of the Setup menu.

Base Font 1
Normal
Bold
<u>Underline</u>
<u>Double Underline</u>
Italic
Outline
Shadow
Small Caps

Base Font 2
Normal
Bold
<u>Underline</u>
<u>Double Underline</u>
Italic
Outline
Shadow
Small Caps

Base Font 3
Normal
Bold
<u>Underline</u>
<u>Double Underline</u>
Italic
Outline
Shadow
Small Caps

Base Fonts and Font Appearances

EXERCISE 1

CHANGING BASE FONTS TO SEE THEIR EFFECTS ON TYPESTYLES

In this exercise, you enter base font codes in a document to see the effect of the changes on the typestyles that have been assigned to terms in the document.

1. Retrieve the TYPESTY2.WP5 document and enter your name.
2. Move the cursor to the two lines that read "*Base Font 2*" and "*Base Font 3*" and enter new base font codes in front of each so that the second and third sections of the document print in typefaces that are different from the one used in the first part (the default base font).
3. Save and print the document. The results you obtain are dependent on the system that you are using but your results should be similar to the figure "Base Fonts and Font Appearances."

EXERCISE 2

CHANGING TYPESTYLES

In this exercise, you change typestyles in a document.

1. Retrieve the TYPESTY3.WP5 document and enter your name.
2. Follow the instructions in the KEY/Strokes box "Changing Font Appearance" to change font appearances so your document is boldfaced and italicized in the same places as the figure "The TYPESTY3 Document."
3. Save and print the document. The results you obtain are dependent on the system that you are using.

KEY/Strokes
Changing Font Appearance
1. Move the cursor to where you want the new appearance to begin. (If formatting existing text, block the text that you want to format.)
2. Either   press **Ctrl-F8** and then press **A** for *Appearance*.
   Or   pull down the Font menu and select *Appearance*.
3. Select any of the styles described in the table "Appearance Styles."
4. If entering new text, type it in, and then use one of the following procedures:
   to turn the format off
   - Press → to move the cursor to the right of the off code, or
   - Press **Ctrl-F8** and then press **N** for *Normal*, or
   - Pull down the Font menu and select *Normal*.

The TYPESTY3 Document

Type Sizes

After completing this topic, you should be able to:
- Explain how type is measured and specified in point sizes
- Describe how you select type sizes for different parts of a document
- Change type sizes in your own documents

▶ T U T O R I A L

In this tutorial, you explore changing font sizes. When you are finished, your printed document should look similar to the figure "WordPerfect's Type Sizes."

GETTING STARTED

1. Retrieve the TYPESIZ1.WP5 document and enter your name.

ASSIGNING A TYPE SIZE

2. Move the cursor under the "*F*" in "*Fine.*"
3. Press **Alt-F4** or **F12** to turn on *Block On* and then press **End** to block the word "*Fine.*"
4. Press **Ctrl-F8** to display the Font menu.
5. Press **S** to select *S*ize.
6. Press **F** to select *F*ine.

ASSIGNING MORE TYPE SIZES

7. Repeat Steps 2 through 6 for each word or phrase and change their size to the one specified. (Do not format the term "*Normal*" since that is the size of the unformatted current font.)

FINISHING UP

8. Save and print the document. Your results will depend on the system you are using.

Fine
Small
Normal
Large
Vry Large
Ext Large

WordPerfect's Type Sizes

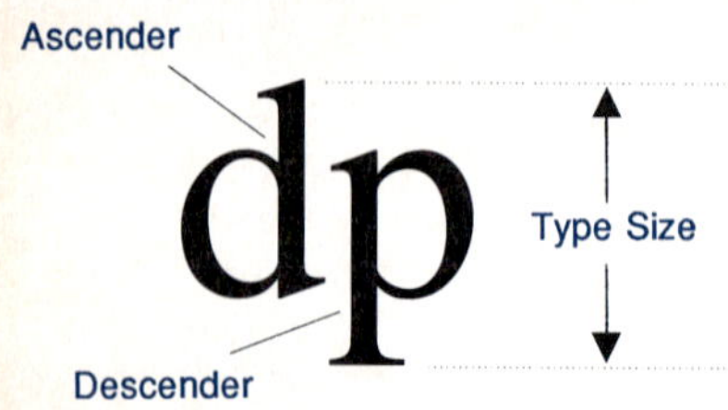

Type Size Measurement

X-Height

Alphabet Length

Here are the alphabet lengths of three typical fonts, all with the same type size.

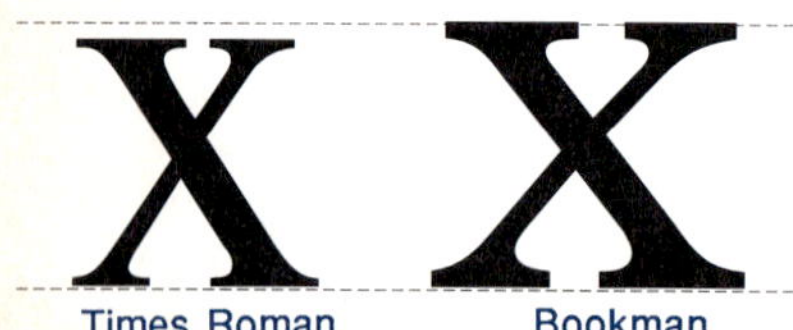

X-Heights Vary from Font to Font

Type size refers to the size of the printed character, and is specified in points. The size is measured vertically, from the top of the type's highest point to its lowest. In most instances this is from the top of ***ascenders*** to the bottom of ***descenders***. For example, the type size might be measured from the top of a lowercase d to the bottom of a lowercase p. In other instances, the uppercase letters are taller than lowercase ascenders so type is measured from the top of one of them.

The ***x-height*** is the height of lowercase letters, not including their ascenders and descenders—in other words, the height of a lowercase letter x. Different typefaces in the same size have different x-heights. This can affect readability. Many people prefer to read characters with a normal x-height. If the x-height is too large, ascenders and descenders are shortened to maintain the font size. These shorter elements provide fewer visual clues to the letters so they can't be read as quickly.

Type Widths

The width of characters, or the space they take up on a line, depends on the proportions of the type. Fonts the same size when measured vertically vary in their horizontal measurements. As a result, some fonts can fit many more characters on a given line than other fonts can even when both are the same size. The width of a complete set of lowercase letters in the same typeface, typestyle, and type size is called the font's ***alphabet length***. This measurement can be found in reference works on fonts and can be used as a rough guide in determining which fonts to use in a given situation. This measurement can be critical when setting chapter titles or headers and footers where line lengths are restricted. The alphabet length also determines the length of a document. Documents printed using fonts with longer alphabet lengths will be longer than the same documents printed with a font with a shorter alphabet length.

Times Roman	abcdefghijklmnopqrstuvwxyz
Helvetica	abcdefghijklmnopqrstuvwxyz
Bookman	abcdefghijklmnopqrstuvwxyz

CHARACTERS PER INCH

Before laser printers became widely available, most documents were printed on daisy-wheel printers or dot-matrix printers with a limited selection of typefaces. Those printers frequently used fixed-pitch characters similar to those on a typewriter. Each character occupied the same space on a line regardless of its width. Because each character occupied the same space, fonts could be specified in characters per inch (cpi). This measurement is not possible with proportionally spaced fonts because the number of characters per inch varies depending on what characters happen to occupy the space being measured. You could fit many more *f*s in a space than *w*'s. Still, on some printers, you will find fonts listed with their size indicated by their cpi, not in points. The smaller the cpi number, the larger the type.

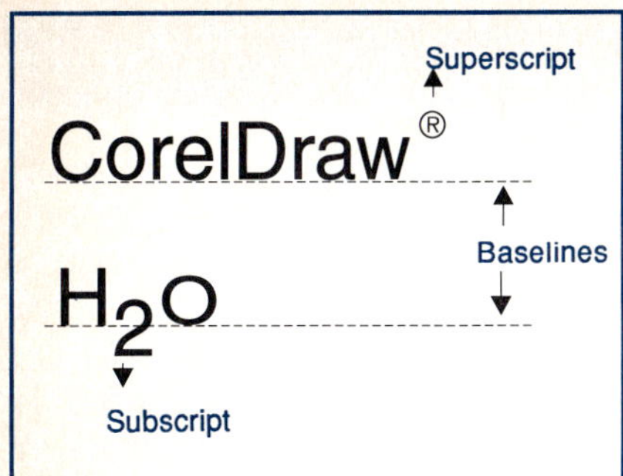

Superscripts and Subscripts

Choosing Type Sizes

Generally, body text is printed in 10-or 12-point type. Once you decide on what size to use for the body text, all other elements can be proportioned or styled to set them off from it.

TYPICAL FONT SIZES

Element	Font Size
Body text	10-12 point
Subheads	12-14 point
Title page	18 point or larger
Captions	9 or 10 point
Footnotes	8 or 9 point
Endnotes	8-10 point
Page numbers	10-12 point
Part opener or Chapter opener	18 point or larger
Headers or footers	8-10 point
Indexes	8 or 9 point
Tables of contents	10-12 point

For example, headings can be emphasized by making them larger or by changing their style. Captions can be set in a type size smaller than the body text or italicized. Page numbers can be printed a few points larger than body text, and boldfaced for emphasis. The table "Typical Font Sizes" lists some starting points to consider when specifying type sizes in a document.

Superscripts and Subscripts

Superscripts and subscripts can be used to print copyright marks, trademark symbols, formulas, and footnote numbers. **Superscripts** (called *superior numbers* or *figures*) are characters that print partially above the x-height of the line of type. **Subscripts** (called *inferior numbers* or *figures*) are characters that print partially below the baseline. Both are usually printed in a font smaller than that used for body text.

Display Type

Typefaces that work well for large blocks of text are called **body type**. These typefaces are easy to read but not very decorative. When you want to attract attention, you use **display type**, a term that is usually reserved for typefaces designed to be used in sizes that are 18 point or larger. In smaller sizes the type may be almost unreadable, especially if used for large blocks of text. This kind of typeface is used in displays and advertisements, and for title pages, chapter openers, and headlines in all kinds of publications.

Display Type
Display type can be ornate and is used for ads and other applications where a lot of visual impact is desired.

Display Type in Small Sizes
As you can tell by trying to read this paragraph, display type is best when used in moderation.

14 point Zapf Chancery

18 point Zapf Chancery

24 point Zapf Chancery

30 point Zapf Chancery

The typefaces that work well for large blocks of text are called body type. These typefaces are easy to read but not very decorative. When you want to attract attention, you use "display type," a term that is usually reserved for typefaces designed to be used in sizes that are 18 points or larger. In smaller sizes the type may be almost unreadable, especially if used for large blocks of text. This kind of typeface is used in displays, advertisements, title pages, chapter openers, and headlines in all kinds of publications.

WordPerfect does not normally allow you to control fonts by specifying specific point sizes. Instead, you specify the point size for the base font, and then change sizes where desired by selecting menu choices that range from fine to extra large. The type sizes that are then printed are relative to the current font. For example, if the current font is 12-point Times Roman, and you select the large font size, the text is printed in the next largest font size, perhaps 14-point Times Roman. If the current font is 10-point type, then large may print at 12 points.

If your system contains numerous font sizes, this lack of control can cause problems for you since the program is selecting font sizes, not you. For example, if you specify a size not on your system, WordPerfect will automatically use the closest available font size. To control font sizes by points, you can enter base font codes wherever you want to change sizes. All base fonts can be selected from a list that indicates the actual point sizes for each font.

KEY/Strokes

Changing Font Sizes

1. Move the cursor to where you want the font size to change. (If formatting existing text, block the text that you want to format.)
2. Either: Press **Ctrl-F8** and then press **S** for **S**ize.
   Or: Pull down the Font menu.
3. Select any of the sizes described in the table "Font Sizes."
4. If entering new text, type it in, and then use one of the following procedures to turn the format off:
   - Press → to move the cursor to the right of the off code, or
   - Press **Ctrl-F8** and then press **N** for **N**ormal, or
   - Pull down the Font menu and select **Normal**.

FONT SIZES

1. *Su**p**rscpt* prints text in a fine size above the center of the line.
2. *Su**b**scpt* prints text in a fine size below the center of the line.
3. *Fine* prints text 60 percent of normal.
4. *Small* prints text 80 percent of normal.
5. *Large* prints text 120 percent of normal.
6. *Vry Large* prints text 150 percent of normal.
7. *Ext Large* prints text 200 percent of normal.

Adjusting WordPerfect's Font Size Ratios

When you select one of the sizes, the font that appears on your printout is controlled to some extent by a setting on the Setup menu. This setting specifies what percent of the normal font is used for each of the menu choices. For example, if the base font is 10-point, the default setting for Fine is 60 percent, so a font of 6-points will be used when you select the

Fine format. If you want, you can change the setting to 80 percent so an 8-point font is used for fine formats. To adjust these settings, you use the Setup menu. If your printer has a large number of fonts, the changes you make can have a big effect. If your printer has only a few fonts, changes will have little effect.

> **➡ KEY/Strokes**
>
> **Changing Font Size Ratios**
>
> 1. Either: Press **Shift-F1** to display the Setup menu.
>   Or: Pull down the File menu and select *Setup*.
> 2. Press **I** for *Initial Settings*.
> 3. Press **P** for *Print Options*.
> 4. Press **S** for *Size Attribute Ratios*.
> 5. Enter percentages for any of the font sizes. (The default settings are listed in the table "Font Sizes.")

▶ EXERCISES

EXERCISE 1

CHANGING BASE FONTS TO SEE THEIR EFFECTS ON TYPE SIZES

In this exercise, you enter base font codes in a document to see the effect of the changes on the typestyles that have been assigned to terms in the document.

1. Retrieve the TYPESIZ2.WP5 document and enter your name.
2. Move the cursor to the lines that read "*Base Font 2*" and "*Base Font 3*" and enter base font codes in front of each that are different from the default font and from each other.
3. Save and print the document. The second and third sections of the document are printed in typefaces that are different from the one used in the first part (the default base font). The type sizes in each section are based on the current font.

EXERCISE 2

CHANGING FONT SIZES

In this exercise, you superscript and subscript characters.

1. Retrieve the TYPESIZ3.WP5 document and enter your name.
2. Follow the instructions in the KEY/Strokes box "Changing Font Sizes" to make the document match the one shown in the figure "Superscript and Subscript Applications."

1. $\frac{1}{2}$

2. Trademark^{TM}

3. Registration$^{®}$

4. 30°F

5. H_2O

6. $1 - \frac{3}{4} = \frac{1}{4}$

Superscript and Subscript Applications

3. Save and print the document. The results you obtain are dependent on the system that you are using.

EXERCISE 3

EXPLORING ALPHABET LENGTHS

In this exercise, you change base fonts to see how the alphabet length varies among fonts.

1. Retrieve the TYPESIZ4.WP5 document and enter your name.
2. Find the two lines that read *"Base Font 2"* and *"Base Font 3"* and enter new base font codes in front of each so that the second and third sections of the document print in typefaces that are different from the one used in the first part (the default base font).
3. Save and print the document. You should see how alphabet lengths vary depending on the typeface you are using.

✔ T Y P E   S I Z E   T I P S

- Fonts are either bit-mapped or scalable. Scalable fonts take up less room on the hard disk and can be scaled to any size within a range, often from 3 or 4 points to well over 100 points.
- You can set the way type sizes are displayed on your screen by changing the Color/Fonts/Attributes settings on the Display menu of the Setup menu.

REVIEW

- Points describe the size of the type.
- Publishers and printers measure type in points and pages in picas.
- Indents, spaces, dashes, and bullets are specified in ems or ens. An em is the square of the font size, about the size of an uppercase letter *M*. An en is half as wide, about the size of an uppercase letter *N*.
- A font is a complete set of characters. It is defined by its typeface (a particular design such as Times Roman or Courier), typestyle (such as normal, italic, or bold), and type size (expressed in points).
- The initial base font is the default font used for all documents or the current document. You change fonts by entering base font codes into the document.
- The current font is the font in effect at the cursor position and is the one that determines font sizes and appearances.

QUESTIONS

TRUE/FALSE

T   F

1. A pica contains exactly 12 points.
2. Points are normally used to specify page layouts.
3. There are about 12 picas in each point.
4. You can change WordPerfect's units of measurement to picas.
5. The term *font* refers to the entire family of type for a given typeface including normal, bold, and italic.
6. The term *typeface* refers to a particular type design such as Times Roman.
7. Serif fonts do not have small cross stokes at the end of main strokes and sans serif typefaces do.
8. Helvetica is a typical sans serif typeface and Times Roman is a typical serif typeface.
9. One of the hallmarks of good design is to use all of the fonts available in one publication.
10. The term *display type* refers to type that salespeople use as samples when selling type.
11. To change the typeface in WordPerfect, you can use the Font menu to apply a new appearance.
12. The term *typestyle* is not used by WordPerfect. Instead, they use the term *font appearance*.

❏ ❏ 13. Typical typestyles are bold and italic.
❏ ❏ 14. When you use WordPerfect's Font menu to change font sizes, you have to specify the size in points.
❏ ❏ 15. All fonts of the same size print the same number of characters per inch.

FILL IN THE BLANK

1. To measure points and picas, you need a(n) ____________.
2. Each pica contains exactly ____________ points.
3. There are about ____________ picas to the inch.
4. A 36-point typeface would be about ____________ inch(es) high.
5. A point is ____________ of an inch.
6. Fonts are described by three basic characteristics that include their ____________, ____________, and their ____________.
7. The overall design of a typeface such as Times Roman is referred to as its ____________.
8. Each typeface has several styles that might include ____________ and ____________.
9. Type sizes are normally given in the unit of measurement called ____________.
10. Large type designed for chapter openers and advertisements is called ____________.
11. To change the typeface in WordPerfect, you change the ____________.
12. Typestyles are categorized as being either italic or ____________.
13. The height of a font not counting its ascenders and descenders is call the ____________.

MATCH THE COLUMNS

1. Helvetica
2. 10 point
3. Bold
4. Point
5. Pica
6. Em
7. En
8. Descender
9. Ascender
10. X-height

__ About 6 to the inch
__ About 72 to the inch
__ Height of lowercase letters, not counting ascenders or descenders
__ One-half the square of the font size
__ The part of a lowercase letter that protrudes above the x-height
__ The part of a lowercase letter that protrudes below the x-height
__ The square of the font size
__ Type size
__ Typeface
__ Typestyle

1. What is the difference between a point and a pica?
2. List three things that you use points to measure.
3. What do you use picas to measure?
4. Describe what ems and ens are.
5. List three things that you specify in ems.
6. List three things that you specify in ens.
7. WordPerfect's points are slightly different from those used elsewhere in the publishing and printing industries. Describe how they are different.
8. What is a font?
9. List and briefly describe three font appearances you can use.
10. Describe a superscript and a subscript.
11. List and describe three terms used to describe fonts.
12. In what units of measurement are font sizes specified?
13. What is the difference between the initial base font and a base font?
14. What is the current font? How does it affect font sizes and appearances?
15. What is the basic difference between a serif and sans serif typeface?
16. What is the basic difference between a roman and italic typestyle?

PROJECTS

There is an old saying that practice makes perfect. When it comes to desktop publishing this is certainly true. There is no substitute for experience. The projects in this section (and those at the end of other chapters) are designed to provide you with this needed experience. As you complete them, you are exposed to most aspects of desktop publishing and learn not only how to format documents but also how to solve problems that may arise.

What You Need

To complete all projects, you retrieve unformatted files from the *Desktop Publishing Disk with WordPerfect 5.1*. The files that you need are listed for each project next to the illustration of the completed document.

How to Use the Projects

Each document to be formatted in the projects is illustrated. Most documents are shown in full, although some long documents have been abbreviated to show only one example of each design element. The numbers on each illustration identify design elements that are then described briefly in the "Formats" section next to the figure. You will have to make choices regarding the fonts to use, so the first project is an inventory of the fonts that are available on your system. After completing this first project you will have a printout that you should retain and use to select fonts for all of the projects that follow.

PROJECT 1

TAKING A FONT INVENTORY

Fonts are printer dependent. This means that the list of fonts from which you can choose depends on which printer you have specified. For this reason, no one can anticipate the fonts that you have to work with. Since fonts will play such an important role throughout this text, here we do an inventory of the fonts that are available.

1. To begin, press **Ctrl-F8** to display the Font menu, then press **F** for *Base* **F***ont*. This displays a list of the fonts available to your printer. The first column on the screen lists the name of the font. Sizes are often specified in points, in cpi (characters per inch for fixed pitch), and as scalable. (The typestyle—bold, italic, and so on—may be indicated in parentheses.)
2. List and describe each of the fonts in the table on the facing page, one on each line. If the fonts are scalable, indicate the range of sizes that you can scale them to.

Font Name	Style	Size

3. Retrieve the FONTLIST.WP5 document and enter your name.

4. Press **Shift**-**F7** to display the Print menu and note the name of the printer following the prompt line *Select Printer*. Press **F7** to return to the Edit screen and enter that name on the prompt line *Printer:*

5. Move the cursor to the line below the heading "*Font Name*" and list each of the fonts you entered in the table above.

6. Move the cursor under the first character in each line where you listed a font, press **Ctrl**-**F8**, then press **F** for *Base Font* to display the list of fonts again. Select the font that is described on that line of your document. Repeat until you have entered a base font code in front of each line of the document.

7. Save and print the document. Retain the printout for your records; you will need it later as a guide to choosing fonts for other exercises and projects. It names and illustrates all of the fonts that are available on your system.

A BUSINESS LETTER

In this project, change the base font for a business letter and then format the letterhead as small caps. Make a printout. Then, delete the base font code, enter a new one, and make another printout. After printing three versions, choose the one that you like the best.

Procedures Used

■ Changing the base font to change the typeface and changing styles to small caps.

Text Files Needed

■ BUSLTR.WP5

Formats

① Enter a base font code for a 12-point serif or sans serif typeface.
② Format the letterhead as small caps.

Tip

■ The ruled line under the letterhead has been entered as a graphics line and will appear on printouts or the View Document screen but not on the Edit screen.

UR OVERDUE INC
110 MISERY LANE
DUNNING, NV 10010

September 19, 1993

Mr. Frank Doe
Late Payment Company
112 Laughing Brook
Avoidance, NJ 23071

Dear Mr. Doe:

We are replying to your letter of June 22, 1992, and recent telephone conversations regarding duplicate payments of $11.33.

Our records indicate that two (2) payments of $11.33 were received and applied to your account, Account Number 100. The adjustment is in process, and you may expect to receive your refund within the next three (3) weeks.

We regret the delay in replying to your correspondence, but in large paperwork operations such as ours, it is extremely difficult to completely avoid incidents of this kind. We will do our utmost to see that they do not recur and that you will be served more promptly and efficiently in the future.

Very truly yours,

A MEMO

In this project, change the base font for the memo and then boldface the headings. Make a printout, delete the base font code, and try another. After printing three versions, choose the one that you like best.

Procedures Used
- Changing the base font.

Text Files Needed
- MEMO1.WP5

Formats
① Enter a base font code for a 12-point serif or sans serif typeface.
② Format the letterhead as extra large.
③ Boldface the side heads.

Tip
- You may want to experiment with a 14-point typeface for memos since larger type is easier to read and the memo is short enough that a larger type won't force text to a second page.

①

②Global Warming Inc.

③

TO:	Our Employees
FROM:	Your Name Director of Human Resource Development
DATE:	JUNE 22, 199X
SUBJECT:	Employee Benefits Update

In speaking with many of our fine associates during recent weeks, I have noticed one topic common to nearly every discussion. Many of us in The Jefferson Company seem to have developed a "healthy" enthusiasm for physical fitness, nutrition, and other health-related issues. This pleases me. The benefits of proper diet and exercise are many and often cited. For this reason I will not belabor the point by listing the numerous physical and psychological benefits of a health-conscious life-style. I will encourage you to utilize the *Free Modern Fitness* VIP membership that is now included in your employee benefit package. This no-cost membership is valid at any of the Modern Fitness locations in the metro area. Individual membership cards may be obtained from the Human Resources office.

Enjoy!

A PERSONAL LETTER

In this project, change the base font for the letter that created a stir when broadcast on a PBS Civil War special. If your system has any script fonts, try one of those to simulate handwriting. If it doesn't, use an italic font. Set the type for the closing paragraph in a different typestyle.

Procedures Used
- Changing the base font and typestyles.

Text Files Needed
- SARAH.WP5

Formats
① Enter a base font code for a 14-point script typeface or a typeface with an italic typestyle.
② Format the last paragraph in a different typeface or typestyle to set it off.

Tip
- If you used a script typeface for the letter, you can set the last paragraph in a normal typeface. If you used an italic typestyle for the document, you can use a normal typestyle.

July 14, 1861
Camp Clark, Washington
My very dear Sarah:

The indications are very strong that we shall move in a few days - perhaps tomorrow. Lest I should not be able to write again, I feel impelled to write a few lines that may fall under your eye when I shall be no more.

I have no misgivings about, or lack of confidence in, the cause in which I am engaged, and my courage does not halt or falter. I know how strongly American Civilization now leans on the triumph of the Government and how great a debt we owe to those who went before us through the blood and sufferings of the Revolution. And I am willing - perfectly willing - to lay down all my joys in this life, to help maintain this Government, and to pay that debt . . .

Sarah, my love for you is deathless, it seems to bind me with mighty cables that nothing but Omnipotence could break; and yet my love of Country comes over me like a strong wind and bears me unresistibly on with all these chains to the battle field.

The memories of the blissful moments I have spent with you come creeping over me, and I feel most gratified to God and to you that I have enjoyed them so long. And hard it is for me to give them up and burn to ashes the hopes of future years, when, God willing, we might still have lived and loved together, and seen our sons grown up to honorable man-hood around us. I have, I know, but few and small claims upon Divine Providence, but something whispers to me - perhaps it is the wafted prayer of my little Edgar, that I shall return to my loved ones unharmed. If I do not my dear Sarah, never forget how much I love you, and when my last breath escapes me on the battle field, it will whisper your name. Forgive my many faults, and the many pains I have caused you. How thoughtless and foolish I have often times been! How gladly would I wash out with my tears every little spot upon your happiness . . .

But, O Sarah! If the dead can come back to this earth and fly unseen around those they loved, I shall always be near you; in the gladdest days and in the darkest nights . . . always, always, and if there be a soft breeze upon your cheek, it shall be my breath, as the cool air fans your throbbing temple, it shall be my spirit passing by. Sarah, do not mourn me dead; think I am gone and wait for thee, for we shall meet again.

Major Sullivan Ballou wrote this letter to his wife Sarah, in Springfield, Rhode Island one week before he was killed at the Battle of Bull Run during the Civil War. During the battle, his leg was shattered by a cannonball while leading a charge and he died on July 21, 1861. The original letter is in the Civil War collection at the Illinois State Historical Library.

SELECTED DICTIONARY ENTRIES

In this project, you change the base font for the document and then boldface the main dictionary entries and italicize the initials that indicate the part of speech. The figure shows only page 1 of a two-page document. The second page should be formatted the same.

Procedures Used
- Changing the base font and font appearances.

Text Files Needed
- DICTION.WP5

Credits
- Bierce, Ambrose, *The Devil's Dictionary*, Dover Publications, NY, 1958

Formats
① Format as a large heading.
② Italicize the introduction.
③ Boldface entries.
④ Italicize parts of speech.

Tip
- Note that the book title in the introduction is not italicized.

---

①—The Devil's Dictionary

② *The Devil's Dictionary was begun in a weekly paper in 1881, and was continued in a desultory way and at long intervals until 1906. In that year a large part of it was published in covers with the title* The Cynic's Word Book, *a name which the author had not the power to reject or the happiness to approve.*

④

From the Preface

③—**Acquaintance**, *n.* A person whom we know well enough to borrow from, but not well enough to lend to. A degree of friendship called slight when the object is poor or obscure, and intimate when he is rich or famous.

Battle, *n.* A method of untying with the teeth a political knot that would not yield to the tongue.

Bigot, *n.* One who is obstinately and zealously attached to an opinion that you do not entertain.

Blackguard, *n.* A man whose qualities, prepared for display like a box of berries in a market--the fine ones on top--have been opened on the wrong side. An inverted gentleman.

Bore, *n.* A person who talks when you wish him to listen.

Brain, *n.* An apparatus with which we think we think. That which distinguishes the man who is content to be something from the man who wishes to do something.

Cartesian, *adj.* Relating to Descartes, a famous philosopher, author of the celebrated dictum, Cogito ergo sum--whereby he was pleased to suppose he demonstrated the reality of human existence. The dictum might be improved, however, thus: Cogito cogito ergo cogito sum--"I think that I think, therefor I think that I am;" as close an approach to certainty as any philosopher has yet made.

Clarionet, *n.* An instrument of torture operated by a person with cotton in his ears. There are two instruments that are worse than a clarionet--two clarionets.

Comfort, *n.* A state of mind produced by contemplation of a neighbor's uneasiness.

Commerce, *n.* A kind of transaction in which A plunders from B the goods of C, and for compensation B picks the pocket of D of money belonging to E.

Confident, Confidante, *n.* One entrusted by A with the secrets of B, confided to him by C.

Connoisseur, *n.* A specialist who knows everything about something and nothing about anything else.

Conservative, *n.* A statesman who is enamored of existing evils, as distinguished from the Liberal, who wishes to replace them with others.

FRESHMAN RULES

In this project, change the base font for a college's freshman rules in the early 1920s. If you have a variety of fonts, try some ornate ones.

Procedures Used
■ Changing the base font.

Text Files Needed
■ FRESHMAN.WP5

Formats
① Base font code for an ornate typeface.
② Format as a very large or extra large heading.

Freshman Rules

Class of 1929

1. Freshman girls shall wear the arm bands at all times.
2. Freshman girls shall get off the walk for upper classmen.
3. Freshman girls shall use no short cuts on the campus.
4. Freshman girls shall use all basement entrances.
5. Freshman girls shall wear no high school pins, rings or other such insignia.
6. Freshman girls shall wear their hats backwards on Monday. (It is compulsory to wear hats on this day).
7. Freshman girls shall use no cosmetics on Tuesday.
8. Freshman girls shall wear rattles around their necks on Wednesday, and rattle them at the approach of a Sophomore girl.
9. Freshman girls shall wear wide, green bows on their hair on Thursday.
10. Freshman girls shall neither walk nor talk with any boys on the campus on Friday.

NOTE. These rules shall be strictly enforced until Christmas vacation, at the end of which time an examination will be given, further information being set forth at a later date.

A MATH DOCUMENT

In this project, superscript the numbers shown in the figure and then make a printout.

Procedures Used
- Superscripting characters.

Text Files Needed
- POWERS.WP5

Formats
① Superscript these items.

Tip
- Superscripted characters are not superscripted on the Edit screen. To see the effects of superscripting, you must use the View Document command or print the document. After formatting some numbers, you can see which have been done by revealing codes.

Exponents and Bases 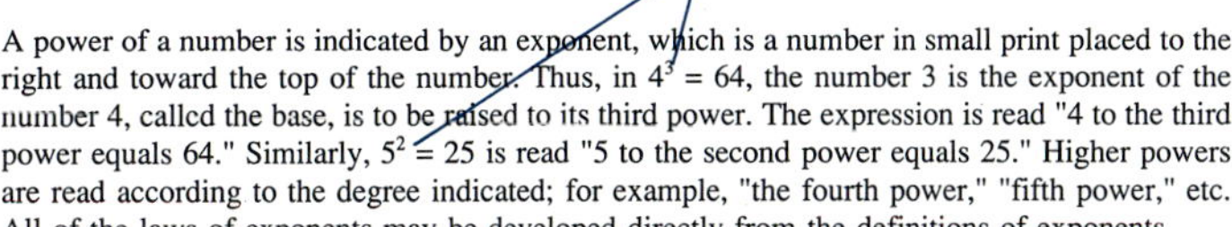

A power of a number is indicated by an exponent, which is a number in small print placed to the right and toward the top of the number. Thus, in $4^3 = 64$, the number 3 is the exponent of the number 4, called the base, is to be raised to its third power. The expression is read "4 to the third power equals 64." Similarly, $5^2 = 25$ is read "5 to the second power equals 25." Higher powers are read according to the degree indicated; for example, "the fourth power," "fifth power," etc. All of the laws of exponents may be developed directly from the definitions of exponents.

Multiplication
To multiply two or more powers having the same base, add the exponents and raise the common base to the sum of the exponents. For example,

$$4^3 \times 4^2 = 4^{(3+2)} = 4^5$$

Division
To divide one power into another having the same base, subtract the exponent of the divisor from the exponent of the dividend. Use the number resulting from this subtraction as the exponent of the base in the quotient. For example,

$$6^7/6^5 = 6^{(7-5)} = 6^2$$

Power of a Power
To find the power of a power, multiply the exponents. For example,

$$(3^2)^4 = 3^{(4 \times 2)} = 3^8$$

Power of a Product
The power of a product is equal to the product obtained when each of the original factors is raised to the indicated power and the resulting power are multiplied together. For example,

$$(3 \times 2 \times 5)^3 = 3^3 \times 2^3 \times 5^3$$

Power of a Quotient
The power of a quotient is equal to the quotient obtained when the dividend and divisor are each raised to the indicated power separately, before the division is performed. For example,

$$(2/3)^3 = 2^3/3^3$$

A BUSINESS CARD

In this project, you format a business card that could be used as camera-ready copy by a printer. You can also enter your own name, address, and phone number in place of the generic text that is already entered in the file when you retrieve it. Be sure to reveal codes when you enter text so you enter it in the correct position relative to codes that are already in the document.

Procedures Used
- Changing typestyles and type sizes.

Text Files Needed
- BUSCARD.WP5

Formats
① Format as large font size with a small caps typestyle.
② Format as a large font size with a bold typestyle.
③ Format as a small font size with a small caps typestyle.

Tip
- Codes have been entered at the top of the document so any text that you enter is centered on the page and kerned. Also the right margin has been changed to 4 inches.

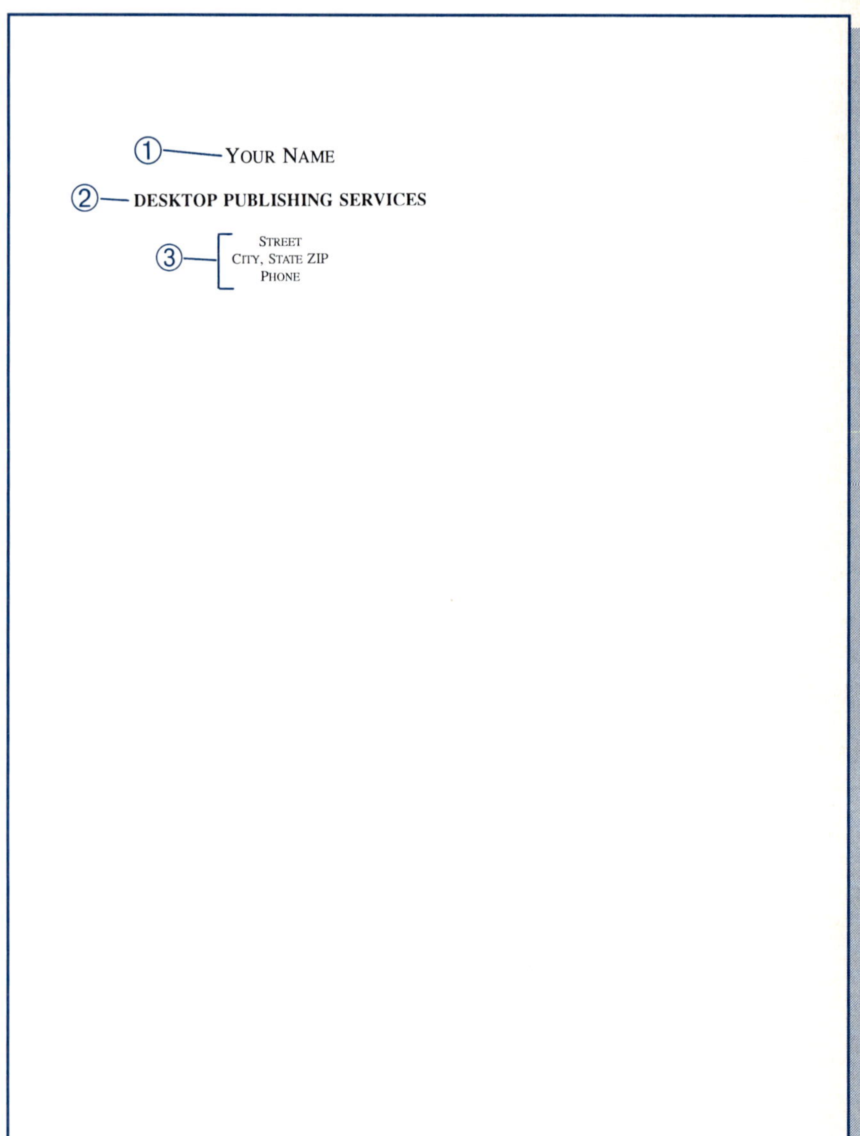

THE DTP ADVISOR NEWSLETTER

This project introduces *The dtp Advisor*, a newsletter featuring announcements of desktop publishing software and hardware. You will work on this newsletter in projects at the end of many chapters of this text, gradually improving it as you proceed. In this project, you specify typefaces, typestyles, and type sizes for various elements in the newsletter.

Procedures Used
- Changing typefaces, typestyles, and type sizes.

Text Files Needed
- ADVISOR.WP5

Formats
① Enter a base font code for a 50-point sans serif typeface such as Helvetica.
② Enter a base font code for a 12-point serif typeface such as Times Roman.
③ Format "*dtp*" in the newsletter's title as italic.
④ Format the headlines for each article so they print bold and in a large size (see Tips).
⑤ Italicize all of the sentences that read "*For more information, contact.*"

Tip
- There are four article headlines that read "*FaceLift For WordPerfect,*" "*PostScript in a Cartridge,*" "*Reduced Magnetic Field Monitor,*" and "*CorelDRAW 2.0 Released.*" You can use the Search command to locate them.

THE *dtp* ADVISOR

FaceLift For WordPerfect

Bitstream Inc. today announced version 1.5 of Bitstream FaceLift for WordPerfect. FaceLift brings enhanced font support to WordPerfect 5.0 and 5.1. The new FaceLift version 1.5 will create high-quality fonts on-the-fly for popular dot-matrix and inkjet printers--like the HP DeskJet, Canon BubbleJet and the IBM ExecuJet--in addition to the existing on-the-fly support for the Hewlett-Packard LaserJet series of printers. FaceLift 1.5 for WordPerfect will be available in the spring of 1991.

In addition to 13 typeface outlines provided in the original FaceLift package, FaceLift 1.5 for WordPerfect will also ship with three Symbol typefaces: ITC Zapf Dingbats Symbol Proportional and Symbol Monospaced. Users will be able to access a total of 698 characters from the Bitstream International Character Set and from these three Symbols typefaces.

FaceLift 1.5 for WordPerfect is an easy-to-use utility that allows users to print high-quality fonts in any size from 2 to 500 point (in quarter point increments) without ever having to leave the application. The fonts are generated at print time, so the need for stored bit-map fonts is eliminated. Based on Bitstream Speedo technology, FaceLift sends characters to printers in both graphics mode (laser, inkjet and dot-matrix printers) and as HP soft fonts (laser printers only). Users have full control over the number and size of soft fonts to be downloaded, depending on the memory available in the printer.

"We are very excited that FaceLift 1.5 for WordPerfect will provide dot-matrix and inkjet users with the same high typographic quality and capabilities that HP LaserJet users have enjoyed with Bitstream type," stated Doug Lloyd, Executive Director at WordPerfect. "That, and the addition of the three new Symbol typefaces makes FaceLift a great companion for WordPerfect."

First-time users can purchase FaceLift 1.5 for WordPerfect for a suggested U.S. list price of $99. Current users of FaceLift 1.0 for WordPerfect can upgrade to version 1.5 for $24.95. In addition to the 16 typefaces included free with FaceLift, users can purchase add-on fonts from the Bitstream Library of 52 typeface packages. Also available is the FaceLift Companion Value Pack, a selection of 24 text and headline faces for a suggested U.S. list price $199.

FaceLift 1.5 for WordPerfect is the newest member of the Bitstream FaceLift product line. The initial product, FaceLift for Windows, shipped in August of 1990. All FaceLift products can share Bitstream typefaces (in Speedo format) stored in a single common subdirectory.

FaceLift for Wordperfect was developed in conjunction with LaserTools Corporation, a privately held company based in Emeryville, CA. LaserTools is a developer of innovative printing enhancement products--tools for printer sharing, printer control, printer acceleration, and font management.

An industry leader in typographic quality and innovative technology, Bitstream licenses fonts and related software to more than 420 hardware manufacturers and software developers worldwide. Its line of retail products is distributed by an extensive network of dealers in the United States and in 18 nations worldwide.

Character &
Line Spacing

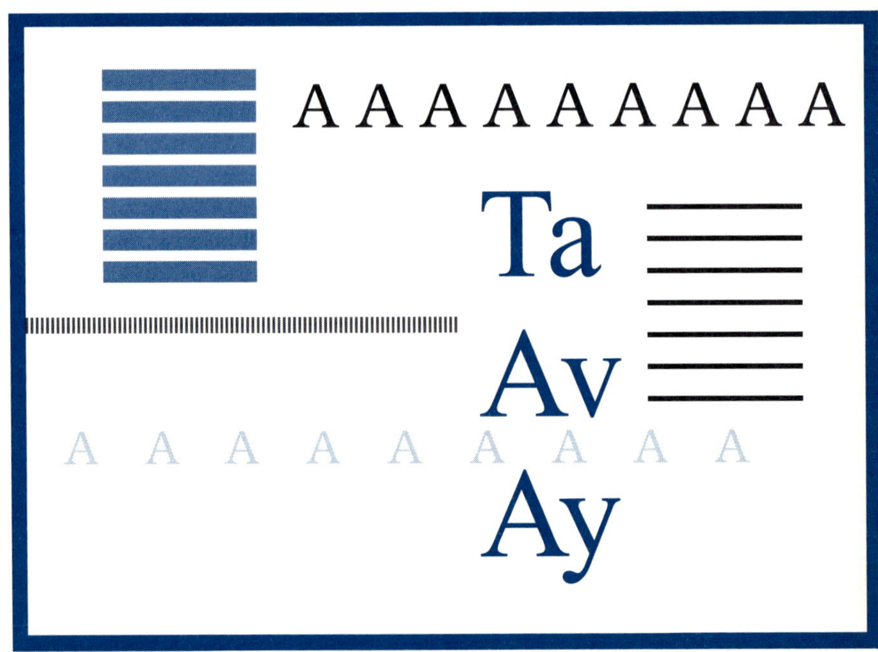

Character Spacing: Kerning

After completing this topic, you should be able to:

- Describe the differences between monospaced and proportionally spaced fonts
- Explain what the term *kerning* means
- Use WordPerfect's Kerning command in your own documents

▶ T U T O R I A L

In this tutorial, you kern some letter pairs to move them closer together. When finished, your printed document should look similar to the figure "Kerned Letter Pairs."

GETTING STARTED

1. Retrieve the KERN1.WP5 document and enter your name.
2. Enter a base font code at the top of the document to change the type size to between 18 and 30 points. (If you do not have fonts this large, use the largest that you do have.)

TURNING KERNING ON

3. Move the cursor under the "*A*" in the "*AT*" on the second row that reads "*AT AW AV LT*" (you leave the first row unkerned).
4. Press **Shift-F8** to display the Format menu.
5. Press **O** for *Other*.
6. Press **P** for *Printer Functions*.
7. Press **K** for *Kerning*.
8. Press **Y** for *Yes*.
9. Press **F7** to return to the Edit screen.

TURNING KERNING OFF

10. Move the cursor under the "*T*" in "*Ta*" on the first row that reads *Ta Ay ij Av*.
11. Repeat Steps 4 through 9 but turn kerning off.

TURNING KERNING ON AGAIN

12. Move the cursor under the "*T*" in "*Ta*" on the second row that reads "*Ta Ay ij Av*."
13. Repeat Steps 4 through 9 to turn kerning back on.

AT AW AV   LT
AT AW AV   LT

Ta Ay   ij   Av
Ta Ay   ij   Av

Kerned Letter Pairs

FINISHING UP

14. Save and print the document. The letter pairs on the second line in each pair of lines should be closer together than the first line. If both lines in each section are the same, your printer or the initial base font does not support kerning. Change the initial base font for the document and make another printout to see if that font is kerned.

▷ D E S K T O P   P U B L I S H I N G   C O N C E P T S

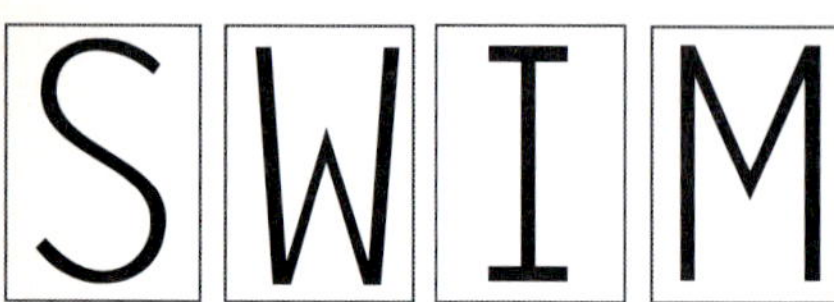

Fixed Pitch

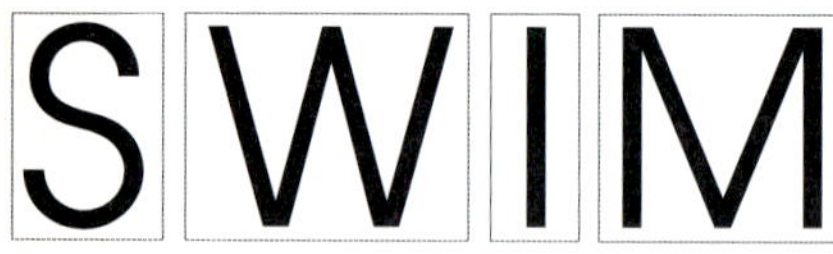

Proportional Spacing

The characters in all fonts are spaced using either fixed-pitch or proportional spacing. **Monospaced** fonts (also called *fixed pitch*) use the same space for each letter, whether a wide *w* or a narrow *i*. **Proportional spacing** varies the space the characters occupy depending on the width of the letter. Therefore, a *w* is given more space than an *i*.

On some programs, you are given additional control over letter spacing. One of the most common is kerning. **Kerning** controls the spacing between specific pairs of letters such as *AV, AW, AY, Ta, Ky*. Some pairs of letters appear farther apart than they really are when they are printed in large type sizes. When kerned, the letters in the pair are moved closer together. This gives a more finished appearance to the text. In the days when one character at a time was set in solid type, individual characters would be notched to move them closer together. Kerning is most often used in titles and chapter openers or wherever large type sizes appear, because **letter spacing** is much more critical in large sizes than it is in small sizes.

▷ W O R D P E R F E C T   P R O C E D U R E S

STATE

Unkerned

STATE

Kerned

Kerning

You can kern text automatically by turning kerning on or you can kern it manually with the Advance command.

Kerning Text Automatically

You can turn kerning on and off anywhere in the document by entering on and off codes. WordPerfect uses the printer resource file that is selected when you add a printer to define which letter pairs are kerned. If this printer definition file does not support kerning, it may be because your printer does not support this feature.

 **K E Y / S t r o k e s**

Turning Kerning On and Off

1. Press **Shift-F8** to display the Format menu.
2. Press **O** for *Other*.
3. Press **P** for *Printer Functions*.
4. Press **K** for *Kerning*.
5. Press **Y** for *Yes* or **N** for *No*.
6. Press **F7** to return to the Edit screen.

Kerned Letters in Solid Type

Kerning Letter Pairs Manually

The Advance command can be used to shift the second character in a pair to the left a specified distance.

Using the Advance Command to Kern Letter Pairs

1. Move the cursor under the second letter in the pair to be kerned.
2. Press **Shift-F8** to display the Format menu.
3. Press **O** for *Other*.
4. Press **A** for *Advance*.
5. Press **L** for *Left* and the prompt reads *Adv. left*.
6. Type the distance (for example **3pt**, or **.042"**) and then press **Enter**.
7. Press **F7** to return to the Edit screen.

► EXERCISES

EXERCISE 1

PRINTING THE KERNING TEST DOCUMENT

WordPerfect comes with a file that allows you to test the kerning capabilities of your system. Retrieve the KERN.TST document.

- On a hard disk system, this file is in the same directory as your WordPerfect printer files.
- On a floppy disk system it is on the *PTR Program* disk.

The file is installed when the Printer Program is installed, so if it isn't on the hard disk, this file may not have been installed along with the program.

Enter a base font code at the top of the document for the font that you want to test. Make a printout to see if your printer supports kerning. If it doesn't, change the base font code and make another printout.

EXERCISE 2

KERNING MANUALLY

In this exercise, you enter advance left codes between letter pairs to move the rightmost letter closer to the left letter.

1. Retrieve the KERN2.WP5 document and enter your name.
2. Enter a base font code at the top of the document to change the type size to about 18 points.
3. Follow the instructions in the KEY/Strokes box "Using the Advance Command to Kern Letter Pairs" to enter an advance left code between

each pair of letters (except in the first column). The advance left distance that you enter for each pair is indicated on the line above the letter pairs. For example, letters in the second column should be advanced left 1 point, in the third column 2 points, and so on.

4. Save and print the document. Compare each column to the first where no advance codes are entered.

P.
PA
T.
Ta
TA
Te
To
Tr
Tu
Tw
Ty
Wa
WA
we
We
Wo
Y.
Ya
yo
Yo

The Most Commonly Kerned Letter Pairs

EXERCISE 3

KERNING THE MOST COMMON LETTER PAIRS

In this exercise, you kern the 20 most frequently kerned letter pairs (according to Frank J. Romano's *TypEncyclopedia*). Use automatic kerning if your system supports it or manual kerning if it doesn't.

1. Retrieve the KERN3.WP5 document and enter your name.
2. Enter a base font code at the top of the document to change the type size to 24 points or larger.
3. Print the document for comparison purposes.
4. Kern each letter pair.
5. Save and print the document. Compare the printout to the first one that you made. (If you hold the pages together up to the light, you can see through them to see slight changes more easily.)

Character Spacing: Tracking

After completing this topic, you should be able to:
- Explain what the term *tracking* means and how it differs from kerning
- Control the letter spacing in your own documents

▶ T U T O R I A L

In this tutorial, you change the word and letter spacing in some headings. When finished, your printed document should look similar to the figure "Letter Spacing."

GETTING STARTED

1. Retrieve the TRACK1.WP5 document and enter your name.

COMPRESSING LETTER SPACING

2. Position the cursor under the "*A*" in "*AVAILABLE*" on the line above the heading "*Condensed.*"
3. Press **Shift**-**F8** to display the Format menu.
4. Press **O** for **O**ther.
5. Press **P** for **P**rinter Functions.
6. Press **W** for **W**ord Spacing and four menu choices are displayed.
7. Press **Enter** to leave word spacing unchanged and the prompt reads *Letter Spacing:* followed by four menu choices.
8. Press **P** to select **P**ercent of Optimal and the prompt reads *Percent of Optimal: 100.*
9. Type **90** and then press **Enter**.
10. Press **F7** to return to the Edit screen.

EXPANDING LETTER SPACING

11. Position the cursor under the "*A*" in "*AVAILABLE*" on the line above the "*Expanded*" heading.
12. Repeat Steps 3 through 10 but type **110** when prompted to enter the percent of optimal setting.

FINISHING UP

13. Save and print the document. Compare the three sections of the document carefully. If there are no differences in the spacing between characters and the length of the words, your printer does not support tracking (at least for the current font).

AVAILABLE

Normal

AVAILABLE

Condensed

AVAILABLE

Expanded

Letter Spacing

▷ D E S K T O P   P U B L I S H I N G   C O N C E P T S

CHAPTER ONE
C H A P T E R   O N E

Tracking
By increasing the spacing between letters and words, you can create special effects. Here, spacing on the first line is normal; on the bottom line it is open.

Sometimes the spacing of characters is not quite right, especially in headings when large size fonts are used. You can control the spacing using a process called **tracking**. Tracking is different from kerning because it affects all characters and can either increase or decrease the space between letters. Kerning affects only specific pairs and usually moves them closer together. A line where spacing has been decreased is called a *close* line. One where it has been increased is called an *open* line. One creative use of tracking is in titles and headings. Putting additional space between characters and words changes the look of the line.

▷ W O R D P E R F E C T   P R O C E D U R E S

To fine-tune the spacing between words and letters, you enter a code where you want the control to begin and one where you want it to end.

→ K E Y / S t r o k e s

Adjusting Word and Letter Spacing

1. Either: Press **Shift-F8** to display the Format menu and press **O** for *Other.*
   Or: Pull down the Layout menu and select *Other.*
2. Press **P** for *Printer Functions.*
3. Press **W** for *Word Spacing* and the prompt reads *Word Spacing* followed by four menu choices.
4. Enter any setting described in the table "Word and Letter Spacing Menu Choices" and the prompt reads *Letter Spacing* followed by four menu choices.
5. Enter any setting described in the table "Word and Letter Spacing Menu Choices."
6. Press **F7** to return to the Edit screen.

WORD AND LETTER SPACING MENU CHOICES

1 **N**ormal uses the spacing recommended by the printer manufacturer.

2 **O**ptimal uses spacing recommended by WordPerfect. For proportionally spaced fonts, spaces are 1/3rd the point size of the font. For example, with a 12-point font, spaces are 4 points.

3 **P**ercent of Optimal adjusts the optimal spacing. Numbers over 100 percent increase spacing while those under 100 decrease spacing.

4 **S**et Pitch specifies how many characters are printed per inch for a specific font.

Adjusting Justification Limits

When WordPerfect justifies text, it first inserts or compresses the spaces between words to fill a line so both left and right margins are even. You can set limits on this expansion and contraction. The limit you set determines the minimum and maximum space that will be inserted between words; when the limit is exceeded, the program then adjusts spacing between letters. The limits that you enter are percentages of the existing space. For example, if you enter 60 percent, no space will be expanded or contracted more than that amount. To allow unlimited expansion, enter any percentage over 999 percent.

> → **KEY/Strokes**
>
> **Justification Limits**
>
> 1. Press **Shift-F8** to display the Format menu.
> 2. Press **O** for *Other*.
> 3. Press **P** for *Printer Functions*.
> 4. Press **J** for *Word Spacing Justification Limits* and the prompt reads *Compressed to (0% - 100%)*.
> 5. Type a compression setting, and then press **Enter**. The prompt reads *Expanded to (100% - unlimited)*.
> 6. Type an expansion setting, and then press **Enter**.
> 7. Press **F7** to return to the document screen.

► EXERCISES

EXERCISE 1

CONTROLLING LETTER SPACING

In this exercise, you control the letter spacing in a document.

1. Retrieve the TRACK2.WP5 document and enter your name.
2. Make a printout for comparison purposes.
3. Move the cursor to the beginning of the title "COMPUTER USERS' CHECKLIST" and follow the instructions in the KEY/Strokes box "Adjusting Word and Letter Spacing" to expand both word and letter spacing to **150**).
4. Move the cursor to the beginning of the first checklist item below the title and change the letter spacing back to Optimal.
5. Make a new printout and compare the two versions. Describe the differences.

EXERCISE 2

MANUALLY SPACING LETTERS

In this exercise, you press the **Spacebar** to enter spaces between letters and words to expand a title.

1. Retrieve the TRACK3.WP5 document and enter your name.
2. Enter a base font code in front of the heading "*Normal*" to print the document in an 18- to 30-point sans serif typeface.
3. In the title "*ADOBE TYPE GUIDE*" below the heading "*With Spaces*," use the **Spacebar** to enter two spaces between letters and three spaces between words.
4. Save and print the document.

Leading: The Space Between Lines

After completing this topic, you should be able to:
- Define the term *leading*
- Explain how WordPerfect's line height, line spacing, and leading commands all control leading
- Change leading in your WordPerfect documents

▶ T U T O R I A L

In this tutorial, you change the space added between lines (called leading). When finished, your printed document should look something like the one in the figure "Leaded Paragraphs."

GETTING STARTED

1. Retrieve the LEADING1.WP5 document and enter your name.

REDUCING LEADING

2. Move the cursor to the top of the document and specify a 10-point initial base font (**Ctrl-F8**).
3. Move the cursor to the beginning of the heading "*10/10.*"
4. Press **Shift-F8** to display the Format menu.
5. Press **L** for *Line*.
6. Press **H** for *Line Height*.
7. Press **F** for *Fixed* and the cursor jumps up to the Line Height line.
8. Type **10p** (for 10 points) and then press **Enter**. (If you reveal codes, you will see that the unit of measurement in the code is displayed in the default unit, for example, *10.02p* or *0.139"*. The line height indicated is also slightly larger than the 10p that you entered because the font has some line spacing built into it.)
9. Press **F7** to return to the Edit screen.

INCREASING LEADING

10. Move the cursor to the headings *10/12, 10/14,* and *10/16* and repeat Steps 4 through 9 but specify **12p**, **14p**, and **16p** (for 12, 14, and 16 points) as the line height.

This paragraph is printed in 10-point type with no leading. When the type and line height are equal, the type is set solid.

This paragraph is printed in 10-point type with 2 points of leading, called 10/12 (10 on 12). This is the type and leading used in many books and magazines.

This paragraph is printed in 10-point type with 4 points of leading, called 10/14 (10 on 14). This gives the text a more open look.

Leaded Paragraphs

FINISHING UP

11. Save and print the document. The line spacing in each paragraph should be different. The first paragraph should be printed with 10-point type on 10-point lines and the following paragraphs with 10-point type on 12-point, 14-point, and 16-point lines.

D E S K T O P   P U B L I S H I N G   C O N C E P T S

Leading

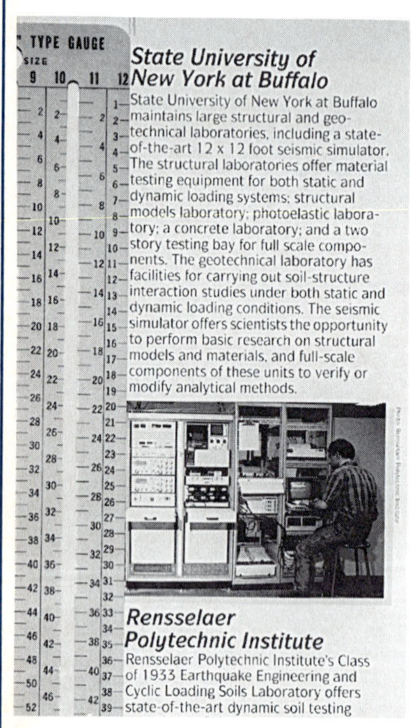

State University of
New York at Buffalo

State University of New York at Buffalo maintains large structural and geo-technical laboratories, including a state-of-the-art 12 x 12 foot seismic simulator. The structural laboratories offer material testing equipment for both static and dynamic loading systems; structural models laboratory; photoelastic labora-tory; a concrete laboratory; and a two story testing bay for full scale compo-nents. The geotechnical laboratory has facilities for carrying out soil-structure interaction studies under both static and dynamic loading conditions. The seismic simulator offers scientists the opportunity to perform basic research on structural models and materials, and full-scale components of these units to verify or modify analytical methods.

Rensselaer
Polytechnic Institute

Rensselaer Polytechnic Institute's Class of 1933 Earthquake Engineering and Cyclic Loading Soils Laboratory offers state-of-the-art dynamic soil testing

Type Gauge

When you print lines of text, even the largest characters on a line are separated from the lines above and below by space so that the lines don't touch or overlap. This blank space is called *leading* (rhymes with "heading"). The term comes from the days when type was set by hand, a character at a time, and the typesetter inserted strips of lead to separate the lines from one another. Leading is important because it helps the eye follow a line of type without being distracted by the lines above and below. If there is too little or too much leading, legibility decreases.

Measuring Leading

Leading is calculated by measuring from the bottom of the x-height on one line of text, called the *baseline*, to the bottom of the x-height on the next line, and subtracting the type size. To determine the leading of a font, underline the baseline on two consecutive lines, measure the distance between the lines in points, and subtract the point size. You can also use the program's Underlining command to underline just below the baseline. (That is why the underline cuts through descenders.)

To measure the leading in a type-set document, you can also use a *type gauge*. These gauges have slots in them for a range of point sizes. You find the slot where the markings line up with the baselines of each line of type and read off the size listed at the top of the slot. Subtract the type size to arrive at the leading used in the document.

Determining the Leading to Use

Leading is normally 2 points for 10- or 12-point type. (If there is more than one type size on a line, leading is calculated for the largest size.) To increase the spacing between lines, you add more leading. For example, if you add 2 points of leading to a 10-point type, the type is said to be set 10 on 12 (written as 10/12). If you add 4 points of leading, the type is said to be set 10 on 14 (written as 10/14). One way to think about this is using a typewriter analogy. Many typewriters have elite type that is 10 points high. When you press the carriage return lever, the paper advances 12 points. This means you type with 10-point type on 12-point lines so you are actually using Elite 10/12 type without knowing it.

When specifying leading, keep the following general rules in mind:

- Longer lines need more leading to make them easier to read.
- Sans serif type requires more leading because it does not have serifs that guide a reader's eye along the line.
- Type with a larger x-height needs more leading to improve its readability.
- Larger type sizes require more leading.

Type with No Leading

If no leading is used, it is said that the text is *set solid*. This setting is frequently specified for title pages and chapter or part openers where large display type is used. For example, 36-point type is said to be set 36 on 36 (36/36) when set solid.

Type on Body

Type Set Solid
When type is set solid, there is no leading between the lines.

This does not mean that lines actually touch, because even when text is set solid there is some space between lines. In the days when type was made of wood or metal, the typeface was created on a body larger than the point size. There was always some space between the top or bottom of each letter and the body on which it was mounted. This space has been retained in electronic versions of fonts.

Carding and Feathering
In some documents, extra space is added between lines or paragraphs to fill out pages that are shorter than called for in the design. Called **short pages**, these are frequently caused by moving lines from one page to another to avoid widows and orphans. The extra added space is called **carding** (because cardboard was originally used to add the space) or **feathering**. Very few programs offer this feature (WordPerfect does not).

Chapter 1 The Beginning

Normal Spacing (24/28)

Chapter 1 The Beginning

Set Solid (24/24)

With WordPerfect, you control leading with three different but related commands: line height, line spacing, and leading.

Line Height
Line height is the term that WordPerfect uses for the distance from the baseline of one line to the baseline of the next. You can set this to Auto to have the program automatically adjust line height when you change font sizes. You can also set it to a fixed height if you want all lines to have the same leading regardless of the type size. However, if you use a fixed line height setting and change font sizes, lines may overlap if the font size is too large for the specified line height.

 **K E Y / S t r o k e s**

Changing Line Height

1. Move the cursor to where you want the line height to change.
2. Either: Press **Shift-F8** and then **L** for *Line.*
   Or: Pull down the Layout menu and select *Line.*
3. Press **H** for *Line Height.*

4. Either: Press **A** for *Auto*.

   Or: Press **F** for *Fixed*, type a line height measurement (for example, **.25** for ¼ inch or **6p** for 6 points between the bottom of one line and the bottom of the next), and then press **Enter**.

5. Press **F7** to return to the Edit screen.

Line Spacing

Line spacing is based on the line height setting. Setting line spacing to 1 makes line spacing the same as the line height setting; setting line spacing to 2 doubles the line height (double spacing); 3 triples it (triple spacing); and so on. To make fine adjustments in line spacing, enter decimals such as 1.1 or 1.2. You can change line spacing for an entire document or for individual paragraphs. WordPerfect displays line spacing on the screen to the nearest whole number. For example, 1.5 spacing is displayed as double spacing. However, in the printed document, the line spacing is whatever you have specified.

→ KEY/Strokes

Changing Line Spacing

1. Move the cursor to where you want the line spacing to change.
2. Either: Press **Shift-F8** and then **L** for *Line*.

   Or: Pull down the Layout menu and select *Line*.
3. Press **S** for *Line Spacing*.
4. Type the desired spacing; for example, type **.5** for half spacing or **2** for double spacing, and then press **Enter**.
5. Press **F7** to return to the Edit screen.

Leading

WordPerfect normally adds leading to lines with the line height setting. However, you can add extra leading to every line (called *primary* leading) and after every hard carriage return (called *secondary* leading). If you add it to every hard carriage return, paragraphs are separated by the specified amount. This is a useful substitute for pressing **Enter** twice at the end of each paragraph because when you press **Enter** to insert a blank line between paragraphs, the paragraphs are always spaced one full line apart. If you use the Leading command instead, you can specify any distance for paragraph spacing, giving you finer control. Paragraphs will be separated by the distance you specify in the Leading command when you press **Enter** only once. They do not appear to be separated on the screen, but they will be separated on your printouts. If you enter the code 1u (for 1 unit) as the leading measurement, WordPerfect inserts one blank line following each hard carriage return that you enter. This is the same as pressing **Enter** twice. You can also enter the codes 2u (for two units), 3u (for three units) and so on to add two or three extra lines in the current type size.

Changing Leading

1. Move the cursor to where you want the spacing between paragraphs to change.
2. Either: Press **Shift-F8** and then **O** for *Other*.

   Or: Pull down the Layout menu and select *Other*.
3. Press **P** for *Printer Functions*.
4. Press **L** for *Leading Adjustment* and the prompt reads *Primary - [SRt]*.
5. Type a setting, and then press **Enter**. The prompt reads *Secondary - [HRt]*.
6. Type the desired space to follow a hard carriage return (type **1u** to insert one line), and then press **Enter**.
7. Press **F7** repeatedly to return to the Edit screen.

WORDPERFECT'S LEADING

WordPerfect treats leading differently for monospaced and proportionally spaced fonts.

If a font is monospaced, any space between lines is built into the font by the font manufacturer. WordPerfect adds no leading to these fonts.

If a font is proportionally spaced, WordPerfect adds 2 points of leading in addition to any space between lines built into the font by the foundry.

Therefore, a 12-point monospaced type has a line height of 12 points and a 12-point proportionally spaced font has a line height of 14 points. These are the heights that are listed when you select Fixed from the Line Height menu (they are automatically converted to the default unit of measurement and are listed as points only if you are using that as the unit).

If you use the leading command to add additional space between lines (primary leading), the additional space is not reflected in the line height setting but is calculated by the program separately.

Baseline Placement for Typesetters

Normally, the baseline of the first line of text on a page falls below the top margin because the top of the text is aligned with the top margin. Changing fonts on the first line will shift the baseline up and down relative to the top margin and the top of the page. When filling out forms or placing items precisely on the page, you set line height to Fixed and position the baseline of the first line at the top margin so all subsequent lines are positioned relative to this fixed position. You should always enter this code in the initial codes screen for the document as described in the KEY/Strokes box "Using the Baseline Placement Command."

→ **K E Y / S t r o k e s**

Using the Baseline Placement Command

1. Press **Shift-F8** to display the Format menu.
2. Press **D** for *Document.*
3. Press **C** for *Initial Codes.*
4. Press **Shift-F8** to display the Format menu.
5. Press **O** for *Other.*
6. Press **P** for *Printer Functions.*
7. Press **B** for *Baseline Placement for Typesetters.*
8. Press **Y** for *Yes* to turn it on or **N** for *No* to turn it off.
9. Press **F7** repeatedly to return to the document.

➤ E X E R C I S E S

EXERCISE 1

MEASURING LEADING

In this exercise, you underline ten consecutive lines of text so you can measure them to calculate the program's leading.

1. Retrieve the LEADING2.WP5 document and enter your name.
2. Block the entire paragraph below the heading (**Alt-F4** or **F12**), and then press **F8** to underline.
3. Save and print the document.
4. Display the base font menu for the document and note the size of the font that is selected. (If your fonts are scalable, you must press **S** for *Select* to see the point size, and then press **F1** to cancel the command.)
5. Measure the distance between the underline on line 1 and the underline on line 11 (in points). Divide the result by 10 and subtract the point size of the base font used in the document to determine the leading used by the program.

EXERCISE 2

CHANGING LINE SPACING AND LINE HEIGHT

In this exercise, you change both line spacing and line height to see how line spacing is based on the line height setting.

1. Retrieve the LEADING3.WP5 document.
2. Move the cursor to the beginning of the first paragraph below the title "The Mayflower Compact." Follow the instructions in the KEY/

Strokes box "Changing Line Spacing" to change the line spacing from single spacing to 1½ spacing.

3. Make a printout.

4. Reveal codes and move the cursor over the line spacing code (*[Ln Spacing:1.5]*) and follow the instructions in the KEY/Strokes box "Changing Line Height" to change the line height to 18-points (**18p**) fixed. When finished, make a printout.

5. Save and print the document. Compare the two printouts and describe the differences.

EXERCISE 3

CHANGING PRIMARY AND SECONDARY LEADING

In this exercise, you use the Leading command to automatically add space following paragraphs.

1. Retrieve the LEADING4.WP5 document and enter your name.

2. Print the document for comparison purposes.

3. Move the cursor to the beginning of the paragraph below the heading. Follow the instructions in the KEY/Strokes box "Changing Leading" to change primary leading to 6 points and secondary leading to 18 points.

4. Save and print the document. Compare the two printouts and describe the differences.

EXERCISE 4

CHANGING SECONDARY LEADING AND ENTERING TEXT

In this exercise, you use the Leading command to automatically add space following paragraphs that you enter.

1. Retrieve the LEADING5.WP5 document and enter your name.

2. Move the cursor to a blank line below the heading and follow the instructions in the KEY/Strokes box "Changing Leading" to change the secondary leading to 12 points.

3. Type the text shown in the box "WordPerfect's Leading," being careful to press **Enter** only once at the end of each paragraph. Paragraphs will remain unseparated on the screen but they will print out with a space between paragraphs even though you did not press **Enter** twice at the end of each paragraph.

4. Save and print the document. Notice how the paragraphs are separated by 12 points.

REVIEW

- Type is either fixed pitch or proportionally spaced. Fixed-pitch type allocates the same width to every character regardless of its size. Proportionally spaced type allocates less space to narrower characters.
- Kerning is a refinement of proportional spacing; it moves pairs of letters closer together if there is room.
- Tracking adjusts the spacing between all characters.
- Line height determines the space from the bottom of one line to the bottom of the next.
- Line spacing specifies if lines are printed single-, double-, or triple-spaced.
- Leading is the distance from the baseline of one line of text to the baseline of the next line minus the type size; it is specified in points.

QUESTIONS

TRUE/FALSE

T F

☐ ☐ 1. Fixed-pitch type allocates the same amount of space for all letters of a given type size.

☐ ☐ 2. Kerning adjusts the spaces between both words and letters.

☐ ☐ 3. Tracking adjusts the spaces between all characters.

☐ ☐ 4. If you want to expand letter spacing, you can use tracking to do so.

☐ ☐ 5. WordPerfect can kern any and all fonts.

FILL IN THE BLANK

1. To control space between specific pairs of letters, you usually use the ___________ command.

2. To expand or compress the spacing between all of the characters in a heading, you usually use the ___________ command.

3. Text that is monospaced has ___________ space allocated to each character regardless of its width.

4. Text that is proportionally spaced allocates space for characters based on their ___________ .

1. Kerning
2. Tracking
3. Fixed pitch
4. Proportionally spaced

__ Same space for each character
__ Adjusts spacing between all characters
__ Space varies depending on character width
__ Adjusts spacing only between specific letter pairs

WRITE OUT THE ANSWERS

1. What is the basic difference between fixed-pitch and proportionally spaced type?
2. What does the term *kern* mean?
3. What is the difference between kerning and tracking?
4. List and describe at least three things you can change that affect leading.
5. What does changing the line height do?
6. What does changing the line spacing do?

CHAPTER 2

PROJECTS

PROJECT 1

KERNING A TITLE PAGE

In this project, you kern a title page and compare the printout with one you made before kerning it to see what differences there are. First, retrieve the document and make a printout. Then enter a kerning on code and print the document again. Then, hold the pages up together against the light to see how (or if) the letters on the second printout are kerned.

Procedures Used
- Entering a kerning on code.

Text Files Needed
- TITLE.WP5

Formats
① Enter a kerning on code at the top of the page.
② Enter a base font code for a large (36- to 50-point) type.
③ Enter a base font code for an 18- to 24-point italic font.
④ Enter a base font code for an 12- to 14-point type and enter your own name.

①②

WordPerfect 5.1 Desktop Publishing

③—*A Quick Reference Guide*

④— Your Name

AUTOMATIC LETTER SPACING

In this project, you use letter spacing codes to space out the letters in a title.

Procedures Used
- Entering letter spacing setting codes.

Text Files Needed
- COVER.WP5

Formats

① Enter a base font code for 12-point Helvetica (or any sans serif typeface you have) and format the title as extra large. Enter two spaces between letters and three spaces between words.

② Format the subtitle as italic.

③ Enter a letter spacing code that specifies letter spacing as 120 percent or optimal.

④ Enter a base font code that specifies an 11-point Helvetica typeface.

Tip
- The figure box represents where an illustration will be placed. It is created with WordPerfect's Graphics command.

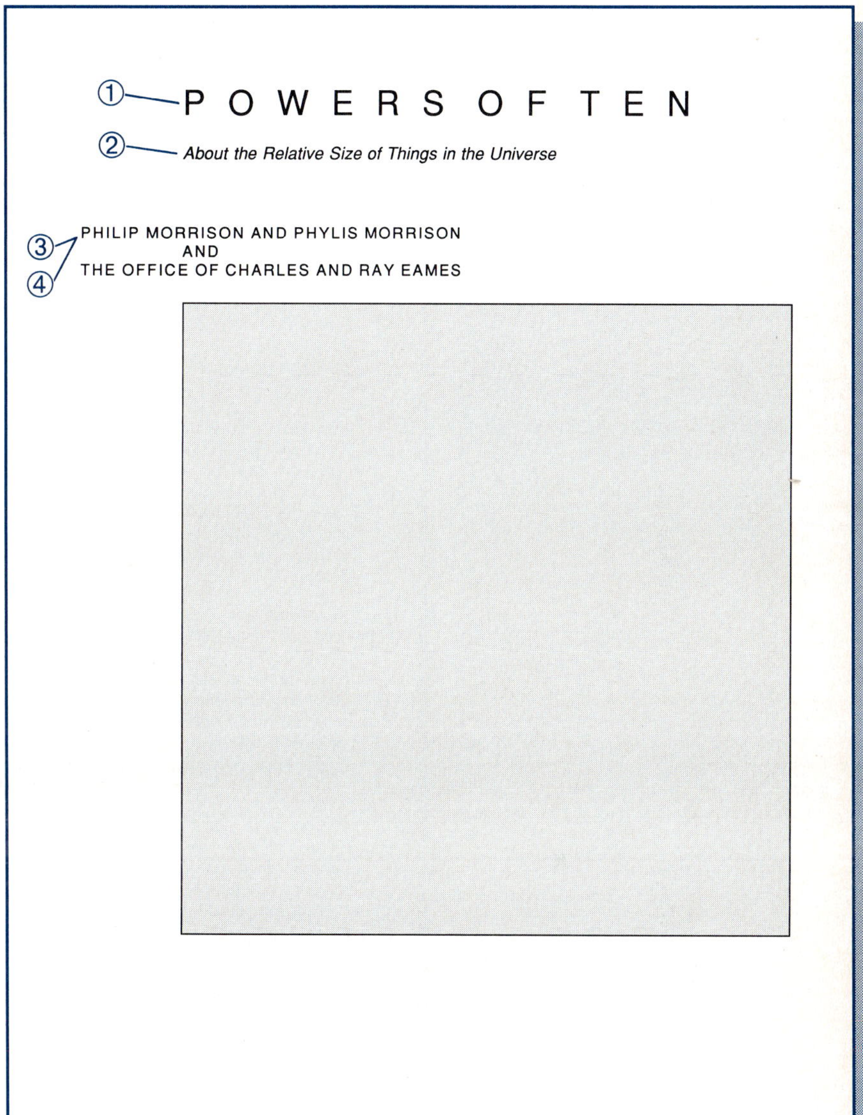

ADDING SECONDARY LEADING

In this project, enter a secondary leading setting of 12 points or 1 line to separate paragraphs instead of using a second hard carriage return.

The Emancipation Proclamation

Whereas, On the twenty-second day of September, in the year of our Lord one thousand eight hundred and sixty-two, a proclamation was issued by the President of the United States, containing, among other things, the following, to wit:

That on the first day of January, in the year of our Lord one thousand eight hundred and sixty-three, all persons held as slaves within any State or designated part of a State, the people whereof shall then be in rebellion against the United States, shall be then, thenceforward, and forever free; and the Executive Government of the United States, including the military and naval authority thereof, will recognize and maintain the freedom of such persons, and will do no act or acts to repress such persons, or any of them, in any efforts they may make for their actual freedom.

That the Executive will, on the first day of January aforesaid, by proclamation, designate the States and parts of States, if any, in which the people thereof, respectively, shall then be in rebellion against the United States; and the fact that any State or the people thereof shall on that day be, in good faith, represented in the Congress of the United States by members chosen thereto at elections where in a majority of the qualified voters of such States shall have participated, shall, in the absence of strong countervailing testimony, be deemed conclusive evidence that such state, and the people thereof, are not then in rebellion against the United States.

Now, therefore I, Abraham Lincoln, President of the United States, by virtue of the power in me vested as Commander-in-Chief, of the Army and Navy of the United States in time of actual armed rebellion against the authority and government of the United States, and as a fit and necessary war measure for suppressing said rebellion, do, on this first day of January, in the year of our Lord one thousand eight hundred and sixty-three, and in accordance with my purpose so to do, publicly proclaimed for the full period of one hundred days, from the day first above mentioned, order and designate as the States and parts of States wherein the people thereof, respectively, are this day in rebellion against the United States, the following, to wit:

Arkansas, Texas, Louisiana (except the parishes of St. Bernard, Plaquemines, Jefferson, St. John, St. Charles, St. James, Ascension, Assumption, Terrebonne, Lafourche, St. Mary, St. Martin, and Orleans, including the City of New Orleans), Mississippi, Alabama, Florida, Georgia, South Carolina, North Carolina, and Virginia (except the forty-eight counties designated as West Virginia, and also the counties of Berkeley, Accomac, Northampton, Elizabeth City, York, Princess Ann, and Norfolk, including the cities of Norfolk and Portsmouth); and which excepted parts are, for the present, left precisely as if this proclamation were not issued.

And by virtue of the power, and for the purpose aforesaid, I do order and declare that all persons held as slaves within said designated States, and parts of States, are, and henceforward shall be, free; States, including the military and naval authorities thereof, will recognize and maintain the freedom of said persons.

THE DTP ADVISOR NEWSLETTER

In this project, you kern the headlines for each of the four articles in the newsletter.

THE *dtp* ADVISOR

FaceLift For WordPerfect

Bitstream Inc. today announced version 1.5 of Bitstream FaceLift for WordPerfect. FaceLift brings enhanced font support to WordPerfect 5.0 and 5.1. The new FaceLift version 1.5 will create high-quality fonts on-the-fly for popular dot-matrix and inkjet printers--like the HP DeskJet, Canon BubbleJet and the IBM ExecuJet--in addition to the existing on-the-fly support for the Hewlett-Packard LaserJet series of printers. FaceLift 1.5 for WordPerfect will be available in the spring of 1991.

In addition to 13 typeface outlines provided in the original FaceLift package, FaceLift 1.5 for WordPerfect will also ship with three Symbol typefaces: ITC Zapf Dingbats Symbol Proportional and Symbol Monospaced. Users will be able to access a total of 698 characters from the Bitstream International Character Set and from these three Symbols typefaces.

FaceLift 1.5 for WordPerfect is an easy-to-use utility that allows users to print high-quality fonts in any size from 2 to 500 point (in quarter point increments) without ever having to leave the application. The fonts are generated at print time, so the need for stored bit-map fonts is eliminated. Based on Bitstream Speedo technology, FaceLift sends characters to printers in both graphics mode (laser, inkjet and dot-matrix printers) and as HP soft fonts (laser printers only). Users have full control over the number and size of soft fonts to be downloaded, depending on the memory available in the printer.

"We are very excited that FaceLift 1.5 for WordPerfect will provide dot-matrix and inkjet users with the same high typographic quality and capabilities that HP LaserJet users have enjoyed with Bitstream type," stated Doug Lloyd, Executive Director at WordPerfect. "That, and the addition of the three new Symbol typefaces makes FaceLift a great companion for WordPerfect."

First-time users can purchase FaceLift 1.5 for WordPerfect for a suggested U.S. list price of $99. Current users of FaceLift 1.0 for WordPerfect can upgrade to version 1.5 for $24.95. In addition to the 16 typefaces included free with FaceLift, users can purchase add-on fonts from the Bitstream Library of 52 typeface packages. Also available is the FaceLift Companion Value Pack, a selection of 24 text and headline faces for a suggested U.S. list price $199.

FaceLift 1.5 for WordPerfect is the newest member of the Bitstream FaceLift product line. The initial product, FaceLift for Windows, shipped in August of 1990. All FaceLift products can share Bitstream typefaces (in Speedo format) stored in a single common subdirectory.

FaceLift for Wordperfect was developed in conjunction with LaserTools Corporation, a privately held company based in Emeryville, CA. LaserTools is a developer of innovative printing enhancement products--tools for printer sharing, printer control, printer acceleration, and font management.

An industry leader in typographic quality and innovative technology, Bitstream licenses fonts and related software to more than 420 hardware manufacturers and software developers worldwide. Its line of retail products is distributed by an extensive network of dealers in the United States and in 18 nations worldwide.

Special Characters & Hyphenation

Special Characters: Those That Are Not on the Keyboard

After completing this topic, you should be able to:
- Explain what special characters are
- List some commonly used special characters
- Enter special characters into your own documents

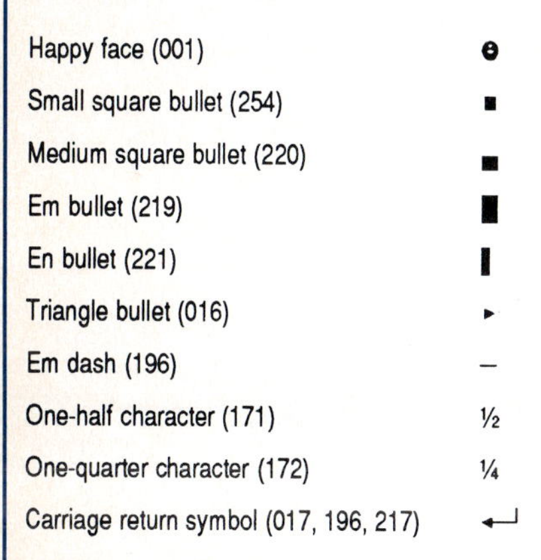

Happy face (001)	☻
Small square bullet (254)	▪
Medium square bullet (220)	▪
Em bullet (219)	▮
En bullet (221)	▮
Triangle bullet (016)	►
Em dash (196)	—
One-half character (171)	½
One-quarter character (172)	¼
Carriage return symbol (017, 196, 217)	↵

Special Characters

In this tutorial, you enter special characters that do not appear on the keyboard. When you are finished, your printout should look similar to the figure "Special Characters."

GETTING STARTED

1. Retrieve the SPECIAL1.WP5 document and enter your name.

ENTER A SPECIAL CHARACTER

2. Move the cursor to the line that reads "*Happy face.*"
3. Press **End** to move to the tab stop.
4. Hold down **Alt**, type **001** (using the numeric keypad, not the numbers above the alphabetic keys), and then release **Alt** to enter a happy face special character. (If the character cannot be displayed on your screen, you will see a square symbol, but the character may still print correctly.)

ENTER A SPECIAL CHARACTER

5. Move the cursor to each of the other lines, and repeat Step 3 (if necessary) and Step 4, but type the numbers in parentheses on the line that you are on. For the last line, you type three sets of characters. Be sure to release the **Alt** key after each three-number sequence.

FINISHING UP

6. Save and print the document. All characters should print on any graphics printer.

There is often a need to use characters that do not appear on the keyboard. These special characters are called **symbols** or **dingbats** and some of them are shown in the table "Special Characters." These characters must be supported by both your program and your printer in order for you to use them, and the font that contains them must be available at the time the document is printed.

SPECIAL CHARACTERS

Character	Examples
Bullets for lists	■ and ●
En and em dashes	– or —
Decorations	✂, ☆, and ➥
Ellipses	…
Math characters and symbols	$\vert$, Σ, $\geq$
Numbers	①, ②, ❶, ❷
Quotes	", ", ', '
Special characters	✔, ™, ®, ©, →

Computers store and process each character using 8 bits of memory so the total number of unique characters that can be stored is 256 (2^8). Since there are many more special characters than just 256, many of them are actually one of the basic 256 characters formatted in a different font to produce a different displayed or printed symbol for the same alphabetic character.

The IBM PC Character Set

A set of 254 characters, called the **IBM character set**, is resident in most IBM PCs and compatibles and these characters are supported by many, but by no means all, printers and programs. A complete list of these characters, and instructions on how to enter them, is in the appendix "The IBM PC Character Set."

Applications of Special Characters

The most frequently used special characters are bullets, dashes, quotes, fractions, and spaces.

Bullets
Bullets are ideal for setting off lists. When you use bullets, make sure they are proportional to the type size being used and centered on the font's x-height. Since bullet sizes vary from font to font, you may have to experiment to find the right size for your document. You may also have to superscript them a little to align them with the center of the font's x-height because some bullets are normally aligned with the font's baseline. Bullets are often followed by em or en spaces before the text begins.

Dashes
Dashes are used to separate phrases. Typists indicate dashes with two hyphens, but in desktop publishing there are two kinds of dashes you can use in a document. Both are longer than a hyphen.

■ Em dashes—often used to indicate an interruption in thought—are used to set off phrases by replacing parentheses, or in headings by replacing hyphens.
■ En dashes are shorter than em dashes and are used to join ranges of numbers such as 1–2, or words to phrases that contain two or more words such as "New York–London."

Quotes and Apostrophes
When you use quotes in a document in standard American usage, you enclose them in double quotation marks. If you then enclose a quotation within a quotation, you enclose it in single quotation marks within double quotation marks. Almost all computer keyboards provide generic kinds of quote marks that look much like inch and foot marks (as in 4" and 4') where there is no distinction between an open quotation and closed quotation mark. There are, however, typographic quotation marks that you should use in place of these in desktop published documents; for example, double quota-

Special Characters and Fonts
The same characters are displayed and printed differently depending on the font used to format them. Here the 26-letter alphabet (in uppercase and lowercase) is shown formatted as Times Roman (left), as Zapf Dingbats (center), and as Symbols (right).

A	a	✡	❀	Α	α
B	b	✚	❂	Β	β
C	c	✛	✳	Χ	χ
D	d	✜	❄	Δ	δ
E	e	✛	❅	Ε	ε
F	f	◆	❆	Φ	φ
G	g	◇	✴	Γ	γ
H	h	★	❉	Η	η
I	i	☆	❊	Ι	ι
J	j	✪	❋	ϑ	φ
K	k	☆	✳	Κ	κ
L	l	✬	●	Λ	λ
M	m	✭	○	Μ	μ
N	n	✮	■	Ν	ν
O	o	✯	❑	Ο	ο
P	p	✰	❐	Π	π
Q	q	✶	❒	Θ	θ
R	r	✸	❏	Ρ	ρ
S	s	✳	▲	Σ	σ
T	t	✳	▼	Τ	τ
U	u	✳	◆	Υ	υ
V	v	✱	❖	ς	ϖ
W	w	✷	◗	Ω	ω
X	x	✸	❘	Ξ	ξ
Y	y	✹	❙	Ψ	ψ
Z	z	✺	❚	Ζ	ζ

• **6 point round bullet**
■ **6 point square bullet**
● **12 point round bullet**
■ **12 point square bullet**

Bullets

Centered Bullet

- **Hyphen**
— **En Dash**
—— **Em dash**

Hyphens and Dashes

tion marks can be set as " and ", and single quotation marks as ' and '. The close quotation mark is also used as an apostrophe. To employ these typographic quotation marks, you must use fonts that contain them.

Fractions
Many documents call for fractions. In a few instances, the needed fractions are available as typographical characters in the font being used and can be set as a single character such as ½ or ¼, sometimes called a case or solid fraction. (WordPerfect includes a number of these fractions in character set 4 as shown in the appendix "WordPerfect Character Sets.") If a needed fraction is not available, you must create the fraction using numbers and a **_solidus_** (the / slash). Fractions entered this way, such as 1/2 or 1/4, have each

part entered as a separate character. You can use superscripting or subscripting, such as $^1/_2$ or $^1/_4$, to improve the appearance of these fractions.

Spaces
Although you normally don't see them, pressing **Spacebar** inserts codes into the document. Certain expressions, though they contain spaces, should not be split to print on different lines. For example,

■ a name such as Henry VIII or Mrs. Wilson
■ a time such as 8 P.M.
■ an address such as 32 Elm Street
■ a formula such as 1 + 1 = 2

To prevent these phrases from splitting, you connect them with **_hard spaces_** (also called _non-breaking spaces_).

½   ¼

Typographic Fractions

$^1/_2$ $^1/_4$

Multi-character Fractions

Fractions
You can enter some fractions as single characters. You must enter others as individual characters separated by a solidus.

WordPerfect has over 1,700 characters that you can print on a graphics-capable printer. These include graphics symbols, Greek letters, foreign currency symbols, and letters with foreign-language accent marks. These are characters that do not appear on your keyboard. If you print a character that is not in one of the fonts available to your printer, WordPerfect prints it as a graphics character. If your printer does not support graphics, you can print only the characters that your printer does support.

You can create special characters in two ways: by typing the character's decimal code on the numeric keypad or by composing them using WordPerfect's Compose command.

Typing the Decimal Code with WordPerfect
You can hold down the **Alt** key and type the decimal code for the character on the numeric keypad (the number keys at the top of the keyboard do not work with this feature). You can enter any of the characters shown in the appendix "The IBM PC Character Set." When you do so, and then release **Alt**, the character is displayed on the screen. For example, to enter an em dash, hold down **Alt**, type **196** on the numeric keypad, then release **Alt**. (Be sure to check that this character prints on your printer before using it in your documents.)

Entering Special Characters by Typing Their Decimal Code

1. Position the cursor where you want to create the special character.
2. Hold down **Alt**.
3. Type the special character's decimal code on the numeric keypad. (See the appendix "The IBM PC Character Set.")
4. Release **Alt** to enter the character.

Composing Characters

You can compose special characters including digraphs such as Æ and æ, symbols such as an L with a hyphen through it, and diacriticals such as á and ö. To do so, you use the Compose command (**Ctrl-V**) and then enter the two characters that you want to combine. (You cannot combine uppercase and lowercase letters.) You can also compose characters from any one of 11 predefined character sets or define a set of your own (see the appendix "WordPerfect Character Sets"). To compose characters from these character sets, you use the Compose command and then enter two numbers separated by a comma. The first number identifies the character set; the second, the character within that set. For example, to enter an up arrow symbol, you type **6,23**.

You can use the Compose command to enter many special characters. For example, after pressing **Ctrl-V** (the prompt reads *Key =*)

■ To insert bullets, type * and then one of the following characters: . (for a small solid bullet), * (for a medium solid bullet), **o** (for a small open bullet), or **O** (for a large open bullet).
■ To insert fractions, type **/2** (for ½) or **/4** (for ¼).
■ To insert double quotation marks, type **4,32** (open) or **4,31** (close).
■ To insert an apostrophe, type **1,9** or **4,28** depending on the font you are using.
■ To insert an en dash, type **4,33**. To enter an em dash, type **4,34**.

If you enter a character that cannot be displayed on your screen, the character is displayed as a square bullet (■). Characters that cannot be displayed may still print correctly.

Composing Special Characters

1. Either: Press **Ctrl-V** from the Edit screen and the prompt reads *Key =*.
   Or: Pull down the Font menu, select *Characters* and the prompt reads *Key =*.
   Or: Press **Ctrl-2** to begin composing from anywhere in the program. (No prompt is displayed.)
2. Either: Type the first and then the second characters.
   Or: Type the number of the character set, a comma, the number of the character, and then press **Enter**.

Entering Hard Spaces

To keep the two or more parts of the phrase together, you enter **hard spaces**. This way, if the phrase does not fit on one line, it all wraps to the next line. To enter a hard space, press **Home**, and then press **Spacebar**.

TO ENTER	PRESS	EXAMPLE
Open quote	Alt-096	'
Close quote	Alt-039	'
Em dash	Alt-196	—
Large bullet	Alt-220	■
Small bullet	Alt-254	■
Triangle bullet	Alt-016	▶
Diamond bullet	Alt-004	♦
Open angle	Alt-060	<
Close angle	Alt-062	>
Pound Sterling	Alt-156	£
Yen symbol	Alt-157	¥
French Franc	Alt-159	ƒ
One-half	Alt-171	½
One-quarter	Alt-172	¼
Division sign	Alt-246	÷
Section	Alt-021	§

Alt-Decimal Number Characters

EXERCISE 1

ENTERING CHARACTERS WITH THE ALT KEY

In this exercise, you use the **Alt** key to enter special characters that you may want to use in your own documents.

1. Retrieve the SPECIAL2.WP5 document and enter your name.
2. Move the cursor to each line, and then press **End** to move to the tab stop.
3. Follow the instructions in the KEY/Strokes box "Entering Special Characters by Typing Their Decimal Code" to enter the characters described in the first column of the document by typing the numbers listed in the second column.
4. When you are finished, make a printout. It should look something like the figure "Alt-Decimal Number Characters."

EXERCISE 2

USING THE COMPOSE COMMAND

In this exercise, you use the Compose command to enter and print special characters.

1. Retrieve the SPECIAL3.WP5 document and enter your name.
2. Move the cursor to each line, and press **End** to move to the tab stop.
3. Follow the instructions in the KEY/Strokes box "Composing Special Characters" to enter the pairs of characters (including the comma) shown in the first column of the document.
4. When you are finished, make a printout. It should look something like the figure "Composed Characters."

EXERCISE 3

SEEING WHAT CHARACTERS YOUR SYSTEM SUPPORTS

The fastest way to see what characters your screen displays and your printer prints is to retrieve the WordPerfect file named CHARACTR.DOC. (On a hard disk system, this file is in the same directory as your

*,.	·
,	•
*,o	o
*,O	O
4,2	■
4,3	·
4,5	¶
4,17	½
4,18	¼
4,22	®
4,23	©
4,28	'
4,29	'
4,31	"
4,32	"
4,41	™
4,43	℞
5,7	☻
5,14	√
5,23	✓
7,6	Σ

Composed Characters

WordPerfect program files. On a floppy disk system, it is on the *Learning/Images* disk.)

With the file on the screen, scroll through it to see what characters your screen displays. Then, make a printout of selected pages (the entire document is 33 pages long). Compare the screen display with the printout. Only characters supported by your system and printer will be displayed or printed. Both the display and the printout change if you change the base font or select a different printer.

✔ SPECIAL CHARACTER TIPS

- On some printers, you can use the Overstrike command to print one character on top of another (for example, L and - to create a pound sterling symbol. To do so, position the cursor where you want to create the special character. Press **Shift-F8** and then **O** for *Other*, **O** for *Overstrike*, and then **C** for *Create* and the prompt reads *[Ovrstk]*. Enter the characters (you can enter up to 30), and then press **Enter**. When you press **F7** to return to the document, only the last character that you typed is displayed on the screen; to see all characters, press **Alt-F3** or **F11**.
- You can search and replace special characters. To do so, when the prompt reads -> *Srch:* create the character the same way you did when you entered it in the document.
- To display a table of the IBM extended character set, press **F3** for help, and then press **Ctrl-V**. Press **Spacebar** when you are finished.

Hyphenation: Improving Word Spacing

After completing this topic, you should be able to:
- Describe what rivers are in justified text and how to avoid them
- Insert hyphens manually into a WordPerfect document
- Automatically hyphenate your own documents and change the hyphenation zone

▶ TUTORIAL

In this tutorial, you print out a document and then hyphenate it and make another printout. By comparing the two documents, you will see the effects of hyphenation.

GETTING STARTED

1. Retrieve the document HYPHEN1.WP5 and enter your name.
2. Print out a copy of the document for comparison purposes.

TURNING HYPHENATION ON

3. Move the cursor to the beginning of the first paragraph below the heading.
4. Press **Shift-F8** and then **L** for *Line*.
5. Press **y** for *Hyphenation*.
6. Press **Y** for *Yes* to turn hyphenation on.
7. Press **F7** to return to the Edit screen.

HYPHENATE THE DOCUMENT

8. Press **Home**, **Home**, ↓ to move the cursor to the end of the document. This hyphenates it automatically. (If the program is set to prompt you, when it finds a word that might be hyphenated, a prompt reads *Position hyphen; Press ESC* followed by the word. A flashing cursor indicates the suggested hyphen position.)
   - Press **Esc** to hyphenate where suggested.
   - Press ← or → to reposition the hyphen, and then press **Esc**.
   - Press **F1** to wrap the entire word to the next line.

FINISHING UP

9. Save and print the document. Circle all of the hyphens in the right margins of each column. Compare those lines with the same lines on the first printout to see hyphenation's effect on word spacing.

▶ D E S K T O P   P U B L I S H I N G   C O N C E P T S

Justification, aligning text flush with both the left and right margins, presents problems when very long words fall at the end of a line or when columns are narrow. If words are not hyphenated, large white spaces may appear on lines where long words have wrapped down to the next line. If this happens on several adjacent lines, a **river** of white space appears. To eliminate large spaces and rivers, you can hyphenate the document. If hyphenation doesn't work, adjust the hyphenation zone so shorter words are hyphenated and more lines will close up. In special circumstances you can increase or decrease word spacing (normal word spacing is about one-third of an em).

Another way to eliminate large white spaces on lines is to have the right margin unjustified. However, the document may still need to be hyphenated to eliminate a very ragged right margin.

Justification

When text is justified in narrow columns, you frequently get "rivers" of white space (left). These can be removed by hyphenating the column (middle) or aligning it flush left with an unjustified right margin (far right).

Justified text is even with both margins. To accomplish this the program inserts spaces of varying lengths between words. These spaces can be very distracting, especially in short lines.	Justified text is even with both margins. To accomplish this the program inserts spaces of varying lengths between words. These spaces can be very distracting, especially in short lines.	Justified text is even with both margins. To accomplish this the program inserts spaces of varying lengths between words. These spaces can be very distracting, especially in short lines.

HYPHENATION TIPS

When hyphenating words, keep the following points in mind when placing the hyphen:

- When possible, hyphenate between syllables.
- Do not hyphenate so that only one or two letters are left at the end of the line or so that fewer than three characters appear at the beginning of the next line.
- Break hyphenated compound terms, such as *computer-based*, only at the hyphen.
- Break nonhyphenated compound words, such as *microcomputer*, only between word parts (between the prefix *micro* and the base word *computer*).
- Do not hyphenate names, other proper nouns, or math formulas.

Check a document carefully after hyphenation. You may find that three or more lines in a row have been hyphenated, forming what appears to be a ladder of hyphens. If this happens, insert or delete a few words or leave a few unhyphenated to interrupt the visual effect.

You should always hyphenate just before printing. The slightest change in the wording or punctuation may change the position of words so that hyphenated words no longer fall at the ends of lines. Since the hyphens are soft hyphens, they do not print out if you revise the text so that they no longer fall at the end of the line. To hyphenate the correct words after editing, you have to hyphenate the document again.

Hyphens can be used to split words or phrases, and you can enter them manually or automatically. Normally, you enter them manually when they belong in a phrase such as *son-in-law*. You use automatic hyphenation to hyphenate words that fall at the ends of lines.

Manual Hyphenation with WordPerfect

You can insert three types of hyphens—hard, soft, and hyphen characters:

- **Hyphen characters**. Phrases hyphenated with hyphen characters split following the hyphen if the words fall at the end of a line, but the hyphens print out regardless of where they fall on the line. For example, to ensure that the phrase *son-in-law* breaks only following hyphens, you enter hyphen characters between the words. You enter a hyphen character by pressing **Hyphen** (-).
- **Hard hyphens**. Words or phrases hyphenated with hard hyphens do not split. If the hyphenated phrase will not fit at the end of a line, the entire phrase wraps to the next line. For example, to keep the entire phrase *son-in-law* on the same line, you enter hard hyphens between the words. You enter a hard hyphen by pressing **Home**, **Hyphen**.
- **Soft hyphens**. Soft hyphens (also called conditional hyphens) are like hyphen characters with one exception: they print and are displayed on the Edit screen only when they fall in the hyphenation zone. If they do fall in this zone, the word or phrase wraps after the soft hyphen, and the hyphen becomes visible at the end of the line. At other times, they can be seen only if you reveal codes. You enter a soft hyphen by pressing **Ctrl**-**Hyphen**. Soft hyphens are also entered when you use the automatic hyphenation feature.

There are two additional codes that you can enter to precisely guide the hyphenation of a document.

- To prevent the hyphenation of a word or phrase, you enter a cancelation hyphenation code at the beginning of the word or immediately after a soft hyphen. You press **Home**, **/** to enter a cancel hyphenation code.
- If you want a word or phrase to be hyphenated only at a specific point (should it be necessary to hyphenate it at all), you can enter

an invisible soft return code. You press **Home**, **Enter** to insert an invisible soft return code.

Automatic Hyphenation with WordPerfect

To hyphenate a document, you move the cursor to where you want hyphenation to begin, and enter a code that turns hyphenation on. As you then scroll through the document, or enter new text, it is automatically hyphenated. WordPerfect looks up each word that falls in the hyphenation zone in its dictionaries to determine possible hyphenation points.

- If you hyphenate the word, the hyphen is the last character on the line; the rest of the word wraps to the beginning of the next line.
- If you do not hyphenate, the entire word wraps to the next line.

You can turn hyphenation on and off at any point in the document if you want some text hyphenated and some not hyphenated. When hyphenating a document, keep the following points in mind:

- To cancel hyphenation when hyphenation is on, press **F1** when the prompt reads *Position hyphen; Press ESC.*
- To turn off hyphenation temporarily when scrolling through a document or when checking spelling, press **F7** when the first hyphenation prompt appears. Hyphenation automatically turns itself back on at the end of the operation.
- If your document contains a hard hyphen or a hard space and hyphenation is on, you may be requested to hyphenate a two-word phrase. Press **F1** to wrap the entire phrase to the next line.

→ **K E Y / S t r o k e s**

Hyphenating a Document

1. Move the cursor to where you want hyphenation to begin or end.
2. Either: Press **Shift**-**F8** and then **L** for *Line.*

   Or: Pull down the Layout menu and select *Line.*
3. Press **y** for *Hyphenation.*
4. Press **Y** for *Yes* to turn hyphenation on.
5. Press **F7** to return to the Edit screen.
6. Press the cursor movement keys to scroll down through the document. If prompting is set to *Always* or *When Required,* when the program finds a word that might be hyphenated, the prompt reads *Position hyphen; Press ESC* followed by the word. A flashing cursor indicates the suggested hyphen position.

   - Press **Esc** to hyphenate where suggested.
   - Press ← or → to reposition the hyphen, and then press **Esc**.
   - Press **F1** to wrap the entire word to the next line.

Changing Prompting During Hyphenation

You can control where hyphens are placed by specifying that you be prompted for each word or only when there is more than one possible hyphenation point. If you specify prompting, when the program finds a word that is a candidate for hyphenation, it pauses and suggests where you might place a hyphen. You have the three options described in the KEY/Strokes box "Hyphenating a Document." You can accept the suggestion, use the directional arrow keys to move the cursor to where you want the hyphen, or tell the program not to hyphenate the word.

Changing Hyphenation Prompting

1. Press **Shift**-**F1** to display the Setup menu.
2. Press **E** for *Environment*.
3. Press **P** for *Prompt for Hyphenation*.
4. Enter any of the settings described in the table "Hyphenation Prompt Choices."
5. Press **F7** to return to the document.

HYPHENATION PROMPT CHOICES

1 Never hyphenates the document without prompting you to confirm.

2 Always prompts you to confirm every hyphenation.

3 When Required prompts you only if there is more than one possible hyphenation point or if WordPerfect cannot determine where the hyphenation point should be.

The Hyphenation Zone

The **hyphenation zone** is an area to both the left and right of the right margin. The width of the hyphenation zone determines the length of words that are candidates for hyphenation. The finer the setting, the shorter the words that are hyphenated and the greater the number of words that are hyphenated. A finer setting reduces the spaces between words when justification is on and the raggedness of the right margin when it is off. When setting the hyphenation zone, keep the following points in mind:

- Words that are candidates for hyphenation begin before or at the left edge of the hyphenation zone and extend past the right edge of the zone.
- Words that begin after the left edge of the zone and extend past the right margin are automatically wrapped to the next line.
- The hyphenation zone determines how far you can move the hyphen when a word is proposed for hyphenation.

WordPerfect's hyphenation zone extends to the left and right of the right margin by the percentage of the total line length that you specify. (The default is 10 percent to the left and 4 percent to the right of the margin.) The percentage figure you enter is based on the total length of

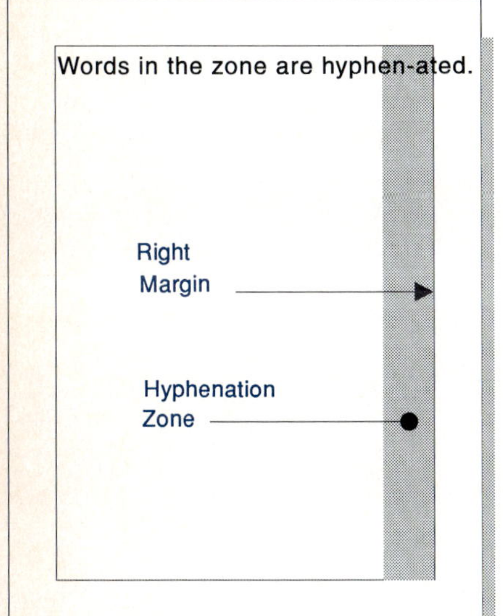

Hyphenation Zone
The hyphenation zone determines which words are candidates for hyphenation. When a word begins at or before the left edge of the zone and extends past the right edge, you are asked if you want to hyphenate it. The narrower the zone, the more words are hyphenated but the less ragged the right margin is.

the line. On a typical 8½-inch page with 1-inch margins, the line length is 6½ inches; 10 percent of that is .65 inch, and 4 percent is .26 inch.

→ **KEY/Strokes**

Changing the Hyphenation Zone

1. Move the cursor to where you want to change the zone.
2. Either: Press **Shift-F8** and then **L** for *Line.*
   Or: Pull down the Layout menu and select *Line.*
3. Press **Z** for *Hyphenation Zone* and the prompt reads *Left.*
4. Type the percentage of the line that is to be used for the left zone (the default is 10 percent), and then press **Enter**. The prompt reads *Right.*
5. Type the percentage of the line that is to be used for the right zone (the default is 4 percent), and then press **Enter**.
6. Press **F7** to return to the Edit screen.

► **E X E R C I S E S**

EXERCISE 1

ENTERING HYPHENS MANUALLY

Enter the document describing compound words shown in the figure "The Hyphen Document." Enter hard hyphens in the compound words.

1. Retrieve the HYPHEN2.WP5 document and enter your name.
2. Using the figure "The HYPHEN Document" as a guide to where hyphens belong, enter hyphen characters in the first paragraph and hard hyphens in the second.
3. Save and print the document.

The HYPHEN Document

> Note that compound words are hyphenated (1) when they consist of a prepositional phrase, for example, "off-center axis," "into-orbit arc"; (2) when "self-" is the first element, for example, "self-sealing," "self-starter"; (3) when a vowel would be doubled, for example, "intra-atomic" (but no hyphen is necessary in compounds such as "intranuclear"); (4) when the compound is a technical unit of measurement ending in "year," "day," "hour," "minute," "second," "mile," "foot," "inch," "pound," "ton," for example, "light-year," "foot-pound."
>
> Terms consisting of a capital letter and a noun are hyphenated only when they are used as attributive adjectives, for example, "I beam" but "I-beam structure"; "X ray" but "X-ray tube." Fractions are hyphenated, for example, "a two-thirds balance," "two-thirds of those present." Do not use a hyphen in compounds containing an adverb ending in "ly," for example, "evenly spaced intervals."

CHANGING THE HYPHENATION ZONE

In this exercise, you change the hyphenation zone and then hyphenate the same document you hyphenated in the tutorial at the beginning of this topic.

1. Retrieve the HYPHEN1.WP5 document.
2. Move the cursor to the beginning of the first paragraph and follow the instructions in the KEY/Strokes box "Changing the Hyphenation Zone" to change the left edge of the zone to 5 percent and the right edge to 0 percent.
3. Move the cursor to the end of the document to hyphenate it, and then make a printout. When finished, compare the printout with the hyphenated one you printed in the tutorial at the beginning of this topic. Are there more hyphens? If the same words are not hyphenated, are the old hyphens still printed? On lines that are hyphenated in both documents, are the hyphens in the same place? Do newly hyphenated lines look more closed up than when unhyphenated?

HYPHENATION TIPS

- To protect a section of your document from hyphenation, for example, a table, enter a hyphenation off code above the section, and a hyphenation on code below the section.
- To remove hyphens from hyphenated words, press **Alt-F3** or **F11** to reveal codes. Delete the soft hyphen (-) or the **[/]** code that was inserted if you pressed **F1** to wrap the entire word to the next line.

REVIEW

- You can enter special characters by holding down **Alt** and typing the character's three-digit decimal number on the numeric keypad.
- Words or phrases hyphenated with hyphen characters (**Hyphen**) split at the hyphen if the words fall at the end of a line.
- Phrases hyphenated with hard hyphens (**Home**, **Hyphen**) do not split. If the hyphenated phrase will not fit at the end of the line, the entire phrase wraps to the next line.
- Soft hyphens (**Ctrl-Hyphen**) print and are displayed on the Edit screen only when they fall in the hyphenation zone, in which case the word or phrase breaks at the soft hyphen, and the hyphen becomes visible.
- Cancel hyphenation codes specify that a word or phrase should not be hyphenated.
- Invisible soft returns specify positions where a word or phrase can be hyphenated if hyphenation is necessary.
- Hyphenation automatically inserts soft hyphens to give a more even look to the right margin or to eliminate white space or rivers of white space in justified text.
- Where words are hyphenated is determined by the hyphenation zone. If a word at the end of a line begins before or at the left edge of the zone and extends past its right edge, you are prompted to hyphenate it.
- A hyphen position is suggested by the program, based on its hyphenation dictionaries.

QUESTIONS

TRUE/FALSE

T   F

❏ ❏   1. The quotation marks that you want to use in desktop published documents are found on the keyboard.

❏ ❏   2. To enter special characters with the **Alt** key, you type the character's decimal number on the number keys above the alphabetic keys on the keyboard.

❏ ❏   3. Composing characters allows you to print over 1,700 characters on any graphics printer.

❏ ❏   4. If you want a hyphenated phrase to split at a hyphen if the entire phrase does not fit at the end of a line, you use hard hyphens.

❏ ❏   5. Soft hyphens are printed regardless of where they fall in the text.

		6.	When you hyphenate a document, you have to enter the hyphens manually.
		7.	When hyphenating a document, you are always prompted to confirm every hyphenation.
		8.	Hyphenating justified text helps eliminate white spaces called *rivers*.
		9.	The hyphenation zone determines how many words are considered for hyphenation.

FILL IN THE BLANK

1. Special characters that do not appear on the keyboard are called ____________ or ____________.
2. Because of the way the computer stores and processes characters, it can store only ____________ total characters.
3. To print more than the number of characters allowed by computers, the basic characters are formatted using a different ____________.
4. Four typical uses of special characters are for ____________, ____________, ____________, and ____________.
5. The quote marks that you want to use in documents are called ____________ quotes.
6. White spaces in justified text that fall near each other on adjacent lines are called ____________.
7. A hyphen that does not allow a phrase to be split at the end of the line is called a(n) ________ ____________.
8. To adjust the number of hyphenated words, you change the ____________.

1. Dingbat
2. Extended character set
3. Piece fraction
4. Split fraction
5. Hard space
6. **Alt** key
7. Compose command
8. Hard hyphen
9. Hyphen character
10. Soft hyphen
11. Hyphenation zone

__ The key used to enter special characters

__ The area at the right margin that determines which words are candidates for hyphenation

__ The 256 characters that a computer can store and process

__ Hyphens that split at the end of the line but print anywhere they fall

__ Hyphens that do not split

__ Hyphens that are displayed and print only when they fall in the hyphenation zone

__ A special character

__ A space that does not break at the end of a line

__ A fraction that is entered as individual characters separated by a solidus

__ A fraction that is a single character

__ A command that allows you to print any of 1,700 characters on a graphics printer

WRITE OUT THE ANSWERS

1. List and briefly describe two ways to create special characters that do not appear on the keyboard.
2. How do you enter special characters using their three-digit decimal code?
3. List three types of hyphens and briefly explain each. Give examples of when you might want to use each type.
4. What is the difference between a hard hyphen and a hyphen character? When would you want to use a hard hyphen? What is the difference between a hyphen character and a soft hyphen?
5. How do you enter an em dash?
6. Why do you hyphenate a document? At what point in its preparation do you do so?
7. What is a hyphenation zone? When are words proposed as candidates for hyphenation?

PROJECTS

PROJECT 1

ENTERING A SPANISH-LANGUAGE DOCUMENT

In this project, you retrieve a Spanish-language document and enter special characters using the **Alt** key and the Compose command. The position of each special character in the file on the screen is indicated with the code *[SC]*. Locate these codes (you can use the Search command) and enter special characters so your printout will match the one shown here. The table "Special Characters" lists the characters used in the document.

Procedures Used
- Entering special characters with the **Alt** key.

Text Files Needed
- SPANISH.WP5

Formats
① Enter a base font code for any typeface you choose.
② Enter special characters in places indicated by the *[SC]* codes.

SPECIAL CHARACTERS

Character	Code
é	**Alt-130**
¨	**Ctrl-V** then **1,7**
ü	**Ctrl-V** then **1,71**
í	**Alt-161**
ñ	**Alt-164**
ó	**Alt-162**
ú	**Alt-163**
ü	**Alt-129**

① ②

The tilde, the dieresis, and the acute accent are the diacritical marks used in Spanish. The tilde is used only over the *n* and *ñ* is a special character representing a special phoneme, the palatal *n*. The dieresis mark (¨), called *diéresis* or *trema* in Spanish, is to be found in a limited number of words, such as *vergüenza* and *argüir*, to indicate that the vowel *u* must be pronounced.

The acute accent is used over a vowel to indicate that it is stressed; it is also used to distinguish homonyms. If there is no accent mark, a word ending in a consonant (including *y*, except *n* and *s*) is stressed on the last syllable; a word ending in a vowel, *n*, or *s* is stressed on the next-to-last syllable. Specifically, the acute accent is used as follows:

1. To indicate that the vowel is stressed.

2. To indicate vowels not forming a diphthong.

3. To distinguish words of the same spelling but of different meanings, for example, *aún* meaning "still" or "yet" and *aun* meaning "even."

4. To distinguish interrogative or exclamatory use from relative or declarative, for example, *cómo* meaning "how?" and *como* meaning "as."

5. To distinguish pronouns from adjectives, for example, *éste* meaning "this one" and *este* meaning "this."

6. Arbitrary or monosyllabic aorists, for example, *di* meaning "I gave."

7. To avoid confusing the word o (or) with the zero, for example, *2 ó 3*, but *dos o tres* meaning "two or three."

USING SPECIAL CHARACTERS IN A CHECKLIST

In this project, you enter checklist characters in a document.

Procedures Used
- Entering special characters with the Compose command.

Text Files Needed
- TRACK2.WP5

Formats
① Enter the character number 23 from Character Set 5 in place of the hyphens.

COMPUTER USERS' CHECKLIST

✓ Correct angle and distance from screen to eyes
✓ Reference material placed near the screen
✓ Reference material and screen same distance from eyes
✓ Screen brightness properly adjusted
✓ Proper overall room lighting
✓ Windows and other sources of bright light shielded
✓ Proper lamps for reference material
✓ Sources of screen reflection eliminated
✓ Fifteen-minute break every two hours for moderate users
✓ Fifteen-minute break every hour for frequent users

THE DTP ADVISOR NEWSLETTER

In this project, you enter registration and trademark characters in the newsletter. The special characters are entered following the first occurrence of the company or product name that is not in a headline or used as the company's name. Finally, you turn on hyphenation so the document is automatically hyphenated at all stages.

Procedures Used

■ Entering special characters with the Compose command.

Text Files Needed

■ ADVISOR.WP5

Formats

① Enter the ® character following the terms "*Bitstream*," "*WordPerfect*," "*HP*," "*DeskJet*," "*IBM*," " *LaserJet*," and "*Dingbats*."

② Enter the ™ character following the terms "*Facelift*," "*Speedo*," and "*Windows*."

③ Enter a hyphen on code at the top of the document.

④ Search for double hyphens (- -) and replace with em dashes.

⑤ Search for inch marks (") and replace with open and close quotation marks ("").

⑥ Search for foot marks (') and replace with apostrophes ('). (No example is shown in the illustration)

Tips

■ You will find it much faster if you use the Search command to locate the first occurrence of each term.

■ After entering the special characters, you may want to experiment with changing their size and superscripting them to adjust their position.

■ The ® code is **4,22** and the ™ code is **4,41**.

THE *dtp* ADVISOR

FaceLift For WordPerfect

Bitstream Inc. today announced version 1.5 of Bitstream® FaceLift™ for WordPerfect® FaceLift brings enhanced font support to WordPerfect 5.0 and 5.1. The new FaceLift version 1.5 will create high-quality fonts on-the-fly for popular dot-matrix and inkjet printers—like the HP® DeskJet® Canon BubbleJet and the IBM® ExecuJet—in addition to the existing on-the-fly support for the Hewlett-Packard LaserJet® series of printers. FaceLift 1.5 for WordPerfect will be available in the spring of 1991.

In addition to 13 typeface outlines provided in the original FaceLift package, FaceLift 1.5 for WordPerfect will also ship with three Symbol typefaces: ITC Zapf Dingbats® Symbol Proportional and Symbol Monospaced. Users will be able to access a total of 698 characters from the Bitstream International Character Set and from these three Symbols typefaces.

FaceLift 1.5 for WordPerfect is an easy-to-use utility that allows users to print high-quality fonts in any size from 2 to 500 point (in quarter point increments) without ever having to leave the application. The fonts are generated at print time, so the need for stored bit-map fonts is eliminated. Based on Bitstream Speedo™ technology, FaceLift sends characters to printers in both graphics mode (laser, inkjet and dot-matrix printers) and as HP soft fonts (laser printers only). Users have full control over the number and size of soft fonts to be downloaded, depending on the memory available in the printer.

"We are very excited that FaceLift 1.5 for WordPerfect will provide dot-matrix and inkjet users with the same high typographic quality and capabilities that HP LaserJet users have enjoyed with Bitstream type," stated Doug Lloyd, Executive Director at WordPerfect. "That, and the addition of the three new Symbol typefaces makes FaceLift a great companion for WordPerfect."

First-time users can purchase FaceLift 1.5 for WordPerfect for a suggested U.S. list price of $99. Current users of FaceLift 1.0 for WordPerfect can upgrade to version 1.5 for $24.95. In addition to the 16 typefaces included free with FaceLift, users can purchase add-on fonts from the Bitstream Library of 52 typeface packages. Also available is the FaceLift Companion Value Pack, a selection of 24 text and headline faces for a suggested U.S. list price $199.

FaceLift 1.5 for WordPerfect is the newest member of the Bitstream FaceLift product line. The initial product, FaceLift for Windows™ shipped in August of 1990. All FaceLift products can share Bitstream typefaces (in Speedo format) stored in a single common subdirectory.

FaceLift for Wordperfect was developed in conjunction with LaserTools Corporation, a privately held company based in Emeryville, CA. LaserTools is a developer of innovative printing enhancement products—tools for printer sharing, printer control, printer acceleration, and font management.

An industry leader in typographic quality and innovative technology, Bitstream licenses fonts and related software to more than 420 hardware manufacturers and software developers worldwide. Its line of retail products is distributed by an extensive network of dealers in the United States and in 18 nations worldwide.

Page Design

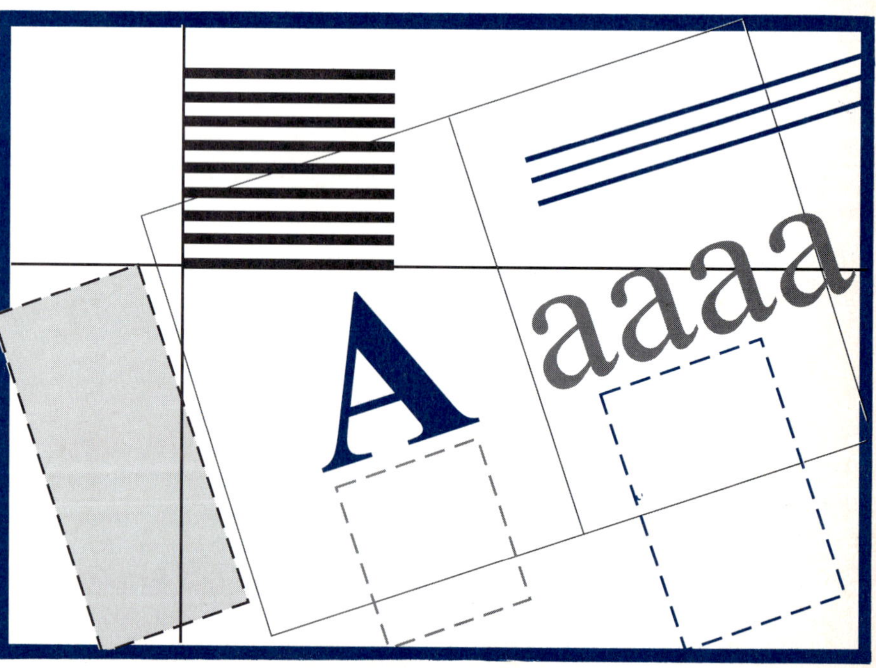

Design

After completing this topic, you should be able to:
- Explain why and how publications are designed
- Describe why a design grid is important
- Describe how design specifications are used

▶ T U T O R I A L

In this tutorial, you use the View Document command to look at two-page spreads.

GETTING STARTED

1. Retrieve the ADVISOR.WP5 document.

VIEWING A DOCUMENT

2. Press **Shift**-**F7** to display the Print menu.
3. Press **V** for *View Document* to display the document.
4. Press **4** for *Facing Pages* to display two-page spreads of the document.
5. Press **PgDn** and **PgUp** to scroll forward and backward through the document.

FINISHING UP

6. Press **F1** to return to the Edit screen.

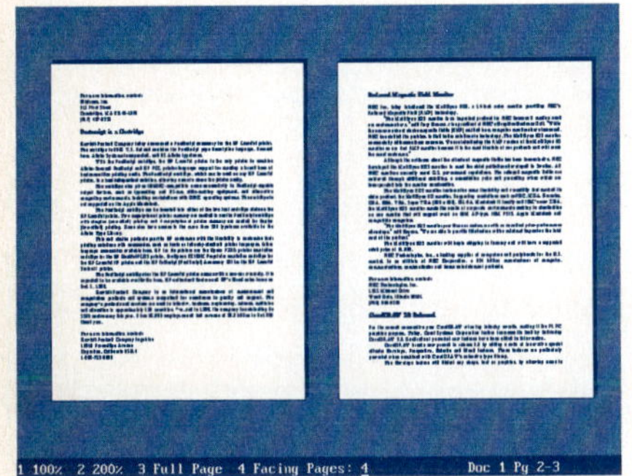

A Two-Page Spread

▶ D E S K T O P   P U B L I S H I N G   C O N C E P T S

Before a manuscript can be published, it must first be designed. Design is the process of specifying how the elements in the publication should look and how they should be organized on the page. When a designer works out a design, he or she usually has a copy of the final manuscript to work from. The designer's first step is to identify all of the elements in the manuscript, which include such things as body text, heads and subheads, illustrations, captions, and tables. The designer then visualizes how the final publication should look given its content and its audience.

Layouts
To help in the design process, the designer creates sketches that show how various elements should be arranged on the page. Early versions

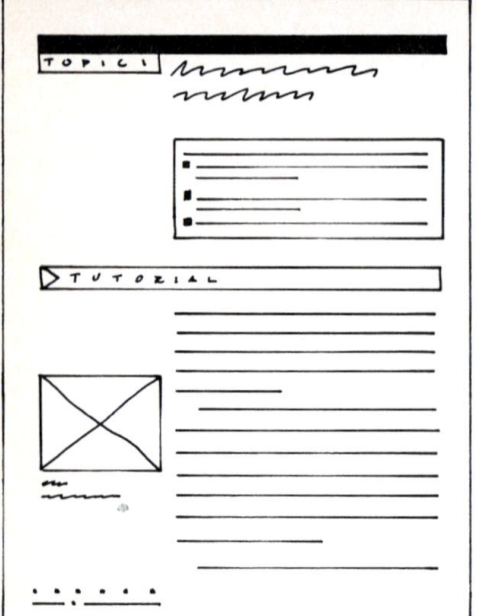

A Thumbnail Sketch

A Two-Page Spread
Two facing pages form the basic unit of design in a publication that is printed on both sides of the page.

A Detailed Layout
If a publication design has to be approved by others, the designer will prepare polished versions of his or her design so others can see how the publication will look in its final form.

are very rough sketches called **thumbnails**.

If the final document is to be printed on both sides of the page, the designer visualizes it in **two-page spreads**. Open any book, and you will immediately see that the left and right facing pages form the basic visual unit. Single pages are the basic unit only when a document is printed on one side of the sheet, like letters and reports are.

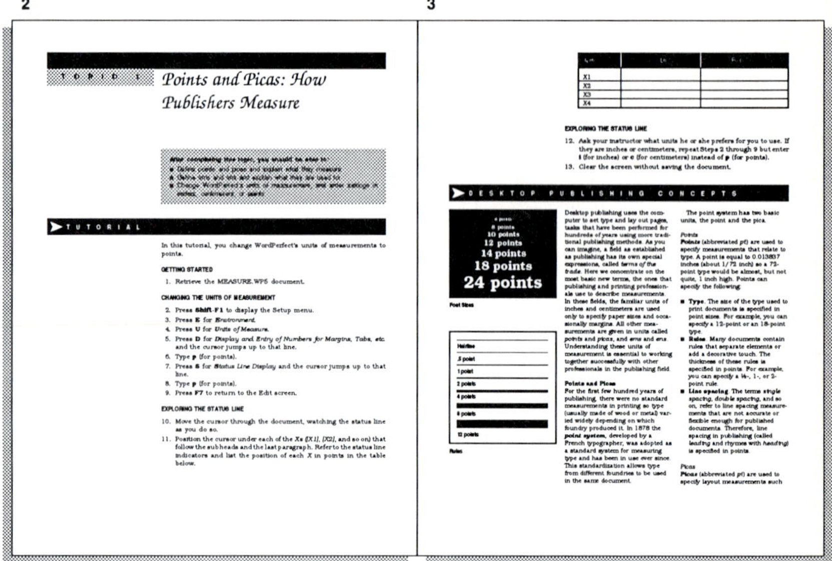

Thumbnails are revised frequently as ideas are developed and design problems are solved. Gradually the sketches become more and more complex until all of the elements are incorporated. If the design has to be approved by a third party, the designer prepares a polished version of the design sketches called a **layout**, or **comp** (for *comprehensive*). The layout clearly shows examples of all elements that will appear in the publication. This layout is then used as a guide when the manuscript is typemarked and set into type.

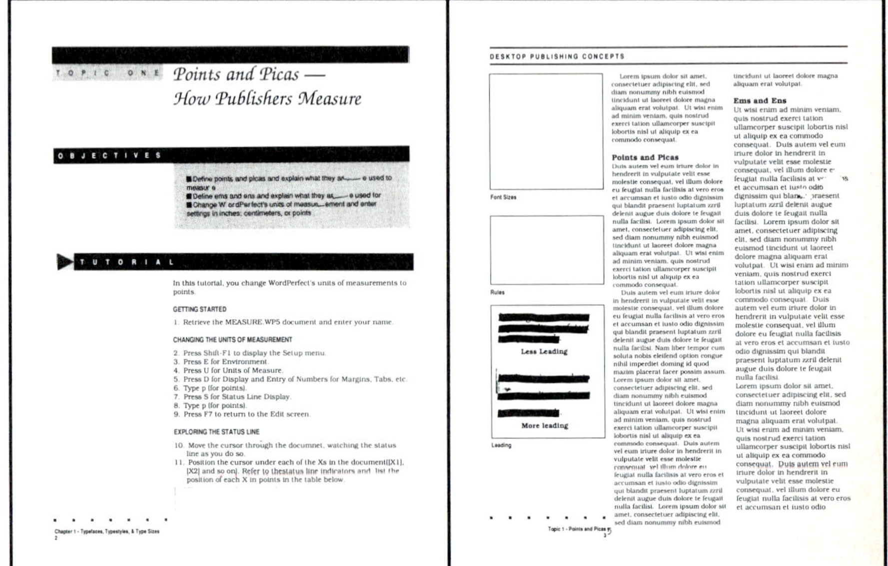

Grids

The design of a printed page is almost always based on a **_grid_**. This grid establishes those characteristics that will be the same throughout the publication and includes the paper size, orientation, number of sides, margins and type page, and the number and width of columns.

The purpose of the grid is to establish consistency throughout the document. A well-designed publication has the same margins, type, spacing, and headings throughout. Readers tend to become subconsciously at ease with a consistent design as they read through a document; sudden changes in the treatment of any elements are visually and aesthetically unsettling.

A Grid
The grid establishes the overall design of the publication.

> ✔ **CHECKLIST FOR CONSISTENCY**
>
> Consistency is important in the design of a publication. It is also important when you are checking to see that the design elements have been applied correctly. When you check through a publication that you are working on, you make a separate pass to check each element for consistency. For example, go though the document once just to check headings, again to check fonts, and so on. When designing or checking, here are some things to consider or check for consistency:
>
> ❑ Margins: top, bottom, inside, outside
> ❑ Column widths and column spacing
> ❑ Table formats and number sequence
> ❑ Headings, all levels
> ❑ Fonts for all elements
> ❑ Illustration number sequence
> ❑ Caption size and position
> ❑ Page number positions
> ❑ Header or footer contents and positions
> ❑ Alignment of numbers in enumerated lists
> ❑ Spacing between elements

Design Specs

Designs involve not only sketches but also the preparation of detailed specifications (called ***design specs***) for each element in the document. When these specs are written on the copy, it is called typemarking or ***markup***. Typemarking may specify the position of subheads (flush left or centered, for example), the typeface, type size, and typestyle, and the space above and below the head.

Design specs are sometimes spelled out in detail right on the manuscript in its margins in a unique color, one that hasn't been used by the copyeditor or others in marking up the manuscript.

A Manuscript with Specifications
Here, a manuscript has been typemarked with the actual specifications written onto it.

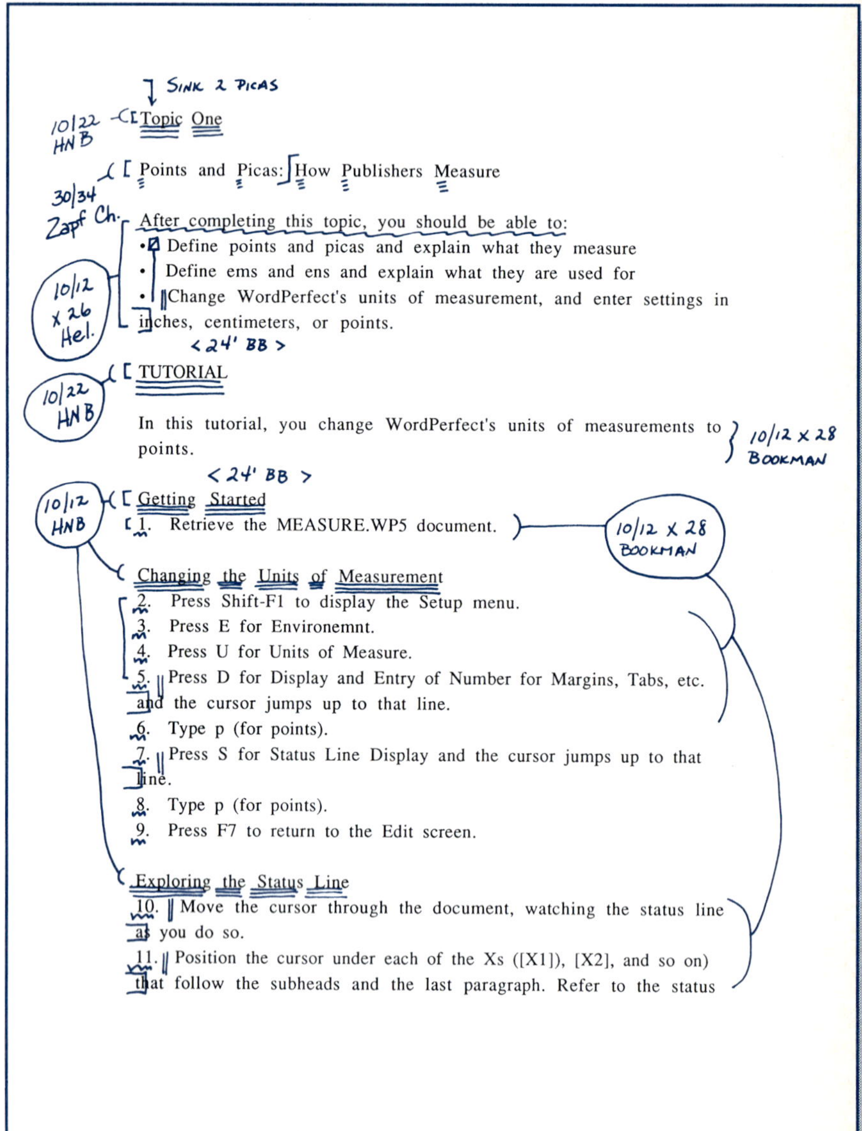

At other times, especially if the document is long, or if the specifications are complicated, they are written out in detail on separate pages and codes are then assigned to each element.

List of Design Specs
When a design is complicated or for or one that has been developed for a long document, design specs are listed separately from the document and given in detail.

CHAPTER OPENER	New right or left
CN	10 pt HNB caps, spell out chapter with arabic fig Letterspace 12 points, ctr in side column. Color: No sink to solid 541, 2 X bleed right CN prints black in 20% screen of 541 13.5 X bleed bottom in side column, 1.5 picas to base of CN from bottom of solid bar
CT	48/58 Zapf Chancery clc, flush left to TA 3.5 picas to base from bottom of solid bar
TOPICS **TN**	Begin new left or right Color: No sink to solid 541, 42.5 X 2 picas TN prints in black in 20% screen of 541 13.5 X 2 in side column top touching solid bar above. TN: 10 pt HNB caps, spell out Topic with arabic fig Letterspace 12 points, ctr in side column in screen.
TT	30/34 X 28 Zapf Chancery clc, no hyphen breaks, flush left to TA, 2 picas to base from bottom of solid bar
TOPIC TAB	On verso pages. To read current Topic Number TN: 10 pt HNB caps, 12 pts letterspaced, spell out topic with arabic fig, drops out of solid band of 541 in side column, 13.5 picas X 4 to bleed top, ctr TN on 13.5
HEADS **A HEAD**	Major Heads: Tutorial, WordPerfect Procedures, Exercises 10 HNB caps. 8 pts letterspaced, 2.5 picas from flush left. Head drops out of solid band of 541 42.5 X 2 picas. Triangle drops out 2 pts from flush left. # above band: 2 pi visual # below band: 1 pica visual
B HEAD	Concepts, Questions types, exercise and project numbers 10 pt HNB caps, 2 pts letterspaced, flush left to either 42.5 or 28 (TA) Concepts head: Fl.L. 42.5; All others, Fl.L. 28 (TA) 6 pts visual # above and below run solid 3 pt rule of 541. # above top rule and below bottom rule: 1 pica visual
B1 HEAD	10/12 X 28 HNB caps, 2 pts letterspaced, flush left, 24 pts bb below. 18 pts bb above (to rule of B head) when following B head.

These codes are written on the manuscript to indicate which specifications relate to which elements.

When the compositor sees a code on the manuscript, he or she refers to the list of specifications for details.

A Manuscript with Codes

Here the same manuscript as the figure "A Manuscript with Specifications" has been typemarked with codes that refer to a separate list of specifications. This approach is better for long documents where styles are repeated throughout.

 Topic One

 Points and Picas: How Publishers Measure

 After completing this topic, you should be able to:
- Define points and picas and explain what they measure
- Define ems and ens and explain what they are used for
- Change WordPerfect's units of measurement, and enter settings in inches, centimeters, or points.

 TUTORIAL

 In this tutorial, you change WordPerfect's units of measurements to points.

 Getting Started
 1.   Retrieve the MEASURE.WP5 document.

 Changing the Units of Measurement
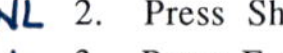 2.   Press Shift-F1 to display the Setup menu.
3.   Press E for Environemnt.
4.   Press U for Units of Measure.
5.   Press D for Display and Entry of Number for Margins, Tabs, etc. and the cursor jumps up to that line.
6.   Type p (for points).
7.   Press S for Status Line Display and the cursor jumps up to that line.
8.   Type p (for points).
9.   Press F7 to return to the Edit screen.

 Exploring the Status Line
10.   Move the cursor through the document, watching the status line as you do so.
11.   Position the cursor under each of the Xs ([X1]), [X2], and so on) that follow the subheads and the last paragraph. Refer to the status

The finished work reflects the specifications that were supplied by the designer.

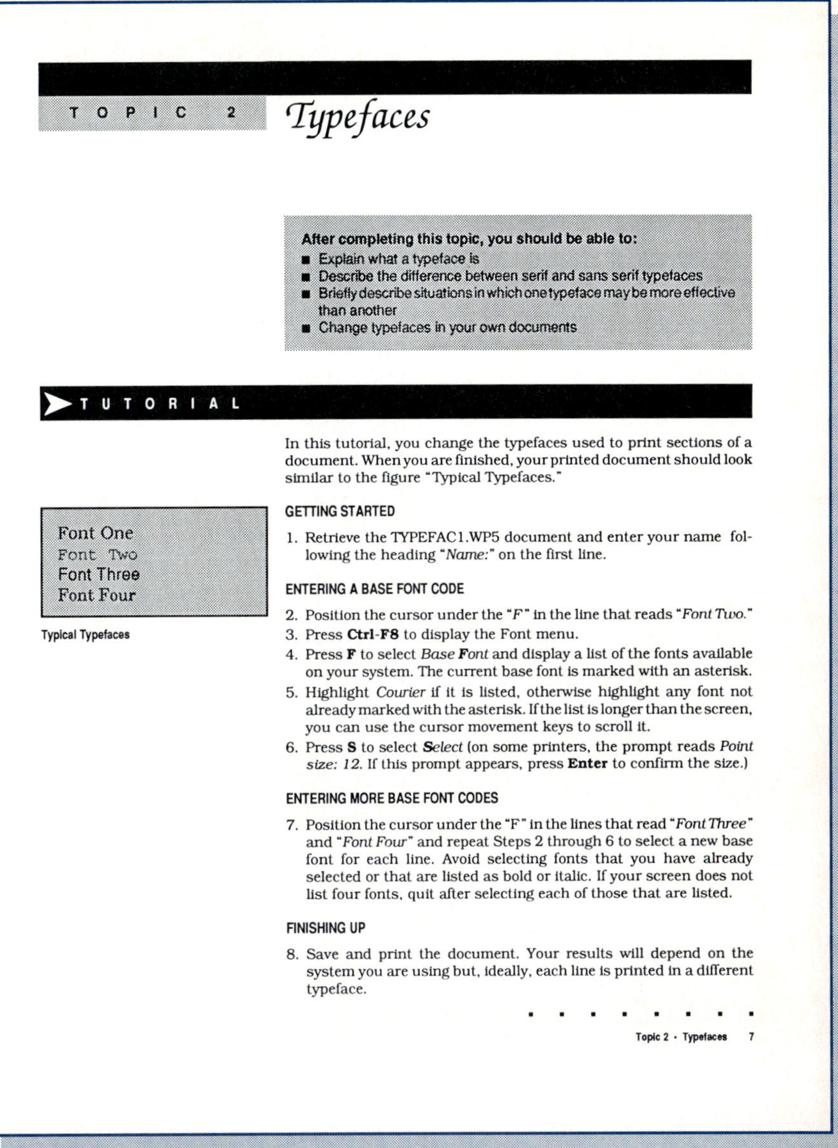

EXERCISE 1

EXPLORING THE WORK OF OTHERS

Locate some books or other publications that you think are well designed. Try to identify what it is about the publication that you like. As you thumb through the books, look for things such as consistency, the use of indents, typefaces, and typestyles. Also see if you can discern a grid that underlies the organization of the elements.

DESIGN SPECS

The elements that are always specified in the design specs include the following:

Fonts

- Typeface, typestyle, and type size.
- All caps, small caps, or caps and lowercase.
- Letter spacing if not the usual.

Vertical Spacing

- Vertical position for elements such as headings. The position of the topmost element on the page is referred to as sinkage (the distance from the top of the type page to the baseline of the element). Other elements are specified in relation to their distance from other elements above or below them.
- Leading specifies the distance between lines of text.

Horizontal Spacing

- Position is specified as being either justified, flush left, flush right, centered, or indented.
- Measure specifies the width of the type line. Full measure means it is to extend across the entire type page.
- Word spacing if not the usual.

The Type Page: Paper Size and Orientation

After completing this topic, you should be able to:
- Define the term *trim size*
- Explain the differences between *portrait mode* and *landscape mode*
- Change paper sizes and types for your own documents

▶ T U T O R I A L

In this tutorial, you change a document's printed orientation from lengthwise (called portrait mode) to sideways (called landscape mode).

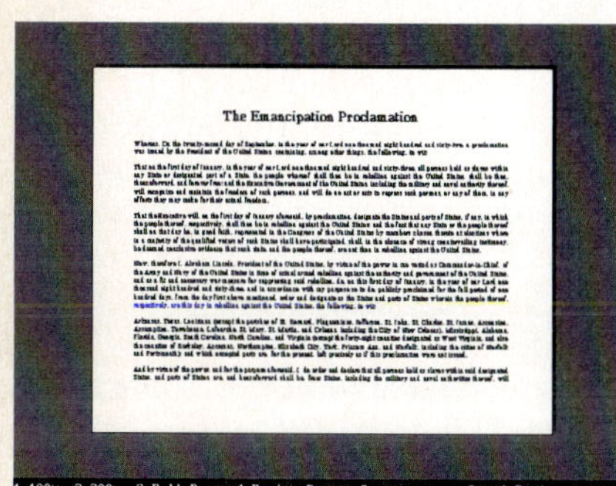
View Document

GETTING STARTED

1. Retrieve the EMANPROC.WP5 document.

VIEWING THE DOCUMENT IN PORTRAIT MODE

2. Press **Shift-F7** to display the Print menu.
3. Press **V** for *View Document* to display the document.
4. Press **F7** to return to the Edit screen.

CHANGING THE DOCUMENT'S ORIENTATION

5. Move the cursor to the top of the document, then press **Shift-F8** to display the Format menu.
6. Press **P** for *Page*.
7. Press **S** for *Paper Size* to display a list of paper sizes from which you can choose.
8. Highlight *Standard - Wide* if it is listed (other landscape orientations are indicated with the term "Wide" in their descriptions or by a larger number listed first in the Paper Size column.) Choose the desired size, and then press **S** for *Select*.
9. Press **F7** to return to the Edit screen.

VIEWING THE DOCUMENT IN LANDSCAPE MODE

10. Press **Shift-F7** to display the Print menu.
11. Press **V** for *View Document* to display the document.
12. Press **F7** to return to the Edit screen.

FINISHING UP

13. Save and print the document.

▷ D E S K T O P   P U B L I S H I N G   C O N C E P T S

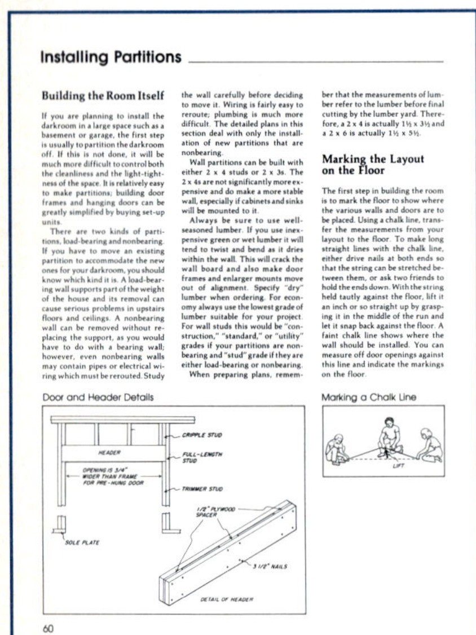

Portrait Mode

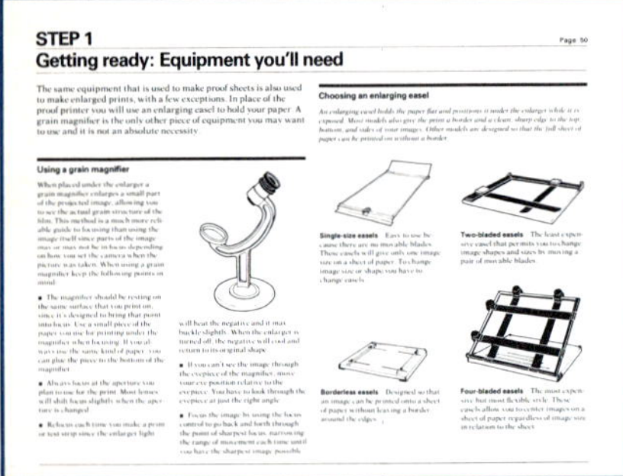

Landscape Mode

In publishing, the size of the finished pages is called the **trim size**. Often, however, the document is printed on larger sheets, which are then folded and trimmed to the desired size. In desktop publishing, most documents are printed on a limited number of page sizes including the following:

- Letter size (8½ by 11 inches)
- Legal size (8½ by 14 inches)
- Double (11 by 17 inches)
- B5 (17.6cm by 25cm)
- A4 (21cm by 29.7cm)

The final size you choose depends both on the document and on the equipment, such as printers and copiers, that you plan on using to process it. For example, most printers will not print double-size sheets. On the other hand, 8½-by-11-inch pages are very flexible. When folded, they make 5½-by-8½-inch pages, ideal for small brochures or programs, for example. If the size of the publication must be a different size from what your equipment can handle, it can be sent to a commercial printer or the pages can be trimmed after printing or copying.

If you print a document on a laser printer, you can print text across the width or length of the page. The direction is called the orientation or mode, and it can be either *portrait mode* or *landscape mode*.

- **Portrait mode** is the orientation of a normal document, that is, text is printed across the width of the page.

- **Landscape mode** (also called *broadside*) rotates the image 90 degrees so that it is printed along the length of the page. This mode is useful when you are printing wide tables, charts, and illustrations that are more horizontal than vertical. When used for this purpose, the left-hand side of the table or chart should print at the bottom of the page. Landscape mode is also ideal when you want to print a four-page 5½-by-8½-inch brochure by printing on 8½-by-11-inch paper and folding it once.

Printing in landscape mode requires landscape fonts. Pages are not printed in this mode by changing the orientation of the paper in the printer. Instead, the computer or printer rotates the entire page in its memory before printing it. Normal (portrait) fonts cannot be rotated like this unless they are designed to do so.

You also have to decide if the final document is to be printed on one side of the page, or on both sides. Printing on both sides saves paper and makes documents look shorter and less intimidating to the reader. If your printer prints both sides of a sheet in a single pass, it is called a **duplex printer**. (Never run already printed sheets through a laser printer a second time to achieve this effect or you may have problems.) If you do not have a duplex printer, you can use a copy machine or send the job out to a commercial printer to print pages back to back.

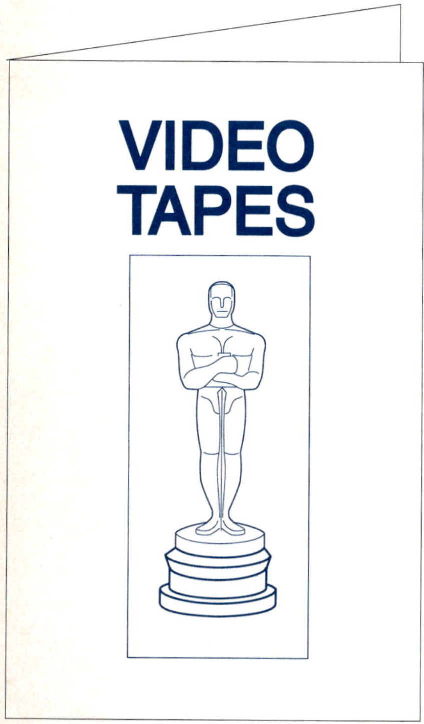

An 8½ by 11-inch Sheet Folded

To change paper sizes or orientations in WordPerfect, you enter a code in the document where you want the change to take place. You select the desired paper size from a menu that lists a variety of forms. The forms listed are those that have been defined for the printer you are using. If you select a different printer, the list of available forms changes. When you select a paper size and type, the definition for that form tells the computer the size of the paper, where the paper is located in the printer, and how the paper is fed to the printer.

The form you select also affects the way the text is displayed on the screen and where page breaks fall. For example, if you select a wide form, your text is displayed wider than normal, so you may have to scroll the screen sideways to edit the document.

→ **K E Y / S t r o k e s**

Changing Paper Size and Type

1. Move the cursor to where you want to change the paper size or type.
2. Either: Press **Shift-F8** and then **P** for *Page*.
   Or: Pull down the Layout menu and select *Page*.
3. Press **S** for *Paper Size* to display a list of paper sizes from which you can choose.
4. Highlight the desired size, and then press **S** for **S**elect.
5. Press **F7** to return to the Edit screen.

Paper Sizes

The Paper Size/Type menu lists several forms on which you can print. (Your menu may vary because the list depends on the printer you are using.)

```
Format: Paper Size/Type

                                                          Font  Double
Paper type and Orientation      Paper Size    Prompt Loc  Type  Sided  Labels

Envelope - Wide                 9.5" x 4"     Yes  Manual  Land  No
Standard                        8.5" x 11"    No   Contin  Port  No
Standard - Wide                 11" x 8.5"    No   Contin  Land  No
[ALL OTHERS]                    Width ≤ 8.5"  Yes  Manual        No








1 Select; 2 Add (Create); 3 Copy; 4 Delete; 5 Edit; N Name Search: 1
```

EXERCISE 1

EXPLORING PAPER SIZES AND TYPES

In this exercise, you change the paper size and type for a document and use the View Document command to explore the results.

1. Retrieve the TYPEFAC1.WP5 document and enter your name.
2. Move the cursor to the top of the document, then follow the instructions in the KEY/Strokes box "Changing Paper Size and Type" to change the paper size and type to any of those listed on the menu other than the one currently selected.
3. Use the View Document command to preview the results, and list any changes that you notice.
4. Delete the *[Paper Sz/Typ:...]* code and select another paper size and type. Again list the changes that you see.

PAPER SIZE AND ORIENTATION TIP

If the form on which you want to print isn't listed on the menu, you can define it, or select *[ALL OTHERS]* from the list and then select a paper size from the list that appears. When you use the *[ALL OTHERS]* code, you can print without defining a form and the document can also be easily printed on other printers.

The Type Page: Margins

After completing this topic, you should be able to:
- Define the terms *type page* and *measure*
- Explain why margin widths and proportions are important
- Describe how margins are set on facing pages
- Change margins in your own documents

▶ T U T O R I A L

In this tutorial, you change margins. When you are finished, your printout should look similar to the illustration "Changing Margins."

GETTING STARTED

1. Retrieve the MARGINS1.WP5 document and enter your name.
2. Make a printout that you can use for comparison purposes at the end of this tutorial. All margin settings on this first printout use WordPerfect's default settings.

SETTING THE LEFT AND RIGHT MARGINS

3. Press **Home** twice and then press ≤ to move the cursor to the top of the document.
4. Press **Shift-F8** to display the Format menu.
5. Press **L** for *Line* to display the Line Format menu.
6. Press **M** for *Margins* and the cursor jumps to the line that reads *Margins - Left*.
7. Type **1.5"** and then press **Enter**. The cursor moves to the line that reads *Right*.
8. Type **1.5"** and then press **Enter**. The cursor moves to the prompt *Selection:*.
9. Press **0** to return to the Format menu (if you return to the Edit screen by mistake, press **Shift-F8** again).

SETTING THE TOP AND BOTTOM MARGINS

10. Press **P** for *Page* to display the Page Format menu.
11. Press **M** for *Margins* and the cursor jumps to the line that reads *Margins - Top*.
12. Type **1.5"** and then press **Enter**. The cursor moves to the line that reads *Bottom*.

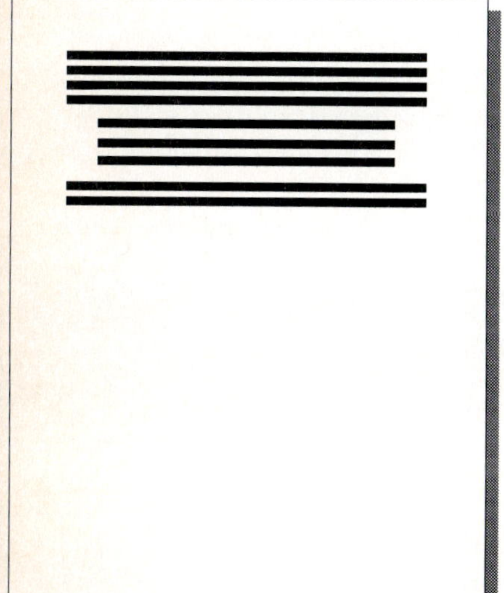

Changing Margins

13. Type **1.5"** and then press **Enter**. The cursor moves to the prompt *Selection:*.

14. Press **F7** to return to the Edit screen.

SETTING MARGINS FOR A SINGLE PARAGRAPH

15. Move the cursor to the blank line between the first and second paragraphs. (The second paragraph begins "*The default settings for the left and right margins...*")

16. Repeat Steps 4 through 8 but set both the left and right margins to 2 inches.

17. Press **F7** to return to the Edit screen. All paragraphs below the new margin code are indented 2 inches from the left and right margins. (If they are not, press ↓ to realign them.)

RESTORING MARGINS TO THEIR ORIGINAL SETTINGS

18. Move the cursor to the blank line between the second and third paragraphs and repeat Steps 4 through 8, resetting the margins to 1½ inches.

19. Press **F7** to return to the document. All paragraphs below this code are realigned with their original margins. (If they are not, press ↓ to realign them.)

FINISHING UP

20. Save and print the document. Compare the printout with the first printout that you made to see the effect of changing margins.

21. Press **Alt**-**F3** or **F11** to examine the codes you entered in the document and compare them with the printout.

▶ DESKTOP PUBLISHING CONCEPTS

Alice's Restaurant
Famous Homemade Ice Cream

Sundaes	Ice Cream Sandwiches	Frappes
	(any flavor)	
Ice Cream Sodas	Milk Shakes	Floats & Malteds

Flavors

Vanilla	Rocky Road	Pistachio
Chocolate	Chocolate Chip	Coffee Almond
Coffee	Chocolate Chocolate Chip	Oreo
Strawberry	Mint Chip	Butter Crunch
Chocolate Almond Fudge	Mocha Chip	Reeses
Banana	Grape Nut	M & M
Bubble Gum	Maple Walnut	Almond Joy
Peppermint Stick	Black Rasberry	Strawberry Cheese
Frozen Pudding	Milky Way	Snickers
Almond Joy	Coffee Almond Fudge	Orange Sherbet
Rasberry Sherbet	Watermelon	Rainbow

Open All Year

Serving You For Over 60 Years

Indoor Seating Available

SEE OUR FOOD MENU ON REVERSE SIDE

The Type Page

When a page is printed, the area that is filled with type is called the **type page** (also called the *text area* or *text page*). The width of the type page is called the **measure**. If a line of text is set so that it runs the entire width of the type page, it is called **full measure**. The type page includes not only body text but all other elements on the page, including the following:

■ Running heads
■ Text column(s)
■ Side heads or marginal notes
■ Footnotes
■ Running footers
■ Page numbers

For long documents that will take a lot of time to read, the width of the type page is very important. Long lines of text are hard to read, so margins should be set so that lines of text include no more than 65 to 70 characters (about 22 to 28 picas wide for 10- or 12-point type). Short lines are also hard to read because of the increased number of line breaks and hyphens. For this reason, lines should be no less than 30 characters. The depth (height) of the type page is determined more by the size of the paper and proportions than by any other criteria.

To establish the type page area, you specify margins. Both their width and proportions have an impact on the visual appeal of a document.

Margin Widths

The width of the margins determines the amount of white space around the type page. The type page, usually printed in black ink, is dark and dense. Leaving **white space** around it opens it up and makes it look more inviting to the reader. If the margins are too narrow, the page looks heavy, busy, and uninviting. White space around the type page sets it off. The more white space there is (within reason) the easier and more inviting the material will look.

Margin Proportions

The proportions of the margins also have an impact. There is an old rule in publishing that the inside, top, outside, and bottom margins follow the proportions of 1½, 2, 3, and 4. As with most design "rules," the best designers violate this one with impunity, but it does reinforce some basic principles.

The bottom margin should be larger than the top margin so the type page is visually centered. If you look at framed photographs in a gallery or museum you will find that

■ TUTORIAL 1   RETRIEVING A DOCUMENT BY ENTERING ITS NAME

One way to retrieve an existing document is to enter its name. Here, use this procedure to retrieve the OVERVIEW.WP5 file from the *Information Processing Lab Manual Student Disk.*

To retrieve a file

Press   **Shift-F10** and the prompt reads *Document to be retrieved:*

Type   **OVERVIEW.WP5** and then press **Enter.**

Result. The document appears on the screen.

■ TUTORIAL 2   GETTING AROUND A DOCUMENT

When you want to edit or format a document, you move the cursor to where you want to make changes. Practice moving the cursor, and notice how the cursor moves through the text. Keys connected with hyphen (for example, **Ctrl-←**) are pressed simultaneously, whereas those separated by commas (for example, **Home**, ↑) are pressed one after the other. Hold down some of the keys to see how they repeat until you release them. If you get lost, just press **Home, Home**, ↑ to move the cursor to the top of the document.

■ TUTORIAL 3   CLEARING THE SCREEN

You clear the screen when you want to retrieve another file from the disk or enter a new one. Here you clear the screen without saving the file.

To clear the screen

Press   **F7** and the prompt reads *Save document? Yes (No)*

Press   **N** and the prompt reads *Exit WP? No (Yes)*

Press   **N** to remain in the program

Result. The document is no longer on the screen.

■ TUTORIAL 4   RETRIEVING A FILE USING LIST FILES

If you cannot recall the name of a file that you want to retrieve, you can display a complete list of the files on a disk. This allows you to look at the filenames, preview the contents of a file, and then retrieve the one you want.

To display the List Files screen

Press   **F5** and the prompt reads *Dir* followed by the current default drive

Press   **Enter** to display a list of the files on the default drive

TUTORIAL 1 RETRIEVING A DOCUMENT BY ENTERING ITS NAME / 1

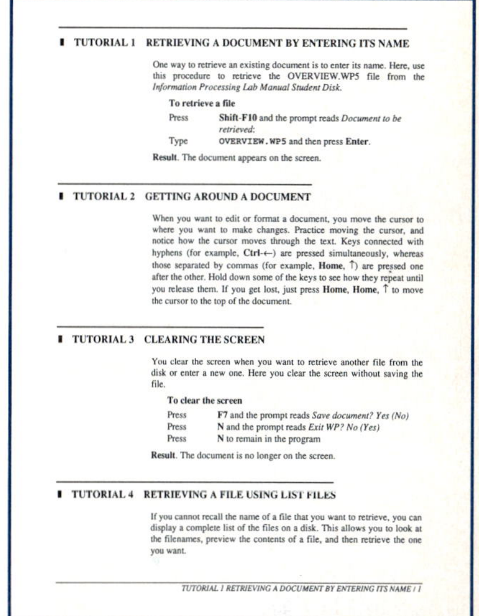

■ TUTORIAL 1   RETRIEVING A DOCUMENT BY ENTERING ITS NAME

One way to retrieve an existing document is to enter its name. Here, use this procedure to retrieve the OVERVIEW.WP5 file from the *Information Processing Lab Manual Student Disk.*

To retrieve a file

Press   **Shift-F10** and the prompt reads *Document to be retrieved:*

Type   **OVERVIEW.WP5** and then press **Enter.**

Result. The document appears on the screen.

■ TUTORIAL 2   GETTING AROUND A DOCUMENT

When you want to edit or format a document, you move the cursor to where you want to make changes. Practice moving the cursor, and notice how the cursor moves through the text. Keys connected with hyphen (for example, **Ctrl-←**) are pressed simultaneously, whereas those separated by commas (for example, **Home**, ↑) are pressed one after the other. Hold down some of the keys to see how they repeat until you release them. If you get lost, just press **Home, Home**, ↑ to move the cursor to the top of the document.

■ TUTORIAL 3   CLEARING THE SCREEN

You clear the screen when you want to retrieve another file from the disk or enter a new one. Here you clear the screen without saving the file.

To clear the screen

Press   **F7** and the prompt reads *Save document? Yes (No)*

Press   **N** and the prompt reads *Exit WP? No (Yes)*

Press   **N** to remain in the program

Result. The document is no longer on the screen.

■ TUTORIAL 4   RETRIEVING A FILE USING LIST FILES

If you cannot recall the name of a file that you want to retrieve, you can display a complete list of the files on a disk. This allows you to look at the filenames, preview the contents of a file, and then retrieve the one you want.

TUTORIAL 1 RETRIEVING A DOCUMENT BY ENTERING ITS NAME / 1

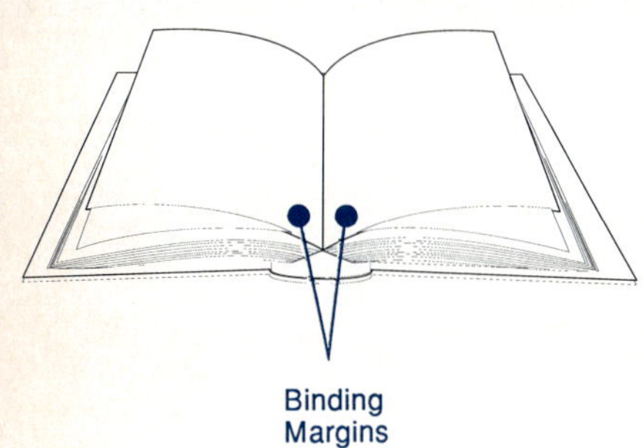

Binding
Margins

the bottom of the mat is wider than the top for this same reason.

The inside margin should be smaller than the outside margin because a bound document is looked at as a series of two-page spreads, not as individual pages. If the combined inside margin widths are too wide, the type pages look visually separated. If the combined width of the inside margins is about the same as the outside margins, the spread looks more balanced.

The actual size of the margins, like their proportions, is subjective.

Margins on Facing Pages

If the document is to be printed on both sides of the sheet and then bound, the margins on the inside of the pages may have to be adjusted to leave room for the binding or to retain the inside/outside margin

proportions that you have specified. The inside margin is sometimes called the **binding margin** or **gutter margin** and it alternates from right to left on facing pages. It is the right margin on even-numbered left-hand pages and the left margin on odd-numbered right-hand pages. There are two ways to control the binding margin: using a binding offset command or mirrored margins.

■ A **binding command** shifts the text block to the left on left-hand pages and to the right on right-hand pages, The net result is to increase the inside margin. This command does not allow you to control the outside margin, however, and works only when you want even margins not counting the binding offset (the distance the block of text is shifted). This is because the binding offset is added to the right margin setting on even pages and the left margin setting on odd pages.

- ■ **Mirrored margins** (not available in WordPerfect) are more powerful. You specify margin settings for inside and outside margins, not left and right margins.

> **MARGIN NAMES**
>
> Although we are used to calling margins *top*, *bottom*, *left*, and *right*, they also have other names. When pages are printed back to back so pages in the document face each other, the terms *inside* and *outside* margins are used instead of *left* and *right* margins. The outside margin is also called the *fore-edge* margin. The inside margin (the edge that is bound) is called the *back*, *binding*, or *gutter* margin. The top margin is called the *head* margin and the bottom is called the *tail* or *foot* margin.

➤ WORDPERFECT PROCEDURES

You change margins for an entire document or for individual paragraphs by entering a margin code. The code is an open code, so it affects all text following it until the end of the document or another margin code occurs.

➔ KEY/Strokes

Changing the Left and Right Margins

1. Move the cursor to where the new margins are to begin. (If it is not at the left margin, the program automatically inserts a hard return code, *[HRt]*, in front of the margin code.)
2. Either: Press **Shift-F8** and then **L** for *Line*.
   Or: Pull down the Layout menu and select *Line*.
3. Press **M** for *Margins* and the prompt reads *Left*.
4. Enter the left margin setting, and then press **Enter**. The prompt reads *Right*.
5. Enter the right margin setting, and then press **Enter**.
6. Press **F7** to return to the Edit screen.

➔ KEY/Strokes

Changing the Top and Bottom Margins

1. Move the cursor to the top of the page where the new setting is to begin (press **Ctrl-Home** then ↑ from anywhere on the page).
2. Either: Press **Shift-F8** and then **P** for *Page*.
   Or: Pull down the Layout menu and select *Page*.
3. Press **M** for *Margins* and the prompt reads *Top*.

Binding Margins

WordPerfect's ***Binding Offset*** command on the Print menu (**Shift**-**F7**) shifts the text to the right on odd-numbered right-hand pages and to the left on even-numbered left-hand pages. The binding offset that you enter is the distance from the edge of the page and is added to the margin settings specified for the document. When you use this command, you can keep margins even on both odd and even pages. To do so, select a binding offset distance and divide it by 2. Enter the result as the binding offset measurement, and add the same amount to the desired left and right margin settings. For example, if you want an inside margin of 1½ inches and outside margin of 1 inch, set the binding offset to .25" and the left and right margins to 1.25". When you print the document, it will be shifted ¼ inch on the page so that the inside (binding) margin is 1½ inches and the outside margin is 1 inch.

► E X E R C I S E S

EXERCISE 1

CHANGING A DOCUMENT'S MARGINS

In this exercise, you change all four margins on a document to 1½ inches.

1. Retrieve the MARGINS2.WP5 document and enter your name.
2. Make a printout of the document for comparison purposes.
3. Move the cursor to the top of the document, then follow the instructions in the KEY/Strokes box "Changing the Left and Right Margins" to change the left and right margins to 1½ inches.
4. Follow the instructions in the KEY/Strokes box "Changing the Top and Bottom Margins" to change the top and bottom margins to 1½ inches.
5. Save and then print the document. Compare the margins on this printout with those on the first printout.

EXERCISE 2

CHANGING BINDING MARGINS

In this exercise, you change the margins and specify a binding offset so back-to-back pages have a 2-inch inside margin and a 1-inch outside margin

1. Retrieve the MARGINS2.WP5 document after completing Exercise 1 where you changed margins.
2. Print the document and when doing so, specify a binding offset of inch.
3. Compare the printout with the second one that you made in Exercise 1. Then, hold the new printed sheets up to the light back to back to see how the inside and outside margins are the same on back-to-back pages.

✔ MARGIN TIPS

- You can add a binding offset to the top of the document instead of the sides. To do so, press **Shift-F8** to display the Format menu, then press **P** for *Page*, **S** for *Paper Size*, and **E** for *Edit* to display the Edit Paper Definition menu. Press **B** for *Binding Edge* and then press **T** for *Top*.
- When entering margin settings, you can enter fractions. For example, to set a margin to 1½ inches, you can type **1.5** or **1 1/2**.

REVIEW

- Design is the process of specifying how each of the elements in a publication should be treated.
- Design begins with ideas expressed in rough thumbnail sketches and is carried through into more detailed and polished layouts.
- Two-page spreads form the basic design units for publications where pages are printed back to back.
- A grid is the underlying structure of a design. It establishes the size and orientation of the paper as well as the margins that frame the type page.
- Designs are spelled out in specifications that explain how each element is to be treated. These design specs are transferred to the copy when it is typemarked.
- The trim size of a document is its final size after printing, binding, and trimming.
- When printing on laser printers, you can use portrait or landscape mode. Portrait mode prints along the short axis of the paper. Landscape mode prints along the longer axis of the sheet.
- Duplex printers can print on both sides of a sheet of paper.
- A paper size/type code changes the size of the paper on which the document is printed.
- The margins determine how much white space is left around the type page. They should be proportioned to provide both balance and white space to the page.
- When a document is to be printed or copied onto both sides of the paper and then bound, the margins should alternate on odd and even pages so that the binding margin remains the same width.

QUESTIONS

TRUE/FALSE

T   F

1. All designs begin with a detailed and polished layout.
2. The grid establishes the overall design of a publication.
3. All documents are designed with the two-page spread as the basic visual unit.
4. Design specs spell out in detail how each element is to be treated.
5. Portrait and landscape modes differ from each other based on the size of the paper used.
6. Landscape mode prints along the longer axis of the paper.

		7.	The type page is the area where body text is printed and does not include headers or footers, which are printed in the margins.
❏	❏	8.	When a line of type extends all the way across the type page it is called a *full measure* line.
❏	❏	9.	All four margins should always be the same width.
❏	❏	10.	If left and right margins are equal and the document is to be printed on one side of the paper, the Binding Offset command must be used.

FILL IN THE BLANK

1. The first stage in designing a publication is to jot down your ideas as ___________ sketches.
2. If you have to present your design ideas to others, you should prepare a more detailed ___________.
3. The basic visual element for publications such as books is called a ___________.
4. The basic element that underlies the design of a publication is called a ___________.
5. If the design of elements must be spelled out in detail, these are called design ___________.
6. The final size of a publication is called the ___________ size.
7. ___________ mode prints text across the short axis of the paper.
8. ___________ mode prints text across the long axis of the paper.
9. A printer that prints on both sides of the paper in one pass is called a ___________ printer.
10. The area of the page in which text is printed is called the ___________.
11. Type set across the entire width of the type page is called full ___________.
12. Space left around the type page is called ___________ space.
13. The margins on the side of the page that are bound are called the ___________ margins.
14. In WordPerfect, you can set the width of the binding margin by using the ___________ command on the Print menu.

1. Thumbnail
2. Layout or comp
3. Grid
4. Design specs
5. Typemarking
6. Trim size
7. Portrait mode
8. Landscape mode
9. Type page
10. Full measure
11. Binding margins

___ Coding copy with design specs for the typesetter
___ The underlying structure of a design
___ Prints across the long axis of a page
___ A polished presentation of a design
___ Prints across the short axis of a page
___ The area of the page where text is printed
___ A rough sketch of a publication's design
___ The final size of a publication
___ Type printed across the full width of the type page
___ The margin on the left side of odd pages and the right side of even pages
___ Detailed descriptions of each element in a design

WRITE OUT THE ANSWERS

1. If you were designing a school newsletter, list and describe at least two steps you would follow.
2. Sketch out a grid and draw in some of the elements that it would contain.
3. Describe the basic difference between portrait and landscape modes. List three types of documents that might work best in each mode.
4. Why would you want all four margins to have different widths?
5. Explain in your own words what a binding margin is and how it works.

PROJECTS

PROJECT 1

PRINTING A VIDEO CATALOG

In this project, you format a catalog for video tapes. You then print it out, trim the pages, and tape them to three 8½-by-11-inch sheets of paper folded so they form a 5½-by-4¼-inch brochure. The first page shown here is actually the back cover for the brochure.

Procedures Used
- Formatting a brochure.

Text Files Needed
- VIDEOCAT.WP5

Formats
① Enter margin codes to set top and bottom margins to 1½ inches and left and right margins to 2 inches.
② Enter a base font code for an 18-point font.
③ Enter a code to horizontally center all text that follows.
④ Enter an advance down code to position the library name down 6¼ inches.
⑤ Format as small caps.

Tip
- The pages are sequenced with the last page first followed by the first page. This is because this would be the correct order if reduced and then folded for use as a cover.

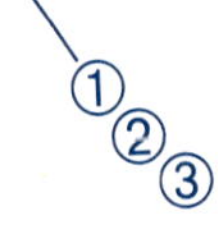

Abbot Public Library

MARBLEHEAD, MASSCHUSETTS

PRINTING A VIDEO CATALOG, CON'T

The front cover has only two words on it.

Formats

① Enter codes to center the title horizontally.

② Enter a base font code for a 48-point font.

Tip

■ The box that prints out has been added using WordPerfect's Graphics commands.

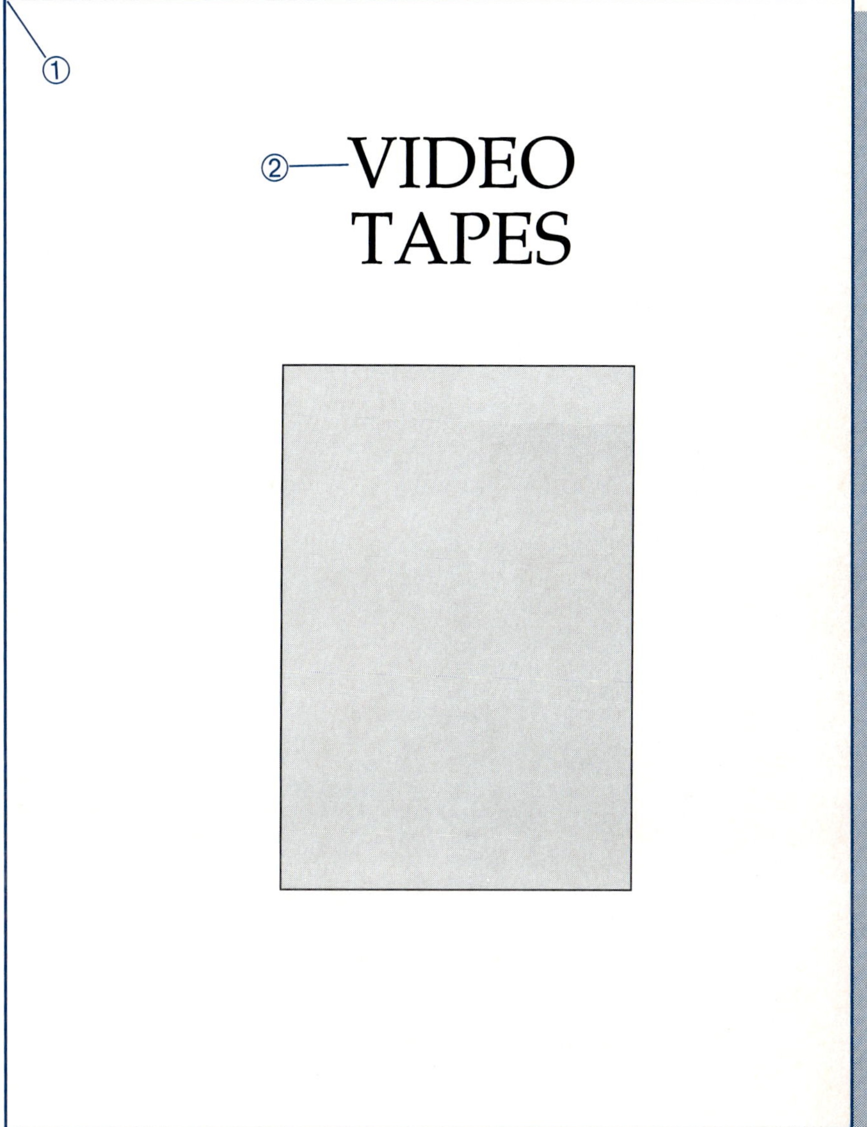

PRINTING A VIDEO CATALOG, CON'T

The four pages for the catalog contain a listing of video tapes available for loan. Only the first page is shown here.

Formats
① Enter a code to left-justify all text that follows.
② Enter a base font code for a 10-point font.

Tip
■ When you print the document, there may not be exactly four pages because of slight variations in font sizes and line heights.

①②

Video/791.437 African/1984	African Queen (1951)	color	103min
Video/791.437 Alexander/1985	Alexander Nevsky (1938)	b/w	108min
Video/791.437 Amadeus/1984	Amadeus (1984)	color	158min
Video/791.437 American/1986	An American in Paris	color	102min
Video/791.437 Bank/1984	The Bank Dick (1940)	b/w	73min
Video/791.437 Battleship/1984	Battleship Potemkin (1925) (silent with music score)	b/w	75min
Video/791.437 Beauty/1985	Beauty and the Beast (1946)	b/w	96min
Video/791.437 Bridge/1985	Bridge on the River Kwai (1957)	color	161min
Video/791.437 Brother/1986	Brother Sun, Sister Moon (1973)	color	121min
Video/791.437 Butch/1984	Butch Cassidy and The Sundance Kid (1969)	color	110min
Video/791.437 Captains/1985	Captains Courageous (1937)	b/w	118min
Video/791.437 Cassablanca/1984	Casablanca (1942)	b/w	103min
Video/791.437 Chariots/1986	Chariots of Fire (1980)	color	121min
Video/791.437 Chosen/1985	The Chosen (1982)	color	121min
Video/791.437 Christmas/1985	A Christmas Carol (1951)	b/w	86min
Video/791.437 Citizen/1982	Citizen Kane (1941)	b/w	119min

THE DTP ADVISOR NEWSLETTER

In this project, you change the margins for the newsletter so they are ½ inch on all sides instead of 1 inch.

Procedures Used
- Changing margins.

Text Files Needed
- ADVISOR.WP5

Formats
① Enter a margin code to set top and bottom margins to ½ inch.
② Enter a margin code to set left and right margins to ½ inch.

---

① ②

THE *dtp* ADVISOR

FaceLift For WordPerfect

Bitstream Inc. today announced version 1.5 of Bitstream® FaceLift™ for WordPerfect.® FaceLift brings enhanced font support to WordPerfect 5.0 and 5.1. The new FaceLift version 1.5 will create high-quality fonts on-the-fly for popular dot-matrix and inkjet printers—like the HP® DeskJet,® Canon BubbleJet and the IBM® ExecuJet—in addition to the existing on-the-fly support for the Hewlett-Packard LaserJet® series of printers. FaceLift 1.5 for WordPerfect will be available in the spring of 1991.

In addition to 13 typeface outlines provided in the original FaceLift package, FaceLift 1.5 for WordPerfect will also ship with three Symbol typefaces: ITC Zapf Dingbats® Symbol Proportional and Symbol Monospaced. Users will be able to access a total of 698 characters from the Bitstream International Character Set and from these three Symbols typefaces.

FaceLift 1.5 for WordPerfect is an easy-to-use utility that allows users to print high-quality fonts in any size from 2 to 500 point (in quarter point increments) without ever having to leave the application. The fonts are generated at print time, so the need for stored bit-map fonts is eliminated. Based on Bitstream Speedo™ technology, FaceLift sends characters to printers in both graphics mode (laser, inkjet and dot-matrix printers) and as HP soft fonts (laser printers only). Users have full control over the number and size of soft fonts to be downloaded, depending on the memory available in the printer.

"We are very excited that FaceLift 1.5 for WordPerfect will provide dot-matrix and inkjet users with the same high typographic quality and capabilities that HP LaserJet users have enjoyed with Bitstream type," stated Doug Lloyd, Executive Director at WordPerfect. "That, and the addition of the three new Symbol typefaces makes FaceLift a great companion for WordPerfect."

First-time users can purchase FaceLift 1.5 for WordPerfect for a suggested U.S. list price of $99. Current users of FaceLift 1.0 for WordPerfect can upgrade to version 1.5 for $24.95. In addition to the 16 typefaces included free with FaceLift, users can purchase add-on fonts from the Bitstream Library of 52 typeface packages. Also available is the FaceLift Companion Value Pack, a selection of 24 text and headline faces for a suggested U.S. list price $199.

FaceLift 1.5 for WordPerfect is the newest member of the Bitstream FaceLift product line. The initial product, FaceLift for Windows,™ shipped in August of 1990. All FaceLift products can share Bitstream typefaces (in Speedo format) stored in a single common subdirectory.

FaceLift for Wordperfect was developed in conjunction with LaserTools Corporation, a privately held company based in Emeryville, CA. LaserTools is a developer of innovative printing enhancement products—tools for printer sharing, printer control, printer acceleration, and font management.

An industry leader in typographic quality and innovative technology, Bitstream licenses fonts and related software to more than 420 hardware manufacturers and software developers worldwide. Its line of retail products is distributed by an extensive network of dealers in the United States and in 18 nations worldwide.

For more information, contact:
Bitstream Inc.
215 First Street
Cambridge, MA 02142-1270
(617) 497-6222

Postscript in a Cartridge

Hewlett-Packard Company today announced a PostScript accessory for the HP LaserJet printer. The cartridge

Paragraph Formats

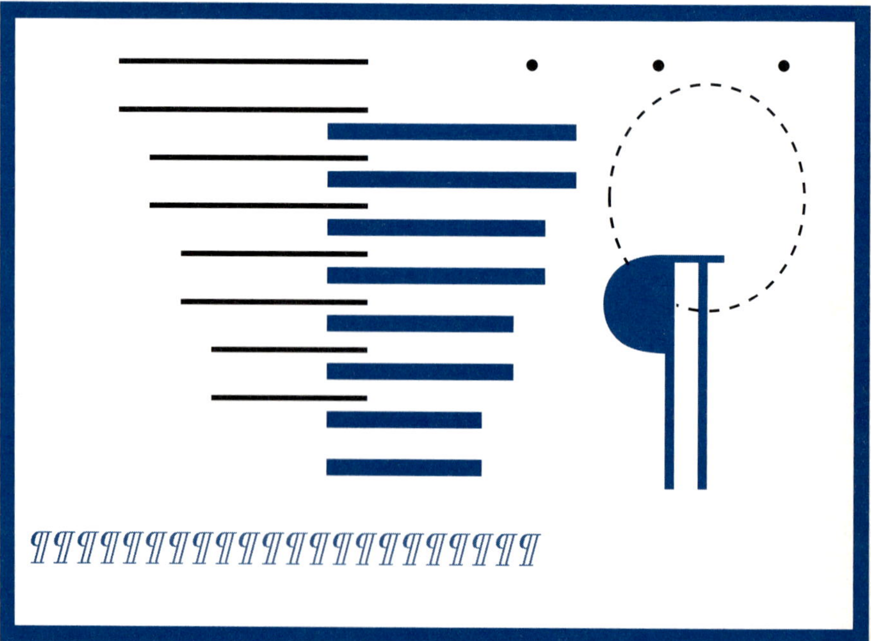

Paragraph Alignment

After completing this topic, you should be able to:
- Describe the four types of horizontal alignments
- Describe vertical centering
- Align text with the margins in your own documents

▶ T U T O R I A L

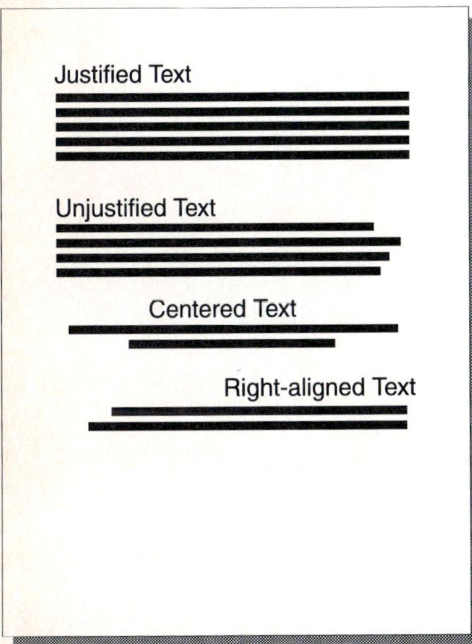

Paragraph Alignments

In this tutorial, you align text with the margins. When you are finished, your printout should look similar to the illustration "Paragraph Alignments."

GETTING STARTED

1. Retrieve the ALIGN1.WP5 document and enter your name.
2. Make a printout for comparison purposes.

TURNING FULL JUSTIFICATION ON

3. Move the cursor under the "*J*" in the heading "*Justified Text.*"
4. Press **Shift-F8** to display the Format menu.
5. Press **L** for *Line* to display the Line Format menu.
6. Press **J** for *Justification*.
7. Press **F** for *Full*.
8. Press **F7** to return to the Edit screen.

TURNING LEFT JUSTIFICATION ON

9. Move the cursor under the "*U*" in the heading "*Unjustified Text.*"
10. Repeat Steps 4 through 7 but specify left justification instead of full.
11. Press **F7** to return to the Edit screen.

CENTERING A LINE OF TEXT

12. Move the cursor under the "*C*" in "*Centered*" in the sentence below the heading "*Centered Text.*"
13. Press **Shift-F6** to center the text.
14. Press ↓ to center the line between the margins.

CENTERING A BLOCK OF TEXT

15. Use **Alt**-**F4** or **F12** to block the entire paragraph under the "*Centered Text*" heading.
16. Press **Shift**-**F6** and the prompt reads *[Just:Center]? No (Yes)*.
17. Press **Y** to center the paragraph.

RIGHT-ALIGNING A LINE OF TEXT

18. Move the cursor under the "*R*" in the heading "*Right-aligned Text*."
19. Press **Alt**-**F6** to right-align the text.
20. Press ↓ to align the line with the right margin.

RIGHT-ALIGNING A BLOCK OF TEXT

21. Use **Alt**-**F4** or **F12** to block the entire paragraph under the "*Right-aligned Text*" heading.
22. Press **Alt**-**F6** to right-align the text and the prompt reads *[Just:Right]? No (Yes)*.
23. Press **Y** to right-align the paragraph.

FINISHING UP

24. Save and print the document. The first paragraph is fully justified, the second has a ragged right margin, the third is centered, and the fourth is aligned with the right margin.

▶ DESKTOP PUBLISHING CONCEPTS

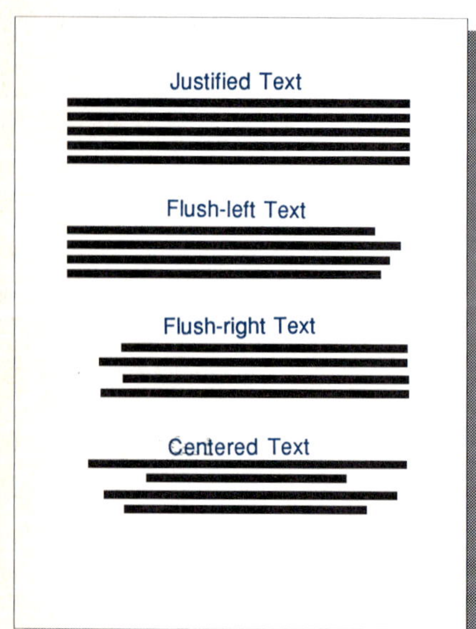

Text Alignments

One of the key elements of a good design is the alignment of paragraphs. Don't think of paragraphs only as blocks of text. Any line, even if it has only a single character, is a paragraph if it ends with a hard carriage return. This means that text, subheads, footnotes, headers, and almost every other element of a document is considered a paragraph. These paragraphs can be aligned on the type page in one of the four ways; justified, flush left, flush right, or centered.

Justified Text

In many circumstances, body text looks best when aligned with both margins, or **justified**. This alignment is frequently used in books and magazines and gives a very finished appearance to a document. The problem with justified text is that to make the lines equal in length, the spaces between words must vary in width. This uneven word spacing makes reading more difficult. To minimize the problem, you can hyphenate the text.

Flush Left Text

In many situations, text is aligned flush with the left margin so the right margin is ragged (called a **ragged-right margin**). This is called **left aligned** or **flush left** and is one of the most popular alignments for body text. Text set in this alignment is very easy to read because all words are evenly spaced even though the lines are of uneven length.

Flush Right Text

In special situations, text can be aligned flush with the right margin so the left margin is ragged (called a **ragged-left margin**). This alignment is called **right aligned** or **flush right** and is used to align page numbers and for special effects, such as aligning headings with the right margin so they stand out.

Centered Text
In special circumstances, text can be centered on the page either horizontally or vertically. This alignment is most often used for titles, headings, subheadings, illustrations, poems, and dedications.

To align large sections of text, you use the Justify command. When you do so without first blocking text, an open code is entered into the document, and all text below the code is formatted with the specified alignment. To end the format, you must enter a different alignment code farther down in the document.

If you first block text, and then use one of the Justify commands, a pair of codes is entered. The one at the beginning of the block turns the new alignment on. The code at the end of the block returns the alignment to what it is above the block.

 **K E Y / S t r o k e s**

Justifying Text

1. Move the cursor to where you want to change the alignment.
2. Either: Press **Shift-F8** and then press **L** for *Line* and press **J** for *Justification.*
   Or: Pull down the Layout menu and select *Line* and then *Justification.*
   Or: Pull down the Layout menu and select *Justify.*
3. Select *Left*, *Center*, *Right*, or *Full*.
4. Press **F7** to return to the document.

WORDPERFECT'S JUSTIFICATION

WordPerfect has changed the meaning of a standard term that can cause confusion. The term *justified text* universally means text that is aligned flush with both the left and right margins. WordPerfect has used this term to refer to codes that align text in four possible combinations: justified, flush left, flush right, and centered. They then use the term *full justification* to distinguish true justified text from the other three alignments.

Aligning Text

If you want to center or right-align a single line or a block of text, you use one of the Align commands (**Shift-F6** to center it or **Alt-F6** to align it flush right).

- If you use one of these commands to align a single line, it inserts a code at the beginning of the line but the center or right alignment ends with the hard carriage return at the end of the line.

- If you block text before using one of these commands, only the block is affected. A code is entered at the beginning of the block to turn the alignment on, and a code is entered at the end of the block to restore the normal alignment that is currently in effect immediately above the newly aligned block.

You can also center text on a specific column. This is useful when preparing tabular material. For example, you can align headings over columns of numbers. You center text on a column by pressing **Tab** to move to a tab stop or **Spacebar** to move to any position on a line. You then press **Shift-F6** and enter your text. You can also use **Tab** or **Spacebar** to push a line of text until the cursor is in the desired column and then press **Shift-F6** to center it.

→ **K E Y / S t r o k e s**

Aligning Text Centered or Flush Right

1. Move the cursor to where you want the alignment to begin:
   - If you are entering new text, move the cursor to a blank line.
   - If you are aligning an existing line, move the cursor under the first character in the line.
   - If you are aligning a block, select the block. (The block can include any part of the first line but must include all of the last line.)
   - If you are centering text on a specific column, press **Tab** or **Spacebar** to move the cursor to that column.
2. Either: Press **Alt-F6** (to right-align) or **Shift-F6** (to center).
   Or: Pull down the Layout menu, select *Align*, and then select *Flush Right* or *Center*.
3. This step depends on the selection that you are aligning.
   - If you are entering text, type it in and then press **Enter** to end the alignment.
   - If you aligned a single line, press ↓ to realign it.
   - If you blocked text, the prompt reads *[Just:Right]? No (Yes)* or *[Just:Center]? No (Yes)*. Press **Y** to align the block of text.

Vertically Centering Text

You can center text vertically on the page between the top and bottom margins. This is useful when you are formatting title pages or section openers. The effects of vertical alignment are seen only on printouts or when using the View Document command on the Print menu; the effects are not displayed on the Edit screen.

→ **K E Y / S t r o k e s**

Centering Text Vertically on the Page

1. Move the cursor to the beginning of the page to be centered vertically (press **Ctrl-Home** and then ↑ from anywhere on the page).

Desktop Publishing with WordPerfect 5.1

Vertically Centered Text

2. Either: Press **Shift-F8** and then **P** for *Page*.

   Or: Pull down the Layout menu and select *Page*.

3. Press **C** for **C**enter Page (top to bottom).

4. Press **Y** or **N**.

5. Press **F7** to return to the Edit screen.

✔ A L I G N M E N T   T I P S

- If you type text in front of a code that you entered to center or align text flush right, the text might not be displayed on the screen (although it will print out). If this happens, press **Alt-F3** or **F11** to reveal codes and the missing text.
- If you have entered an open code to turn on center or right justification, you cannot use WordPerfect's center, flush right, or tab align features. You also cannot hyphenate centered or right justified text.
- When you are using justified text, hard spaces prevent the program from inserting unwanted soft spaces in formulas and computer commands. To enter a hard space, press **Home** and then press **Spacebar**.

▶ E X E R C I S E S

EXERCISE 1

CENTERING HEADINGS AND LEFT-JUSTIFYING PARAGRAPHS

In this exercise, you center headings in a document. You then align each of the ten paragraphs flush left.

1. Retrieve the ALIGN2.WP5 document and enter your name.

2. Follow the instructions in the KEY/Strokes box "Aligning Text Centered or Flush Right" to center the heading "*BILL OF RIGHTS*" at the top of the document.

3. Follow the instructions in the KEY/Strokes box "Aligning Text Centered or Flush Right" to center the two lines above each amendment that contain the amendment number and title.

4. Save and then print the document.

5. Follow the instructions in the KEY/Strokes box "Justifying Text" to left justify the text for each amendment (but not the centered headings), and then print the document.

6. Compare the two printouts. If you like the look of the unjustified version better than the justified one, save the document; otherwise, clear the screen without saving it.

EXERCISE 2

CENTERING A POEM

In this exercise, you center a poem on the page both horizontally and vertically.

1. Retrieve the ALIGN3.WP5 document and enter your name.
2. Move the cursor to the top of the document, then follow the instructions in the KEY/Strokes box "Centering Text Vertically on the Page" to center the poem and heading vertically on the page.
3. Move the cursor to the first character in the poem's title, then follow the instructions in the KEY/Strokes box "Justifying Text" to center the poem horizontally on the page.
4. Save and print the document. The poem and the document heading are centered vertically and horizontally on the page.

EXERCISE 3

CENTERING TEXT ON COLUMNS

In this exercise, you center text on columns instead of between the margins. When you are finished, your results should look similar to those shown in the figure "The ALIGN4 Document."

1. Retrieve the ALIGN4.WP5 document and enter your name.
2. Type in the column headings "Item," "List Price," and "Net Price," shown in the figure "The ALIGN4 Document," following the instructions in the KEY/Strokes box "Aligning Text Centered or Flush Right" to center the headings on the decimal tab stops in the second and third columns of numbers.
3. Save and print the document.

The ALIGN4 Document

Item	List Price	Net Price
Computer (IBM)	$3,500.00	$2,750.00
Laser Printer (HP)	2,100.50	1,500.25
Display Monitor (NEC)	1,000.75	800.35

Tab Stops

After completing this topic, you should be able to:
- Describe the different types of tab stops you can use to align text
- Align text with tab stops in your own documents
- Set tab stops to align your text

▶ T U T O R I A L

In this tutorial, you change tab stops and then use them to align text and decimals. (When you set tab stops, you can do so in inches or points. The numbers given are not equivalents since the tab setting line has only selected markings and those are given to simplify your setting the stops.)

GETTING STARTED

1. Retrieve the TABS1.WP5 document and enter your name.

DISPLAYING THE TAB RULER

2. Press **Ctrl-F3** to display the Screen menu.
3. Press **W** for *Window*, and the prompt reads *Number of lines in this window: 24.*
4. Press ↑ once to display the ruler at the bottom of the screen, and then press **Enter** to return to the document.

SETTING TAB STOPS

5. Press **Home** twice and then press ↑ to move the cursor to the beginning of the document.
6. Press **Shift-F8** to display the Format menu.
7. Press **L** for *Line* to display the Line Format menu.
8. Press **T** for *Tab Set* to display the Tab Settings screen.
9. Press **Home** twice and then press ← to move the cursor to the beginning of the line.
10. Press **Ctrl-End** to delete all tab stops.
11. Press → to move the cursor to +1" (or +100p).
12. Press **L** to enter a left-aligned tab stop.
13. Press → to move the cursor to +3" (or +200).
14. Press **D** to enter a decimal tab stop.
15. Press → to move the cursor to +5.5" (or +396).

16. Press **R** to enter a right-aligned tab stop.

17. Press **F7** twice to return to the document. The new tab stops appear on the ruler at the bottom of the screen.

ENTERING TAB-ALIGNED TEXT

18. Enter the table shown in the figure "The TABS1 Document" below the heading. Be sure to press **Tab** to move the cursor to each of the three tab stops when entering the three columns of data on each line.

FINISHING UP

19. Save and print the document. To remove the tab ruler from the bottom of the screen, press **Ctrl**-**F3** to display the Screen menu, and then press **W** for *Window*. The prompt reads *Number of lines in this window: 23.* Press ↓ and then press **Enter**.

The TABS1 Document
This is the document that you enter in this tutorial.

ITEM	PRICE	# AVAILABLE
Computer	$2,000.00	5000 in stock
Printer	600.25	100 in stock
Modem	75.76	24 in stock

▶ D E S K T O P   P U B L I S H I N G   C O N C E P T S

Item	Number
Disks	1100
Books	890
Cables	11

Aligned with Spaces

Item	Number
Disks	1100
Books	890
Cables	11

Aligned with Tabs

Wrong and Right Tab Alignments

Using tab stops to align or indent text is critical. If you align or indent text with the **Spacebar**, your document may print poorly. This is because printers used in desktop publishing printers use proportionally spaced type, which means that each character occupies a different-width space. Columns that appear aligned on the screen will not be aligned on a printout. If you use tab stops to align columns, they print correctly.

Types of Tab Stops
When you set tab stops, you have the choice of three possible alignments: left, right, and centered. The choice depends on the material you are tabbing. For example, text is usually left aligned in columns, but column headings over numbers may be centered.

If you are aligning numbers that contain decimal points, you can also set decimal tab stops. When you enter numbers at these stops, all of the decimal points in a column are aligned. Decimal tab stops are also used to align numbers or letters in enumerated lists. Many programs allow you to change the alignment character so you can align any specified character and not just decimal points. This makes it possible to align commas, pound signs (#), and so on.

Dot Leaders
Dot leaders are characters that fill the space between tabbed columns. They connect rows and make it easier for the eye to move from one column to the next without getting lost. In some programs (but not WordPerfect), you can even choose the character used as the leader.

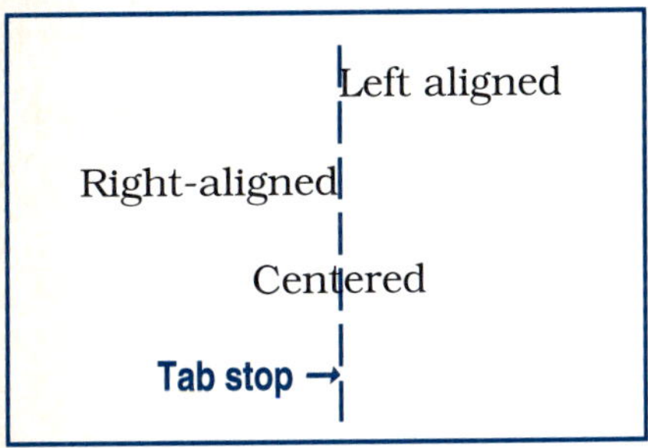

Tab Alignments

The Ruler
The ruler can be displayed to indicate tab stops (with triangles), left and right margins ([and]), and left or right margins that are in the same position as tab stops ({ and }).

```
Part 1 ....................... 1
Part 2 ..................... 10
Part 3 ..................... 20

Part 1 _______________ 1
Part 2 _______________ 10
Part 3 _______________ 20
```

Dot Leaders

```
Numbers            100|00
                    50|00
                     1|00

List numbers          1|
                     10|
                    100|

List letters          A|
                      B|
                      C|
```

Decimal Tabs Alignments

You can align text and numbers with tab stops, indent text to them, or change them where needed.

The Tab Ruler

You can display a ruler that indicates the positions of margins and tab stops. If you change tab stops or margins at any point, the indicators on the ruler change as you move through the document. On the ruler, triangles indicate tab stops, brackets ([and]) indicate the left and right margins, and braces ({ and }) indicate a left or right margin and tab stop in the same position.

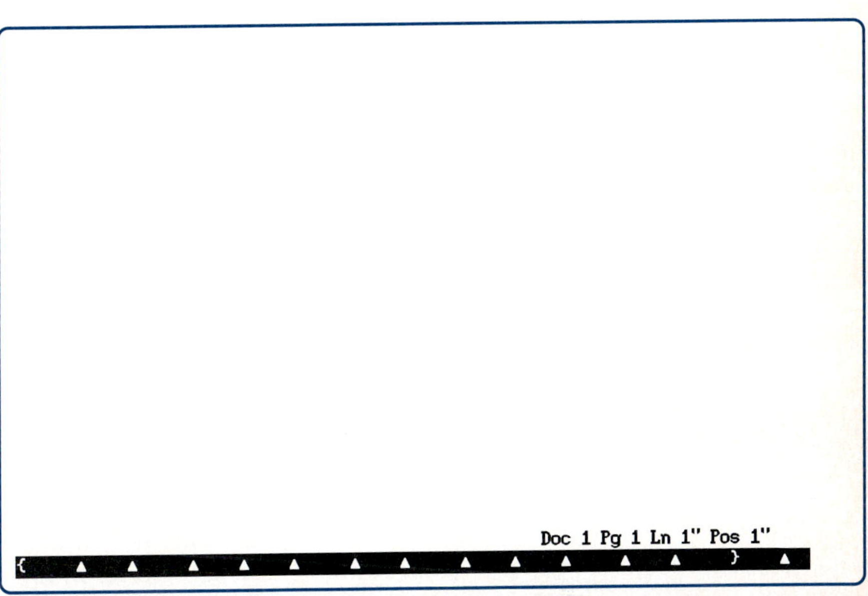

➡ **K E Y / S t r o k e s**

Displaying and Removing the Ruler

1. Either: Press **Ctrl-F3** and then press **W** for **Window**.
   Or: Pull down the Edit menu and select **Window**.
   The prompt reads *Number of lines in this window:*
2. Either: Press ↑ once to display the ruler at the bottom of the screen. (Pressing it more than once divides the screen into two windows.)
   Or: Press ↓ to remove the ruler. (On most, but not all, systems the prompt should read *Number of lines in this window: 24.*)
3. Press **Enter** to return to the Edit screen.

Aligning Text with Tab Stops

All tab stops are initially set every ½ inch, and text tabbed to these tab stops is left aligned. You can align text or numbers with these tab stops as you enter the text or after you have entered it.

- To align text with a tab stop as you enter the text, press **Tab** until the cursor is in the desired tab column, and then type the text. If you type enough text to reach past the right margin, the second and subsequent lines wrap back to and align with the left margin, not with the tab stop.
- To align text with a tab stop after you have entered the text, position the cursor under the first character in the text to be aligned. When you then press **Tab** the cursor and all text to its right moves to the next tab stop. You must be in insert mode to do this. If you are in typeover mode, pressing **Tab** just moves the cursor through the text.

TAB ALIGNMENT SHORTCUTS

Although you can set decimal, center, and right-aligned tab stops, you can also align text in a variety of ways using regular left-aligned tab stops.

- To align the decimal points in numbers such as $10.95, press **Ctrl-F6** instead of **Tab** to move the cursor to the tab stop. The status line then reads *Align char = .* Type the number and then press **Tab** or **Ctrl-F6** to move to the next tab stop, or press **Enter** to end the line.
- To center text on a left-aligned tab stop, press **Tab** to move the cursor to the tab, press **Shift-F6**, then type the text.
- You can right-align text with a left-aligned (or decimal) tab stop. To do so, press **Ctrl-F6** to move the cursor to the tab stop, and then type the text without entering an alignment character.

Dollar signs	$10
	$100
	$1000
Numbers	10
	100
	1000
Commas	1,000
	10,000
Pound Signs	# 1
	# 10
	# 100
	# 1000

Alignment Characters

Decimal Tabs and Alignment Characters

Columns of numbers, including those containing decimal points, can be aligned with **decimal tab stops**. WordPerfect's default setting is to align decimal points (periods), but you can change the alignment character to any character on the keyboard including spaces. For example, you can align columns based on commas (,), pound signs (#), dollar signs ($), or a specific letter. This is useful when you are writing to a country such as France, which uses commas where we use decimal points, and vice versa. Whereas we would write 1,000.50, in France they would write 1.000,50.

To align numbers with decimal tabs:

1. Position decimal tab stops in the desired columns (see "Setting Tab Stops" in this topic).
2. Press **Tab** to move the cursor to the decimal tab position, and the status line reads *Align char = .* to indicate that you are in a decimal tab column.
3. Enter the part of the number preceding the decimal point. As you do so, the numbers you enter move to the left while the cursor remains in the decimal tab column.
4. Enter a decimal point using the period key (or any other alignment character that you have specified).

5. Type the numbers that follow the decimal point. As you do so, the decimal remains fixed in place, and all numbers are entered to the right of it.

Changing the Alignment Character

1. Move the cursor to where you want the alignment character to change.
2. Either: Press **Shift-F8** and then press **O** for *Other*.

   Or: Pull down the Layout menu and select *Other*.
3. Press **D** for *Decimal/Align Character*.
4. Enter the new alignment character using any key on the keyboard, including a space (the default is the period), and then press **Enter** twice.
5. Press **F7** to return to the Edit screen.

Setting Tab Stops

You can set up to 40 tab stops in a document and set them anywhere up to 54½ inches from the left edge of the page. The tab stops you enter remain in effect until the end of the document or until you enter another tab setting code below them.

To change tab stops, you display the Tab Settings screen. With this screen displayed, you have several options.

The Tab Settings Screen

The Tab Settings screen displays the tab stops in effect at the cursor's position. The instructions at the bottom of the screen tell you how to delete and set new tab stops.

```
Left
   Center
      Right
            100.10

               . . . . . Left
               . . . . . . Center
               . . . . . . . . Right
               . . . . . . . . . . .100.10




.....L....C.....R....D.............L....C.....R....D...............................
  !     ^     !     ^     !     ^     !     x     !     ^     !     ^     !
0"         +1"         +2"         +3"         +4"         +5"         +6"         +7"
Delete EOL (clear tabs); Enter Number (set tab); Del (clear tab);
Type; Left; Center; Right; Decimal; .= Dot Leader; Press Exit when done.
```

- You can press **T** and specify if tab stops are relative (the default) or absolute.
  - ***Relative tab stops*** shift if you change the left margin so they always stay the same distance from the margin. For example, if you have a relative tab stop ½ inch from the left margin and then increase the left margin by ½-inch, the tab stop shifts to the right ½ inch. When you are setting relative tabs, the *0″* indicator shows where the left margin is positioned. Tabs to the left of the left margin are indicated with negative signs (-1, -2) and those to the right with plus signs (+1, +2).
  - ***Absolute tab stops*** are set relative to the left edge of the paper you print on, so they do not shift when you change the left margin. When you are setting absolute tabs, the *0″* indicator shows where the left edge of the page is positioned.
- You can move the cursor along the ruler line and enter tab stop codes. Enter an **L** for a left-aligned tab, a **C** for a centered tab, an **R** for a right-aligned tab, or a **D** for a decimal tab stop.
- To delete a specific tab stop, move the cursor under it and press **Del**.
- To specify dot leaders, highlight any tab stop code and press the period (you can press it again to remove dot leaders). The tab stop on the Tab Settings screen is displayed in reverse video to indicate that dot leaders have been specified. Dot leaders will then be inserted whenever you press **Tab** to move the cursor to that tab stop in the document.
- You can move the cursor anywhere on the ruler line and press **Ctrl-End** to delete all tab stops to the cursor's right. This is helpful when you want to reset all tabs.
- To enter a single tab stop, type its position in inches, and then press **Enter**. If you enter a fractional tab stop position, such as ½, enter it as **0.5**, and not **.5** since a leading period indicates a dot leader.
- To enter tab stops at regular intervals, type the beginning position in inches, a comma, the interval in inches, and then press **Enter**. For example, type **1,1** and then press **Enter** to set tab stops every inch beginning at a left margin of 1 inch. The type of tab stop set with this command depends on the type of tab stop set in the beginning position.
  - If no tab is set there, this command enters left aligned tabs (L).
  - To set another type, enter that type in the beginning position before using this command. For example, press **D** at 1 inch; then type **1,1** and press **Enter** to set decimal tab stops every inch.
- To move a tab code, position the cursor under it, then hold down **Ctrl** and press → or ←.

Setting Tab Stops

1. Move the cursor to where the new tab stops are to take effect.
2. Either: Press **Shift**-**F8** and then press **L** for *Line*.
   Or: Pull down the Layout menu and select *Line*.
3. Press **T** for *Tab Set* to display the Tab Settings screen.
4. Move the cursor to the desired position on the ruler, and then use the tab stop editing commands described in the table "Tab Stop Editing Commands" to enter the tab stop codes described in the table "Tab Stop Codes."

   Press **T** at any point to display the Tab Type menu, and press **A** for *Absolute* or **R** for *Relative*.
5. Press **F7** to return to the Edit screen.

TAB STOP EDITING COMMANDS

To Move the Cursor on the Ruler to	Press
Left edge of screen	**Home**, ←
Right edge of screen	**Home**, →
Left or right one tab stop	↓ or ↑
Left edge of ruler line	**Home**, **Home**, ←
Right edge of ruler line	**End**

To Delete Tab Stops	Press
At cursor's position	**Del**
From cursor to end of line	**Ctrl**-**End**
All tab stops	**Home**, **Home**, ←, **Ctrl**-**End**

TAB STOP CODES

Alignment	Code
Text left-aligns	**L**
Text centers on tab stop	**C**
Text right-aligns	**R**
Text aligns with decimal or other specified alignment character	**D**
Text left-aligns (with dot leader)	**L** then **.** (period)
Text centers (with dot leader)	**C** then **.** (period)
Text right-aligns (with dot leader)	**R** then **.** (period)
Text aligns with decimal or other specified alignment character (with dot leader)	**D** then **.** (period)

✔ | TAB TIPS

- To align text with tab stops so that the alignment doesn't change if you change tab stop types, use hard tab codes. When setting tabs:
  - To enter a hard left-aligned tab code, press **Home**, **Tab**
  - To enter a hard centered tab code, press **Home**, **Shift-F6**
  - To enter a hard flush-right tab code, press **Home**, **Alt-F6**
  - To enter a hard decimal tab code, press **Ctrl-F6**
- On enhanced keyboards, you can move the cursor left or right on the ruler by holding down **Alt** and pressing ← or →. However, do not use the arrow keys on the numeric keypad to do so.
- On enhanced keyboards, you can move a tab stop on the ruler by positioning the cursor over it, holding down **Ctrl** and pressing ← or →. However, do not use the arrow keys on the numeric keypad to do so.
- When aligning text in columns with the Tab key, you can change the distance between columns on the screen by changing the display pitch. This is helpful if text overlaps on the screen where tabs, indents, and column margins have been entered. Changing the display pitch affects only the document on the screen. It does not affect printouts. To change the display pitch, press Shift-F8 to display the Format menu. Press D for Document, and then press D for Display Pitch. Press Y to have the pitch adjusted automatically, or press N and then enter the pitch you want to use. Decreasing the pitch, for example, from .09 inch to .07 inch, expands the lines horizontally; increasing it compresses them.

Table of Keyboard Characters

Character	Name
'	apostrophe
"	quotation mark
^	circumflex
`	grave
~	tilde
|	vertical bar
_	underscore
{}	braces
[]	brackets
()	parentheses
@	at sign
#	pound sign
*	asterisk
/	backslash
\	slash
-	hyphen
=	equal
+	plus
<>	angle brackets
:	colon
;	semicolon

The TABS2 Document

The TABS3 Document

EXERCISE 1

FORMATTING A TABLE WITH TABBED COLUMNS

In this exercise, you format a table that names the special characters on the computer keyboard.

1. Retrieve the TABS2.WP5 document and enter your name.
2. Make a printout for comparison purposes. Note how the rightmost heading does not align correctly over its column.
3. Move the cursor to the top of the document, then follow the instructions in the KEY/Strokes box "Setting Tab Stops" to change the tab stops so that there is only one left tab set at 2 inches.
4. Save and print the document. Compare this printout with the first one that you made. If your columns are too far apart, move the tab stop and make another printout.

EXERCISE 2

FORMATTING A TABLE WITH TWO TABBED COLUMNS

In this exercise, you format a document that has two tabbed columns.

1. Retrieve the TABS3.WP5 document and enter your name.
2. Make a printout to see how the document is currently formatted. The columns are poorly spaced and would also be better if they were right aligned rather than left aligned as they are now. Using a ruler, calculate where tab stops should be set to leave about ½-inch between the columns when they are aligned with right-aligned tabs.
3. Follow the instructions in the KEY/Strokes box "Setting Tab Stops" to change the tab stops to your calculated positions. (Be sure to insert the new code to the right of, or below, the original tab code.)
4. Save and print the document.

	Current Jobs	New Jobs
8 years or less	6%	4%
1—3 years of high school	12%	10%
4 years of high school	40%	35%
1—3 years of college	20%	22%
4 years or more of college	22%	30%
Total	100%	100%

EXERCISE 3

CHANGING THE ALIGNMENT CHARACTER

In this exercise, you change the alignment character to colons to correctly align the colons in a memo heading.

1. Retrieve the TABS4.WP5 document and enter your name.
2. Print the document for comparison purposes. Try to enter data following the "*To:*" heading and watch how alignment is affected.
3. Follow the instructions in the KEY/Strokes box "Setting Tab Stops" to set a decimal tab stop at 1 inches and delete any other tab stops. (Be sure to insert the new code to the right of, or below, the original tab code.)
4. Follow the instructions in the KEY/Strokes box "Changing the Alignment Character" to change the alignment character to a colon.
5. Now, try to enter data again. The colons should remain in a fixed position.
6. Save and print the document.

EXERCISE 4

ADDING DOT LEADERS

In this exercise, you add dot leaders to a table of contents.

1. Retrieve the TABS5.WP5 document and enter your name.
2. Move the cursor to the immediate right of the tab stop code already in the document, then follow the instructions in the KEY/Strokes box "Setting Tab Stops" to change the right-aligned tab stop so dot leaders are added.
3. Save and print the document.

Paragraph Indenting and Spacing

After completing this topic, you should be able to:
- Describe the types of indents that you can use in a document
- Describe different ways to visually separate paragraphs
- Indent and space paragraphs in your own document

► T U T O R I A L

In this tutorial, you indent text. When you are finished, your printout should look similar to the illustration "Types of Indents."

GETTING STARTED

1. Retrieve the INDENTS1.WP5 document and enter your name.

INDENTING THE FIRST LINE OF PARAGRAPHS

2. Move the cursor to the blank line between the first and second paragraphs under the heading "*I. Indented Paragraphs.*"
3. Press **Del** to delete the *[HRt]* code that separates the paragraphs with a blank line, then press **Tab** to indent the first line of the paragraph to the first tab stop.
4. Move the cursor to the blank line between the second and third paragraphs, and then repeat Step 3.

INDENTING A PARAGRAPH FROM THE LEFT MARGIN

5. Move the cursor to the beginning of the first paragraph under the heading "*II. Single and Double Indents.*"
6. Press **F4** to move the cursor and the paragraph to the first tab stop. (If necessary, press ↓ to realign the text so all lines in the paragraph are indented ½ inch from the left margin.)

INDENTING A PARAGRAPH FROM BOTH MARGINS

7. Move the cursor to the beginning of the second paragraph that begins "*You can also indent...*"
8. Press **Shift-F4** twice to move the cursor and the first line of the paragraph to the second tab stop. (If necessary, press ↓ to reform

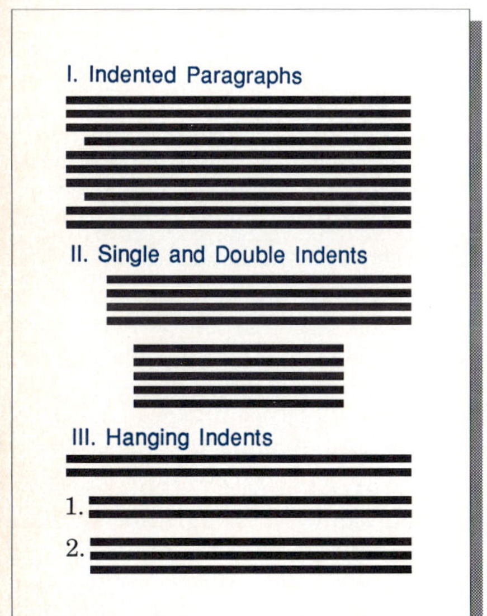

Types of Indents

the existing text so that both sides of the paragraph are indented 1 inch.)

ENTERING HANGING INDENTS

9. Move the cursor to the space following the period in the item numbered 1.
10. Press **Del** to delete the space.
11. Press **F4** to indent the paragraph. (If necessary, press ↓ to reform the rest of the paragraph.)
12. Move the cursor to the space following the period in the item numbered 2. in the next paragraph and repeat Steps 10 and 11.

FINISHING UP

13. Save and print the document.

▶ D E S K T O P   P U B L I S H I N G   C O N C E P T S

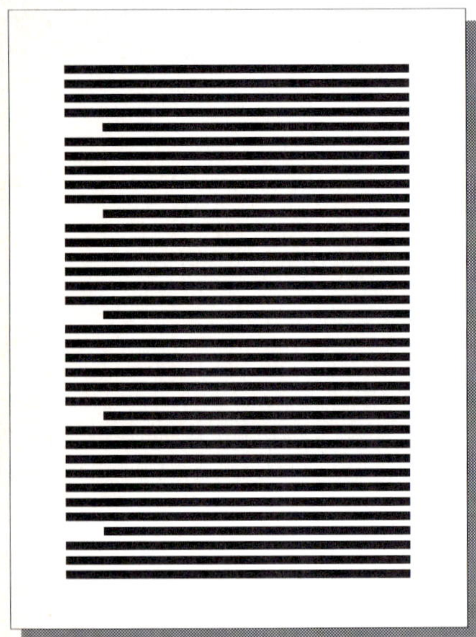

Indented Paragraphs

One basic design decision that has to be made for each publication is how to separate paragraphs from one another so they stand out. There are three basic styles—indented paragraphs, block-style paragraphs, or hanging indents. You can, of course, use a combination of styles within a publication.

Indented Paragraphs

Indented paragraphs (also called *plain paragraphs*) have the first line indented from the left margin and all other lines flush with the margin. The individual paragraphs in a series of paragraphs are indicated by the indents. Because there is no white space between paragraphs, this format gives a solid look to text. If you use this style, both the first paragraph in the document and paragraphs following subheads are frequently not indented, but this is a matter of choice. Indents are usually proportional to the size of the type and the measure. For example, text in 10- and 12-point type is normally indented 1 em space if the type column is up to 27 picas wide, 1 picas for pages between 28 to 35 picas, and 2 picas for columns over 36 picas. These amounts can be reduced for smaller type and increased for larger type. If different type sizes appear in the manuscript, you can use em indents even though it will cause the absolute size of the indent to vary slightly.

Block-Style Paragraphs

Block-style paragraphs (also called *flush paragraphs*) use extra spacing between paragraphs to set them off. This extra space can be entered as a blank line or you can use the program's leading command to automatically add space between paragraphs. Changing leading is the preferred approach because you have much more control over the amount of space between the paragraphs. If you do change leading, the traditional spacing between paragraphs is equal to the size of the type plus leading. For example, if you are using 10/12 type, the spacing between paragraphs would be 12 points. If you are printing in two or more columns, be sure to use this leading or an even multiple, such as 24 or 36, so that lines in the side-by-side columns remain aligned and pages end at the same place on the paper.

Single and Double Indents

Extracts or quotes can be set off from the rest of the text to make them stand out better. One way is to indent them slightly (about 1 to 2 picas) from the left margin or from

Block Paragraphs

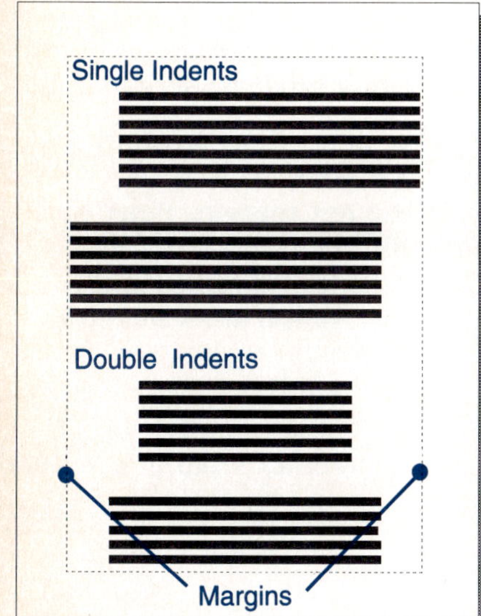

Single and Double Indents

both the left and right margins (called a ***double indent***). (Another way is to add 2 or 3 points of additional spacing above and below them, and set them in a smaller type size than that used for the body text.)

Hanging Indents

Hanging indents (also called *outdents*, *reverse indents*, or *flush-and-hang paragraphs*) are paragraphs that have the first line a specified distance from the left margin and all other lines indented by an additional amount.

One of the major applications of hanging indents are for bulleted or

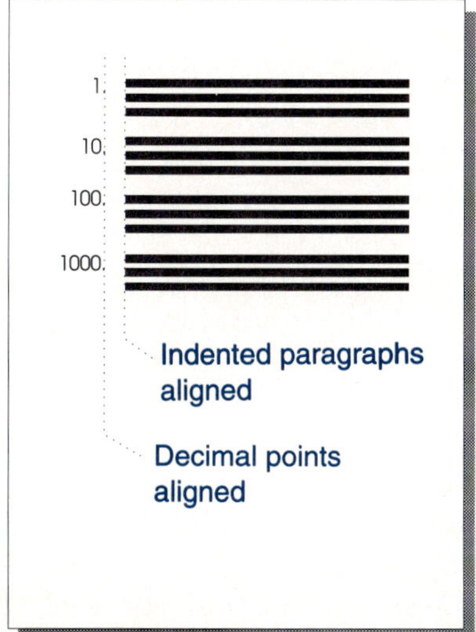

Enumerations

subsequent lines, the lines are called ***turnovers***. There is a variety of ways to indent turned over lines. If the list has more than one level, first lines of subsequent levels should align vertically with the indented line above.

Widows and Orphans

If the last line of a paragraph prints by itself at the top of a page or column, it is a ***widow***. If the first line of a paragraph prints by itself at the bottom of a page or column, it is an ***orphan***. In most situations, both should be avoided.

To remove widows or orphans, you can move another line to the same page to accompany it. If you do not

numbered lists called ***enumerations***. The bullets or numbers in the list stand off by themselves, but the text following them is indented and aligned. When you use hanging indents to create enumerations, the largest number you use determines the minimum amount of the indent that you specify for all entries. Also, there must be room to the left of any aligned decimal points for the largest number used in the list.

Another application of hanging indents is for sideheads, subheads that protrude out into the margin so they stand out from the text.

When a hanging indent is used in text that wraps to a second and

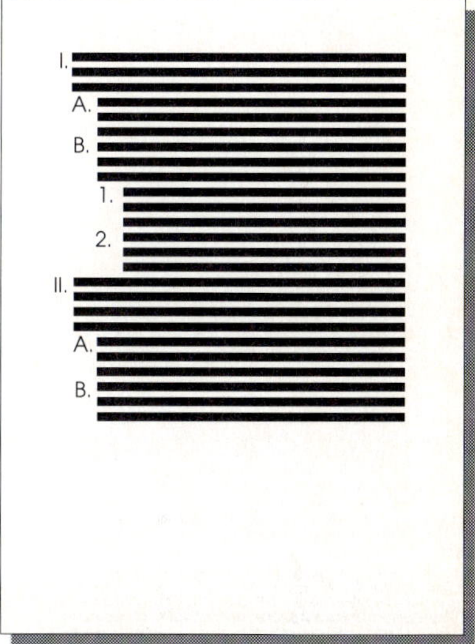

Aligning Turnovers in Hanging Indents

allow single lines by themselves, no three-line paragraphs will be split; the entire paragraph will move to the next page if it will not print on the current page. Moving lines like this presents a problem, however, if you want the text on every page to end at the same place on the sheet. If you move lines from one page to the next, you will create a ***short page***. The solution is to leave two facing pages short instead of just one. To do so, you may have to work backward, moving lines to the next page, until all pages end together when looked at as two-page spreads.

Because of the problems caused by preventing widows and orphans, they are sometimes considered acceptable in text that isn't justified because they do not stand out. In justified text, they are frequently permitted if they almost fill the line. If your widows are very short lines, you can try to remove them in one of the following ways:

- Edit the copy to remove enough characters so that the widow moves up to the line above. This is by far the easiest approach if you have the right to do so. If you don't have this authority, ask the writer or someone else in charge of the project.
- Force a second word down to accompany the single word, although this may affect word spacing on the line you force it down from if the line is justified.
- Hyphenate a word above to change line lengths slightly.

You normally indent with either the Indent (**F4**) key or the **Tab** key, although you can use the Margin Release command (**Shift**-**Tab**) in special situations. Each time you press these keys, the paragraph is indented 1 tab stop. To change the distance your text is indented from the margins, change the tab stops.

Indents affect all text up to the next hard carriage return (you may have to press ↓ to realign the paragraph). If you indent new text, all text that you enter is affected until you press **Enter**. This automatically ends the indent and returns the cursor to the left margin.

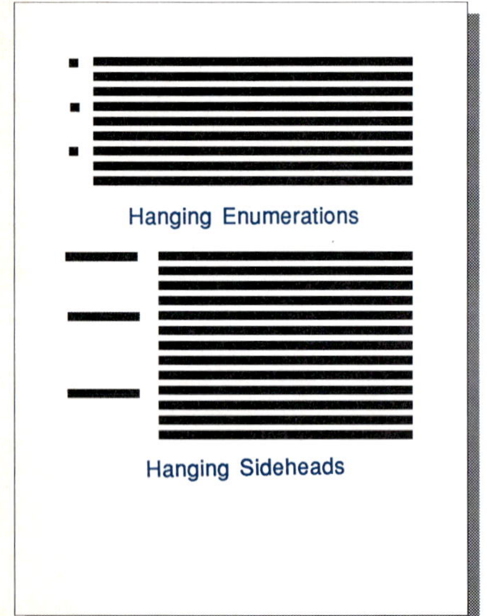

Hanging Indents

Indents

You can indent the first line of a paragraph, indent the entire paragraph from the left margin, or indent the entire paragraph from both margins.

- To indent the first line of a paragraph, move the cursor to the beginning of the first line, and then press **Tab**.
- To indent an entire paragraph from the left margin, move the cursor to the beginning of the paragraph, and then press **F4**.
- To indent an entire paragraph from both left and right margins, move the cursor to the beginning of the paragraph and then press **Shift**-**F4**.

Hanging Indents

There are two procedures that you can use to enter a hanging indent as you enter text:

- Type the text to be left hanging; for example, type **1**, and then press **F4** to insert an indent code. Type the rest of the paragraph, and then press **Enter**.
- Press **F4** to move the cursor to the desired tab stop, and then press **Shift**-**Tab** to move the cursor back to the previous tab stop to the left. Type the text to be left hanging, press **Tab**, type the rest of the paragraph, and then press **Enter**.

To create a hanging indent in existing text, move the cursor to the place in the first line where you want text to begin indenting, press **F4** to insert an indent code, and then press ↓ to reform the rest of the paragraph.

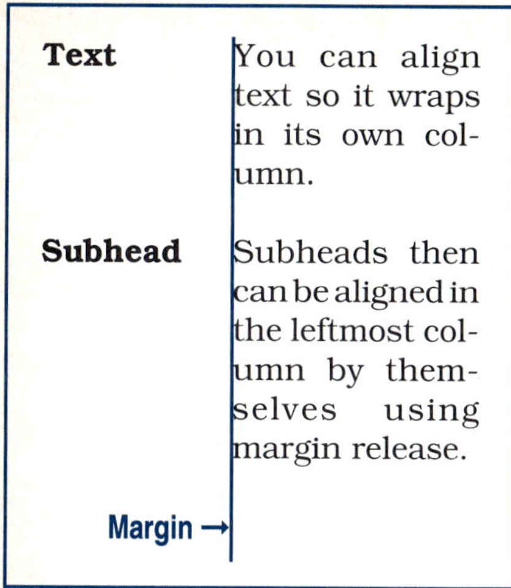

Margin Release

Hanging Indents with the Margin Release Command

You can enter text to the left of the left margin with the **_Margin Release_** (**Shift**-**Tab**) command. Each time you use this command, the cursor moves one more tab stop to the left until it reaches the last tab stop.

Margin release is a useful procedure when you are working with a page design that uses one-third of the page for the headings and two-thirds for the text. You can set the left margin one-third in and all of the body text will then align correctly in the wider column. When you enter a subhead, you then press **Shift**-**Tab** to move the cursor to a tab stop set at the left margin of the narrow column. If the subheads are short, they can be set on the same line as the opening line of the paragraph they relate to. If they are longer, they can be set on a line by themselves. If they are on the same line as the first line in the paragraph, set a left tab stop at the left margin setting and press **Tab** at the end of the subhead to ensure that the first line of the paragraph remains aligned.

If you use the Margin Release command and then enter new text, pressing **Enter** ends the margin release and the cursor returns to the left margin. If you enter text that wraps, the second and subsequent lines of the paragraph are aligned with the left margin.

→   K E Y / S t r o k e s

Indenting Text

- To indent the first line of a paragraph, move the cursor to the beginning of the first line, and press **Tab**.
- To indent an entire paragraph, move the cursor to the beginning of the paragraph, and press **F4**.
- To double indent a paragraph, move the cursor to the beginning of the paragraph, and press **Shift-F4**.
- To enter a hanging indent, use one of the following procedures.
  - Type the text to be left hanging; for example, type **1**, and then press **F4** to insert an indent code. Type the rest of the paragraph, and then press **Enter** to return the cursor to the left margin and end indenting.
  - Press **F4** to move the cursor to the desired tab stop, and then press **Shift-Tab** to move the cursor back to the left margin. Type the text to be left hanging, and then press **Tab**. Type the rest of the paragraph, and then press **Enter** to move the cursor to the left margin and end indenting.
- To enter text to the left of the left margin, move the cursor to the left margin and press **Shift-Tab** to move the cursor to the next tab stop to its left.

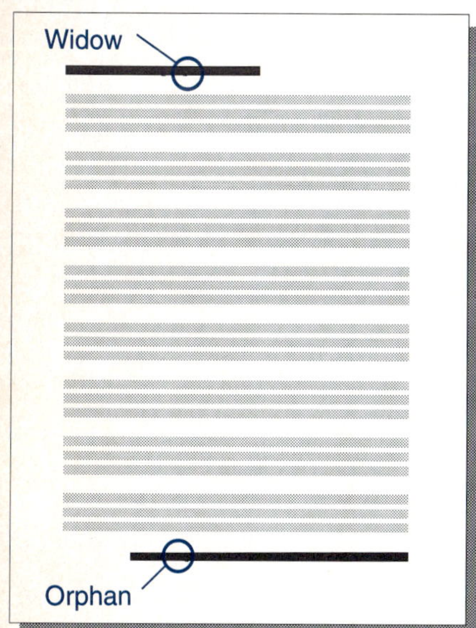

Widows and Orphans

Widows and Orphans

You prevent widows and orphans by entering an open code into the document where you want protection to begin. Then, if WordPerfect calculates that the first or last line of a paragraph is to print at the bottom or top of a page or column by itself, it moves another line to accompany it. You can also enter a code elsewhere in the document to turn protection off.

KEY/Strokes

Turning Widow and Orphan Protection On or Off

1. Move the cursor to where you want to turn widow and orphan protection on or off.
2. Either: Press **Shift-F8** and then press **L** for *Line*.
   Or: Pull down the Layout menu and select *Line*.
3. Press **W** for *Widow/Orphan Protection*.
4. Either: Press **Y** to turn protection on.
   Or: Press **N** to turn protection off.
5. Press **F7** to return to the Edit screen.

EXERCISES

EXERCISE 1

INDENTING AN ENUMERATED LIST

In this exercise, you indent items in an enumerated list. When you are finished, your document should look similar to the figure "The IN-DENTS2 Document."

1. Retrieve the INDENTS2.WP5 document and enter your name.
2. Set tab stops. When you display the tab ruler with units of measurement set to inches, each inch is divided into sections with periods. Delete all existing tab stops, then enter a decimal tab stop at the third period to the right of 0". Set left-aligned tab stops at the fifth and eighth periods.
3. Insert a tab code in front of each number to align it with the decimal tab stop. (Insert two tab codes in front of the bulleted items following point 3 under the heading "*MEMOS*.")
4. Insert an indent code following the period in each number (and following bullets in the memos section) and delete the existing space in that position.
5. Save and print the document.

Name:
Date: August 21, 1991
Filename: INDENTS2.WP5
Topic: Indents

BLOCK-STYLE LETTERS

1. Margins. Set all margins to 1 inch or more.
2. Dateline. Enter the dateline at the left margin on a block style letter. Press **Enter** four times after entering the date.
3. Letter Address. Enter the letter address flush with the left margin. Use the two-letter state abbreviations, space twice, and enter the ZIP code. Press **Enter** two times after the last line.
4. Salutation. Enter the salutation flush with the left margin. No punctuation is used after the salutation in a block style letter. Press **Enter** two times after entering the salutation.
5. Body Text. Body text is single spaced with no paragraph indentions. Press **Enter** twice at the end of each paragraph.
6. Closing. Enter the closing flush with the left margin, and then press **Enter** four times.
7. Signature Line. Enter flush with the left margin, and then press **Enter** two times.
8. Identification. Enter your reference initials and document filename flush with the left margin a double space below the signature line. Use lowercase letters for the reference initials with no punctuation or spacing between them. Press **Enter** to end the line.

MODIFIED BLOCK-STYLE LETTERS

1. Margins. Set all margins to 1 inch or more.
2. Tab Stops. Set a left-aligned tab stop centered between the left and right margins.
3. Dateline. Enter the date at the tab stop, then press **Enter** four times.
4. Letter Address. Enter the letter address flush left. Press **Enter** four times after the last line.
5. Salutation. Enter the salutation flush left, and then press **Enter** two times. (No punctuation is required after the salutation.)
6. Body Text. Enter body text single spaced, and press **Enter** twice at the end of each paragraph. Paragraphs may be indented five spaces.
7. Closing. Tab the signature line to the tab stop. Press **Enter** twice after entering the line.
8. Signature. Press **Tab**, enter the signature line, then press **Enter** twice.
9. Identification. Enter your reference initials flush left. Use lowercase letters for the reference initials with no punctuation or spacing between them.

SIMPLIFIED STYLE LETTERS

1. Margins. Set all margins to 1 inch or more.
2. Dateline. Enter the dateline flush left, and then press **Enter** four times.
3. Letter Address. Enter the letter address flush left. Press **Enter** three times after the last line.
4. Subject Line. Enter the subject line flush with the left margin in all capital letters without

the word subject. Press **Enter** three times after it is entered.

5. Body Text. Single-space the body text but double space between paragraphs. No paragraph indentions are used. Press **Enter** four times after the last line of the body text.
6. Signature. Enter the signature line in all capital letters. Press **Enter** two times before keyboarding the reference initials.
7. Identification. Enter your reference initials and document filename flush with the left margin a double space below the signature line. Use lowercase letters for the reference initials with no punctuation or spacing between them.

MEMOS

1. Left and Right Margins. Set left and right margins to 1 inch.
2. Top and Bottom Margins. Set the top margin at 1½ inches.
3. Side Headings.
    - Enter side headings in all capital letters.
    - Double-space between the side headings.
    - Triple-space between the last heading and the body of the memo.
    - Press **Spacebar** five spaces before entering the TO heading.
    - Press **Spacebar** three times before entering FROM and DATE.
    - Begin SUBJECT at the left margin.
    - Enter two spaces following colons in the side headings.
4. Body Text. Body text is single spaced and flush with the left margin. Double-space between paragraphs.
5. Identification. Enter your reference initials and document filename a double space below the last line of the body text.

EXERCISE 2

INDENTING PARAGRAPHS ON MULTIPLE LEVELS

In this exercise, you indent three levels of items so the second two levels each align with the turn on the level above. When you are finished, your results should look similar to the figure "The INDENTS3 Document."

1. Retrieve the INDENTS3.WP5 document and enter your name.
2. Set tab stops. When you display the tab ruler with units of measurement set to inches, each inch is divided into sections with periods. Delete all existing tab stops, then enter decimal tab stops at the third, sixth, and ninth periods to the right of 0". Set left-aligned tab stops at the fifth and eighth periods, and at the 1" marker.
3. Use the Search command to replace all periods followed by spaces with periods followed by indent codes (or do so manually).
4. Insert tab codes in front of each level to move it to the appropriate decimal tab stop.
5. Save and print the document.

Name:
Date: August 21, 1991
Filename: INDENTS3.WP5
Topic: Hanging indents at various levels

   I. If there is more than one level of indent, each subsequent level should align with the indent of the level above.

      A. If there is more than one level of indent, each subsequent level should align with the indent of the level above.

      B. If there is more than one level of indent, each subsequent level should align with the indent of the level above.

         1. If there is more than one level of indent, each subsequent level should align with the indent of the level above.

         2. If there is more than one level of indent, each subsequent level should align with the indent of the level above.

  II. If there is more than one level of indent, each subsequent level should align with the indent of the level above.

      A. If there is more than one level of indent, each subsequent level should align with the indent of the level above.

      B. If there is more than one level of indent, each subsequent level should align with the indent of the level above.

         1. If there is more than one level of indent, each subsequent level should align with the indent of the level above.

         2. If there is more than one level of indent, each subsequent level should align with the indent of the level above.

EXERCISE 3

ALIGNING TEXT TO THE LEFT OF THE LEFT MARGIN

In this exercise you use the Margin Release command to align text to the left of the left margin. When you are finished, your results should look similar to the figure "The INDENTS4 Document."

1. Retrieve the INDENTS4.WP5 document and enter your name.
2. Change the left margin to 3 inches.
3. Delete all tab stops, then enter left-aligned tabs at -2" (or -148p) and +.3" (or +22p).
4. Follow the instructions in the KEY/Strokes box "Indenting Text" to align the subheads to the left of the left margin. (One subhead, "Hanging Indents," is on the second page.)
5. Save and print the document.

The INDENTS4 Document

Name:
Date: August 21, 1991
Filename: INDENTS4.WP5
Topic: Aligning subheads with the Margin Release command

One basic design decision that has to be made for each publication is how to separate paragraphs from one another so they stand out. There are three basic styles: indented paragraphs, block-style paragraphs, or hanging indents. You can, of course, use a combination of styles within a publication.

Indented Paragraphs

Indented paragraphs (also called plain paragraphs) have the first line indented from the left margin and all other lines flush with the margin. The individual paragraphs in a series of paragraphs are indicated by the indents. Because there is no white space between paragraphs, this format gives a solid look to text. If you use this style, the first paragraph in the document and paragraphs following subheads are frequently not indented but this is a matter of choice. Indents are usually proportional to the size of the type and the measure. For example, 10- and 12-point type are normally indented 1 em space if the type column is up to 27 picas wide, 1½ picas for pages between 28-35 picas, and 2 picas for columns over 36 picas. These amounts can be reduced for smaller type and increased for larger type. If different type sizes are used in the manuscript, you can use em indents, even though it will cause the absolute size of the indent to vary slightly.

Block-Style Paragraphs

Block-style paragraphs (also called flush paragraphs) use extra spacing between paragraphs to set them off. This extra space can be entered as a blank line or you can use the program's leading command to automatically add space between paragraphs. Changing leading is the preferred approach because you have much more control over the amount of space between the paragraphs. If you do change leading, the traditional spacing between paragraphs is equal to the size of the type plus leading.

Single and Double Indents

Extracts can be set off from the rest of the text to make them stand out better. One way is to indent them slightly (about 1 to 2 picas) from the left margin or both the left and right margins (called a double indent). Another way is to add 2 or 3 points of additional spacing above and below them, and set them in a smaller type size than that used for the body text.

Hanging Indents

Hanging indents (also called outdents, reverse indents, or flush-and-hang paragraphs) are paragraphs that have the first line a specified distance from the left margin and all other lines (called runover lines) indented by an additional amount.

The major applications of hanging indents are bulleted or numbered lists called enumerations. The bullets or numbers in the list stand off by themselves, but the text following them is indented and aligned.

When you use hanging indents to create enumerations, the largest number you use determines the minimum amount of the indent that you specify for all entries. Also, there must be room to the left of any aligned decimal points for the largest number used in the list.

Title Pages, Section Openers, and Subheadings

After completing this topic, you should be able to:

- Describe some characteristics of title page designs
- Describe ways to set off subheads from body text
- Create your own title pages and section openers
- Space and position subheads in your own documents

▶ TUTORIAL

In this tutorial, you format a title page so all of its elements are spaced using margin and advance commands. When you are finished, your printout should be similar to the figure "A Typical Title Page."

GETTING STARTED

1. Retrieve the TITLEPG1.WP5 document and enter your name.

SET THE LEFT MARGIN

2. Move the cursor to the upper left-hand corner of the screen.
3. Press **Shift-F8** to display the Format menu.
4. Press **L** for *Line* to display the Line Format menu.
5. Press **M** for *Margins* and the cursor jumps to the line that reads *Margins - Left.*
6. Type **2"** and then press **Enter** twice. The cursor returns to the prompt that reads *Selection:*
7. Press **F7** to return to the Edit screen.

ADVANCE THE TITLE DOWN

8. Move the cursor to the "*C*" in "*Casy & Williams.*"
9. Press **Shift-F8** to display the Format menu.
10. Press **O** for *Other.*
11. Press **A** for *Advance.*
12. Press **D** for *Down* and the prompt reads *Adv. down.*
13. Type **2.5"** (for 2½ inches) and then press **Enter**. (The text is not moved down on the screen but it will be moved down on the printout.)

Casy & Williams, Inc.
A Five-Year Plan

By: Your Name
Date: 00/00/92
Filename: TITLEPG1.WP5
Topic:

A Typical Title Page

14. Press **F7** to return to the Edit screen.

ADVANCE THE HEADING IN AND DOWN

15. Move the cursor to the "*N*" in "*Name:*" in the heading.
16. Repeat Steps 3 through 7 but specify a left margin of **4"**.
17. Repeat Steps 9 through 14 but specify **3"** for the distance to be advanced down.

CHANGE FONTS

18. Move the cursor to the top of the document.
19. Press **Ctrl-F8** to display the Font menu.
20. Press **F** for *Base Font*.
21. Highlight any font that is 18 points or greater (or the largest that you have), and then press **S** for *Select*. (If you select a scalable font and are prompted to enter its size, type **36** and then press **Enter**.)
22. Move the cursor to the "*N*" in "*Name:*" in the heading.
23. Repeat Steps 19 through 21 but specify a font of 12 points.

FINISHING UP

24. Save and print the document. Measure the spacings in the document and compare them with the codes that you entered into the document file.

> **D E S K T O P   P U B L I S H I N G   C O N C E P T S**

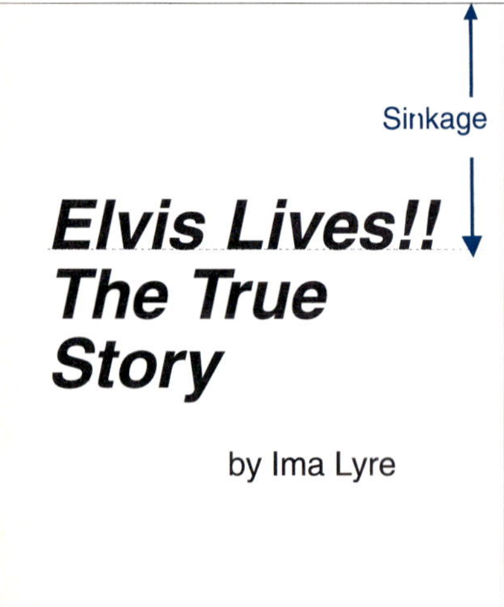

Sinkage

When you publish pamphlets, reports, manuals, books, or newsletters, you frequently have to design title pages, section openers, and subheadings.

Title Pages

Reports, books, and manuals frequently have both half-title pages that list just the book title and title pages that list the title, author, and publisher or issuing company.

■ Title pages always start on new pages.
■ Title text is usually set down from the top of the type page to the baseline of the first line of the title by a distance referred to as **sinkage**.
■ Titles and other text on the title page should not be justified (called full justification in WordPerfect), and words should not be hyphenated.

■ You can be very creative with type sizes and alignments on these pages but the type usually relates to the type used elsewhere in the document.
■ If a work has a subtitle, you can set it in a different typestyle to separate it from the main title so punctuation is not required.
■ If the work is copyrighted, it should have a copyright notice that includes the special character, ©. This notice is usually placed on the page following the title page.

Section Openers

The most decorative elements in a publication are frequently the section openers such as part and chapter opening pages. These elements break up the publication into smaller units so it is less intimidating and easier to find material.

SUMMARIES OF AGENCY PROGRAMS

Section Openers

Initial Letters

YOU can use the first character in a paragraph following
the chapter title as a decorative element by setting it in a
larger type size so it extends
above the line.

Stickup Caps

A Level Subheads

B Level Subheads

C LEVEL SUBHEADS

D Level Subheads

Run-in Heads. These are
used only for the lowest
level of subheadings.

Subhead Levels

- Section openers are usually set in display type that is larger than the type used elsewhere in the publication.
- The typestyle can be different from that used elsewhere in the publication but it should be visually compatible.
- Section titles should not be justified and words should not be hyphenated.
- Title text can be sunk below the top of the type page the same distance as text on the title page.
- If sections are numbered, you do not have to repeat the words "Chapter" or "Part" for each section if you don't want to.
- These pages always begin on a new page.
- The section number and title may be the only things on that page, or they may be accompanied by an introduction or the beginning of the text in the section.
- You can use the first character in a paragraph following the chapter title as a decorative element by setting it in a larger type size so it extends above the line (called a **stickup cap** or *stickup initial*) or drops below it (called a **drop cap** or *drop initial*). If it drops below, the lines below are affected. The baseline of the initial letter should be even with the baseline of the second or third line in the paragraph. If you use a stickup or drop cap, you can set the rest of the first word in small caps.

Subheadings
Most long documents or chapters are broken up into sections using subheadings. The level of these subheads is usually specified with letters, for example, A-heads, B-heads, C-heads, and so on. Subheads are usually set on their own line and their level can be established using several formats that include case; typefaces, styles, and sizes; and alignments.

One type of subheading is called a **run-in head** (also called a *run-in side head*). It is actually the first word, phrase, or sentence in a paragraph that is highlighted, usually in italics or bold followed by a period or extra space, so it stands out. Run-in subheads are always used in the text as the lowest-level heading. However, they can also be used in tables and figure captions.

When you work with subheads you should think about their spacing, style, and position.

Subhead Spacing
The space above and below a subhead not only sets it off from the body text so it stands out, but the space also associates it with the text below that it relates to.

- The space above the heading should be larger than the space below. For example, you can specify 2 picas above and 1 pica below. These proportions visually associate the heading with the text that follows rather than the text that precedes it.
- The space added above and below the subhead should be an even multiple of the type size so pages or columns with headings don't end at a different position than pages or columns without them. For example, if you are using 12-point type, adding 8 points above and 4 points below makes the heading and its extra space an even two lines.

Subhead Styles
Each level of subhead should be unique and all headings at the same level should have identical formats. When designing subheads, keep the following points in mind:

- Heads can be set using the same typeface in the same size as that used for the body text. Alternatively, if the body text is a serif type, the headings can be sans serif.
- Keep in mind that all cap heads may run longer than lines with upper- and lowercase letters. Also, all cap heads are harder to read because the ascenders and descenders that provide visual clues are lacking.

Emily

EMILY

Subhead Case
Words that have all uppercase letters are harder
to read than words that have lowercase letters.

- In some cases, the number of heading levels varies from section to section. For example, some sections may have A-, B-, and C-heads and others just two levels. In these cases, you can format the headings in the later sections as B- and C-heads, without using the A-head format.
- Sections can be numbered in a variety of styles. For example, they can be numbered sequentially 1, 2, 3; or using numbers with levels 1.1.1, 1.1.2, and so on.

Subhead Positions
You can position subheads in a variety of ways as long as each level uses its own alignment consistently. However, there are certain positions in which subheads should not fall and there are ways to treat the text that follows them.

- You can use various alignments to highlight headings on the page. If the subhead continues past the first line, all but the first line are called runover lines (this same term is used with indents). Typical alignments include the following:
  - Flush left
  - Drop-line
  - Inverted pyramid
  - Hanging indented
  - Indented
  - Block with last line centered
- Subheads should be followed by at least 2 lines of text at the bottom of a page or column.
- The first line of text following a subhead can be flush left even if the first lines in other paragraphs are indented. However, this is not a hard-and-fast rule and many publications indent all paragraphs.

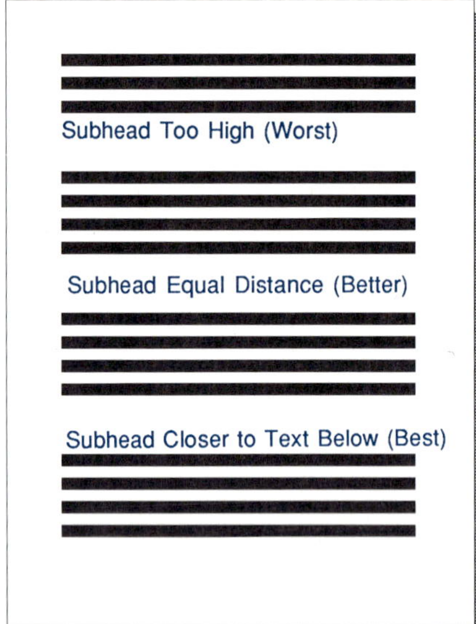

Subhead Spacing

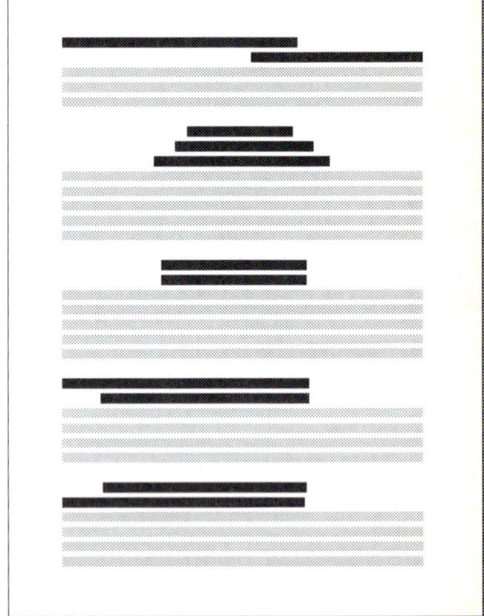

Subhead Alignments

▶ W O R D P E R F E C T   P R O C E D U R E S

When creating title pages and section openers (and even covers), you may want to sink the title to a fixed position on the page. You can do so by using the Advance command. The Advance command shifts the specified text up, down, left, or right a specified distance or to a specific place on the page. You do not see the effects of this command on the screen. To see the effects, use the View document command or make a printout.

Using the Advance Command

1. Move the cursor to the beginning of the text you want advanced.
2. Press **Shift-F8** to display the Format menu.
3. Press **O** for *Other*.
4. Press **A** for *Advance*.
5. Make any of the choices described in the table "Advance Command Menu Choices."
6. Type a distance for the text to move, and then press **Enter**.
7. Press **F7** to return to the Edit screen.

ADVANCE COMMAND MENU CHOICES

1 *Up* moves the text up following the code.
2 *Down* moves the text down following the code.
3 *Line* moves the text following the code a specified distance down from the top edge of the paper (not from the top margin). For example, if you enter 2 inches, the text is printed 2 inches down from the top of the page.
4 *Left* moves the text left following the code.
5 *Right* moves the text right following the code.
6 *Position* is the same as *Line* but specifies the distance to be moved horizontally from the left edge of the paper.

► E X E R C I S E S

EXERCISE 1

SPACING SUBHEADS

In this exercise, you space subheads so that they are separated from the text above and below.

1. Retrieve the TITLEPG2.WP5 document and enter your name.
2. Move the cursor to each subhead, then follow the instructions in the KEY/Strokes box "Using the Advance Command" to enter advance down codes. Enter one advance down code in front of each subhead to advance it down 16-points. Enter another advance down code at the end of each subhead (except the E level head) to advance the following text down 8 points (16 + 8 is equal to 24 points or two lines).
3. Save and print the document.

The TITLEPG2 Document

Section Opener

To distinguish levels of subheads, you can change case, typestyles, and indents. The formats you select should visually indicate the levels of each element.

A-Level Subheads

To distinguish levels of subheads, you can change case, typestyles, and indents. The formats you select should visually indicate the levels of each element.

B-Level Subheads

To distinguish levels of subheads, you can change case, typestyles, and indents. The formats you select should visually indicate the levels of each element.

C-LEVEL SUBHEADS

To distinguish levels of subheads, you can change case, typestyles, and indents. The formats you select should visually indicate the levels of each element.

D-LEVEL SUBHEADS

To distinguish levels of subheads, you can change case, typestyles, and indents. The formats you select should visually indicate the levels of each element.

E-Level Subheads. To distinguish levels of subheads, you can change case, typestyles, and indents. The formats you select should visually indicate the levels of each element.

EXERCISE 2

ALIGNING SUBHEADS

In this exercise, you align subheads with the margins.

1. Retrieve the TITLEPG3.WP5 document and enter your name.
2. Using the commands you have learned about centering, indenting, and aligning flush right, align each of the heads so that they look similar to those in the figure "The TITLEPG3 Document."
3. Save and print the document.

Name:
Date: August 21, 1991
Filename: TITLEPG3.WP5
Topic: Subhead Alignments

There are a variety of ways to lay out subheads so that they are distinctive.

SUBHEADS
                              THE DROP-LINE TYPE

The choices include **drop-line**, **inverted pyramid**, reverse indent, indented, and block with the last line centered.

                    SUBHEADS CAN BE
                       AN INVERTED
                        PRYAMID

The choices include drop-line, **inverted pyramid**, reverse indent, indented, and block with the last line centered.

SUBHEADS CAN BE FORMATTED AS A HANGING INDENT
        JUST LIKE THIS ONE

The choices include drop-line, inverted pyramid, **hanging indent**, indented, and block with the last line centered.

        SUBHEADS CAN ALSO HAVE THE FIRST LINE
INDENTED LIKE THIS

The choices include drop-line, inverted pyramid, reverse indent, **indented**, and block with the last line centered.

                    SUBHEADS CAN BE
                   ARRANGED LIKE A
                    SQUARE BLOCK

The choices include drop-line, inverted pyramid, reverse indent, indented, and **block with the last line centered**.

R E V I E W

- Text can be aligned with the left or right margin, centered, or justified. When text is aligned flush with the left or right margin, the other margin is ragged. Justified text (called full justification in WordPerfect) is flush with both the left and right margins.
- Vertical centering centers the text on a page between the top and bottom margins.
- Tab stops indent text and align tables and lists. You can set tab stops so that text tabbed to them aligns flush left, aligns flush right, or is centered.
- Decimal tabs align columns of numbers containing decimal points.
- The alignment character is the character that is aligned when text is tabbed to a decimal tab stop. It is initially the period, but you can change it to any other character.
- You set tab stops by revising the ruler line and inserting a tab code into the document.
- Block-style paragraphs are separated from one another by space. You can vary the amount of space with the leading command.
- Paragraphs can be indented so that the first line is indented from the rest of the paragraph, the entire paragraph is indented from the left margin or from the left and right margins, or the first line is kept aligned with the left margin and the rest of the paragraph is indented.
- Hanging indents are often used for enumerated lists so that the number is left hanging while the rest of the paragraph is indented and aligned.
- The Margin Release command is used to enter text to the left of the left margin.
- A widow is the last line of a paragraph printed by itself at the top of a page. An orphan is the first line of a paragraph printed by itself at the bottom of a page. When the Widow On/Off Protection command is on, these are prevented from occurring.
- The text on title pages and section openers should not be justified or hyphenated. The title can be set down from the top of the type page at a distance called *sinkage*.
- Subheads should be spaced so they are closer to the text that follows than the text that precedes them. The added space should be an even multiple of the font size being used so pages all end at the same point.
- Subhead levels should be distinguished from one another by alignment, case, or typestyles.

QUESTIONS

TRUE/FALSE

T   F

1. WordPerfect uses the term *justification* the same way publishers and printers use the term.

2. WordPerfect's default setting for tab stops is every half inch.

3. It is faster and better to align text by pressing the **Spacebar** rather than with tab stops.

4. Absolute tab stops are set in relation to the left margin and change when you change the margin.

5. Block-style paragraphs are separated from one another by space.

6. A double indent is indented two tab stops from the left margin.

7. A hanging indent has the first line indented and the rest of the paragraph left hanging.

8. A widow is a single line of text at the top of a page or column.

9. An orphan is a single line of text at the top of a page or column.

10. Short pages are caused by paper that is not long enough.

11. To indent text in WordPerfect, you use the **F4** key.

12. Indents should always be proportional to the size of the type being used.

13. The Margin Release command undoes all margin settings in a document.

14. You can use the Margin Release command to enter side heads.

15. A title should always be set on a page by itself.

16. A section opener should always be on a page by itself.

17. Subhead levels are specified by letters, for example, A-level, B-level, and so on.

18. Higher-level subheads should be set in much larger type than lower-level subheads.

19. A run-in head is actually part of a paragraph and not set on a line by itself.

20. Subheads should be closer to the paragraph that follows than to the one that precedes.

21. Each level of subhead should have a unique appearance so it can be distinguished from other levels.

1. Text that is even with both margins is called ____________.
2. The margin that is not justified is called a(n) ____________ margin.
3. If you want to align numbers that contain decimal points, you set ____________ tab stops.
4. If you want characters to fill the space when you press **Tab**, you specify ____________.
5. Tab stops in WordPerfect that change when you change margin settings are called ____________ tab stops.
6. Tab stops in WordPerfect that do not change when you change margins are called ____________ tab stops.
7. Default tab stops are set every ____________ inch.
8. Paragraphs that are separated from one another with spaces are called ____________-style paragraphs.
9. An indent from both left and right margins is called a(n) ____________ indent.
10. An indent where the first line remains flush with the left margin and the rest of the paragraph is indented is called a(n) ____________ indent.
11. Indents should be one ____________ space in width so they are proportional to the size of the type being used.
12. A last line of a paragraph that prints by itself at the top of a page or column is called a ____________.
13. A first line of a paragraph that prints by itself at the bottom of a page or column is called a ____________.
14. If you move lines from one page to the next to eliminate widows, you create a ____________ page.
15. The Margin Release command can be used to enter ____________.
16. The page in a publication that lists the title, author, and publisher is called a ____________ page.
17. Subhead levels are usually referred to by ____________.
18. Subheads should have ____________ space above than below.

MATCH THE COLUMNS

1. Justified text
2. Ragged-right margin
3. Decimal tab stop
4. Dot leaders
5. Alignment character
6. Relative tab stop

___ A large initial that extends below a line of text

___ A large initial that extends above a line of text

___ A tab stop used to align numbers with decimal points

___ Allows you to enter text to the left of the left margin

___ First line of a paragraph by itself at the bottom of the page or column

___ Last line of a paragraph by itself at the top of the page or column

7. Absolute tab
   stop
8. Indented
   paragraph
9. Block-style
   paragraph
10. Double indent
11. Hanging indent
12. Widow
13. Orphan
14. Margin release
15. A-head
16. Stickup initial
17. Drop cap

__ Paragraphs that are separated by spaces
__ Paragraphs that are visually separated by indents
__ Tabs that change when margins change
__ Tabs that remain fixed when the left margin changes
__ Text that has the first line less indented than the rest of the paragraph
__ Text that is aligned with both margins
__ Text that is flush left
__ Text that is indented from both margins
__ The character that is aligned at a tab stop
__ The characters that fill the space between tabbed columns
__ The highest-level subhead

WRITE OUT THE ANSWERS

1. List four ways in which you can align text, and give some examples of when you might want to use the alignments.
2. What does it normally mean to say that text is justified? In what four ways can you justify text with WordPerfect?
3. What is a ragged margin?
4. When would you use tab stops?
5. In what ways can you align text with a tab stop?
6. Describe two procedures for centering text on tab stops.
7. When would you use decimal tab stops?
8. Describe two procedures for aligning decimal points in numbers with tab stops.
9. List and describe the choices you have when setting tab stops.
10. List and describe three ways to indent text.
11. What is a hanging indent? What is it used for?
12. Describe three ways to create a hanging indent.
13. What command do you use to enter text to the left of the left margin?

PROJECTS

PROJECT 1

USING INITIAL CAPS

In this project, you format the first letter in the paragraph following the heading so that it is very large or extra large.

Procedures Used
- Using larger initial caps in each paragraph.

Text Files Needed
- INITCAPS.WP5

Formats
① Format opening letters in each stanza as extra large.

Tips
- You might want to experiment with new base fonts to make as attractive a printout as you can.
- The space between the first and second lines in each paragraph may be greater than the space between other lines because the larger font used for the opening letter has more leading built into it.

The Star-Spangled Banner

I

①——Oh, say can you see by the dawn's early light
What so proudly we hailed at the twilight's last gleaming?
Whose broad stripes and bright stars thru the perilous fight,
O'er the ramparts we watched were so gallantly streaming?
And the rocket's red glare, the bombs bursting in air,
Gave proof through the night that our flag was still there.
Oh, say does that star-spangled banner yet wave
O'er the land of the free and the home of the brave?

II

①——On the shore, dimly seen through the mists of the deep,
Where the foe's haughty host in dread silence reposes,
What is that which the breeze, o'er the towering steep,
As it fitfully blows, half conceals, half discloses?
Now it catches the gleam of the morning's first beam,
In full glory reflected now shines in the stream:
'Tis the star-spangled banner! Oh long may it wave
O'er the land of the free and the home of the brave!

III

①——And where is that band who so vauntingly swore
That the havoc of war and the battle's confusion,
A home and a country should leave us no more!
Their blood has washed out their foul footsteps' pollution.
No refuge could save the hireling and slave
From the terror of flight, or the gloom of the grave:
And the star-spangled banner in triumph doth wave
O'er the land of the free and the home of the brave!

IV

①——Oh! thus be it ever, when freemen shall stand
Between their loved home and the war's desolation!
Blest with victory and peace, may the heav'n rescued land
Praise the Power that hath made and preserved us a nation.
Then conquer we must, when our cause it is just,
And this be our motto: "In God is our trust."
And the star-spangled banner in triumph shall wave
O'er the land of the free and the home of the brave!

A DESKTOP PUBLISHING QUIZ

In this project, you format a desktop publishing quiz using tab stops and hanging indents. This figure shows page 1 of the two-page document.

Procedures Used
- Indents and dot leaders.

Text Files Needed
- DTP-QUIZ.WP5

Formats
① Enter a decimal tab stop at .6 inch (with dot leaders), and left-aligned tab stops at .8 inch and 2.5 inches.
② Use **Tab** to align numbers with decimal tab stop.
③ Use **F4** to align text with left-aligned tab stop.

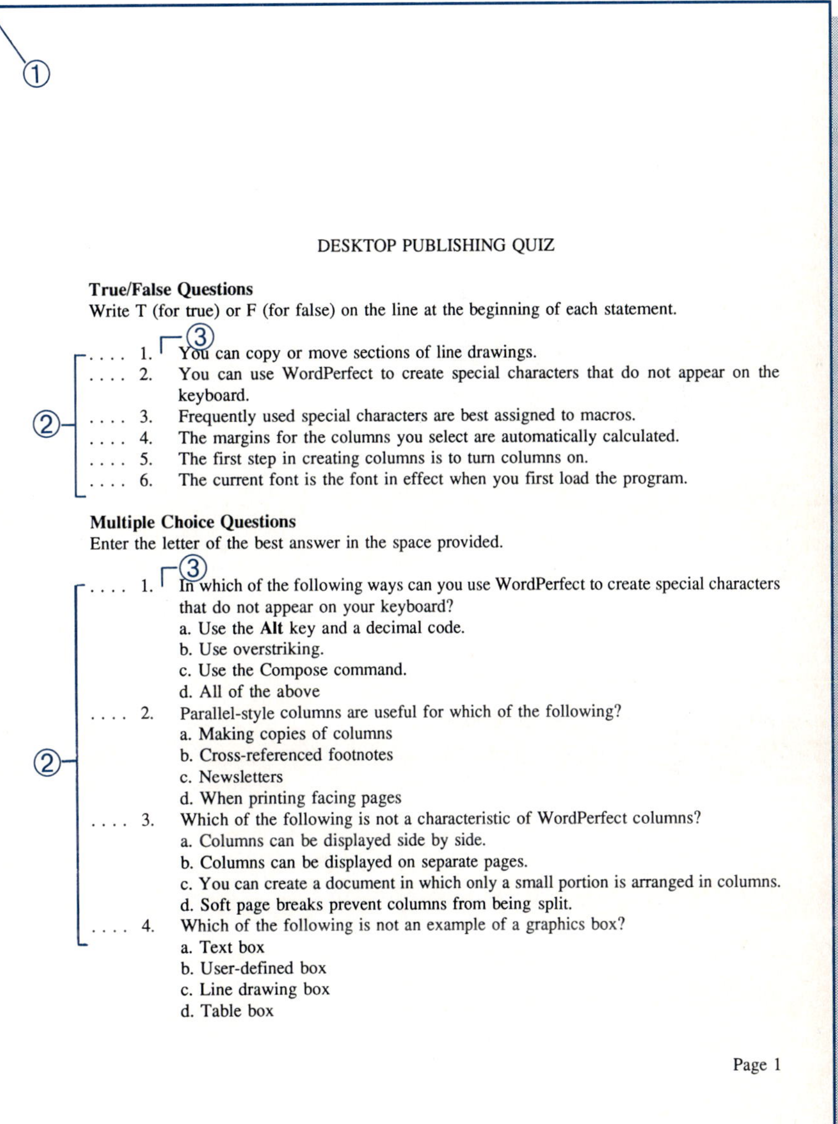

DESKTOP PUBLISHING QUIZ

True/False Questions
Write T (for true) or F (for false) on the line at the beginning of each statement.

.... 1. You can copy or move sections of line drawings.
.... 2. You can use WordPerfect to create special characters that do not appear on the keyboard.
.... 3. Frequently used special characters are best assigned to macros.
.... 4. The margins for the columns you select are automatically calculated.
.... 5. The first step in creating columns is to turn columns on.
.... 6. The current font is the font in effect when you first load the program.

Multiple Choice Questions
Enter the letter of the best answer in the space provided.

.... 1. In which of the following ways can you use WordPerfect to create special characters that do not appear on your keyboard?
a. Use the **Alt** key and a decimal code.
b. Use overstriking.
c. Use the Compose command.
d. All of the above
.... 2. Parallel-style columns are useful for which of the following?
a. Making copies of columns
b. Cross-referenced footnotes
c. Newsletters
d. When printing facing pages
.... 3. Which of the following is not a characteristic of WordPerfect columns?
a. Columns can be displayed side by side.
b. Columns can be displayed on separate pages.
c. You can create a document in which only a small portion is arranged in columns.
d. Soft page breaks prevent columns from being split.
.... 4. Which of the following is not an example of a graphics box?
a. Text box
b. User-defined box
c. Line drawing box
d. Table box

Page 1

A DESKTOP PUBLISHING QUIZ, CON'T

This figure shows how to format the second page of the test.

Formats

① Use **F4** to align text with left-aligned tab stop.

② Use **Tab** to align numbers with decimal tab stop.

③ Use **F4** to align text with left-aligned tab stop.

④ Use **F4** to align numbers with decimal tab stop

Tip

■ If you press **F4** to move text to a decimal tab stop with a dot leader setting, no dot leader is entered.

Matching Questions

Enter the letter preceding one of the terms below in the space preceding each question.

①
a. parallel
c. figure
e. newspaper

①
b. overstrike
d. line draw

②

③
. . . . 1. Function that allows you to print two or more characters in the same position on a page.
. . . . 2. Columns in which text flows continually up and down.
. . . . 3. Columns in which text appears side by side.
. . . . 4. Graphic box used for graphic images and charts.
. . . . 5. Feature that allows you to create organizational charts.

Fill In the Blank Questions

Choose the best answer from the words listed below to fill in the blanks in the following sentences.

①
turn columns off
turn columns on
images
define columns
indented
initial font

①
fonts
enter or retrieve text
hard carriage return
tables of numbers
GoTo

④

③
1. When you use the Line Draw function to draw boxes around text, enter the text so that each line ends with a _____________________ and is _____________________ from the left margin.
2. If line drawings do not print, try changing _________.
3. The four basic steps to creating columns are:
   1. _____________________________________
   2. _____________________________________
   3. _____________________________________
   4. _____________________________________
4. Graphics boxes may contain _____________ and _____________.
5. To move between columns, use the _______________ command with the left and right arrow keys.
6. The _____________________ is the default font for your document.

Page 2

FORMATTING A SECTION OPENER PAGE

In this project, you format a section opener page for a chapter on clouds.

Procedures Used
- Changing base fonts and using the advance down code.

Text Files Needed
- CLOUDS1.WP5

Formats
① Enter a margin code to set left margin to 3 inches.
② Enter an advance down code to advance text down 2 inches.
③ Enter a base font code for 18-point font.
④ Enter a base font code for 127-point font (or the largest you have).
⑤ Enter a base font code for 60-point type (or smaller than the chapter number).

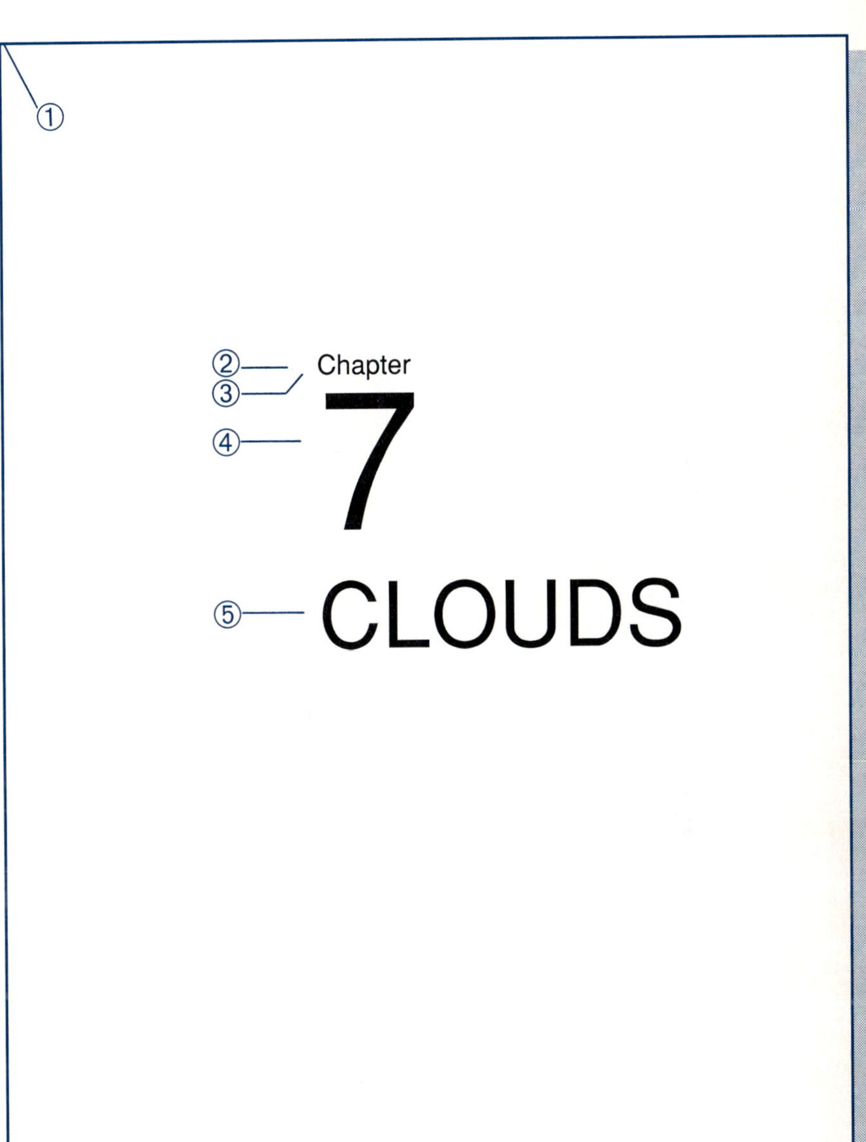

ALIGNING SUBHEADS WITH THE MARGIN RELEASE COMMAND

In this project, you set the left margin to 3 inches and a relative tab stop at -2 inches (after clearing all other tab stops). You then use the Margin Release command to align the subheads with the single tab stop to the left of the left margin.

Procedures Used
- Margin Release command.

Text Files Needed
- CLOUDS2.WP5

Formats
① Enter a base font code of 10-point Helvetica or a similar font.
② Enter a margin code to set the left margin to 3 inches and the right margin to 1 inch.
③ Enter a tab stop code that has a single relative left-aligned tab stop at -2 inches.
④ Use the Margin Release command to move subheads out into the left column.

Tip
- There is a heading "*LOW CLOUDS*" on page 2 and a heading "*CLOUDS WITH EXTENSIVE VERTICAL DEVELOPMENT*" on page 3 that are not shown in the figure.

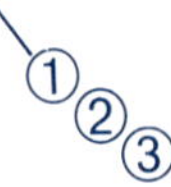

Clouds, to almost everyone, have some meaning. But to you as a pilot, clouds are your weather "signposts in the sky." They give you an indication of air motion, stability, and moisture. Clouds help you visualize weather conditions and potential weather hazards you might encounter in flight. Let's examine these "signposts" and how to identify them.

For identification purposes, you need be concerned only with the more basic cloud types, which are divided into four "families." The families are: high clouds, middle clouds, low clouds, and clouds with extensive vertical development. The first three families are further classified according to the way they are formed. Clouds formed by vertical currents in unstable air are *cumulus* meaning *accumulation* or *heap*; they are characterized by their lumpy, billowy appearance. Clouds formed by the cooling of a stable layer are *stratus* meaning *stratified* or *layered*; they are characterized by their uniform, sheetlike appearance. In addition to the above, the prefix *nimbo-* or the suffix *-nimbus* means raincloud. Thus stratified clouds from which rain is falling are *nimbostratus*. A heavy, swelling cumulus type cloud which produces precipitation is a *cumulonimbus*. Clouds broken into fragments are often identified by adding the suffix *-fractus*; for example, fragmentary cumulus is *cumulus fractus*.

The high cloud family is cirriform and includes cirrus, cirrocumulus, and cirrostratus. They are composed almost entirely of ice crystals. The height of the bases of these clouds ranges from about 16,500 to 45,000 feet in middle latitudes. Figures 45 through 47 are photographs of high clouds.

Cirrus
Cirrus are thin, featherlike ice crystal clouds in patches or narrow bands. Larger ice crystals often trail downward in well-defined wisps called "Mares tails." Wispy, cirruslike, these contain no significant icing or turbulence.

Cirrocumulus
Cirrocumulus are thin clouds, the individual elements appearing as small white flakes or patches of cotton. May contain highly supercooled water droplets. Some turbulence and icing.

Cirrostratus
Cirrostratus is a thin whitish cloud layer appearing like a sheet or veil. Cloud elements are diffuse, sometimes partially striated or fibrous. Owing to their ice crystal makeup, these clouds are associated with halos—large luminous circles surrounding the sun or moon. No turbulence and little if any icing. The greatest problem flying in cirriform clouds is restriction to visibility. They can make the strict use of instruments mandatory.

In the middle cloud family are the altostratus, altocumulus, and nimbostratus clouds. These clouds are primarily water, much of which may be supercooled. The height of the bases of these clouds ranges from about 6,500 to 23,000 feet in middle latitudes. Figures 48 through 52 are photographs of middle clouds.

ALIGNING DICTIONARY ENTRIES AS HANGING INDENTS

In this project, you set tab stops and use indents to format a dictionary of terms used in home building.

Homeowner's Glossary of Building Terms[1]

A   **Acoustical Tile**   Special tile for walls and ceilings made of mineral, wood, vegetable fibers, cork, or metal. Its purpose is to control sound volume while providing cover.

Air Duct   Pipes that carry warm air and cold air to rooms and back to furnace or air conditioning system.

Ampere   The rate of flow of electricity through electric wires.

Apron   A paved area, such as the juncture of a driveway with the street or with a garage entrance.

B   **Backfill**   The gravel or earth replaced in the space around a building wall after foundations are in place.

Balusters   Upright supports of a balustrade rail.

Balustrade   A row of balusters topped by a rail, edging a balcony or a staircase.

Baseboard   A board along the floor against walls and partitions to hide gaps.

Batt   Insulation in the form of a blanket, rather than loose filling.

Batten   Small thin strips covering joints between wider boards on exterior building surfaces.

Beam   One of the principal horizontal wood or steel members of a building.

Bearing Wall   A wall that supports a floor or roof of a building.

Bib or Bibcock   A water faucet to which a hose may be attached, also called a hose bib or sill cock.

Bleeding   Seeping of resin or gum from lumber. This term is also used in referring to the process of drawing air from water pipes.

Brace   A piece of wood or other material used to form a triangle and stiffen some part of a structure.

Braced Framing   Construction technique using posts and cross-bracing for greater rigidity.

Brick Veneer   Brick used as the outer surface of a framed wall.

Bridging   Small wood or metal pieces placed diagonally between floor joists.

Building Paper   Heavy paper used in walls or roofs to dampproof.

Built-Up Roof   A roofing material applied in sealed, waterproof layers, where there is only a slight slope to the roof.

Butt Joint   Joining point of two pieces of wood or molding.

Bx Cable   Electricity cable wrapped in rubber with a flexible steel outer covering.

---

[1]U.S. Department of Housing and Urban Development, Washington, DC 20410

FORMATTING A TITLE PAGE

In this project, you format a two-page title page for a book on North American Indians.

Procedures Used
■ Changing margins, base fonts, and letter spacing.

Text Files Needed
■ INDIANS.WP5

Formats
① Enter a code for left and right margins of   inch.
② Enter a code for a top margin of 2 inches and a bottom margin of 1 inch.
③ Enter a base font code for 30-point typeface.
④ Enter a code to change letter spacing to 150 percent of optimal.
⑤ Enter a base font code of 10-point typeface. Also, enter a code to return letter spacing to optimal.
⑥ Align flush right.

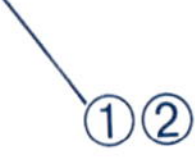

Handbook of North American Indians

FORMATTING A TITLE PAGE, CON'T

In this project, you format a title page following the designer's specifications.

Formats

① Enter a code for a top margin of 1 inches and a bottom margin of 1 inch. Enter a code for a left margin of 1 inches and a right margin of 1 inch. Enter a code to change letter spacing to 150 percent of optimal.

② Enter a base font code for 42-point type. Enter a code to change letter spacing to optimal.

③ Enter a base font code for 10-point type.

④ Specify an italic typestyle.

⑤ Enter a code to change letter spacing to 150 percent of optimal.

Tip

■ The figure box below the volume editor's name has been added using WordPerfect's graphics command. It indicates where an illustration should be placed.

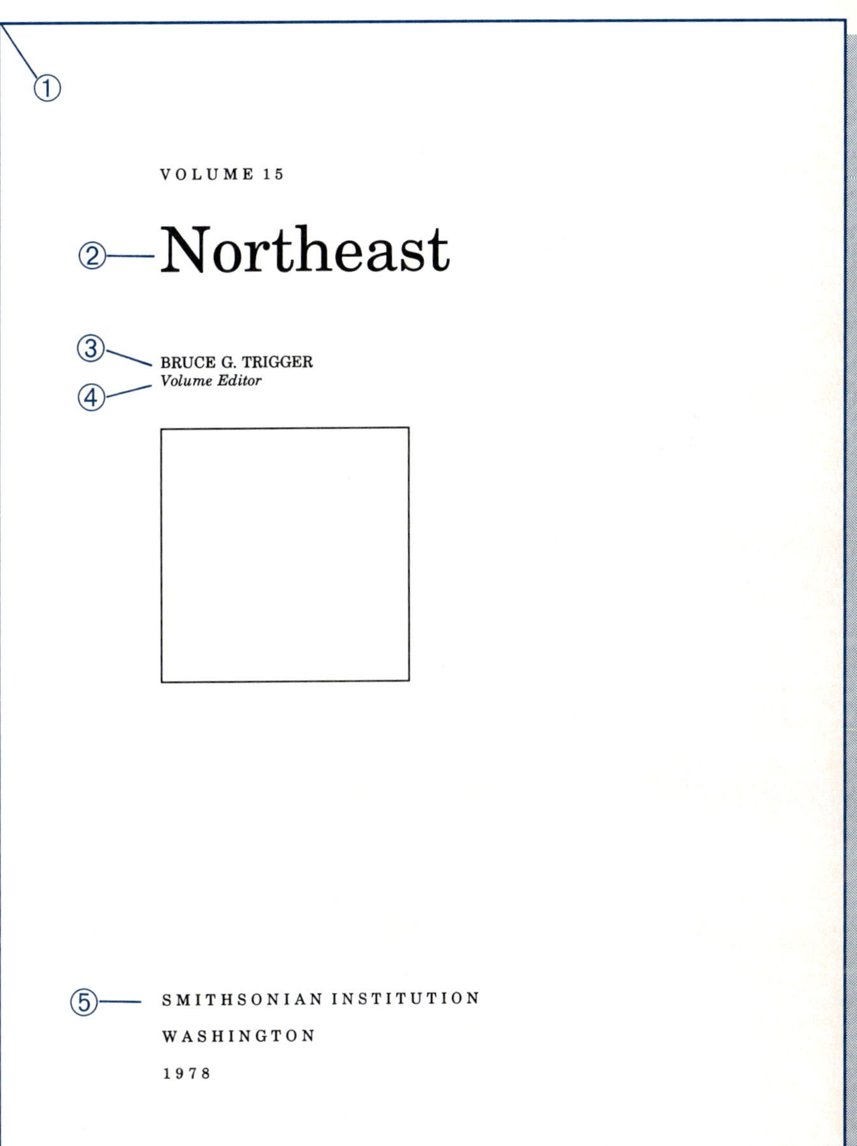

THE DTP ADVISOR NEWSLETTER

In this project, you align and indent text and subheads throughout the newsletter.

Procedures Used
- Setting tab stops.
- Indenting text.
- Aligning text.

Text Files Needed
- ADVISOR.WP5

Formats

① Enter a tab code that contains only two left-aligned tab settings, one at the left margin and one at 1 pica (which you enter by typing **1/6"**).

② Enter a code to turn widow/orphan protection on.

③ Center the newsletter's title.

④ Enter a left justification code in front of each of the four article headlines and the "*Staff*" heading at the end of the document.

⑤ Enter a full justification code after each of the four article headlines and the "*Staff*" heading.

⑥ Indent each of the four headlines and the "*Staff*" heading.

Tip
- You enter a tab stop at 1 pica by typing **1/6"** because 1 inch contains 6 picas. WordPerfect automatically does the division for you and displays 12p or .167 inch.

THE *dtp* ADVISOR

FaceLift For WordPerfect

Bitstream Inc. today announced version 1.5 of Bitstream® FaceLift™ for WordPerfect.® FaceLift brings enhanced font support to WordPerfect 5.0 and 5.1. The new FaceLift version 1.5 will create high-quality fonts on-the-fly for popular dot-matrix and inkjet printers—like the HP® DeskJet,® Canon BubbleJet and the IBM® ExecuJet—in addition to the existing on-the-fly support for the Hewlett-Packard LaserJet® series of printers. FaceLift 1.5 for WordPerfect will be available in the spring of 1991.

In addition to 13 typeface outlines provided in the original FaceLift package, FaceLift 1.5 for WordPerfect will also ship with three Symbol typefaces: ITC Zapf Dingbats® Symbol Proportional and Symbol Monospaced. Users will be able to access a total of 698 characters from the Bitstream International Character Set and from these three Symbols typefaces.

FaceLift 1.5 for WordPerfect is an easy-to-use utility that allows users to print high-quality fonts in any size from 2 to 500 point (in quarter point increments) without ever having to leave the application. The fonts are generated at print time, so the need for stored bit-map fonts is eliminated. Based on Bitstream Speedo™ technology, FaceLift sends characters to printers in both graphics mode (laser, inkjet and dot-matrix printers) and as HP soft fonts (laser printers only). Users have full control over the number and size of soft fonts to be downloaded, depending on the memory available in the printer.

"We are very excited that FaceLift 1.5 for WordPerfect will provide dot-matrix and inkjet users with the same high typographic quality and capabilities that HP LaserJet users have enjoyed with Bitstream type," stated Doug Lloyd, Executive Director at WordPerfect. "That, and the addition of the three new Symbol typefaces makes FaceLift a great companion for WordPerfect."

First-time users can purchase FaceLift 1.5 for WordPerfect for a suggested U.S. list price of $99. Current users of FaceLift 1.0 for WordPerfect can upgrade to version 1.5 for $24.95. In addition to the 16 typefaces included free with FaceLift, users can purchase add-on fonts from the Bitstream Library of 52 typeface packages. Also available is the FaceLift Companion Value Pack, a selection of 24 text and headline faces for a suggested U.S. list price $199.

FaceLift 1.5 for WordPerfect is the newest member of the Bitstream FaceLift product line. The initial product, FaceLift for Windows,™ shipped in August of 1990. All FaceLift products can share Bitstream typefaces (in Speedo format) stored in a single common subdirectory.

FaceLift for Wordperfect was developed in conjunction with LaserTools Corporation, a privately held company based in Emeryville, CA. LaserTools is a developer of innovative printing enhancement products—tools for printer sharing, printer control, printer acceleration, and font management.

An industry leader in typographic quality and innovative technology, Bitstream licenses fonts and related software to more than 420 hardware manufacturers and software developers worldwide. Its line of retail products is distributed by an extensive network of dealers in the United States and in 18 nations worldwide.

For more information, contact:
Bitstream Inc.
215 First Street
Cambridge, MA 02142-1270
(617) 497-6222

Postscript in a Cartridge

Columns

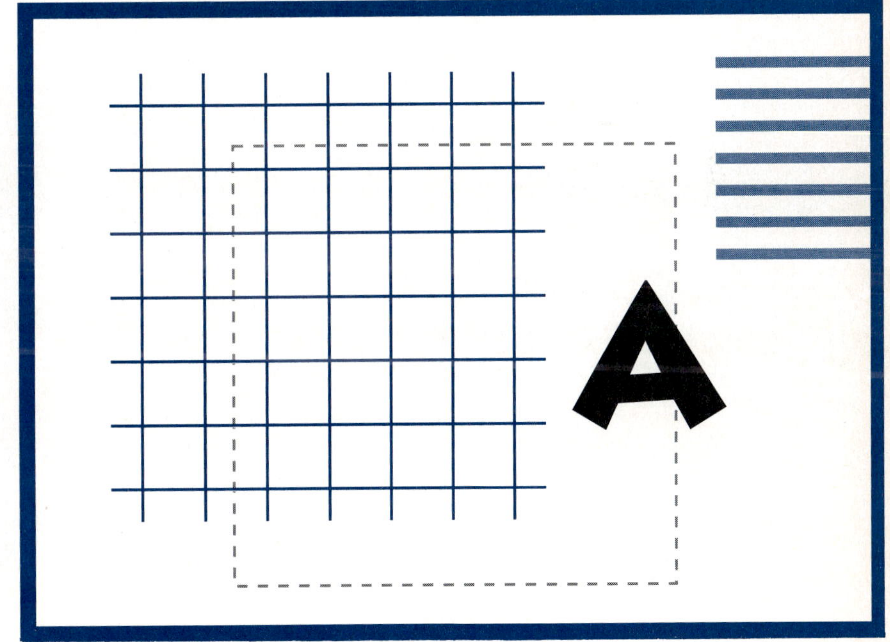

Columns: Newspaper-Style

After completing this topic, you should be able to:
- Describe newspaper-style columns
- Format text in newspaper-style columns in your own documents
- Edit text in columns

▶ T U T O R I A L

In this tutorial, you enter and edit text in newspaper-style columns. When you are finished, your document should look similar to the illustration "Newspaper Columns."

GETTING STARTED

1. Retrieve the NEWSCOL1.WP5 document and enter your name.

DEFINING COLUMNS

2. Move the cursor to the top of the document.
3. Press **Alt**-**F7** to display the Columns/Tables menu.
4. Press **C** for *Columns*.
5. Press **D** for *Define* to display the Text Column Definition screen and menu. The default column settings specify two columns with .5 inch separating them. This default setting is the one you want to use.
6. Press **0** (zero) to return to the Columns/Tables menu.

TURNING COLUMNS ON

7. Press **O** for *On* to turn columns on.
8. Scroll down through the text to reform it into columns. (If the columns are not displayed side by side on your screen, a default setting has been changed. To restore it, refer to the KEY/Strokes box "Turning the Column Display On and Off.")

FINISHING UP

9. Save and print the document.

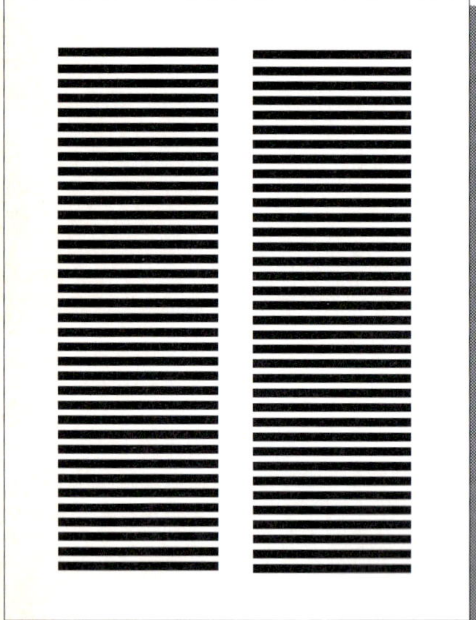

Newspaper Columns

```
Name:
Date: July 26, 1991
Filename: NEWSCOL1.WP5
Topic: Newspaper-style Columns

Newspaper-style columns (also called
snaking columns) are those you see in
newspapers, newsletters, and books. Text
flows from column to column. As you enter
text, it gradually fills the first column. When
that column is full, text flows into the next
column. When the last column on the page
is full, text starts to fill the first column on
the next page. If you add text to or delete
text from any of the columns, the remaining
text adjusts to keep the columns full.

Many publications are designed with text in
a single column. However, double columns
may accommodate more text per page. The
shorter lines allow you to use a smaller type
and less spacing between lines without
losing readability.

G:\NEWSCOL1.WP5
```

```
words. If the document is hyphe
lines will end in hyphens. All
detract from one's ease of read
space between columns should be
enough to visually separate the
reading but not so great that t
look like completely separate e
the page.

When you are laying out columns
step is to calculate their widt
spaces (gutters) between them.
follow these steps;

1.  Determine the number of col
    say you want three columns.

2.  Determine the space between
    columns. Let's say it is 2

3.  Determine the width of the
    Let's say it is 40 picas.

4.  Calculate the total space f
    Doc 1 Pg 1 Ln 1" Pos 1"
```

▷ D E S K T O P   P U B L I S H I N G   C O N C E P T S

Newspaper-style columns (also called ***snaking columns***) are those you see in newspapers, newsletters, and books (and in the section you are now reading). As you enter text, it gradually fills the first column. When that column is full, text flows into the next column. When the last column on the page is full, text starts to fill the first column on the next page. If you add text to or delete text from any of the columns, the following text moves up or down in the columns.

Many publications are designed with text in a single column. However, double columns may accommodate more text per page. The shorter lines allow you to use a smaller type and less spacing between lines without losing readability.

The type page can be wider when you use two columns. With 12-point type, the type page should be no wider than 27 picas. Printing on 8½-by-11-inch paper with 1-inch margins gives a line length of 6½ inches or about 39 picas, too long to be read comfortably. When set in two columns, the text page can be specified as 41 picas. Even with 1 pica separating the columns (the space between the columns is called a ***gutter***), each column is 20 picas, giving a total type measure of 40 picas. With three columns of 13 picas each, you have 39 picas of text. Also, the space between columns should be large enough to visually separate them when reading but not so much that the columns look like completely separate elements on the page.

You should generally use no more than two or three columns at most, because columns that are too narrow cause serious reading problems—frequent line breaks, few words to the line, among other visual annoyances. In addition, if text is justified, there may be frequent large gaps between words. If the document is hyphenated, many lines will end in hyphens. All of these detract from one's ease of reading.

When you are laying out columns, the first step is to calculate their width and the spaces (gutters) between them. To do so, follow these steps.

1. Determine the number of columns. Let's say you want three columns.
2. Determine the space between the columns. Let's say it is 1 pica.

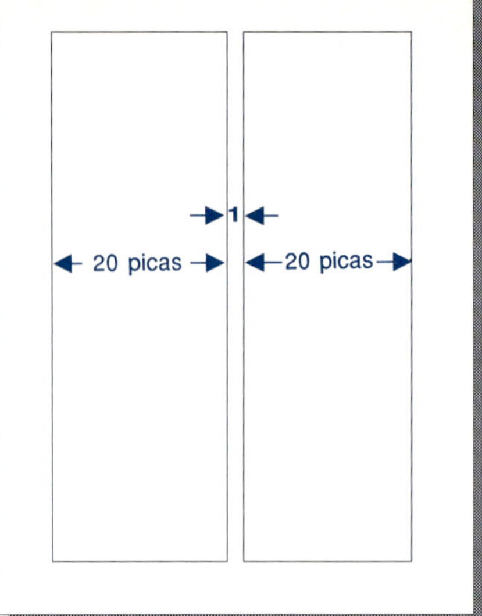

Two Columns

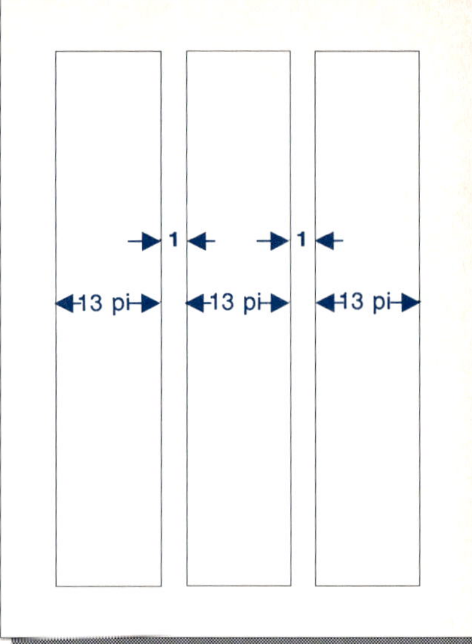

Three Columns

3. Determine the width of the type page. Let's say it is 41 picas.
4. Calculate the total space for column gutters. The number of gutters is always 1 less than the number of columns. For example, for three columns having 1 picas between them, the total gutter space is 2.
5. Subtract the total gutter space calculated in Step 4 from the width of the type page to calcu-

late the space available for columns. For example, subtract 2 picas for gutters from the 41 pica type page width to get 39 picas available for columns themselves.
6. Divide the total space available for columns calculated in Step 5 by the number of columns. For example, divide 39 picas by 3 and you get column widths of 13 picas each.

► W O R D P E R F E C T   P R O C E D U R E S

To format text in more than one column, you follow two basic steps:

1. Define the columns by entering a column definition code above where you want columns to begin. You can do this before or after you enter text.
2. Turn columns on by entering a column on code below the definition code.

→ K E Y / S t r o k e s

Defining Text Columns and Turning Them On

1. Move the cursor to where columns are to begin.
2. Press **Alt-F7** to display the Columns/Tables menu.
3. Either: Press **C** for *Columns* and then **D** for *Define* to display the Text Column Definition screen and menu.

Text Column Definition Screen and Menu
The Text Column Definition screen and menu allow you to specify the type of columns and their spacing on the page.

```
Text Column Definition

   1 - Type                               Newspaper

   2 - Number of Columns                  2

   3 - Distance Between Columns

   4 - Margins

   Column    Left      Right     Column    Left      Right
     1:      1"        4"          13:
     2:      4.5"      7.5"        14:
     3:                            15:
     4:                            16:
     5:                            17:
     6:                            18:
     7:                            19:
     8:                            20:
     9:                            21:
    10:                            22:
    11:                            23:
    12:                            24:

Selection: 0
```

COLUMN DEFINITION MENU CHOICES

1 *Type* specifies newspaper, parallel, or parallel-with-block-protect columns.
- **1** *Newspaper* allows text to flow from the bottom of one column to the top of the next.
- **2** *Parallel* is for side-by-side paragraphs. Any or all of the columns can be longer than a page.
- **3** *Parallel with **Block** Protect* prevents soft page breaks from splitting a paragraph. If any column contains a paragraph that extends past the bottom margin, the group of parallel paragraphs is moved to the top of the next page.

2 *Number of Columns* specifies the number of columns and sets the default margins for columns of equal widths.

3 *Distance Between Columns* specifies the distance between columns. The default is .5 inches.

4 *Margins* changes the default margins that are automatically suggested when you enter the number of columns. Enter the left and right margins for each column, and then press **F7** to return to the Columns/Tables menu. You can set the left margin of the first column and the right margin of the last column to set columns wider or narrower than the regular document margins. The margin settings made on the Text Column Definition screen take precedence over the margins set for the document.

Entering or Editing Text in Columns

You can use the commands described in the table "Column Cursor Movement Commands" to move between and around the columns when entering or editing text. The only new command you need to know is **Ctrl-Enter**. This is similar to entering a hard page break in single-column text. Pressing **Enter** by itself moves the cursor down within a column. When you want to start a new column, you press **Ctrl-Enter**. If you do so in existing text, this command moves the cursor, and any text to its right, to the next column.

COLUMN CURSOR MOVEMENT COMMANDS

Action	Press
Start a new column	**Ctrl-Enter**
Move the cursor to the previous column	**Ctrl-Home**, ←
Move the cursor to the next column	**Ctrl-Home**, →
Move the cursor to the first column	**Ctrl-Home**, **Home**, ←
Move the cursor to the last column	**Ctrl-Home**, **Home**, →

If you set tab stops while using newspaper-style columns, set relative tabs. This way, the tabs are set the same in each column. If you set absolute tab stops, they are set relative to the left edge of the page, not to the column margins.

Turning Columns On or Off

Once columns are defined, you can turn them on or off anywhere in the document below the definition code. When you turn them back on, you do not have to define them again unless you want to change the column layout. A column definition code affects all columns turned on below it to the end of the document or to the next column definition code.

➔ **K E Y / S t r o k e s**

Turning Column Mode On and Off Below a Definition Code

1. Move the cursor anywhere in the document below a column definition code.
2. Either: Press **Alt-F7**, then **C** for *Column*, then press **O** for *On* or **f** for *Off.*

   Or: Pull down the Layout menu, select *Columns*, and then select *On* or *Off.*

If you have a long document and want to format only part of it in multiple columns, you can avoid confusion if you follow these steps:

1. Define the columns but don't turn them on.
2. Move the cursor down to where you want the columns to end, and enter a code to turn columns off.
3. Move the cursor up to where you want columns to begin and enter a code to turn the columns on. When you now move the cursor down

through the document, the text below the column off code will not be displayed in columns.

Column Display

Columns are always printed side by side, but you can change the way they are displayed on the screen. They can be displayed either side by side, just as they print, or on separate pages. To switch between these two displays, you change a default setting. You can scroll through and edit the document more quickly when the columns are displayed on separate pages.

KEY/Strokes

Turning the Column Display On and Off

1. Press **Shift-F1** to display the Setup menu.
2. Press **D** for *Display* to display the Display menu.
3. Press **E** for *Edit-Screen Options*.
4. Press **S** for *Side-by-side Columns Display*.
5. Press **Y** to display the columns side by side or **N** to display columns in a single column.

NEWSPAPER COLUMN TIP

When aligning text in columns, you can change the distance between columns on the screen by changing the display pitch. This is helpful if columns overlap.

➤ EXERCISES

EXERCISE 1

PRINTING A DOCUMENT IN THREE COLUMNS

In this exercise, you format a document in three columns and make a printout. **Do not save this version of the document**.

1. Retrieve the NEWSCOL1.WP5 document that you formatted in the tutorial at the beginning of this topic.
2. Delete the existing column definition code. Then, follow the instructions in the KEY/Strokes box "Defining Text Columns and Turning Them On" to format it in three newspaper-style columns of equal width.
3. Print the document and then clear the screen without saving it.

EXERCISE 2

EDITING COLUMNS OF TEXT

In this exercise, you edit and format text that is formatted in two columns.

1. Retrieve the NEWSCOL1.WP5 document that you formatted in Exercise 1.
2. Use the keystrokes described in the table "Column Cursor Movement Commands" to move the cursor through the document and add or delete its contents or formats as you see fit. Feel free to experiment. Don't worry about the changes you make. For example, insert or delete paragraphs or change tab stop settings for the indented items in the two numbered lists.
3. Save and print the document.

Columns: Parallel-Style

After completing this topic, you should be able to:
- Describe parallel-style columns and when to use them
- Use parallel-style columns in your own documents

►TUTORIAL

In this tutorial, you enter and edit text in parallel-style columns. When you are finished, your document should look similar to the illustration "Parallel-Style Columns."

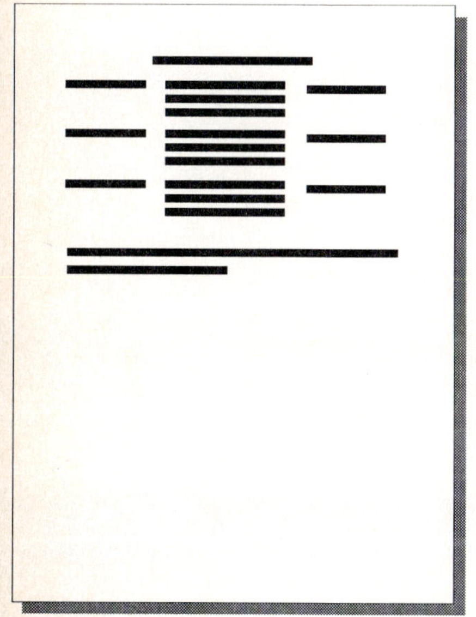

Parallel-Style Columns

GETTING STARTED

1. Retrieve the PARCOLS1.WP5 document and enter your name.

DEFINING THE COLUMNS

2. Move the cursor to the blank line above the name "*Dennis Hogan.*"
3. Press **Alt-F7** to display the Columns/Tables menu.
4. Press **C** for *Columns*.
5. Press **D** for *Define* to display the Text Column Definition screen and menu.
6. Press **T** for *Type*.
7. Press **P** for *Parallel*.
8. Press **N** for *Number of Columns*.
9. Type **3** and then press **Enter**. The prompt reads *Selection:*. Notice that all of the margin settings are set automatically.
10. Press **0** (zero) to return to the Columns/Tables menu.
11. Press **O** for *On* to turn the columns on and return to the document. The status line displays *Col 1*.

FORMATTING THE FIRST ROW OF PARALLEL COLUMNS

12. Move the cursor to the space following the name "*Dennis Hogan*" and press **Ctrl-Enter** to move the cursor and the text following it to the next column.
13. Move the cursor to the end of the ZIP code line and press **Ctrl-Enter** to move the cursor and the text following it to the next column.
14. Move the cursor to the end of the first phone number and press **Ctrl-Enter** to move the cursor and the text following it back to the first column.

FORMATTING THE OTHER ROWS OF PARALLEL COLUMNS

15. Repeat Steps 12 through 14 after moving the cursor to the appropriate position in each of the next two rows of data.

TURNING COLUMNS OFF

16. Move the cursor under the "*N*" in "*Note*" and press **Alt**-**F7** to display the Columns/Tables menu.
17. Press **C** for *Columns*.
18. Press **f** for *Off*.

FINISHING UP

19. Save and print the document. Your results should match the figure "The Parallel-Style Columns Displayed on Your Screen" except for line breaks in the last paragraph.

The Parallel-Style Columns Displayed on Your Screen

You format this document in this tutorial.

```
Name:
Date: July 26, 1991
Filename: PARCOLS1.WP5
Topic: Parallel Columns

                        NAMES AND ADDRESSES

Dennis Hogan            Lakeside Industries          716-555-1212
                        100 Elm Street
                        Westfield, NY  10010

Nancy Benjamin          Wordcraft, Inc.              403-555-1212
                        52 Seneca Road
                        Oakland, CA  90020

Liz Kendall             Office Tech Inc.             313-555-1212
                        15500 Main Street
                        Muncie, IN  47030

Note:   This list of names and addresses is current as of January 1, 1992.  Any c
found by calling Dennis Hogan.



A:\PARCOLS1.WP5                          Doc 1 Pg 1 Ln 1" Pos 1"
```

▶ D E S K T O P   P U B L I S H I N G   C O N C E P T S

Parallel-style columns (also called *side-by-side columns*) align related text side by side. This style is used when showing the same text in two languages; annotating a script with marginal notes; or creating tables of text for schedules, product descriptions, and the like. Text does not flow from one column to another, as in newspaper-style columns. You enter and edit text in each column independently. The text in each column wraps within that column. If the text in one column is longer than the text on the same row in adjacent columns, all rows below are moved down so they start on their own line. Parallel columns are ideal when you want to use a two-column layout with headings in one column and body text in the other. When headings are arranged like this in relation to the text, they are called ***side heads***.

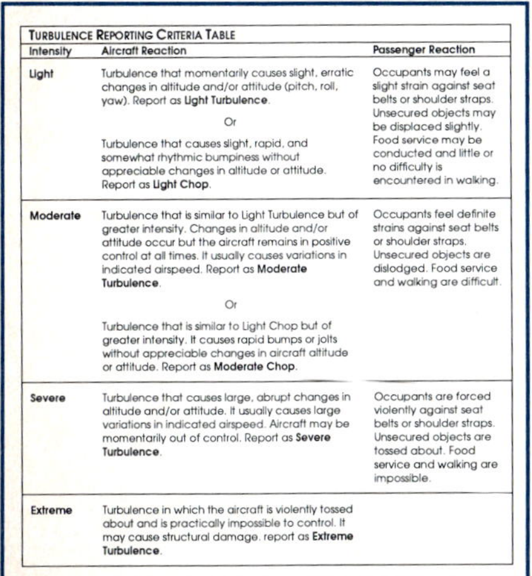

TURBULENCE REPORTING CRITERIA TABLE

Intensity	Aircraft Reaction	Passenger Reaction
Light	Turbulence that momentarily causes slight, erratic changes in altitude and/or attitude (pitch, roll, yaw). Report as **Light Turbulence**. Or Turbulence that causes slight, rapid, and somewhat rhythmic bumpiness without appreciable changes in altitude or attitude. Report as **Light Chop**.	Occupants may feel a slight strain against seat belts or shoulder straps. Unsecured objects may be displaced slightly. Food service may be conducted and little or no difficulty is encountered in walking.
Moderate	Turbulence that is similar to Light Turbulence but of greater intensity. Changes in altitude and/or attitude occur but the aircraft remains in positive control at all times. It usually causes variations in indicated airspeed. Report as **Moderate Turbulence**. Or Turbulence that is similar to Light Chop but of greater intensity. It causes rapid bumps or jolts without appreciable changes in aircraft altitude or attitude. Report as **Moderate Chop**.	Occupants feel definite strains against seat belts or shoulder straps. Unsecured objects are dislodged. Food service and walking are difficult.
Severe	Turbulence that causes large, abrupt changes in altitude and/or attitude. It usually causes large variations in indicated airspeed. Aircraft may be momentarily out of control. Report as **Severe Turbulence**.	Occupants are forced violently against seat belts or shoulder straps. Unsecured objects are tossed about. Food service and walking are impossible.
Extreme	Turbulence in which the aircraft is violently tossed about and is practically impossible to control. It may cause structural damage. report as **Extreme Turbulence**.	

Example of Parallel-Style Columns

Text Column Definition Screen and Menu
The Text Column Definition screen and menu allow you to specify the type of columns and their spacing on the page.

Parallel-style columns are created just like newspaper-style columns; you just make different menu selections. The basic steps are:

1. Define the columns by entering a column definition code above where you want columns to begin. You can do this before or after you enter text.
2. Turn columns on by entering a Column On code below the definition code.

Defining Text Columns and Turning Them On

1. Move the cursor to where columns are to begin.
2. Press **Alt-F7** to display the Columns/Tables menu.
3. Either: Press **C** for *Columns* and then **D** for *Define* to display the Text Column Definition screen and menu.

   Or: Pull down the Layout menu, select *Columns*, and then select *Define*.

4. Enter any of the settings described in the table "Column Definition Menu Choices," then press **F7** to return to the Columns/Tables menu.
5. Press **O** for *On* to turn the columns on and return to the document.

```
Text Column Definition

    1 - Type                              Newspaper

    2 - Number of Columns                 2

    3 - Distance Between Columns

    4 - Margins

    Column    Left      Right     Column    Left      Right
      1:      1"        4"          13:
      2:      4.5"      7.5"        14:
      3:                            15:
      4:                            16:
      5:                            17:
      6:                            18:
      7:                            19:
      8:                            20:
      9:                            21:
     10:                            22:
     11:                            23:
     12:                            24:

Selection: 0
```

COLUMN DEFINITION MENU CHOICES

1 Type specifies newspaper, parallel, or parallel-with-block-protect columns.

- *1 Newspaper* allows text to flow from the bottom of one column to the top of the next.

- **2** *Parallel* is for side-by-side paragraphs. Any or all of the columns can be longer than a page.
- **3** *Parallel with* **Block** *Protect* prevents soft page breaks from splitting a paragraph. If any column contains a paragraph that extends past the bottom margin, the group of parallel paragraphs is moved to the top of the next page.

2 *Number of Columns* specifies the number of columns and sets the default margins for columns of equal widths.

3 *Distance Between Columns* specifies the distance between columns. The default is .5 inch.

4 *Margins* changes the default margins that are automatically suggested when you enter the number of columns. Enter the left and right margins for each column, and then press **F7** to return to the Columns/Tables menu. You can set the left margin of the first column and the right margin of the last column to set columns wider or narrower than the regular document margins. The margin settings made on the Text Column Definition screen take precedence over the margins set for the document.

Entering or Editing Text in Columns

You can use the commands described in the table "Column Cursor Movement Commands" to move between and around the columns when entering or editing text. The only new command you need to know is **Ctrl-Enter**. This is similar to entering a hard page break in single-column text. Pressing **Enter** by itself moves the cursor down within a column. When you want to start a new column, you press **Ctrl-Enter**. If you do so in existing text, this command moves the cursor, and any text to its right, to the next column.

COLUMN CURSOR MOVEMENT COMMANDS

Action	Press
Start a new column	**Ctrl-Enter**
Move the cursor to the previous column	**Ctrl-Home**, ←
Move the cursor to the next column	**Ctrl-Home**, →
Move the cursor to the first column	**Ctrl-Home**, **Home**, ←
Move the cursor to the last column	**Ctrl-Home**, **Home**, →

If you set tab stops while using parallel-style columns, set relative tabs. This way the tabs are set the same in each column. If you set absolute tab stops, they are relative to the left edge of the page, not the column margins.

Turning Columns On or Off

Once columns are defined, you can turn them on and off anywhere in the document below the definition code. When you turn them back on, you do not have to define them again unless you want to change the column layout. A column definition code affects all columns turned on below it to the end of the document or to the next column definition code.

Turning Column Mode On and Off Below a Definition Code

1. Move the cursor anywhere in the document below a column definition code.
2. Either: Press **Alt-F7** then **C** for *Column*, then press **O** for *On* or **f** for *Off*.

   Or:　　Pull down the Layout menu, select *Columns* and then select *On* or *Off*.

Column Display

Columns are always printed side by side, but you can change the way they are displayed on the screen. They can either be displayed side by side, just as they print, or on separate pages. To switch between these two displays, you change a default setting. When columns are displayed on separate pages, you can scroll through and edit the document more quickly.

Turning the Column Display On and Off

1. Press **Shift-F1** to display the Setup menu.
2. Press **D** for *Display* to display the Display menu.
3. Press **E** for *Edit-Screen Options*.
4. Press **S** for *Side-by-side Columns Display*.
5. Press **Y** to display them side by side or **N** to display them in a single column.

► E X E R C I S E S

EXERCISE 1

FORMATTING TEXT USING PARALLEL-STYLE COLUMNS

In this exercise, you define parallel-style columns for a document, then turn them on and off as needed to format sections in two equal parallel columns.

1. Retrieve the PARCOLS2.WP5 document and enter your name.
2. Move the cursor to the top of the document and follow the instructions in the KEY/Strokes box "Defining Text Columns and Turning Them On" to define two parallel-style columns of equal width.
3. Move the cursor to the section headed "*Omission*" then move it under the "*B*" in "*Biased*" in this section of the document. Follow the

instructions in the KEY/Strokes box "Turning Column Mode On and Off Below a Definition Code" to turn the columns on.

4. Format the first section in parallel-style columns as shown in the figure "The PARCOLS2 Document." (You may have to reveal codes and delete any extra hard carriage return codes that keep columns from beginning on the same row.)

5. Move the cursor to the beginning of the heading *"Equal Treatment"* and turn columns off.

6. Move the cursor under the *"B"* in *"Biased"* in this section of the document. Follow the instructions in the KEY/Strokes box "Turning Column Mode On and Off Below the Definition Code" to turn the columns on again.

7. Format the second section in columns as shown in the figure "The PARCOLS2 Document." (There are a few lines on the second page which are not shown in the figure.)

8. Save and print the document.

The PARCOLS2 Document

Name:
Date: September 11, 1991
Filename: PARCOLS2.WP5
Topic: Parallel Columns

Sexism in writing includes sins of omission as well as sins of commission and bias in thought and concept as well as language. The portrayal of roles and life situations as exclusively masculine or exclusively feminine or the more subtle omission of women as participants in the action is just as much bias as is the general use he or man to characterize all human beings. These guidelines contain "checklists" of things to look for in reading or editing a manuscript as well as specific kinds of expressions to change or avoid.

Omission

Check the descriptive and illustrative material--the example used to illustrate concepts, and the description of processes, social structures, and typical situations. Here are some examples of what to look for, accompanied by some possible unbiased alternatives.

Biased	**Unbiased**
The pioneers crossed the desert with their women, children, and possessions.	Pioneer families crossed the desert carrying all their possessions.
Radium was discovered by a woman, Marie Curie.	Marie Curie discovered radium.
When setting up his experiment, the researcher must always check his sample for error.	When setting up an experiment, a researcher must always check for sampling error.

Equal Treatment

Check the use of adjectives and modifiers: Do those used for women consistently create a negative impression or betray a patronizing attitude? Are women mentioned consistently as an afterthought?

Biased	**Unbiased**
Though a woman, she ran the business effectively.	She ran the business effectively.
The little girls played with the boys.	The girls played with the boys; the children played; the little girls played with the little boys.

FORMATTING SIDE HEADS USING PARALLEL-STYLE COLUMNS

In this exercise, you use parallel-style columns to print side heads in one column and body text in another.

1. Retrieve the PARCOLS3.WP5 document and enter your name.
2. Move the cursor to the top of the document, then follow the instructions in the KEY/Strokes box "Defining Text Columns and Turning Them On" to define two parallel columns. Set the margins for the left column at 1 inch and 2½ inches and the right column at 3 inches and 7½ inches. (Pressing **Enter** moves the cursor from setting to setting in the margin section.)
3. Move the cursor to the first character in "DESKTOP PUBLISHING CONCEPTS" and follow the instructions in the KEY/Strokes box "Turning Column Mode On and Off Below the Definition Code" to turn the columns on.
4. Format the document as shown in the figure "The PARCOLS3 Document." (The heading "*Hands-On Exercises*" on page 2 should also be formatted as a side head.) You will have to reveal codes and delete some hard carriage return codes in each column to align the text in parallel columns with each other.
5. Save and print the document.

Name:
Date: September 11, 1991
Filename: PARCOLS3.WP5
Topic: Parallel Columns

D E S K T O P P U B L I S H I N G CONCEPTS	Parallel-style columns (also called side-by-side columns) align related text side by side. This style is used when showing the same text in two languages; annotating a script with marginal notes; or creating tables of text for schedules, product descriptions, and the like. Text does not flow from one column to another, as in newspaper-style columns. You enter and edit text in each column independently. The text in each column wraps within that column. If the text in one column is longer than the text on the same row in adjacent columns, all rows below are moved down so they start on their own line. Parallel-style columns are ideal when you want to use a two column layout so headings are in one column and body text in another.
W O R D P E R F E C T PROCEDURES	Parallel-style columns are created just like newspaper-style columns, you just make different menu selections. The four basic steps are
	1. Define the columns by entering a column definition code above where you want columns to begin. You can do this before or after you enter text.
	2. Turn columns on by entering a Column On code below the definition code.
	3. Enter or edit text. You can use the commands described in the table "Column Cursor Movement Commands" to move between and around the columns when entering or editing text. Pressing **Enter** moves the cursor down within a column. When you want to start a new column, parallel to the one you are currently entering, you press **Ctrl-Enter**.
	4. Turn columns off if you want to enter single-column text below the columns. Once columns are defined, you can turn them on or off anywhere in the document. When you turn them back on, you do not have to define them again unless you want to change the column layout. Column definition codes affect all columns turned on below them to the end of the document or to the next column definition code.
PARALLEL-STYLE COLUMN TIPS	■ If you want to set tab stops while using newspaper- or parallel-style columns, set relative tabs. This way, the tabs are set the same in each column. If you set absolute tab stops, they are relative to the left edge of the page, not the column margins.

EXERCISE 3

EDITING COLUMNS OF TEXT

In this exercise, you edit text that is formatted in two columns.

1. Retrieve the PARCOLS3.WP5 document.
2. Use the keystrokes described in the table "Column Cursor Move-ment Commands" to move the cursor through the document and edit it. For example, set tab stops at .3 inch and indent all of the numbered and bulleted items.
3. Save and print the document.

- When aligning text in columns, you can change the distance between columns on the screen by changing the display pitch. This is helpful if columns overlap.
- To move or copy a parallel-with-block-protect-style column, block the *[BlockPro:On]* and *[BlockPro:Off]* codes along with the text. Do not use the *Tabular Column* selection on the Move menu to move text columns, or the text will not be retrieved correctly.

REVIEW

- In newspaper-style columns, text flows from the bottom of one column to the top of the next.
- In parallel-style columns, paragraphs are entered side by side.
- You can print text in more than one column by defining the columns and then turning them on.
- To start a new column, you press **Ctrl-Enter**.
- To move the cursor between columns, you press **Ctrl-Home** then the left or right arrow key.

QUESTIONS

TRUE/FALSE

T   F

1. Newspaper-style columns are best for aligning text side by side.

2. You have to define columns before you can turn them on.

3. When you define columns you must also specify where they begin and end.

4. You can use the Setup menu to specify if columns are displayed side by side on the screen or not.

5. Newspaper-style columns allow you to fit more text on the same page while retaining readability.

6. Every time you want to use columns in a document, you have to redefine them.

7. The space between columns is called the gutter margin.

8. Parallel-with-block-protect columns are the same as parallel-style columns but soft page breaks are prevented within a column entry.

9. Column margins do not have to be the same as the page margins.

10. When setting tab stops, you use relative tabs so they are the same in each column.

1. If you want text to flow smoothly from one column to the next, you use ___________-style columns.
2. If you want text aligned side by side, you use ___________-style columns.
3. Before you can use columns, you must first ___________ them and then ___________ them ___________.
4. To start a new column, you press ___________.
5. To move the cursor between columns, before you press the left or right arrow key, you press ___________.
6. A code to turn columns on must be positioned ___________the code that defines the columns.
7. If you want tab stops to be the same in each column, you set ___________tab stops.

MATCH THE COLUMNS

1. Newspaper-style columns	__ Keys you press before pressing the left or right arrow keys to move from one column to the next
2. Parallel-style columns	__ Keys you press to start a new column
3. **Ctrl**-**Enter**	__ Tab stops that will be the same in each column
4. **Ctrl**-**Home**	__ Text flows from one column to the next
5. Gutter margin	__ Text is aligned side by side
6. Relative tab stops	__ The space between columns

WRITE OUT THE ANSWERS

1. What two kinds of columns can you create? What is the difference between them?
2. List and describe the five basic steps you would follow to create a newspaper-style document.
3. When entering parallel-style columns, what command do you use to move the cursor and the text to its right to a new column?
4. Describe the steps you follow to calculate column widths.

PROJECTS

PROJECT 1

PRINTING A DOCUMENT USING NEWSPAPER-STYLE COLUMNS

In this project, you format a document using two newspaper-style columns. After retrieving the document, reveal codes and delete margin and tab stop codes that you may have entered in a previous project. Then use Search to locate and delete all margin release codes.

Procedures Used
- Formatting a document in newspaper-style columns.

Text Files Needed
- CLOUDS2.WP5

Formats
① Enter a column definition code to create two newspaper-style columns of equal widths. Then, enter a code to turn them on.

Clouds, to almost everyone, have some meaning. But to you as a pilot, clouds are your weather "signposts in the sky." They give you an indication of air motion, stability, and moisture. Clouds help you visualize weather conditions and potential weather hazards you might encounter in flight. Let's examine these "signposts" and how to identify them.

IDENTIFICATION
For identification purposes, you need be concerned only with the more basic cloud types, which are divided into four "families." The families are: high clouds, middle clouds, low clouds, and clouds with extensive vertical development. The first three families are further classified according to the way they are formed. Clouds formed by vertical currents in unstable air are *cumulus* meaning *accumulation* or *heap*; they are characterized by their lumpy, billowy appearance. Clouds formed by the cooling of a stable layer are *stratus* meaning *stratified* or *layered*; they are characterized by their uniform, sheetlike appearance. In addition to the above, the prefix *nimbo-* or the suffix *-nimbus* means raincloud. Thus stratified clouds from which rain is falling are *nimbostratus*. A heavy, swelling cumulus type cloud which produces precipitation is a *cumulonimbus*. Clouds broken into fragments are often identified by adding the suffix *-fractus*; for example, fragmentary cumulus is *cumulus fractus*.

HIGH CLOUDS
The high cloud family is cirriform and includes cirrus, cirrocumulus, and cirrostratus. They are composed almost entirely of ice crystals. The height of the bases of these clouds ranges from about 16,500 to 45,000 feet in middle latitudes. Figures 45 through 47 are photographs of high clouds.

Cirrus
Cirrus are thin, featherlike ice crystal clouds in patches or narrow bands. Larger ice crystals often trail downward in well defined wisps called "Mares tails." Wispy, cirruslike, these contain no significant icing or turbulence.

Cirrocumulus
Cirrocumulus are thin clouds, the individual elements appearing as small white flakes or patches of cotton. May contain highly supercooled water droplets. Some turbulence and icing.

Cirrostratus
Cirrostratus is a thin whitish cloud layer appearing like a sheet or veil. Cloud elements are diffuse, sometimes partially striated or fibrous. Owing to their ice crystal makeup, these clouds are associated with halos—large luminous circles surrounding the sun or moon. No turbulence and little if any icing. The greatest problem flying in cirriform clouds is restriction to visibility. They can make the strict use of instruments mandatory.

MIDDLE CLOUDS
In the middle cloud family are the altostratus, altocumulus, and nimbostratus clouds. These clouds are primarily water, much of which may be supercooled. The height of the bases of these clouds ranges from about 6,500 to 23,000 feet in middle latitudes. Figures 48 through 52 are photographs of middle clouds.

Altocumulus
Altocumulus are composed of white or gray-colored layers or patches of solid cloud. The cloud elements may have a waved or roll-like appearance. Some turbulence and small amount of icing.

Altostratus
Altostratus is a bluish veil or layer of clouds. It is often associated with altocumulus and sometimes gradually merges into cirrostratus. The sun may be dimly visible through it. Little or no turbulence with moderate amounts of ice.

Altocumulus Castellanus
Altocumulus castellanus are middle-level convective clouds. They are characterized by their billowing tops and comparatively high bases. They are a good indication of midlevel instability. Rough turbulence with some icing.

Standing Lenticular Altocumulus Clouds
Standing lenticular altocumulus clouds are formed on the crests of waves created by barriers in the wind flow. The clouds show little movement, hence the name *standing*. Wind, however, can be quite strong blowing through such clouds. They are characterized by their smooth, polished edges. The presence of these clouds is a good indication of very strong turbulence and should be avoided. Chapter 9, "Turbulence," further explains the significance of

USING PARALLEL COLUMNS FOR SIDE HEADS

In this project, you format the same document that you formatted in Project 1. After retrieving the document, delete the column definition code. Then format it using two parallel-style columns so you can have side heads in one column and body text in the other.

Procedures Used

■ Formatting a document in parallel-style columns.

Text Files Needed

■ CLOUDS2.WP5

Formats

① Enter a column definition code to create two parallel columns and turn them on. Set the margins for the first column at 1 inch (left) and 3 inches (right). Set the margins for the second column at 3½ inches (left) and 7½ inches (right).

② Place all uppercase headings in the first column as side heads. (The headings *"Middle Clouds," "Low Clouds,"* and *"Clouds with Extensive Vertical Development"* on the second and subsequent pages should also be formatted as side heads.) All body text should be in the right column.

---

①

Clouds, to almost everyone, have some meaning. But to you as a pilot, clouds are your weather "signposts in the sky." They give you an indication of air motion, stability, and moisture. Clouds help you visualize weather conditions and potential weather hazards you might encounter in flight. Let's examine these "signposts" and how to identify them.

② **IDENTIFICATION**

For identification purposes, you need be concerned only with the more basic cloud types, which are divided into four "families." The families are: high clouds, middle clouds, low clouds, and clouds with extensive vertical development. The first three families are further classified according to the way they are formed. Clouds formed by vertical currents in unstable air are *cumulus* meaning *accumulation* or *heap*; they are characterized by their lumpy, billowy appearance. Clouds formed by the cooling of a stable layer are *stratus* meaning *stratified* or *layered*; they are characterized by their uniform, sheetlike appearance. In addition to the above, the prefix *nimbo-* or the suffix *-nimbus* means raincloud. Thus stratified clouds from which rain is falling are *nimbostratus*. A heavy, swelling cumulus type cloud which produces precipitation is a *cumulonimbus*. Clouds broken into fragments are often identified by adding the suffix *-fractus*; for example, fragmentary cumulus is *cumulus fractus*.

② **HIGH CLOUDS**

The high cloud family is cirriform and includes cirrus, cirrocumulus, and cirrostratus. They are composed almost entirely of ice crystals. The height of the bases of these clouds ranges from about 16,500 to 45,000 feet in middle latitudes. Figures 45 through 47 are photographs of high clouds.

Cirrus
Cirrus are thin, featherlike ice crystal clouds in patches or narrow bands. Larger ice crystals often trail downward in well defined wisps called "Mares tails." Wispy, cirruslike, these contain no significant icing or turbulence.

Cirrocumulus
Cirrocumulus are thin clouds, the individual elements appearing as small white flakes or patches of cotton. May contain highly supercooled water droplets. Some turbulence and icing.

Cirrostratus
Cirrostratus is a thin whitish cloud layer appearing like a sheet or veil. Cloud elements are diffuse, sometimes partially striated or fibrous. Owing to their ice crystal makeup, these clouds are associated with halos—large luminous circles surrounding the sun or moon. No turbulence and little if any icing. The greatest problem flying in cirriform clouds is restriction to visibility. They can make the strict use of instruments mandatory.

THE DTP ADVISOR NEWSLETTER

In this project, you format the newsletter so it prints in two columns below the newsletter's title.

THE *dtp* ADVISOR

FaceLift For WordPerfect

Bitstream Inc. today announced version 1.5 of Bitstream® FaceLift™ for WordPerfect.® FaceLift brings enhanced font support to WordPerfect 5.0 and 5.1. The new FaceLift version 1.5 will create high-quality fonts on-the-fly for popular dot-matrix and inkjet printers—like the HP® DeskJet,® Canon BubbleJet and the IBM® ExecuJet—in addition to the existing on-the-fly support for the Hewlett-Packard LaserJet® series of printers. FaceLift 1.5 for Word-Perfect will be available in the spring of 1991.

In addition to 13 typeface outlines provided in the original FaceLift package, FaceLift 1.5 for WordPer-fect will also ship with three Symbol typefaces: ITC Zapf Dingbats® Symbol Proportional and Symbol Monospaced. Users will be able to access a total of 698 characters from the Bitstream International Char-acter Set and from these three Symbols typefaces.

FaceLift 1.5 for WordPerfect is an easy-to-use utility that allows users to print high-quality fonts in any size from 2 to 500 point (in quarter point incre-ments) without ever having to leave the application. The fonts are generated at print time, so the need for stored bit-map fonts is eliminated. Based on Bitstream Speedo™ technology, FaceLift sends characters to printers in both graphics mode (laser, inkjet and dot-matrix printers) and as HP soft fonts (laser printers only). Users have full control over the number and size of soft fonts to be downloaded, depending on the memory available in the printer.

"We are very excited that FaceLift 1.5 for Word-Perfect will provide dot-matrix and inkjet users with the same high typographic quality and capabilities that HP LaserJet users have enjoyed with Bitstream type," stated Doug Lloyd, Executive Director at WordPerfect. "That, and the addition of the three new Symbol typefaces makes FaceLift a great companion for WordPerfect."

First-time users can purchase FaceLift 1.5 for WordPerfect for a suggested U.S. list price of $99. Current users of FaceLift 1.0 for WordPerfect can upgrade to version 1.5 for $24.95. In addition to the 16 typefaces included free with FaceLift, users can purchase add-on fonts from the Bitstream Library of 52 typeface packages. Also available is the FaceLift Companion Value Pack, a selection of 24 text and headline faces for a suggested U.S. list price $199.

FaceLift 1.5 for WordPerfect is the newest member of the Bitstream FaceLift product line. The initial product, FaceLift for Windows,™ shipped in August of 1990. All FaceLift products can share Bitstream typefaces (in Speedo format) stored in a single common subdirectory.

FaceLift for Wordperfect was developed in con-junction with LaserTools Corporation, a privately held company based in Emeryville, CA. LaserTools is a developer of innovative printing enhancement products—tools for printer sharing, printer control, printer acceleration, and font management.

An industry leader in typographic quality and innovative technology, Bitstream licenses fonts and related software to more than 420 hardware manufac-turers and software developers worldwide. Its line of retail products is distributed by an extensive network of dealers in the United States and in 18 nations worldwide.

For more information, contact:
Bitstream Inc.
215 First Street
Cambridge, MA 02142-1270
(617) 497-6222

Postscript in a Cartridge

Hewlett-Packard Company today announced a Post-Script accessory for the HP LaserJet printer. The cartridge is $995 V.S. list and contains the PostScript page description language, licensed from Adobe Systems Incorporated, and 35 Adobe typefaces.

With the PostScript cartridge, the HP LaserJet printer is the only printer to combine Adobe-licensed PostScript and HP PCL printer-language support for meeting a broad base of business-office printing needs. The PostScript cartridge, which can be used on any HP LaserJet printer, is a host-independent solu-tion, allowing users to share the printer easily.

Page Numbers, Headers, Footers, & Footnotes

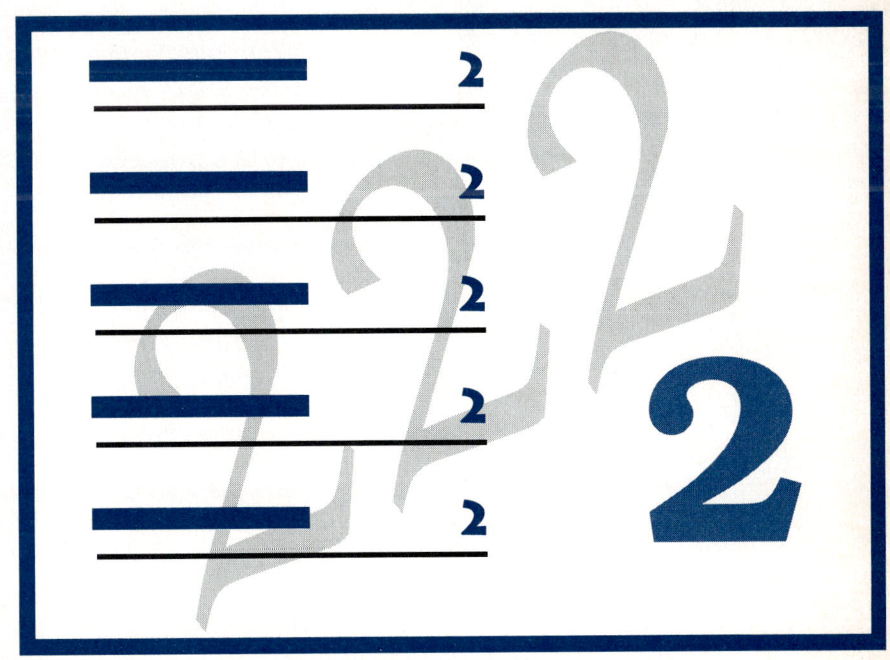

Page Numbers

After completing this topic, you should be able to:
- Define the term *folio*
- Describe possible page number positions and styles
- Print page numbers in your own documents

Page Numbers

In this tutorial, you add page numbers to a document. When you are finished, your printout should look similar to the illustration "Page Numbers."

GETTING STARTED

1. Retrieve the PAGENUMB.WP5 document and enter your name.

TURNING PAGE NUMBERS ON

2. Press **Home** three times, and then press ↑ to move the cursor to the beginning of the document above all codes.
3. Press **Shift-F8** to display the Format menu.
4. Press **P** for *Page* to display the Page Format menu.
5. Press **N** for *Page Numbering* to display the Page Numbering menu.
6. Press **P** for *Page Number Position No page number* to display an illustration of page numbering options.
7. Press **6** to enter page numbers at the bottom center of the page and return to the Page Numbering Format menu.

SPECIFY A NEW PAGE NUMBER

8. Press **N** for *New Page Number*.
9. Type **i** and then press **Enter**.
10. Press **F7** to return to the Edit screen.

SPECIFYING ANOTHER NEW PAGE NUMBER

11. Move the cursor to the beginning of the first line of the first poem on page 2 following the hard page break *[HPg]* code.
12. Press **Shift-F8** to display the Format menu.
13. Press **P** for *Page* to display the Page Format menu.
14. Press **N** for *Page Numbering* to display the Page Numbering menu.
15. Press **N** for *New Page Number*.

16. Type **2** and then press **Enter**.

17. Press **F7** to return to the Edit screen.

FINISHING UP

18. Save and print the document. The document is printed on two pages. Page 1 is numbered at the bottom center with a Roman i, and page 2 is numbered in the same position with an Arabic 2.

▶ DESKTOP PUBLISHING CONCEPTS

There are two types of page numbers that you can use in a document: Arabic (1, 2, 3) and Roman (i, ii, iii). In publishing, page numbers are called **folios**, and if they are printed on the bottom of the page they are called **drop folios**. If a page is counted and a page number is printed on it, that page number is called an **expressed folio**. If the page is counted, but no page number is printed on it, that page is considered to have a **blind folio**. When designing page numbers, you have to consider their position, style, and sequence.

Page Number Positions

The position of page numbers determines how easily a reader can find a specific page.

■ Page numbers should be printed on the outside edges of the page for easy reference, although they can also be indented or centered.

■ If the document is to be printed on both sides of the page, page numbers should alternate from one side to the other on right- and left-hand pages so that they remain near the outside margin. When page numbers alternate like this, they are said to be *mirrored* because one side is like a mirror image of the other.

■ Blind folios are frequently specified for title pages and section openers.

Page Numbers on Facing Pages

Page Number Styles

To make page numbers stand out, you can vary the type used to print them or use different types of numbers.

■ Page numbers are sometimes printed in bold or bold italic type in a size 1 or 2 points larger than the body text so they are easy to find.

■ In frontmatter, such as prefaces, introductions, and tables of contents, you can use lowercase Roman numerals on the numbered pages. If you do so, the first page of text should then be numbered 1 (using Arabic numbers).

Page Number Sequences

Some pages always have page numbers, but on others they are optional.

■ All leaves (sides of the sheets) are counted in the page numbering system—even those that are not numbered.

■ Page numbers are frequently omitted from the title page, copyright page, section opening pages, and blank pages.

■ Page numbers are sometimes printed as drop folios on pages that contain only tables or illustrations.

WordPerfect prints page numbers only if you tell it to. You can turn page numbering on and then back off anywhere in a document by entering open codes. When you do so, you can also specify where on the page they will print relative to the margins. The figure "The Page Number Position Menu" shows some of the page number positions you can specify. Page numbers are not displayed on the Edit screen but are added as the document is printed. They can be previewed with the View Document command, and their codes can be seen when you reveal codes.

After you turn on page numbering, you can start a new page number sequence anywhere in your document. When you do so, you can specify whether numbers are printed as Arabic numerals (1, 2, 3), lowercase Roman numerals (i, ii, iii), or uppercase Roman numerals (I, II, III).

Page numbers are printed in the text area of the page. The amount of space left available for text is reduced by the line height specified for the page number plus 1/6 inch.

➡ **K E Y / S t r o k e s**

Turning Page Numbers On or Off

1. Move the cursor to the beginning of the page (above all other codes) where page numbers are to be turned on or off (press Ctrl-**Home** and then press ↑ from anywhere on the page).
2. Either: Press **Shift**-**F8** and then press **P** for *Page*.
   Or: Pull down the Layout menu and select *Page*.
3. Press **N** for *Page **N**umbering* to display the Page Numbering menu.
4. Make any of the choices described in the table "Page Numbering Menu Choices."
5. Press **F7** to return to the document.

PAGE NUMBERING MENU CHOICES

1 ***N**ew Page Number* specifies the page number that is to be printed on the page in which the cursor is positioned and the style it is to be printed in. All subsequent pages are numbered in sequence beginning with the specified number. Type the new page number in the style you want to use and then press **Enter**. For example,
   - Type **1**, **2**, or **3** for Arabic.
   - Type **i**, **ii**, or **iii** for lowercase Roman.
   - Type **I**, **II**, or **III** for uppercase Roman.
2 *Page Number **S**tyle* allows you to combine the page numbers with text, for example, *Page 1 of 5*, *Page: 1*, *Page 1 of Chapter 1*. To do so, you enter text with the ^B code (press **Ctrl-B** to enter the code). To combine with text, for example, to print **Page: #**, type **Page:**, press **Spacebar**, and then press **Ctrl-B**.

3 *Insert Page Number* inserts the ^B code into the document at the cursor's position using the format specified in *2 Page Number Style*. You can also enter the code by pressing **Ctrl-B**. When the document is printed, this ^B code is replaced with a page number. You can enter this code anywhere in the document, including in headers and footers.

4 *Page Number* **Position** specifies the position in which page numbers are printed or that there be no page numbering.

The Page Number Position Menu

The Page Number Position menu illustrates your page number position choices. For example, selecting **1** prints page numbers in the upper left-hand corner of every page. Selecting **4** prints them in the upper left-hand corner of even-numbered pages and the upper right-hand corner of odd-numbered pages.

```
Format: Page Number Position


    Every Page                  Alternating Pages
  ┌─────────────┐        ┌─────────────┐ ┌─────────────┐
  │ 1   2   3   │        │ 4           │ │           4 │
  │             │        │             │ │             │
  │             │        │ Even        │ │        Odd  │
  │             │        │             │ │             │
  │ 5   6   7   │        │ 8           │ │           8 │
  └─────────────┘        └─────────────┘ └─────────────┘


    9 - No Page Numbers




Selection: 0
```

Suppressing Page Numbers

If you enter page numbers, you can discontinue them or suppress them on selected pages.

→ **K E Y / S t r o k e s**

Suppressing Page Numbers

1. Move the cursor to the beginning of the page where page numbers, headers, or footers are to be turned off (press **Ctrl-Home** and then ↑ from anywhere on the page).
2. Either: Press **Shift-F8** and then **P** for *Page*.

   Or: Pull down the Layout menu and select *Page*.
3. Press **u** for *Suppress (this page only)*.
4. Select one of the choices listed on the screen. (To select choices 1 and 2, you merely press the number of the option. To select choices 3 through 8, press the number and then **Y** or **N**.)
5. Press **F7** once or twice to return to the Edit screen.

The Suppress Menu
The Suppress menu lists options for suppressing page numbers, headers, and footers on selected pages.

```
Format: Suppress (this page only)

     1 - Suppress All Page Numbering, Headers and Footers

     2 - Suppress Headers and Footers

     3 - Print Page Number at Bottom Center   No

     4 - Suppress Page Numbering              No

     5 - Suppress Header A                    No

     6 - Suppress Header B                    No

     7 - Suppress Footer A                    No

     8 - Suppress Footer B                    No




Selection: 0
```

SPECIFYING PAGES TO BE PRINTED

When you enter the name of the file to be printed or select it from the List Files screen and menu, the prompt reads *Page(s): (All)*. You can either press **Enter** to print the entire document or specify selected page numbers and then press **Enter** to begin printing. When specifying only certain pages, use the following procedures. (Do not enter spaces in the page specifications, for they may create problems.)

- To print sections where you have specified Roman numbering, enter Roman numerals. For example, to print page 2, type **ii**; to print pages 2 through 5, type **ii-v**; and to print pages 1, 5, and 10, type **i,v,x**.
- If you have specified new page numbers anywhere in the document, those changes divide the document into sections. To print selected pages, follow the preceding rules, but add section numbers followed by a colon. For example, to print pages 2 through 5 in an introduction, and pages 2 through 5 in the second and third sections of the document, type **1:2-5,2:2-5,3:2-5**.

Sections are numbered sequentially beginning at 1 unless you have used both Roman (i, ii, iii) and Arabic (1, 2, 3) numbers in the document. In these cases, each numbering style is numbered separately. For example, to print pages 2 through 5 in an introduction numbered with Roman numerals and pages 2 through 5 in the second and third sections of the document numbered with Arabic numerals, type **1:ii-v,1:2-5,3:2-5**.

EXERCISE 1

ADDING PAGE NUMBERS TO A DOCUMENT

In this exercise, you add page numbers to a document.

1. Retrieve the EMANPROC.WP5 document and enter your name on a blank line at the end of the document.
2. Reveal codes and delete the *[Paper Sz/Type:...]* code that you may have entered in a previous tutorial.
3. Move the cursor to the top of the document, then follow the instructions in the KEY/Strokes box "Turning Page Numbers On and Off" to add page numbers so that they print at the bottom center of each page in uppercase Roman numerals.
4. Print the document.
5. Follow the instructions in the KEY/Strokes box "Suppressing Page Numbers" to suppress the page numbers on page 1.
6. Save and print the document again.

EXERCISE 2

ADDING MIRRORED PAGE NUMBERS

In this exercise, you add mirrored page numbers to a document.

1. Retrieve the NEWSCOL1.WP5 document.
2. Move the cursor to the top of the document, then follow the instructions in the KEY/Strokes box "Turning Page Numbers On and Off" to add page numbers so that they print on the outside edges at the bottom of odd and even pages.
3. Save and print the document. Hold the pages up back to back and you'll see that the page numbers are printed on the outside of both pages.

✔ PAGE NUMBER TIPS

- If you change page numbers throughout a document, the status line indicates the renumbered page sequence, not the consecutive page number beginning at the first page.
- You can force an odd or even page number on a page. When you do so, you move the cursor to the page and specify that it be odd or even. If necessary, the program then inserts a blank page in front of the page so that it prints as specified. For example, if you force an odd number on page 2, the page becomes page 3, and a blank page 2 is inserted when you print the document. To force an odd or even page break, move the cursor to the top of the page where you want the change to take effect, and then press **Shift**-**F8** to display the Format menu. Press **P** for *Page*, and then press **o** for *Force Odd/Even Page*. Press **O** for *Odd* or **E** for *Even*, and then press **F7** to return to the Edit screen.

Headers and Footers

After completing this topic, you should be able to:
- Define the terms *headers*, *footers*, *running headers*, and *running footers*
- Describe some typical contents of headers and footers
- Describe possible header and footer alignments
- Enter headers and footers in your own documents

▶ T U T O R I A L

In this tutorial, you enter headers and footers. When you are finished, your printout should look similar to the illustration "Headers and Footers."

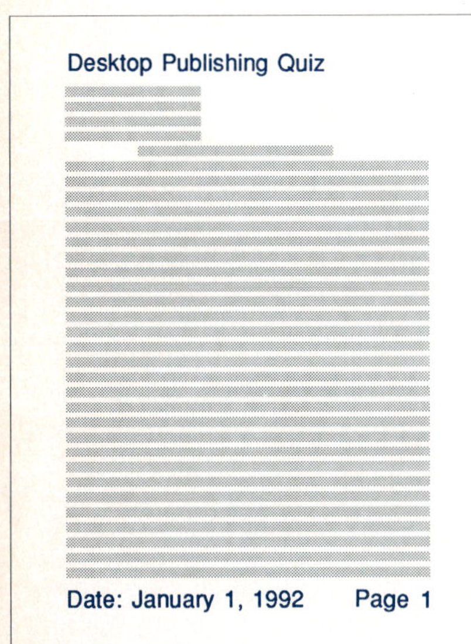

Headers and Footers

GETTING STARTED

1. Retrieve the DTP-QUIZ.WP5 document.

ENTERING A HEADER

2. Press **Home** twice and then press ↑ to move the cursor to the top of the first page.
3. Press **Shift-F8** to display the Format menu.
4. Press **P** for *Page* to display the Page Format menu.
5. Press **H** for *Headers*.
6. Press **A** for *Header A*.
7. Press **P** for *Every Page* and the header entry screen appears.
8. Type **Desktop Publishing Quiz**.
9. Press **F7** to return to the Page Format menu.

ENTERING A FOOTER WITH DATE AND PAGE CODES

10. Press **F** for *Footers*.
11. Press **A** for *Footer A*.
12. Press **P** for *Every Page*.
13. Type **Date:** and then press **Spacebar**.
14. Press **Shift-F5** to display the Date menu.
15. Press **C** for *Date Code*.
16. Press **Alt-F6** to align the cursor with the right margin.
17. Type **Page:** and then press **Spacebar**.
18. Press **Ctrl-B** to enter a code to number pages.

19. Press **F7** twice to save the footer text and return to the Edit screen.

FINISHING UP

20. Save and print the document. The header prints at the top of the page and is aligned with the left margin. The footer prints both the date and page number using the codes you entered.

▶ D E S K T O P   P U B L I S H I N G   C O N C E P T S

Headers

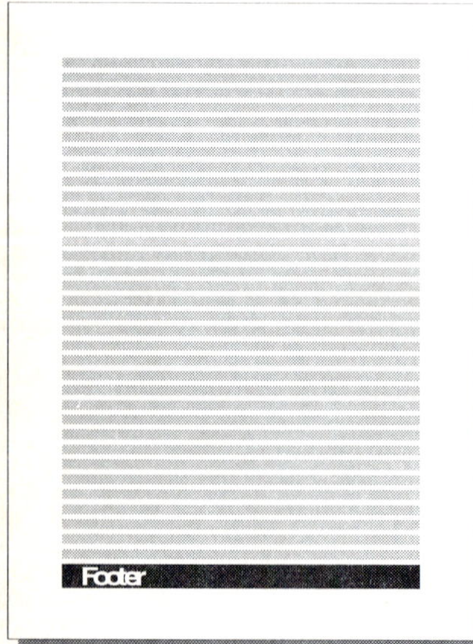

Footers

Headers consist of text printed at the top of the type page and *footers* at the bottom. If they print on more than one page in a sequence, they are called *running headers* and *running footers*. Both headers and footers help readers know where they are in the document. This is especially important in catalogs, manuals, or books that are used as references.

When designing headers and footers, you should keep the following points in mind:

- The size of the type should allow the longest header or footer to fit within the type page. It should not be larger than the body text or boldfaced because it should blend into the background and not detract from the other elements on the page.
- If a page number is printed as part of the header or footer, it can be separated from the header or footer text by at least 1 em space.
- You do not normally use headers or footers on the following pages:
  - Display pages such as title pages and copyright pages.
  - The first page of a table of contents or preface
  - Part titles and chapter openers
  - Pages that contain only illustrations or tables

Header and Footer Contents

Headers or footers indicate sections of the document. Possible contents include the combinations shown in the table "Header and Footer Contents." Basically, the more detailed the information in the document, the more specific the information required in the headers or footers.

HEADER AND FOOTER CONTENTS*

Right or Odd Pages	Left or Even Pages
Frontmatter	
Contents	Contents
Preface	Preface
Text Pages	
Document title	Chapter title
Chapter title	Part title
Subhead	Chapter title
Chapter title	Chapter title
Subhead	Subhead
Author of book or section	Title of book or section
Backmatter	
Appendix letter or number	Appendix title
Appendix	Appendix
Glossary	Glossary
Bibliography	Bibliography
Index	Index

* Adapted from *The Chicago Manual of Style*

When headers or footers refer to subheads on pages where there are more than one subhead, the left-hand pages should refer to the first subhead on the page, right-hand pages should refer to the last item on the page. This is the same system used in dictionaries.

Header and Footer Positions

Headers or footers can be aligned with the inside or outside margins or centered between them. However, if the document is to be printed on both sides of the page, the placement of the headers and footers may be affected. To keep them symmetrical (if they are not centered) they may have to alternate from one side to the other on odd-numbered (right-hand) pages and even-numbered (left-hand) pages. When the headers and footers alternate like this, they are said to be mirrored.

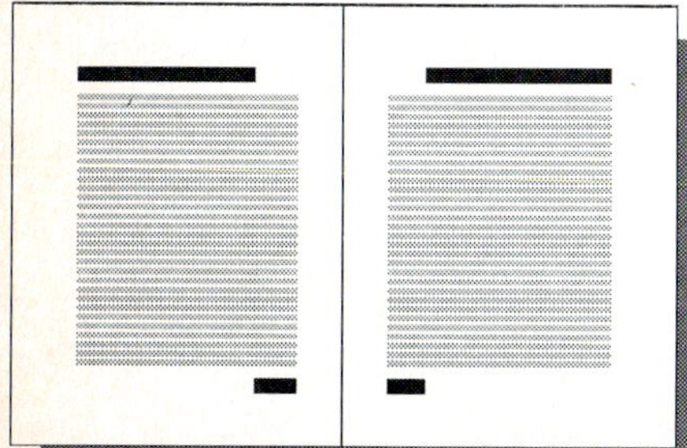

Headers and Footers on Facing Pages

You can add two headers and two footers to each page of your document. They are printed where the first or last line of text would normally be printed with 1/6 inch inserted to separate them from the text below or above them. Headers or footers are not displayed on the Edit screen but you can preview them with the View Document command or reveal codes to see their codes. When entering headers or footers, keep the following points in mind:

- Headers or footers print from the place where you enter them to the end of the document or to the next header or footer code that changes or discontinues them.
- The header or footer code must be placed at the top of the page it is to begin on. If the code is not at the top of the page, it will not print until the next page. To be sure the code stays at the top of the page, enter a hard page break immediately before the code if it isn't at the top of the document.
- When entering headers or footers, you can press **Enter** to insert blank lines above or below the header to add extra space between it and the text. This is useful when you use two headers or footers on the same page and want to keep them on separate lines.
- Your headers or footers can be longer than a single line of text.
- You can enter page numbers in headers or footers by pressing **Ctrl-B**. This inserts a ^B code. When you print the document, the page number is printed in the position of the code. If you also turn on page numbers with the Page Format menu, you will have two page numbers printed on each page; to avoid this, turn off normal page numbering.
- You can enter a date or a time in a header or footer using the date and time commands that enter text or codes. To do so, position the cursor in the header or footer, press **Shift-F5**, and then press **T** for *Date Text* or **C** for *Date Code* or pull down the Tools menu and select *Date Text* or *Date Code*. (To enter a time you have to use the Date Format command.) The advantage of using codes to enter dates and times is that they change automatically each time the document is retrieved or printed; thus, it is easier to keep track of the various versions of the same document.
- When you enter headers and footers, the program normally aligns them flush left. To change the alignment, use the commands to center or align them flush right. For example, if you enter two headers or two footers so that they print on the same pages, keep them short, and use the Flush Right command (**Alt-F6**) to align one of them with the right margin so that they do not overlap on the printout.

Entering Headers or Footers or Discontinuing Them

1. Move the cursor to the top of the page (above all other codes) where you want the headers or footers to begin (press **Ctrl-Home** and then ↑).
2. Either: Press **Shift-F8** and then **P** for *Page*.
   Or: Pull down the Layout menu and select *Page*.
3. Either: Press **H** for *Headers*.
   Or: Press **F** for *Footers*.
4. Select the header or footer type described in the table "Header and Footer Types and Occurrences."
5. Press the number indicating the occurrence of the header or footer (see the table "Header and Footer Types and Occurrences"), and the blank header/footer screen appears.
6. Type the header or footer text (you can enter up to one full page of text), press **Shift-F5** to enter the date or time, or press **Ctrl-B** to enter a code to number pages.
7. Press **F7** twice to save the header or footer text and return to the Edit screen.

Editing Headers or Footers

1. Move the cursor to below where the header code is located in the document. (The program searches from the cursor toward the top of the document for the next header or footer code, and that is the header or footer displayed.)
2. Either: Press **Shift-F8** and then **P** for *Page*.
   Or: Pull down the Layout menu and select *Page*.
3. Either: Press **H** for *Headers*.
   Or: Press **F** for *Footers*.
4. Select either header or footer type, and then press **E** for *Edit* to display the next header or footer above the cursor.
5. Edit the header or footer text.
6. Press **F7** twice to save the header or footer text and return to the Edit screen.

Type

1 *Header **A*** or *Footer **A*** displays the occurrence menu so you can print, edit, or discontinue a header or footer.
2 *Header **B*** or *Footer **B*** displays the occurrence menu so you can print, edit, or discontinue a second header or footer.

Occurrence

1 ***D****iscontinue* discontinues headers or footers for the rest of the document.
2 *Every **P**age* prints headers or footers on every page.
3 ***O****dd Pages* prints headers or footers only on odd pages.
4 *Even Pages* prints headers or footers only on even pages.
5 ***E****dit* displays the header or footer for editing.

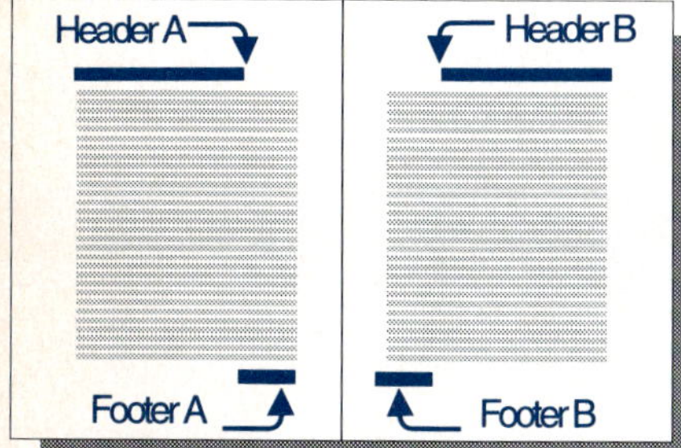

Mirrored Footers

Mirrored Headers and Footers

To print headers or footers on a document to be printed or copied on both sides of the paper, align them so that they appear on the outside corners. To do so, enter an A header or footer, align it flush left, and specify even pages. Then enter a B header or footer, align it flush right, and specify odd pages.

Suppressing Headers and Footers

If you enter headers or footers, you can suppress them on selected pages.

→ KEY/Strokes

Suppressing Headers or Footers

1. Move the cursor to the beginning of the page where page numbers, headers, or footers are to be turned off (press **Ctrl-Home** and then ↑ from any place on the page).
2. Either: Press **Shift-F8** and then **P** for *Page*.
   Or: Pull down the Layout menu and select ***P****age*.
3. Press **u** for *Suppress (this page only)*.
4. Select one of the choices listed on the screen. (To select choices 1 and 2, you merely press the number of the option. To select choices 3 through 8, press the number and then **Y** or **N**.)
5. Press **F7** once or twice to return to the Edit screen.

The Suppress Menu

The Suppress menu lists options for suppressing page numbers, headers, and footers on selected pages.

```
Format: Suppress (this page only)

     1 - Suppress All Page Numbering, Headers and Footers

     2 - Suppress Headers and Footers

     3 - Print Page Number at Bottom Center   No

     4 - Suppress Page Numbering              No

     5 - Suppress Header A                    No

     6 - Suppress Header B                    No

     7 - Suppress Footer A                    No

     8 - Suppress Footer B                    No




Selection: 0
```

▶ E X E R C I S E S

EXERCISE 1

EDITING HEADERS AND FOOTERS

In this exercise, you enter base font codes in the headers and footers. These codes affect only the headers and footers, not the body text.

1. Retrieve the DTP-QUIZ.WP5 document that you added headers and footers to in the tutorial at the beginning of this topic.
2. Follow the instructions in the KEY/Strokes box "Editing Headers or Footers" to display the Header A text that you entered in the tutorial. Enter a base font code in front of the text for a 10-point typeface.
3. Follow the instructions in the KEY/Strokes box "Editing Headers or Footers" to display the Footer A text that you entered in the tutorial. Enter a base font code in front of the text for a 10-point typeface.
4. Save the document, then print just the first page.

EXERCISE 2

ADDING MIRRORED FOOTERS

In this exercise, you enter mirrored footers that alternate from side to side on odd- and even-numbered pages so they always print flush with the outside margin.

1. Retrieve the DTP-QUIZ.WP5 document.
2. Reveal codes and delete the existing Footer code.

3. Follow the instructions in the KEY/Strokes box "Entering Headers or Footers or Discontinuing Them" to add a Footer A that reads *Page ^B* on odd pages only and align it flush right.

4. Follow the instructions in the KEY/Strokes box "Entering Headers or Footers or Discontinuing Them" to add a Footer B that is aligned flush left on even pages only and reads *Page ^B*.

5. Save and print the document. Hold the pages up back to back and you will see how the page numbers will be on the outside edges of the pages if the document were printed on both sides of the paper and bound like a book.

✔ HEADER AND FOOTER TIPS

- If you have specified that page numbers be printed, the headers or footers might print on the same line as the page numbers or even print over them. To avoid this, change the page number position.
- Headers and footers print where the first and last lines of text normally print. To change the line on which they print,
  - Press **Enter** when the header or footer is displayed on the screen to insert blank lines above or below it.
  - Change the top or bottom margins. For example, you normally have 1-inch top and bottom margins. If you print a header, it prints just below the top margin, and the program adds 1/6 inch below it before the first line of text. If you change the top margin to 3/4 inch, the header prints higher on the page.
- Most format commands work in headers and footers just as they do in normal text. You can boldface or underline text, center or align it with the right margin, and so on.
- To search for or replace text in headers and footers, use the Extended Search (**Home**, then **F2**) command.

Footnotes and Endnotes

After completing this topic, you should be able to:
- Describe the differences between footnotes and endnotes
- List and describe footnote and endnote options
- Enter footnotes and endnotes in your own documents

▶ T U T O R I A L

In this tutorial, you enter footnotes. When you are finished, your printout should look similar to the illustration "A Typical Footnote."

GETTING STARTED

1. Retrieve the SPECIAL3.WP5 document.

ENTERING A FOOTNOTE

2. Move the cursor to the end of the "*Topic:*" line.
3. Press **Ctrl-F7** to display the Footnote menu.
4. Press **F** for *Footnote*.
5. Press **C** for *Create*, and the screen goes blank except for the number *1*.
6. Type **Characters that cannot be displayed on the screen are displayed as small squares**.
7. Press **F7** to return to the Edit screen. The number *1* at the cursor's position is the footnote reference number.
8. To see the footnote code, press **Alt-F3** or **F11**. Highlight the code *[Footnote:1;[Note Num]* to display the first 50 characters of the footnote. It ends with *...]*, indicating that there is more to the footnote that is not displayed. Press **Alt-F3** or **F11** to return to the Edit screen.

ENTERING A SECOND FOOTNOTE

9. Move the cursor to the end of the line where the date is displayed.
10. Repeat Steps 3 through 5 to display the footnote screen, then type **This date changes each time the document is retrieved because it has been entered as a code, not as text**.
11. Press **F7** to return to the Edit screen. The new footnote is now numbered *1*. Move the cursor down through the text to reform the paragraph, and the number of the original footnote changes from *1* to *2*.

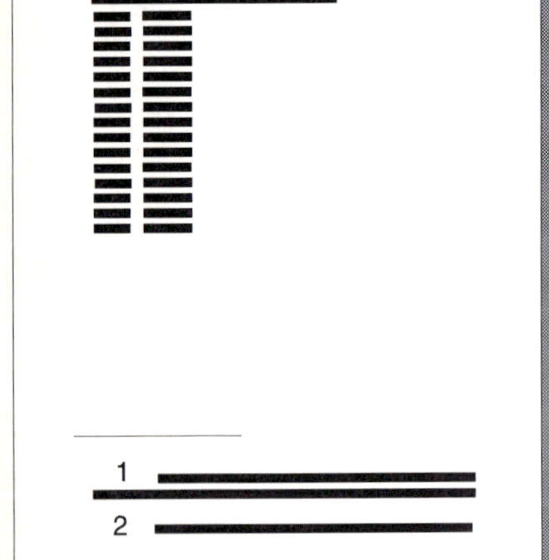

A Typical Footnote

12. Save and print the document. The footnotes you entered are printed at the bottom of the page.

▶ DESKTOP PUBLISHING CONCEPTS

Footnotes consist of numbered text printed at the bottom of the page on which a matching reference number appears in the body text. ***Endnotes*** are just like footnotes, but instead of printing at the bottom of the page with the matching reference number, they are printed at the end of a section, or at the end of the document. When you insert a new footnote or endnote or delete an old one, all footnote or endnote references that follow are automatically renumbered.

Footnotes are often set at least 2 points smaller than the body text, but should not be less than 8 points. Footnotes should be separated from the last line of text on the page by enough space to make them stand out, usually a minimum of 2 picas spacing. An optional hairline rule can also be used to separate them from the body text. Endnotes are often set smaller than body text but not as small as footnotes.

If a footnote must continue to a second page, it is usually preceded by a rule that extends the full width of the type page.

▶ WORDPERFECT PROCEDURES

You can enter footnotes and endnotes anywhere in a document by entering codes.

Footnotes

Footnotes print in the text area of the document, not in the bottom margin. If the footnote is too long to print on a page, ½ inch of it prints on the same page as the reference number, and the rest of the footnote prints on the next page. If there is not enough room to print the first ½ inch of the footnote, both the footnote and the text line that contains the reference number move to the next page.

Endnotes

Endnotes print below the last hard carriage return on the last page of the document. To print endnotes on a separate page, put a hard page break (**Ctrl-Enter**) after the last line of text in the document. To add a heading, type it on the last page, and then press **Enter** two or three times so that the first endnote prints that number of lines below the heading.

If you do not want endnotes to print at the end of the document, you can enter a code wherever you do want them to print. This is useful when you want endnotes to print together at the end of sections rather than at the end of the document. To enter an endnote code, press **Ctrl-F7** to display the Footnote menu, and then press **P** for *Endnote Placement*. The prompt reads *Restart endnote numbering? Yes (No)*. Press **Y** to have endnotes restart numbering below the code, or **N** to have endnotes continue in numerical order. This command inserts a comment into the document followed by a hard page break code so that any following text is printed on a separate page. To calculate the space to be occupied by the endnotes, press **Alt**-**F5** to display the Mark Text menu. Press **G** for *Generate*, and then press **G** for *Generate Tables, Indexes, Automatic References, etc.* Press **Y** to generate the space. A new comment is inserted that shows the amount of space occupied by the endnotes.

After entering footnotes or endnotes, you can edit them. When you use the command to edit a footnote or an endnote, the program searches for the next note following the cursor and asks if you want to edit that note. You can either press **Enter** to accept the suggested number, or enter a new number and then press **Enter**.

➡️ **K E Y / S t r o k e s**

Entering or Editing Footnotes or Endnotes or Changing Options

1. Move the cursor to where you want the footnote or endnote reference to appear in the document or above where you want to change the style of all footnotes and endnotes.
2. Either: Press **Ctrl**-**F7** and then **F** for *Footnote* or **E** for *Endnote*.
   Or: Pull down the Layout menu and select *Footnote* or *Endnote*.
3. Make one of the selections described in the table "Footnote and Endnote Menu Choices."

FOOTNOTE AND ENDNOTE MENU CHOICES

1 *C*reate displays the footnote or endnote screen. Type the note, then press **F7** to return to the Edit screen.

2 *E*dit displays the prompt *Footnote number?* or *Endnote number?* followed by the number of the next note. Press **Enter** to edit the suggested number (or letter if you have changed the numbering method), or enter the number (or letter) of another note, and then press **Enter**. The note is displayed on the screen. Edit it, and then press **F7** to return to the Edit screen.

3 *N*ew Number displays the prompt *Footnote number?* or *Endnote number?* Enter a new number, and then press **Enter**. This overrides automatic numbering, for example, when different parts of the same document are kept in separate files but you want numbering to be consecutive when you print them out.

4 *O*ptions displays the Footnote Options or Endnote Options menu. Use any of the choices described in the table "Footnote and Endnote Options." (Only some of the options are offered for endnotes.) When you are finished changing options, press **F7** to return to the Edit screen.

Footnote and Endnote Options

You can specify options that include changing the spacing between or within notes, changing starting numbers, or changing the line that separates the notes from the document portion of the page.

The Footnote Options Menu
The Footnote Options menu allows you to specify where and how footnotes are printed.

```
Footnote Options

    1 - Spacing Within Footnotes              1
              Between Footnotes               0.167"

    2 - Amount of Note to Keep Together       0.5"

    3 - Style for Number in Text              [SUPRSCPT][Note Num][suprscpt]

    4 - Style for Number in Note                  [SUPRSCPT][Note Num][suprscpt

    5 - Footnote Numbering Method             Numbers

    6 - Start Footnote Numbers each Page      No

    7 - Line Separating Text and Footnotes    2-inch Line

    8 - Print Continued Message               No

    9 - Footnotes at Bottom of Page           Yes



Selection: 0
```

The Endnote Options Menu
The Endnote Options menu allows you to specify where and how endnotes are printed.

```
Endnote Options

    1 - Spacing Within Endnotes               1
              Between Endnotes                0.167"

    2 - Amount of Endnote to Keep Together    0.5"

    3 - Style for Numbers in Text             [SUPRSCPT][Note Num][suprscpt]

    4 - Style for Numbers in Note             [Note Num].

    5 - Endnote Numbering Method              Numbers








Selection: 0
```

FOOTNOTE AND ENDNOTE OPTIONS

1 Spacing Within/Between Footnotes/Endnotes controls the line spacing within and between the notes. For the spacing within notes, type **1** for single spacing, **1.5** for 1½ spacing, **2** for double spacing, and so on. For the spacing between notes, enter a distance; for example, type **.2** for a spacing of 2/10 inch.

2 Amount of Note/Endnote to Keep Together controls the number of lines kept together on the same page when part of the footnote continues onto another page. Enter a measurement; for example, type **1** to keep 1 inch of the note on the page.

FOOTNOTE AND ENDNOTE OPTIONS (CONTINUED)

3 *Style for Number in* **Text** controls the style of the footnote or endnote reference numbers in the text area of the document. For example, you can change font sizes or appearances.

4 *Style for Number in* **Note** works just like **3** *Style for Number in* **Text** but you can also enter spaces to indent them from the left margin.

5 *Footnote/Endnote Numbering* **Method** controls the way footnotes are numbered. Press **N** for **N**umbers, **L** for **L**etters, or **C** for **C**haracters to specify other characters. If you press **C**, you can specify as many as five characters. (The default is a single asterisk.) If you specify a single character, such as the asterisk, the number of characters indicates the sequence. For example, * indicates the first reference, ** the second, and *** the third. If you specify more than one character, they cycle to indicate the sequence. For example, if you specify * and #, the first reference is *, the second #, the third **, the fourth ##, and so on.

6 *Start Footnote Numbers Each* **Page** specifies whether footnote numbers run consecutively throughout the document or start over on each page of the document.

7 **L**ine *Separating Text and Footnotes* controls whether a line separates footnotes from the last line of the document. Type **N** for **N**o *line*, **2** for **2**-*inch line*, or **M** for **M**argin to Margin to print a line across the entire page.

8 *Print* **C**ontinued Message prints *(Continued...)* on the last line of the first page and *(...Continued)* on the first footnote line of the following page if the footnote continues to the next page.

9 *Footnotes at* **B**ottom of Page specifies where footnotes are to be printed on pages that are not full. You can specify that they be printed at the bottom of the page or just below the last line of text on the page.

▶ E X E R C I S E S

EXERCISE 1

EDITING A FOOTNOTE

In this exercise you edit the footnotes that you entered in the tutorial at the beginning of this topic.

1. Retrieve the SPECIAL3.WP5 document that you added footnotes to at the beginning of this topic.

2. Follow the instructions in the KEY/Strokes box "Entering or Editing Footnotes or Endnotes or Changing Options" to edit the first footnote. After the word "*retrieved*" insert the phrase **or printed**. When you are finished, press **F7** to return to the Edit screen.

3. Save and print the document

ENTERING AN ENDNOTE

In this exercise, you enter an endnote in a document to see where it prints out.

1. Retrieve the ALIGN2.WP5 document.
2. Follow the instructions in the KEY/Strokes box "Entering or Editing Footnotes or Endnotes or Changing Options" to enter an endnote that states **All amendments passed unanimously** following the "*BILL OF RIGHTS*" heading.
3. Save and print the document. Notice where the endnote prints out.

> ✔ **FOOTNOTE/ENDNOTE TIPS**
>
> - If headers or footers do not print in a specified font, it is because the new base font code is positioned after the header or footer code. Headers and footers always print in the base font in effect at the place where their code is entered.
> - To see an entire footnote, use the View Document command on the Print menu, or print the page on which its reference number appears. To print all endnotes, print the last page of the document.
> - To search and replace in footnotes and endnotes, use the Extended Search command. To do so, press **Home** and then **F2** to search or **Alt**-**F2** to replace.
> - You can permanently change the footnote and endnote options by changing the Initial Codes setting on the Initial Settings menu of the Setup menu.

- You can print page numbers on multipage documents. They can be printed at the top or bottom of the page and aligned flush left, centered, or flush right. You can also print them on odd or even pages only or alternate them (called *mirrored*) for a document that is to be copied on both sides of the paper so that they appear only on the outside corner of each page.
- A page number that is printed at the bottom of the page is called a *drop folio.*
- You can choose any of three numbering styles: Arabic, uppercase Roman, or lowercase Roman.
- You can start or stop page numbers anywhere in the document and suppress them on individual pages.
- Headers and footers are printed at the top and bottom of the page. When printed on more than one page, they are called running heads and running feet.
- You can enter codes into headers and footers that automatically calculate and print the date and time or the page number.
- To print headers or footers on alternate sides of pages, use a Header or Footer A aligned flush left on even-numbered pages and a Header or Footer B aligned flush right on odd-numbered pages.
- Footnotes are numbered references printed at the bottom of the page.
- Endnotes are numbered references printed at the end of the document or a section within the document.
- If you insert or delete footnote or endnote reference numbers in the document, all the following reference numbers adjust automatically.

TRUE/FALSE

T F

1. WordPerfect is set to automatically print page numbers on every page without your telling it to do so.

2. Page numbers can be printed anywhere on the type page.

3. A page number printed at the bottom of the page is called a *drop folio.*

4. If a page is counted in the page numbering sequence but it does not have a printed page number, it is called a *blind folio.*

5. Headers are printed at the top of the document and footers at the bottom.

❑ ❑   6. Headers and footers in WordPerfect are printed in either the top or bottom margin.

❑ ❑   7. The main purpose for headers or footers is to provide decoration.

❑ ❑   8. In WordPerfect you can enter two headers, and two footers on each page.

❑ ❑   9. Mirrored headers or footers are in the same position on odd and even pages.

❑ ❑   10. The only difference between footnotes and endnotes is where they print in a document.

FILL IN THE BLANK

1. A page number printed at the bottom of the page is called a ____________.

2. If a page is counted in the page numbering sequence but does not have a printed page number, the page number is called a ____________ folio.

3. To print the same text at the top of every page, you create a ____________.

4. To print the same text at the bottom of every page, you create a ____________.

5. If headers or footers print on more than one page they are called ____________ heads or ____________ feet.

6. When headers and footers on alternate odd and even pages are aligned with the inside or outside margins, they are said to be ____________.

7. To enter a code into a header or footer that automatically numbers pages, you press ____________.

8. To enter a code in headers or footers that calculates and prints the date, you press ____________.

9. If you want notes to print at the bottom of the page on which you enter the reference number, you specify ____________.

10. If you want notes to print at the end of the document, you specify ____________.

1. Drop folio
2. Folio
3. Blind folio
4. Mirrored page numbers
5. Headers
6. Footers
7. Running headers or footers
8. **Ctrl-B**
9. **Shift-F5**
10. Footnotes
11. Endnotes

___ A page number

___ A page number that is counted but not printed on the page

___ Headers or footers that are aligned with the inside or outside margins on odd and even pages

___ Headers or footers that print on more than one page

___ Keys you press to display a menu from which you can choose a date code to enter dates in headers and footers

___ Keys you press to enter a code that calculates and prints the page number

___ Notes that print at the end of the document

___ Notes that print on the same page as their reference numbers

___ Page numbers printed at the bottom of the page

___ Text printed at the bottom of the page

___ Text printed at the top of the page

WRITE OUT THE ANSWERS

1. What do you have to do to have WordPerfect print page numbers on each page of a document?
2. List and describe at least two options available for page numbering control.
3. What are headers and footers? Why are they used?
4. What are headers and footers that appear on more than one page called?
5. List and describe some options you have when printing headers and footers.
6. Assume that your document is to be printed on both sides of the page and then bound. How do you align headers and footers so that they are on the outside edge of each page?
7. What is the difference between a footnote and an endnote?
8. What happens to a footnote reference number if you insert a new reference number above it?
9. List the steps you would follow to edit a footnote.
10. List the steps you would follow to change the spacing between footnotes.

PROJECTS

PROJECT 1

ENTERING A DOCUMENT ON FOOTNOTE FORMATS

In this project, you enter footnotes that do not refer to specific works but provide the form and identify the elements that you should use in your citations.

Procedures Used
- Entering footnotes.

Text Files Needed
- FOOTFORM.WP5

Formats
① Enter a footnote code with the corresponding text shown in the footnotes at the bottom of the document.

1. Book with one author[1] — ①
2. Book with two or three authors[2]
3. Book with a corporate author[3]
4. Work in several volumes or parts[4]
5. Works in an anthology or a collection[5]
6. Article in a reference work[6]
7. Article from a weekly, biweekly, or monthly magazine or newspaper[7]
8. Article from a daily newspaper[8]
9. Film[9]
10. Interview[10]

---

[1]First Last, <u>Title</u> (City, State: Publisher, copyright date), pages.

[2]First Last, First Last, and First Last, <u>Title</u> (City, State: Publisher, copyright date), pages.

[3]Name of Corporation, <u>Title</u> (City, State: Publisher, copyright date), pages.

[4]First Last, <u>Title</u>, Volume or Part (City, State: Publisher, copyright date), pages.

[5]First Last, "Title of Article," in <u>Title of Publication</u>, ed. (City, State: Publisher, copyright date), pages.

[6]"Title of section," <u>Title of Book</u>, copyright or edition date.

[7]First Last, "Title of Article," Name of Periodical, date, section, page, column.

[8]First Last, "Title of Article," Name of Newspaper, date of issue, page.

[9]First Last, dir., <u>Film Title</u>, with Major Actor, Studio, date or release.

[10]Personal interview with Title, First Last, date.

ADDING MIRRORED PAGE NUMBERS IN FOOTERS

In this project, you enter mirrored page numbers in footers.

Procedures Used
■ Entering page numbers in mirrored footers.

Text Files Needed
■ CLOUDS2.WP5

Formats
① Enter a Footer A code. It should specify even page numbers flush left. The footer should read "*^B Clouds.*" Format the *^B* code as boldface and change its size to Large. Enter a base font code in front of the footer text for a 10-point typeface.
② Enter a Footer B code that sets odd page numbers flush right. The footer should read "*Clouds ^B.*" Format the *^B* code as boldface and change its size to Large. Enter a base font code in front of the footer text for a 10-point typeface.

Tip
■ If your headers or footers do not print, check the location of the header and footer codes. They should be at the top of the page.

Clouds, to almost everyone, have some meaning. But to you as a pilot, clouds are your weather "signposts in the sky." They give you an indication of air motion, stability, and moisture. Clouds help you visualize weather conditions and potential weather hazards you might encounter in flight. Let's examine these "signposts" and how to identify them.

IDENTIFICATION

For identification purposes, you need be concerned only with the more basic cloud types, which are divided into four "families." The families are: high clouds, middle clouds, low clouds, and clouds with extensive vertical development. The first three families are further classified according to the way they are formed. Clouds formed by vertical currents in unstable air are *cumulus* meaning *accumulation* or *heap*; they are characterized by their lumpy, billowy appearance. Clouds formed by the cooling of a stable layer are *stratus* meaning *stratified* or *layered*; they are characterized by their uniform, sheetlike appearance. In addition to the above, the prefix *nimbo-* or the suffix *-nimbus* means raincloud. Thus stratified clouds from which rain is falling are *nimbostratus*. A heavy, swelling cumulus type cloud which produces precipitation is a *cumulonimbus*. Clouds broken into fragments are often identified by adding the suffix *-fractus*; for example, fragmentary cumulus is *cumulus fractus*.

HIGH CLOUDS

The high cloud family is cirriform and includes cirrus, cirrocumulus, and cirrostratus. They are composed almost entirely of ice crystals. The height of the bases of these clouds ranges from about 16,500 to 45,000 feet in middle latitudes. Figures 45 through 47 are photographs of high clouds.

Cirrus
Cirrus are thin, featherlike ice crystal clouds in patches or narrow bands. Larger ice crystals often trail downward in well defined wisps called "Mares tails." Wispy, cirruslike, these contain no significant icing or turbulence.

Cirrocumulus
Cirrocumulus are thin clouds, the individual elements appearing as small white flakes or patches of cotton. May contain highly supercooled water droplets. Some turbulence and icing.

Cirrostratus
Cirrostratus is a thin whitish cloud layer appearing like a sheet or veil. Cloud elements are diffuse, sometimes partially striated or fibrous. Owing to their ice crystal makeup, these clouds are associated with halos—large luminous circles surrounding the sun or moon. No turbulence and little if any icing. The greatest

Clouds **1**

THE DTP ADVISOR NEWSLETTER

In this project, you add a footer to the newsletter that gives its issue date, page number, and volume number.

Procedures Used
- Entering footers.

Text Files Needed
- ADVISOR.WP5

Formats

① Enter a code to print a footer on every page. When the footer screen is displayed, enter *SPRING 1993*, center a code to print page numbers, then right align *Volume 1/Number 1*. Format the footer so that it prints in small caps in 10-point type.

Tip

- The footer code should be positioned after the margin setting code and before the column definition code.

① # THE *dtp* ADVISOR

FaceLift For WordPerfect

Bitstream Inc. today announced version 1.5 of Bitstream® FaceLift™ for WordPerfect.® FaceLift brings enhanced font support to WordPerfect 5.0 and 5.1. The new FaceLift version 1.5 will create high-quality fonts on-the-fly for popular dot-matrix and inkjet printers—like the HP® DeskJet,® Canon BubbleJet and the IBM® ExecuJet—in addition to the existing on-the-fly support for the Hewlett-Packard LaserJet® series of printers. FaceLift 1.5 for Word-Perfect will be available in the spring of 1991.

In addition to 13 typeface outlines provided in the original FaceLift package, FaceLift 1.5 for WordPer-fect will also ship with three Symbol typefaces: ITC Zapf Dingbats® Symbol Proportional and Symbol Monospaced. Users will be able to access a total of 698 characters from the Bitstream International Char-acter Set and from these three Symbols typefaces.

FaceLift 1.5 for WordPerfect is an easy-to-use utility that allows users to print high-quality fonts in any size from 2 to 500 point (in quarter point incre-ments) without ever having to leave the application. The fonts are generated at print time, so the need for stored bit-map fonts is eliminated. Based on Bitstream Speedo™ technology, FaceLift sends characters to printers in both graphics mode (laser, inkjet and dot-matrix printers) and as HP soft fonts (laser printers only). Users have full control over the number and size of soft fonts to be downloaded, depending on the memory available in the printer.

"We are very excited that FaceLift 1.5 for Word-Perfect will provide dot-matrix and inkjet users with the same high typographic quality and capabilities that HP LaserJet users have enjoyed with Bitstream type," stated Doug Lloyd, Executive Director at WordPerfect. "That, and the addition of the three new Symbol typefaces makes FaceLift a great companion for WordPerfect."

First-time users can purchase FaceLift 1.5 for WordPerfect for a suggested U.S. list price of $99. Current users of FaceLift 1.0 for WordPerfect can upgrade to version 1.5 for $24.95. In addition to the 16 typefaces included free with FaceLift, users can purchase add-on fonts from the Bitstream Library of 52 typeface packages. Also available is the FaceLift Companion Value Pack, a selection of 24 text and headline faces for a suggested U.S. list price $199.

FaceLift 1.5 for WordPerfect is the newest member of the Bitstream FaceLift product line. The initial product, FaceLift for Windows,™ shipped in August of 1990. All FaceLift products can share Bitstream typefaces (in Speedo format) stored in a single common subdirectory.

FaceLift for Wordperfect was developed in con-junction with LaserTools Corporation, a privately held company based in Emeryville, CA. LaserTools is a developer of innovative printing enhancement products—tools for printer sharing, printer control, printer acceleration, and font management.

An industry leader in typographic quality and innovative technology, Bitstream licenses fonts and related software to more than 420 hardware manufac-turers and software developers worldwide. Its line of retail products is distributed by an extensive network of dealers in the United States and in 18 nations worldwide.

For more information, contact:
Bitstream Inc.
215 First Street
Cambridge, MA 02142-1270
(617) 497-6222

Postscript in a Cartridge

Hewlett-Packard Company today announced a Post-Script accessory for the HP LaserJet printer. The cartridge is $995 V.S. list and contains the PostScript page description language, licensed from Adobe Systems Incorporated, and 35 Adobe typefaces.

With the PostScript cartridge, the HP LaserJet printer is the only printer to combine Adobe-licensed PostScript and HP PCL printer-language support for

Spring 1993   1   Volume 1/Number 1

Graphics

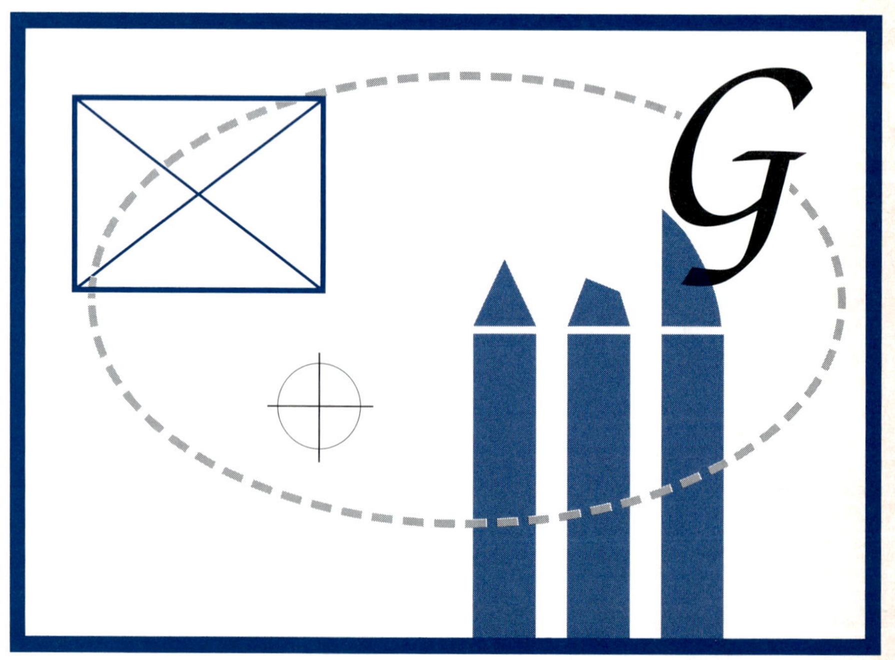

Ruled Lines

After completing this topic, you should be able to:
- Describe typical applications for ruled lines
- Insert graphics lines into your documents
- Use WordPerfect's Line Draw command in your own documents

▶ T U T O R I A L

In this tutorial, you add ruled lines to the subheads in a document. When you are finished, your printout should look similar to the illustration "Ruled Subheads."

GETTING STARTED

1. Retrieve the RULES1.WP5 document and enter your name.

ADDING A RULED LINE OVER A SUBHEAD

2. Move the cursor to the blank line above the subhead that reads "*Lines.*"
3. Press **Alt-F9** to display the Graphics menu.
4. Press **L** for *Line*.
5. Press **H** for *Horizontal* to display the Horizontal Line menu.
6. Press **Enter** to accept all defaults. (You can use the *View Document* command on the Print menu to see the line.)

ADDING MORE RULED LINES

7. Move the cursor to the blank lines above the subheads that read "*Boxes*" and "*Inserting Graphics Lines.*"
8. Repeat Steps 3 through 6 for each subhead.

SEPARATING THE RULED LINES AND SUBHEADS

9. Save and print the document.
10. Reveal codes and move the cursor to the beginning of the subhead that reads "*Lines.*"
11. Press **Shift-F8** to display the Format menu.
12. Press **O** for *Other*.
13. Press **A** for *Advance*.
14. Press **D** for *Down* and the prompt reads *Adv. down.*
15. Type **3p** and then press **Enter**.

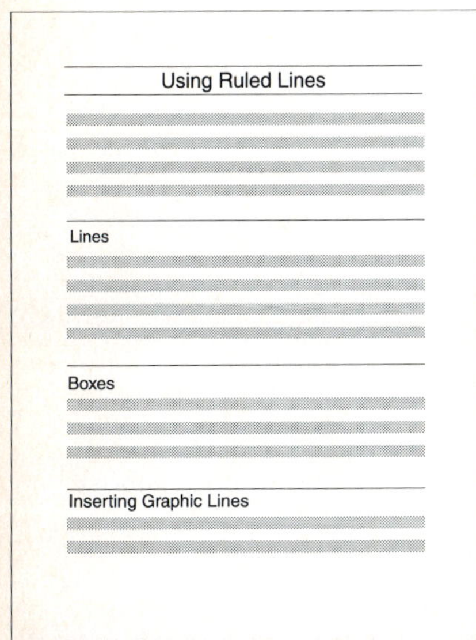

Ruled Subheads

16. Press **F7** to return to the Edit screen.

17. Move the cursor to the beginning of the subheads that read *"Boxes"* and *"Inserting Graphics Lines"* and repeat Steps 11 through 16.

FINISHING UP

18. Save and print the document. Compare this printout with the first one that you made in Step 9. The headings should now be moved down 3 points from the graphics line.

▶ D E S K T O P   P U B L I S H I N G   C O N C E P T S

Pull-quotes are short extracts from the text that are repeated, frequently in a boldface type, and set off from the other text with rules above and below.

Pull-Quotes

Item	Model 10	Model 20
Hard Disk		■
Floppy Disk	■	
EGA Display	■	
VGA Display		■
286 CPU	■	
386 CPU		■
CD ROM		■
20 Mhz	■	
33 MHz		■

Tables

Many publications use ruled lines to set off various elements or to separate sections. You can use lines above, below, or both above and below text elements. Typical applications include subheads, pull-quotes, and tables.

If you use rules with subheads, it is usually best to place the rule above the head, not below it. When below the head, it separates the subhead from the text that follows. If you use one line above and another below, making the one above darker or thicker associates the subhead more closely with the text that follows.

Pull-quotes are short extracts from the text that are repeated, frequently in a boldface type, and set off from the other text with rules above and below. These are widely used in newsletters, newspapers, and magazines to fill out short columns.

Tables are made more readable by adding rules to separate sections. Horizontal rules are used in almost all tables, and vertical rules are used in some. Vertical rules are also frequently used to separate columns when a document is printed in more than one column.

When using lines, here are some points to consider.

- The weight of the rules used above or below text should be proportional to the size of the type.
- Rules can range in density from light gray to black. If they are wide enough, they can also contain text. The density of the text is important to ensure its readability. White text is more readable in dark gray or black rules (called ***dropped-out text***) and dark text is more readable in light gray rules.
- Rules can span the full page horizontally or vertically or you can specify where they start and what length they should be.

▶ W O R D P E R F E C T   P R O C E D U R E S

8 Point Subhead

12 Point Subhead

Rule Weights

There are two ways to enter lines in a document: by inserting graphic lines or by drawing them in.

Graphics Lines

The graphics line feature allows you to place horizontal or vertical lines on a page and specify both their thickness and their density. Unlike lines that you draw, these lines work with all fonts and you can specify that they automatically adjust to changes in margins. To control the space between the text that follows or precedes a graphics line, use advance up or advance down codes on the Other Format menu (**Shift-F8**, *Other*, *Advance*)

Inserting Graphics Lines

1. Position the cursor where you want a horizontal or a vertical line to appear (or anywhere on the page if you are setting the line's position relative to the edges of the page).
2. Either: Press **Alt-F9**, then **L** for *Line*, and then **H** for *Horizontal* or **V** for *Vertical.*
   Or: Pull down the Graphics menu, select *Line*, and then select *Create Horizontal* or *Create Vertical.*
3. Select any of the settings described in the table "Graphics Line Menu Choices."
4. Press **F7** to return to the Edit screen.

GRAPHICS LINE MENU CHOICES

1 *Horizontal Position* positions the line.
- **1** *Left* prints the line flush with the left margin, and you have to specify a length for the line.
- **2** *Right* prints the line flush with the right margin, and you have to specify a length for the line.
- **3** *Center* centers the line between the margins, and you have to specify a length for the line.
- **4** *Full* prints the line so that it is flush with the left and right margins, and the length of the line adjusts automatically when you change margins and do not specify a length.
- **5** *Set Position* specifies where the line should start relative to the left edge of the paper.

2 *Vertical Position* is the same as **1** *Horizontal Position* but controls vertical position and length of the line. For example, the *Set Position* choice prints the line starting at the distance specified from the top of the paper.

3 *Length of Line* determines how long the line is. When printing a horizontal line, the line length is calculated from the margin specified by the Horizontal Position command. If you specified the *Full* choice, the line automatically prints from margin to margin.

4 *Width of Line* specifies how thick the line is.

5 *Gray Shading (% of black)* specifies how dark the printed line appears. 100% is the darkest, and 0% is the lightest.

Once you have entered a graphics line, you may find that you need to edit it to change its position, length, width, or shading. To do so, you use the Graphics Line Edit command.

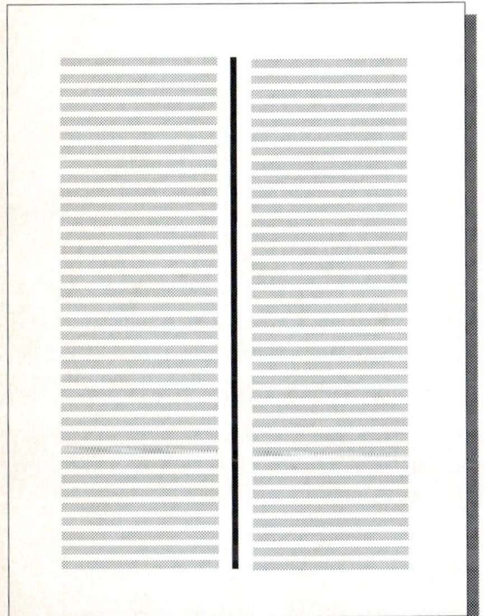

Columns Separated by a Line

Editing Graphics Lines

1. Position the cursor below or to the right of the graphics line that you want to edit. (The program searches toward the top of the document.)
2. Either: Press **Alt**-**F9**, then **L** for *Line*, and then **o** for *Horizontal* or **e** for *Vertical*.

   Or: Pull down the Graphics menu, select *Line*, and then select *Edit Horizontal* or *Edit Vertical*.
3. Revise any of the settings described in the table "Graphics Line Menu Choices."
4. Press **F7** to return to the Edit screen.

Text in Lines

WordPerfect allows you to print text within graphics lines. There are three basic steps to doing this.

1. Begin by entering a graphics line wide enough to hold the text. The gray shading that you specify is important, and you can vary it from 0 percent (white) to 100 percent (black). If you want to print black text in the line, a light gray is best. If you want to print white text in the line, dark gray or black is best.
2. Enter the text below the line and place an advance up code in front of it to move it up into the line when it is printed. For example, if you enter a code for a 1-inch graphics line in a document, you then enter the line of text immediately below it. Placing a code to advance the line of text up .6 inch will print it right in the middle of the graphics line.
3. Specify a text color. If you are printing white text in a dark-gray or black line, you use the Font menu to assign colors to text (this feature is not supported by all printers). To print white text dropped out of a black border, move the cursor in front of the text to be dropped out, press **Ctrl**-**F8** to display the Font menu, then press **C** for *Print Color*. Press **W** for *White* to print the text in white, then press **F7** to return to the document. (Be sure to enter a code at the end of the text to restore it to black.)

Line Drawing

WordPerfect has a Line Draw command that you can use to create lines and boxes. These drawn lines are more limited than graphics lines because they don't adjust when you change margins and they are hard to use in conjunction with text. They also work only when printing in a monospaced font such as Courier. If you use a proportional font, the lines will not print correctly in relation to the text. However, line drawing makes it possible to do some things, such as drawing organizational charts, that you can't do with graphics lines.

To draw lines, you select the character you want to work with. You then use the directional arrow keys to move the cursor around the screen and paint a line with the selected character. There is a command

Black and White Text Printed in Lines with Varying Gray Shading

that lets you erase any lines you have mistakenly entered and one that allows you to move the cursor without drawing a line. When using Line Draw, here are some points to keep in mind.

- Use left justification only; full justification may cause problems.
- You can copy or move sections of line drawings with the Rectangular Block commands.
- To box text, enter the text so that each line ends with a hard carriage return and is indented one or more spaces from the left margin. Often it is easier first to draw the boxes and then use typeover mode to insert text in them. When you do so, do not press **Enter** to end lines. Instead, use the cursor movement keys to move the cursor to the beginning of the next line.

Drawing Lines

1. Either: Press **Ctrl-F3** and then **L** for *Line Draw*.

   Or: Pull down the Tools menu and select *Line Draw*.
2. Select any of the menu choices described in the table "Line Draw Menu Commands" to draw and edit lines.
3. Press the arrow keys to move the cursor.
4. When you are finished, press **F7** to remove the menu and return to the Edit screen.

LINE DRAW MENU COMMANDS

1 | selects the character that draws single lines.

2 ‖ selects the character that draws double lines.

3 * selects the character that draws lines with asterisks or any other character specified with the Change command.

4 *Change* displays a list of additional characters that you can draw with. When you select a character, it replaces the asterisk on the Line Draw menu. Type the number of your choice, and you then return to the Line Draw menu. You can also press **O** for *Other*, and the prompt reads *Solid character:* Hold down **Alt** and type any character's ASCII code on the numeric keypad.

5 *Erase* erases lines when the cursor is moved through them.

6 *Move* allows you to move the cursor around the screen without drawing or erasing lines.

EXERCISE 1

ADDING RULED LINES TO A TABLE

In this exercise, you add ruled lines to set off a table's column heads and to end the table.

1. Retrieve the RULES2.WP5 document and enter your name.
2. Print out the document and measure the width that the lines should be to span the six columns of data. (The distance varies slightly depending on the typeface you are using. It should be slightly over 6 inches or 430 points.)
3. Insert a blank line between the table title and the column heads. Then follow the instructions in the KEY/Strokes box "Inserting Graphics Lines" to enter a horizontal line on the blank line. The line's characteristics should be:
   - Horizontal position: left
   - Length of line: your measurement
   - Width of line: 2 points
4. Insert a blank line between the table column heads and the table body, then insert a horizontal line on the blank line. The line's characteristics should be:
   - Horizontal position: left
   - Length of line: your measurement
   - Width of line: 1 point
5. Enter a horizontal line at the end of the table. The line's characteristics should be:
   - Horizontal position: left
   - Length of line: your measurement
   - Width of line: 2 points
6. Enter advance down codes on the line below each of the top two graphic lines to move the text that follows down 3 points.
7. Save and print the document.

EXERCISE 2

CREATING AN ORGANIZATIONAL CHART

In this exercise, you use the Line Draw commands to create the organizational chart shown in the figure "Organizational Chart." To complete this exercise, you need access to a monospaced or line draw font. If you do not have one of these, your drawing will look fine on the screen but will print out of alignment.

1. Retrieve the RULES3.WP5 document and enter your name above the title "*President.*"
2. Enter a base font code at the top of the document to print in a monospaced typeface such as Courier or a line draw font.

3. Before drawing lines, use the **Spacebar** to align the text as follows:
   - Enter two spaces to the left of the department label "*Marketing*."
   - Enter ten spaces between the department labels "*Marketing*," "*Finance*," and "*Manufacturing*."
   - Center the "*VP*"s above the three department names.
   - Center your name and title over the "*VP of Finance*."
   - Insert three blank lines between your title and the titles of the three people below you on the chart.
4. Save the document so you can clear the screen and retrieve it to start over if you encounter serious problems.
5. Follow the instructions in the KEY/Strokes box "Drawing Lines" to draw the lines shown in the figure.
6. Save and print the document. To adjust alignments, you can insert and delete spaces to shift elements about in the drawing.

Organizational Chart

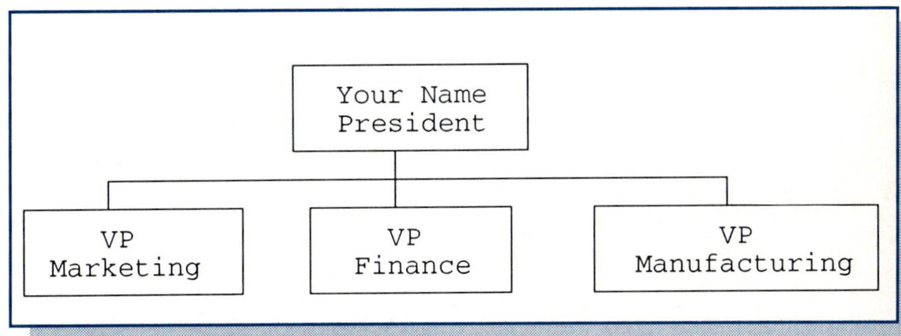

EXERCISE 3

ADDING RULED LINES TO AN ACCOUNTING DOCUMENT

In this exercise, you enter ruled lines to separate sections of the table of accounting terms as shown in the figure "Accounting Terms."

1. Retrieve the RULES4.WP5 document and enter your name.
2. Print out the document and measure the length that the lines should be (it varies depending on the typeface you are using).
3. Follow the instructions in the KEY/Strokes box "Inserting Graphics Lines" to enter a horizontal line between the table title and the column heads. The line's characteristics should be:
   - Horizontal position: left
   - Length of line: your measurement
   - Width of line: 4 points
4. Enter a horizontal line between the table column heads and the table body. The line's characteristics should be:
   - Horizontal position: left
   - Length of line: your measurement
   - Width of line: 2 points
5. Enter horizontal lines between each of the other entries in the table. The line's characteristics should be:
   - Horizontal position: left
   - Length of line: your measurement
   - Width of line: 1 point

(Tip. It's faster to enter one line and then copy it to the other rows. After you copy it once, move to the next place you want it, press **Shift-F10**, and then press **Enter** to copy it again.)

6. Enter a horizontal line at the end of the table. It should be aligned left, as long as your measurement, and 4 points wide.

   - Horizontal position: left
   - Length of line: your measurement
   - Width of line: 4 points

7. Enter advance down codes on the lines below each of the graphics lines to move the text that follows down 3 points. (Again, it's faster to enter one code and then copy it where needed.)

8. Save and print the document.

Accounting Terms

Exhbit 1. Table of Debit and Credit Entries

Type of Account	If the transaction will decrease the Account, enter it as a:	If the transaction will increase the account, enter it as a:	Typical Balance
Asset	credit	debit	debit
Liability	debit	credit	credit
Capital	debit	credit	credit
Income	debit	credit	credit
Expense	credit	debit	debit

✔ GRAPHICS LINE TIPS

- If you print graphics on a dot-matrix printer, vertical lines may appear broken. To correct this, set the line height to .125 inch or 8 lines per inch.
- To add boxes around your text, or even to print a light screen over it so that it stands out, use text boxes or tables.
- To add vertical and horizontal ruled lines in tabular tables or parallel-style columns, consider using the Tables Create command.

Line Art and Halftones

After completing this topic, you should be able to:

- Incorporate graphics images into your own documents
- Describe different types of graphics options that you can use
- Edit graphics that you have inserted into the document

▶ T U T O R I A L

In this tutorial, you integrate graphics into a document. When you are finished, your printout should look similar to the illustration "Newspaper Headline."

GETTING STARTED

1. Retrieve the LINEART.WP5 document and enter your name in the heading and in the text in place of the current text *"Your Name."*

CREATING A FIGURE BOX

2. Move the cursor to the line immediately below the line that reads *"in Desktop Publishing!"*
3. Press **Alt-F9** to display the Graphics menu.
4. Press **F** for *Figure*.
5. Press **C** for *Create* to display the Graphics Definition screen and menu.
6. Press **F** for *Filename*, and the prompt reads *Enter filename:*.
7. Press **F5**, enter the path to the drive/directory where you store your document files, and then press **Enter** to display a list of the files.
8. Highlight *EX0104.CGM* and press **R** for *Retrieve*.
9. Press **H** for *Horizontal Position*.
10. Press **F** for *Full*.
11. Press **F7** to return to the Edit screen. The figure number and the top of the figure box are displayed on the screen.
12. Use the Print menu's View Document command to preview your results. You see that the figure is below the text as you would expect. Press **F7** to return to the Edit screen.

MOVING THE TEXT DOWN TO WHERE WE WANT IT

13. Press **Alt-F3** or **F11** to reveal codes and move the cursor to the beginning of the line with your name on it in the headline *"Your Name Wins Award in Desktop Publishing!"*

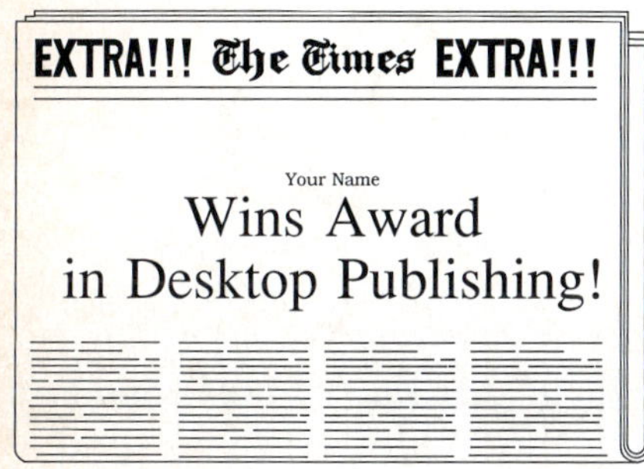

Newspaper Headline

14. Press **Shift**-**F8** to display the Format menu.
15. Press **O** for **O**ther to display the Other menu.
16. Press **A** for **A**dvance.
17. Press **D** for **D**own and the prompt reads *Adv. down 0*.
18. Type **2.5"** and then press **Enter**.
19. Press **F7** to return to the Edit screen.

MOVING THE IMAGE BACK OVER THE TEXT

20. Move the cursor to the beginning of the line with the figure box code *[Fig Box:1;EX0104.CGM;]* on it.
21. Repeat Steps 14 through 16, then enter an advance up code that advances the graphic up **3"**.

FINISHING UP

22. Save the document.
23. Use the Print menu's View Document command to preview your results. The text should now be positioned within the graphic. Press **F7** to return to the Edit screen.
24. Enter a base font code above the headline to make it 40 points (if you do not have fonts that large, use the largest size you do have). Use the View Document command again to preview your work. Continue experimenting until you have the text and graphic the way you like them.
25. Save and print the document. Printing graphics can take a long time on some printers. Ask your instructor if you should make a printout. If you do so, when you display the Print menu again check the *Graphics Quality* setting. The setting can be *Draft*, *Medium*, or *High* quality (listed from fastest/poorest quality to slowest/highest quality). If you want to print the graphic with another resolution, press **G** for **G**raphics Quality, change the setting, and then press **F** for **F**ull Document.

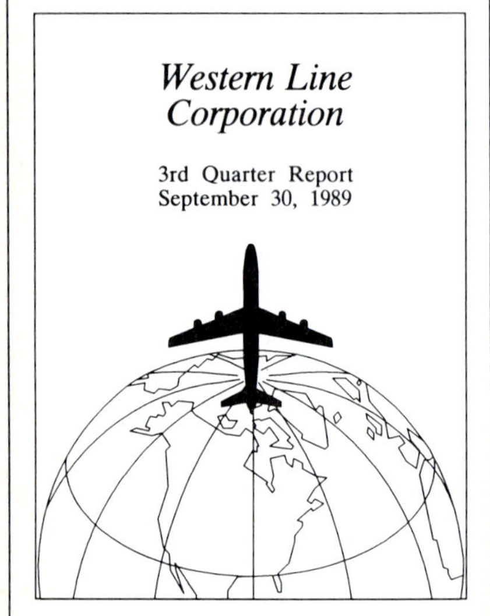

Graphics and Text Combined
("Courtesy of Islandview/MCI."
Picture Pak is a trademark of Imageline,
Inc. copyright Imageline, Inc. 1991.)

▷ D E S K T O P   P U B L I S H I N G   C O N C E P T S

WARNING

This cabinet contains extremely high voltage components. Do not open if you are not an authorized technician.

Sidebar

Illustrations can add greatly to the interest level of a publication. For example, charts, maps, and graphs can provide detail in a compressed form, photographs can show people or places, or line drawings can add decoration. You can also use graphics for such things as letterheads and facsimile signatures. Traditionally, a page or part of a page in the document was left blank, and the illustration was prepared separately and then inserted, or pasted in. Now, it is possible to integrate graphics so they print in position as the document is being printed.

Graphics can be placed in boxes. (In WordPerfect this is done automatically.) Boxes are used, as lines are, to set off elements of a design. Typical uses include sidebars, charts, and graphics.

Sidebars are small sections of text related to but not included in the body text. Sidebars can be set off by being enclosed in a box. When you do so, be sure you leave margins between the box and the text.

Charts can use boxes and text to illustrate such things as the structure of organizations. It is best to prepare these on separate paint or draw programs and import them as graphics into a document.

When using boxes, here are some points to consider.

- Boxes can be varied in their design by changing elements such as line thickness and shading.

- Boxes can use **drop shadows** to make them stand out and lead the reader's eye to the caption.

Boxed Graphics
Here are four variations on boxes showing changes in thickness and shading as well as a drop shadow.

WordPerfect allows you to integrate graphics directly into your document. You can also use this feature to put text in boxes.

WordPerfect Clip Art
WordPerfect includes many graphics images, called clip art, that you can integrate into a document. The images are stored in files with the extension .WPG. On a hard disk system, these files are usually stored in the same directory as the WordPerfect program files. On a floppy disk system, they are stored on the *Learning/Images* floppy disk.

Incorporating Images into Documents
To incorporate a graphics image into a document, the graphic must be in a file on the disk. To insert the graphic into a document, you insert a code where you want it to print. This code refers to the name of the graphic's file on the disk and specifies such formats as position and size. You can enter these codes in the main body of your document, in headers and footers, and in footnotes and endnotes. After you enter a graphics box, an outline of the box and its number is displayed on the screen. To see the box exactly as it will print, you use the Print menu's View Document command. To edit the contents of the figure box, you use the *Edit* choice on the Graphics Definition menu (see the table "Graphics Definition Menu Choices").

You can choose from five types of graphics boxes and retrieve text or graphics into any of them. The box type does not refer to the contents of the box but to the numbering system assigned to each type and its default settings, such as border styles and shading. For example, figure boxes are automatically numbered *1, 2, 3,* and so on and have single lines on all four sides. Table boxes are numbered *I, II, III,* and so on and have thick rules above and below. You can change any of these styles from the Options menu, but each box type will be numbered consecutively, independently of the other box types. If you want figures to be numbered consecutively, regardless of their contents, use the same box type. To use different styles for different contents, specify different box types as follows:

- Figure boxes are normally used for graphics images and charts. These boxes have default lines on all four sides.
- Table boxes can be used for tables of numbers. These boxes have default lines at top and bottom.
- Text boxes can be used for quotes, excerpts, or any other section of text you want to draw attention to. These boxes have default lines at top and bottom with a screen printed between them.

Clip Art

These illustrations show the clip art files included with the WordPerfect 5.1 program. You can insert any of them into your documents by specifying their filenames (and path to the disk drive they are stored on) on the Graphics Definition screen.

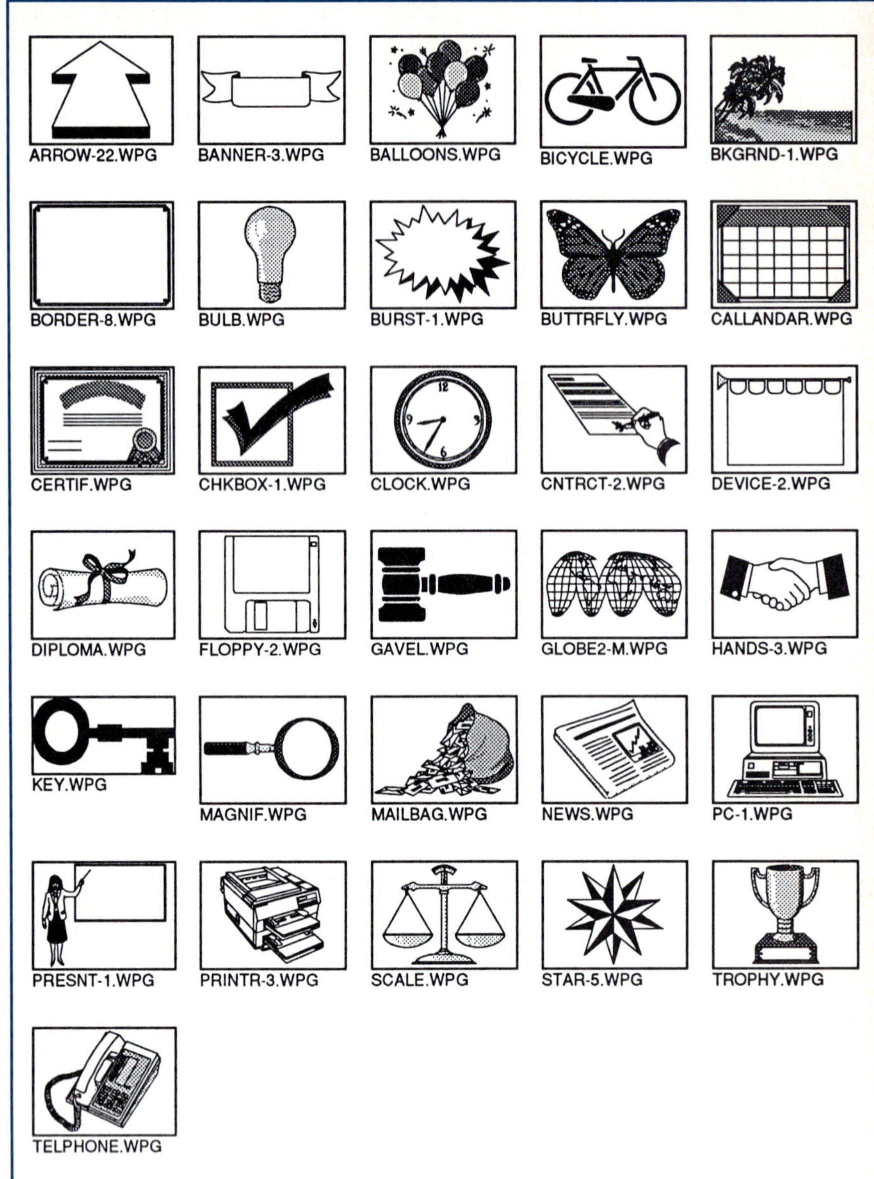

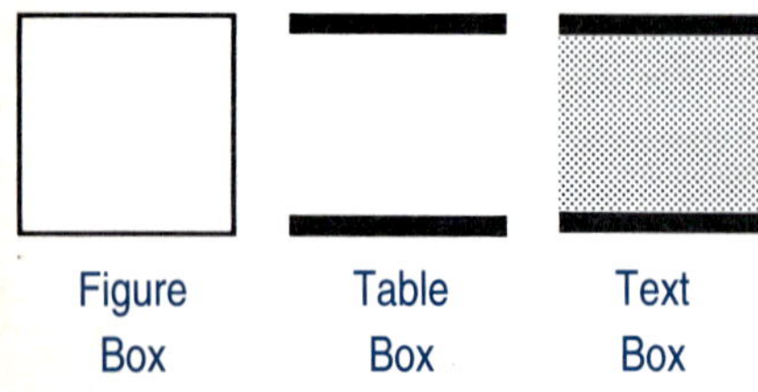

WordPerfect Graphic Box Defaults

- User-defined boxes can be used for any series of text or captions that you want numbered independently from the other types. These boxes have no default line or screen settings.
- Equation boxes are used to enter mathematical equations. (This feature is not covered in this text.)

The *Contents* choice on the Graphics Definition menu gives you the option of embedding a graphics file into a document or linking it. If you embed it, the size of the document may increase dramatically, since graphics files can be quite large. This will slow down scrolling, saving, and editing. If you link the graphic, it is not included in the document until the document is printed. This keeps the size of the document file smaller, but if you want to send the document file to someone else, you also have to send the graphics files that are linked to it.

Creating or Editing a Graphics Box

1. Position the cursor where you want the box to appear or above the figure where you want to change options or figure numbers.
2. Either: Press **Alt-F9** to display the Graphics menu.

   Or: Pull down the Graphics menu.
3. Select a box type.
4. Either: Press **C** for *Create*, and then define the box using the menu selections described in the table "Graphics Definition Menu Choices" and shown in the figure "The Graphics Definition Screen and Menu."

   Or: Press **E** for *Edit*, and the prompt reads *Figure number?* Type the number or the figure that you want to edit, and then press **Enter**. Edit the box using the menu selections described in the table "Graphics Definition Menu Choices" and shown in the figure "The Graphics Definition Screen and Menu."
5. Press **F7** to return to the Edit screen.

The Graphics Definition Screen and Menu
The Graphics Definition screen and menu lists the choices you use to specify the name of the graphic file to be inserted, add a caption, define the type, and specify its size and position on the page.

```
Definition: Figure

    1 - Filename

    2 - Contents              Empty

    3 - Caption

    4 - Anchor Type           Paragraph

    5 - Vertical Position     0"

    6 - Horizontal Position   Right

    7 - Size                  3.25" wide x 3.25" (high)

    8 - Wrap Text Around Box  Yes

    9 - Edit



Selection: 0
```

GRAPHICS DEFINITION MENU CHOICES

1 *Filename* is the name of the graphic or text file you want to incorporate. After you select *Filename*, the prompt reads *Enter filename:*. You can then press **F5**, **Enter** to list files. (The directory that is displayed is determined by the *Location of Files* setting on the Setup menu.) Highlight the desired file, and press **R** for *Retrieve*. If you do not enter a filename, the box is left empty. When editing, you can also delete the filename to delete the contents of the box while leaving the box itself intact.

2 *Contents* specifies how the graphic is saved and the type of data that can be placed in a graphics box.

- **1** *Graphic* saves the graphics image as part of the document.
- **2** *Graphic on Disk* keeps a graphic stored in its own file on the disk and accesses it during printing.
- **3** *Text* allows you to place both text and formatting codes in the graphics box.
- **4** *Equation* specifies that the equation editor be displayed so that you can create or edit equations.

3 *Caption* displays a screen on which you type a caption for the figure. The caption screen also displays a numbering code (and the calculated number), which automatically numbers the figure in sequence. You can leave this code intact or delete it if you do not want your box numbered. If you delete it and then want to restore it, press **Alt**-**F9**. You cannot enter captions for graphics boxes that you place in headers and footers or footnotes and endnotes.

4 *Anchor Type* specifies how the graphics box interacts with text.

- **1** *Paragraph* boxes (the default type) move with the text that wraps around them. When you select this type, the code is automatically entered at the beginning of the paragraph containing the cursor. If the box will not fit on the current page, it is printed at the top of the next page, but the paragraph containing the code will not move to follow it.
- **2** *Page* boxes stay fixed on a specified page. Be sure that the code is entered at the top of the page if you want it to print on the current page. When you select this option, the prompt reads *Number of pages to skip:*. If you enter **0**, it prints on the current page, entering **1** prints it on the next page, and so on.
- **3** *Character* boxes are treated like other characters in a line of text. Text is interrupted by the box when the document is printed. This box type is the only one permitted in footnotes and endnotes.

5 *Vertical Position* options are based on the anchor type you selected in **4** *Anchor Type* .

- Paragraph boxes are offset from the first line of the paragraph containing the code by the distance you enter. The default shown on the screen is the current distance of the cursor from the top of the paragraph. If the box will not fit on the page, the offset is changed to keep the box positioned within the paragraph. You control how far it can move with the *Minimum Offset from Paragraph* command on the box type's Options menu.
- Page boxes can be aligned with the top or bottom of the page, centered, or offset a specified distance from the top of the page.
- Character boxes can be aligned so that the text on the same line is aligned with the top, center, or bottom of the box.

6 *Horizontal Position* options are also based on the anchor type you selected.

- Paragraph boxes can be aligned with the left or right edge or centered in the area where the text wraps. You can also specify that it expand to fill the area. The area it aligns with is determined by the margins unless you use indents, columns, or other boxes that affect the area.
- Page boxes can be aligned with margins or columns or a specified position. When aligning with columns, you can also

enter a range of columns to have it span more than one. For example, type **1-2** to expand the box across columns 1 and 2.

- Character boxes do not need to be aligned; they automatically align with the character to their immediate left.

7 *Size* sets the box's width or height, or both. If you set either the width or height, the other size is set automatically. If a box contains text, you cannot select the height setting.

8 *Wrap Text Around Box* specifies if the box is to be ignored when text is printed. If set to *Yes*, text wraps around the box (up to 100 boxes per page). If set to *No*, the box outline is not shown on the Edit screen, and text prints over the box. You can use this setting to print one graphic over another. Just enter the codes side by side, and then set all but the last to *No*.

9 *Edit* displays the contents of the graphics box on the screen. It also displays an editor that is determined by the box type. See the table "Graphics Edit Menu Choices."

Superimposing Graphics

Occasionally, you may want to print a graphic over text, or over another graphic. There are two ways to do so: using advance codes and turning the *Wrap Text Around Box* choice off on the Graphics Definition menu.

- To superimpose text and graphics, use an advance up code to move text (or another graphic) up so it prints over a graphic.

- Set the *Wrap Text Around Box* choice of the Graphics Definition menu to *No*. When you do so, the box outline is not shown on the Edit screen, and the graphic will print over any text or graphic that follows. To print the graphic over text, the text should be below the graphic. You can position the text correctly by inserting blank lines above it or by using advance codes. You can also use this setting to print one graphic over another. Just enter the codes side by side, and then set all but the last to *No*.

Positioning Graphics with Columns

When you insert a graphic, the Graphics Definition menu allows you to center it on the page or align it with the left or right margins. Normally these choices are sufficient. However, if you want to precisely position the graphic, as you might when working with a document formatted in columns, you can specify that its anchor type is Page. This allows you to set both the vertical and horizontal distances relative to the edges of the paper. You can also display the Horizontal Position menu and choose *Columns* to position it relative to two or more columns. You can then specify that it be aligned left, right, center, or full in these columns. For example, to position a graphic in the center of a two-column document, specify its vertical position as centered and its horizontal position as centered in columns 1 and 2. The two columns of text will then wrap around either side of the graphic.

If the graphic is so placed in the document that text flows around it, the text is called a **run-around**, or it is said to **wrap around** the graphic.

Text Wrapped Around Graphic

Rotating Graphics

Editing Graphics

WordPerfect has the limited selection of graphics editing procedures described in the table "Graphics Edit Menu Choices." You can use these commands to edit line drawings and photographs or the contents of text boxes. To use these commands, follow the steps in the KEY/Strokes box "Creating or Editing a Graphics Box," and then press **E** for **Edit**.

GRAPHICS EDIT MENU CHOICES

- If the box contains text, the text editor is displayed, and you can enter and edit the text just like any other document. If your printer supports rotated fonts, you may also press **Alt-F9** to display a menu that allows you to specify their rotation.
- If the box contains a graphic, the editor's menu has five editing commands. (Press **Ins** to control the degree of change these controls have.)

1 **M**ove moves the figure within the box when you press the arrow keys or enter horizontal and vertical distances as positive or negative numbers.

2 **S**cale expands or contracts the image by the percentage you specify for the X (horizontal) and Y (vertical) axes. You can also scale the image without choosing this command, by pressing **PgUp** (to expand) or **PgDn** (to contract). You cannot scale bit-mapped images.

3 **R**otate rotates the image the number of degrees that you specify. When you enter a number (or leave it set to 0) and then press **Enter**, you can specify if you want the image mirrored or not. A mirrored image is flopped horizontally around the vertical axis. You can also rotate the image without choosing this command by pressing the **+** (clockwise) or **-** (counterclockwise) on the numeric keypad.

4 **I**nvert On/**I**nvert Off reverses the colors of bit-mapped images. White becomes black, and black becomes white.

5 **B**lack & White turns color display on or off.

Changing Graphics Options

Once you have placed graphics in a document, you can use the Options command to change their borders, spacing, and numbering systems. Graphics options codes are open codes, so they affect all graphics boxes of the same type from the code to the end of the document or to the next options code. Therefore, to affect a graphic's appearance, the options code must be above the graphic's code.

 **KEY/Strokes**

Using Graphics Options

1. Position the cursor above the figure where you want to change options or figure numbers.
2. Either: Press **Alt-F9** to display the Graphics menu.
   Or: Pull down the Graphics menu.
3. Select a box type.
4. Press **O** for **Options**, and then define the options using the menu

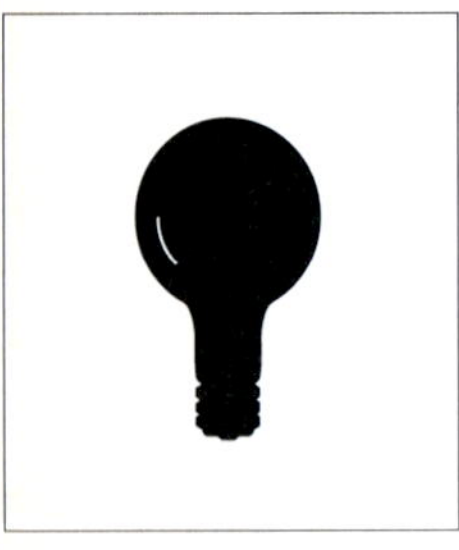

Original

Inverted

Inverting Graphics

The Graphics Options Screen and Menu
The Graphics Options screen and menu allow you to set options for all figures that follow the code that you enter.

```
Options: Figure

        1 - Border Style
                Left                    Single
                Right                   Single
                Top                     Single
                Bottom                  Single
        2 - Outside Border Space
                Left                    0.167"
                Right                   0.167"
                Top                     0.167"
                Bottom                  0.167"
        3 - Inside Border Space
                Left                    0"
                Right                   0"
                Top                     0"
                Bottom                  0"
        4 - First Level Numbering Method   Numbers
        5 - Second Level Numbering Method  Off
        6 - Caption Number Style           [BOLD]Figure 1[bold]
        7 - Position of Caption            Below box, Outside borders
        8 - Minimum Offset from Paragraph  0"
        9 - Gray Shading (% of black)      0%

Selection: 0
```

GRAPHICS OPTIONS MENU CHOICES

1 Border Style sets the border style for the four sides of the box.

2 Outside Border Space sets the distance between the border of the box and the text in the document.

3 Inside Border Space sets the distance between the box and the figure within it.

4 First Level Numbering Method sets the numbering style for the first level of numbering in captions.

5 Second Level Numbering Method sets the numbering style for the second level of numbering in captions.

6 Caption Number Style sets the numbering style used in captions. You can enter text and the numbers **1** and **2** to specify where two levels of numbers print. For example, type **Figure 1** to have figures numbered *Figure 1*, *Figure 2*, and so on. Type **Figure 1-2** to specify both first and second numbering levels. You can also assign font attributes to the numbers.

7 Position of Caption specifies if the caption is to be printed above or below the figure and inside or outside the box.

8 Minimum Offset from Paragraph adjusts the vertical position when a box does not fit at the bottom of a page. This setting specifies how far up into a paragraph a box can move before it is shifted to the top of the next page.

9 Gray Shading (% of black) specifies the amount of shading printed over the figure in the box. 0% is no screen, and 100% is black. If your printer supports only one level of shading, enter 100%.

▶ E X E R C I S E S

EXERCISE 1

ADDING A GRAPHIC TO A DOCUMENT

In this exercise, you enter a graphic into a checklist of computer users'
tips. The graphic you will use is a WordPerfect graphic that is installed
along with the program. These graphics are usually stored in the same
directory as your WordPerfect files. You will have to specify the path to
the graphics file when placing it into the document.

1. Retrieve the TRACK2.WP5 document.
2. Follow the instructions in the KEY/Strokes box "Creating or Editing
   a Graphics Box" to add the CHKBOX-1.WPG graphic between the
   heading and the first item in the list. Specify that it be a figure box,
   centered horizontally, and 3 inches wide (allow the height to be set
   automatically).
3. Use **Enter** to move all of the text that follows the code to below the
   graphics box.
4. Save and print the document.

EXERCISE 2

CREATING A TEXT BOX

In this exercise, you retrieve a document on the disk into a text box that
you create on the screen.

1. Retrieve the TEXTBOX1.WP5 document and enter your name.
2. Follow the instructions in the KEY/Strokes box "Creating or Editing
   a Graphics Box" to create a text box on a blank line below the heading
   block and display the Graphics Definition Menu for that choice.
3. Enter the filename TEXTBOX2.WP5 to retrieve that file into the box.
   (You may have to specify a path to the drive/directory where the file
   is stored.)
4. Press **E** for *Edit* to see the text in the box, then press **F7** to return to
   the Text Box Definition menu.
5. Specify that the horizontal position is left.
6. Set the width to 2 inches (allow the height to be adjusted automatically).
7. Return to the Edit screen, and then save and print the document.
8. Follow the instructions in the KEY/Strokes box "Using Graphic
   Options" to enter a text box options code above the text box code. The
   code should specify that the gray shading be 0% and that the box has
   single border styles for the left and top and thick border styles for the
   bottom and right.
9. Save and print the document. It should now be printed in a drop
   shadow box without any gray shading over it.

REMOVING GRAPHICS BORDERS

In this exercise, you remove the border from the graphic in a document.

1. Retrieve the LINEART.WP5 document and enter your name.
2. Enter a figure options code above the figure box code that removes the borders from the art.
3. Save and print the document.

✔ GRAPHICS TIPS

- You can control the quality of printed graphics using the Print menu.
- The text in text boxes is not updated if you revise the file the text box refers to. To update the text in the box, you must edit the text box, press **F** for *Filename*, and then press **Enter** to reload the file. You will be prompted *Replace contents with [FILENAME]? No (Yes)*. Press **Y** to update.
- To create a list of graphics boxes and their captions automatically (without first marking them), you can enter a list definition code anywhere in the document, and then generate lists 6 through 10. To generate a list of figure boxes, enter a definition code for List 6; for table boxes, List 7; for text boxes, List 8; user-defined boxes, List 9; and, for equation boxes, list 10.
- If your document contains graphics and they do not print completely on a laser printer, you might need to add memory to your printer. A full page of graphics requires at least 1 megabyte of memory in the printer. In the meantime, reduce the size or number of the graphics.
- If your dot-matrix printer will not print text and graphics in the same pass, use the *Do Not Print* choice on the Print menu's *Graphics Quality* and *Text Quality* choices to print the document in two passes. On the first pass, print text without graphics. Then reinsert the paper in the printer, and print graphics without text.

Graphics Image Manipulations

After completing this topic, you should be able to:
- Explain the differences between line art and halftones
- Describe ways to obtain graphics images
- Describe the differences between line copy and continuous-tone copy
- Describe the differences between bit-mapped and vector images
- Add captions and position them relative to the figure
- Scale and crop graphics images

➤ T U T O R I A L

In this tutorial, you edit a figure box to add a caption.

GETTING STARTED

1. Retrieve the LINEART.WP5 document.

CHANGING GRAPHICS OPTIONS

2. Press **Alt-F9** to display the Graphics menu.
3. Press **F** for *Figure*.
4. Press **E** for *Edit* and the prompt reads *Figure number?*
5. Type **1** and then press **Enter** to display the Definition menu for Figure 1.
6. Press **C** for *Caption* and the box caption screen is displayed.
7. Press **Spacebar** to insert a space and then type **This headline appeared in a major daily newspaper**.
8. Press **F7** twice to return to the Edit screen

FINISHING UP

9. Save and print the document. The figure box prints with its new caption.

When working with graphic images, you should understand the basic types, how they are stored in files, how you add captions, and scale or crop art so that it fits the space available for it.

Types of Illustrations

All graphic illustrations fall into one of two classes, line copy or continuous-tone copy.

Line Copy

Line copy is art that contains only solids, lines, and text. These graphics can be scanned or printed just like the text. No special procedures are involved, even when the job is printed by a commercial printer.

Continuous Tone Copy

Continuous tone copy contains a wide range of tones and gradations in tones. These tones range from light to dark in a series of unbroken steps. When you scan continuous-tone copy, it is broken up into dots so it can be printed on a laser printer. For better results, however, you can have a printer shoot it through a **halftone screen** like those used to reproduce photographs and other halftones for books and magazines. When the image is photographed through a screen, it is broken up into dots of varying sizes, large dots for dark areas and small dots for light ones. The plates made from the resulting screened halftones can then print a range of gray tones. If you look through a magnifying glass at a published photograph in a magazine or book, you can see these dots very clearly. The number of lines in the screen determines the quality of the image. The finer the screen, the more detailed the image. Most newspapers use coarse screens with 100 to 133 lines per inch. Books use finer screens of between 133 to 150 lines per inch. Art and photography books, where high quality is desired, use screens with 200 to 300 lines per inch.

If you have a print made of a halftone screened piece of art, it is called a **velox**. You can treat a velox just as if it were line art because it is already broken up into dots that can be printed. This technique is used for jobs where ease of preparation and speed are more important than quality. Quality suffers because this approach works only when coarse screens are used. If the screen is too fine, the dots that make up the image will run together when printed, and the result will be muddy, blurred looking images.

Obtaining Graphics Images

There are four ways of obtaining images to be incorporated into your documents.

- You can buy "clip-art" files that have been especially created for use in desktop publishing. These images are already in a ready-to-use digitized form on disks.
- You can scan the image into a file on the disk. When you scan art for distribution to others, be sure that it is not **copyrighted**. If it is (and most published art is copyrighted), you are violating the owner's rights by using it without written permission.
- You can create the image on the screen with an interactive paint or draw program, or create it with a spreadsheet like Lotus 1-2-3. You then save it in a file on the disk.
- You can use a program that captures any image that can be displayed on the screen. You first load the capture program and then any applications program. You then display on the screen the graphic you want to include in the document. With the graphic on the screen, you press designated keys to save the graphic in a file on the disk.

Types of Graphics Files

Graphics images are stored in a wide variety of file formats, many of

Line Art

Halftone
(Courtesy of Richard Ashley Photography)

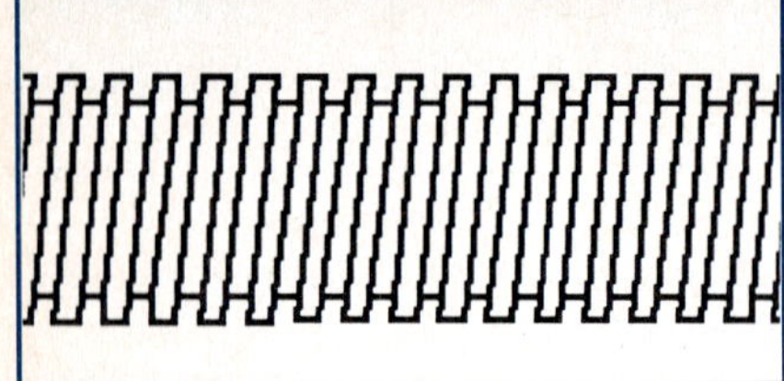

Bit Mapped Image

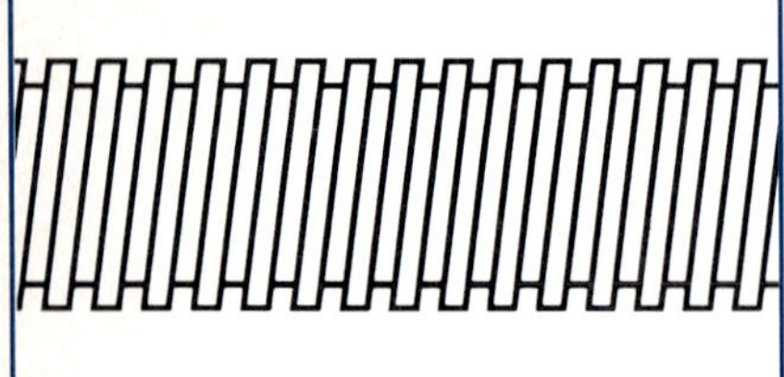

Vector Graphic Image

which are specific to the program that created them. To understand these formats, it is important to understand the differences between bit-mapped graphics and vector graphics.

Bit-Mapped Graphics
Bit-mapped graphics (also called *images* or *paint-type* graphics) are stored as an arrangement of dots, each of which is called a **pixel** (for *picture element*.). Many of the images that you encounter in desktop publishing are bit-mapped because this is the format used by scanners and paint programs. These graphics are easy to edit, because programs like PC Paintbrush can be used to add, delete, or move individual pixels. The problem with bit-mapped graphics is that they can never be printed at a resolution greater than the resolution used to capture them. For example, if you scan them at 300 dots per inch (dpi), you can never print them at 1200 dpi. They also don't always scale well—enlarging or shrinking them may cause degradation of the image. Leading bit-mapped graphics programs store images in one of the following formats:

- Most scanners save their files in the tagged-image-file-format (TIFF) that has the extension TIF. One of the big advantages of this format is that graphics are printed in the correct scale even when the input and output devices have different resolutions.
- PC PaintBrush is one of the leading paint programs, so many programs support its file format. These files have the extension PCX.
- Microsoft Paint and some other programs save their files in the bit-mapped format. These files have the extension BMP.

Vector Graphics
Vector graphics images are stored as mathematical formulas. These graphics are created on programs such as Lotus 1-2-3, Microsoft Excel, AutoCAD, Adobe Illustrator, and CorelDRAW (the terms *design*, *illustrator*, or *draw* in a program's title indicates that it is a vector program). Vector images are created when the program draws lines between points, called *nodes*, like a connect-the-dots puzzle.

The best thing about vector images is that they always print at the resolution offered by the printer. If its resolution is higher than the resolution of the program that created the image, the printed resolution will be higher.

Leading vector graphics programs include the following formats:

- Lotus 1-2-3 graphics have the file extension PIC and Microsoft Excel graphics have the extension XLC.
- Encapsulated PostScript files have the extension EPS.
- Computer Graphics Metafile graphics have the extension CMG.
- Microsoft Windows graphics files have the extension WMF.

Converting Graphics
Since many programs have their own unique file formats, conversion programs have been developed to convert one format into another. For example, Hijack converts bit-mapped files created on the following systems into any of the other listed formats (their extensions are in parentheses):

- Amiga (IFF files)
- CompuServe Image Format (GIF files)
- HP Laserjet (HPC files)
- Lotus (PIC files)
- Macintosh (MacPaint files)
- PC Paintbrush (PCX files)
- PostScript (PSC files)
- Scanner (TIFF files)
- Text (TXT files)

You can also convert vector graphics images to bit-mapped images. To do so, you use the program that created them to print them to a disk file.

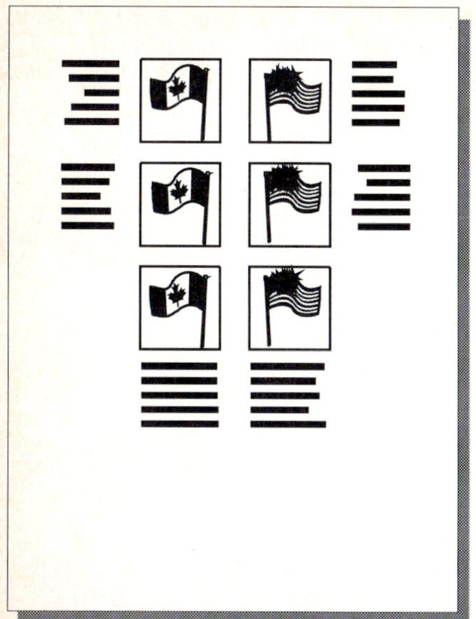

Caption Positions and Alignment

Scaling Angles

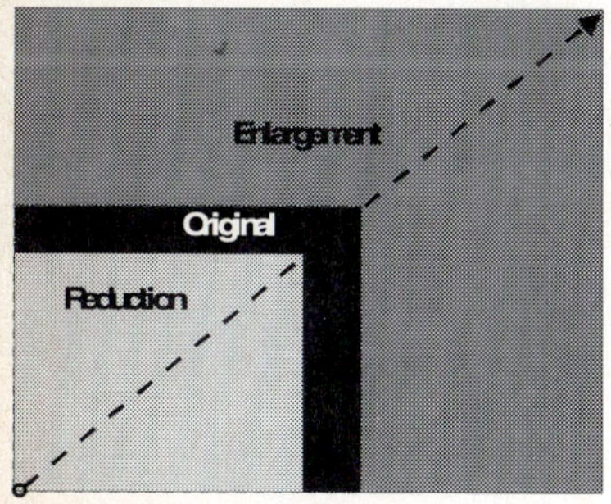

Scaling Mechanically

All art is scaled on the diagonal. If you draw a diagonal line through a copy of an original piece of art you can use horizontal and vertical lines to calculate reductions and enlargements.

Captions

When you incorporate graphics, you can add captions and position them above, below, or to either side of the graphic.

- If the publication has many illustrations, it usually helps the reader if they are numbered and all references to the graphics from the text refers to them by their number.
- All graphics should be positioned below, and as close as possible to, the references to them in the text.
- Figure numbers and captions are usually placed below the figure unless there is room to put them side by side to save space. If side by side with the figure, the caption can be aligned flush left or right. If the caption is narrow, justified text may have large white spaces between words or too many hyphens if you choose to hyphenate it.
- If the caption refers to parts of the illustration, it should do so as *upper left*, *lower right*, and so on, with the position in italics.
- Credit lines should be used whenever the name of the source is known. If you do not list these credits next to your figures, you can list them in the frontmatter or at the end of the document.

Scaling Graphics

When you include a graphic in a document, you can specify any size that you want to print it at. This is called *scaling* the graphic. When you scale graphics, you need to understand how you specify sizes while retaining proportions.

When scaling a graphic you specify either a new size or a percentage for reduction or enlargement. For example, if you change a figure's size within WordPerfect, you must enter sizes. If you send a graphic to a service bureau or printer for reduction or enlargement, they may want the new size specified as a percentage of the original.

Specifying a New Size

To calculate the new size of a graphic that is to be enlarged or reduced, you can use a mechanical or a mathematical approach.

To calculate a new size mechanically, follow these steps:

1. Lay a piece of translucent paper over the original image and draw a box around it (draw lightly so you don't mar the original).
2. Draw a diagonal line through the lower left-hand and upper right-hand corners.
3. To calculate a reduction, measure the desired new width on the lower edge of the box and draw a vertical line up to the diagonal.
4. Draw a horizontal line over to the left side of the box. Measure the distance from the bottom of the box to the place where the horizontal line that you drew intersects it; that is the new height.

You use the same approach when calculating an enlargement, but you must first extend the left and bottom lines of the box.

You can also calculate sizes using a *scaling angle*. You lay this device over the original art and adjust the angles so they are perfectly square and set to the same size. You then lock them into position, and slide them open or closed on the diagonal slide bar. When you adjust one of them to the desired new width or depth, you can read the new size off the scaled angles.

To calculate a new size mathematically, you use the formula *Original Height:Original Width::New Height:New Width*, which means that the original height is to the original width as the new height is to the new width. To use the formula, you substitute measurements in picas or inches for three of the variables and then calculate the missing number. For example, if the original is 8 by 10 inches and you want to reduce it to print in a 4-inch-wide column, you substitute the following numbers:

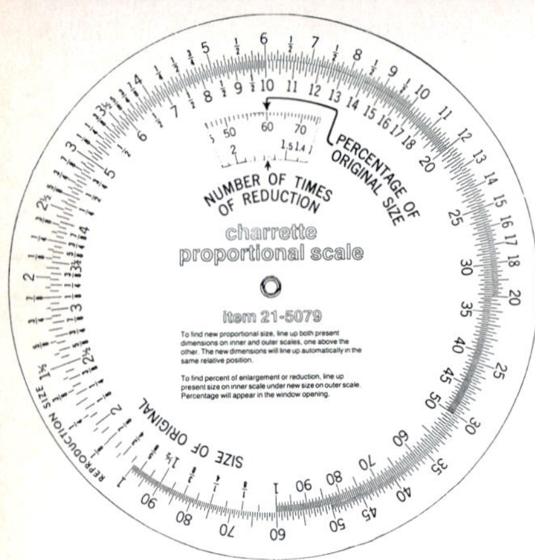

Proportional Scale

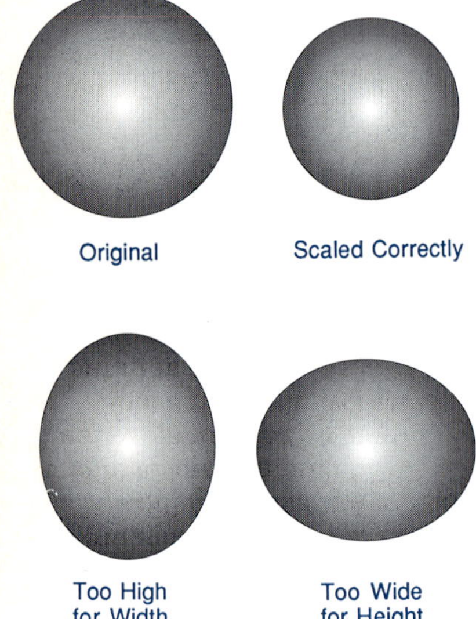

Original

Scaled Correctly

Too High for Width

Too Wide for Height

Aspect Ratios

Cropping

A pair of cropping Ls is used to determine the best part of the photograph to use (left). Then the photograph is cropped for use in a publication (right).

Original Height:Original Width::New Height:New Width

8:10::4:New Width

You then multiply the inner two numbers (10 x 4); in this example you get 40. You then divide this result by the single outer number (8) to find that the new width (the depth of the reduced figure) is 5 inches.

Specifying a Percentage for Reduction or Enlargement

To calculate a reduction or enlargement as a percentage, you use the Pythagorean theorem $A^2 + B^2 = C^2$. The steps are as follows:

1. Calculate the diagonal of the original. For example, if a graphic is 8 by 10 inches, square each number and add the results. In this example, 8^2 is 64 and 10^2 is 100. Adding these together gives you 164. To calculate the diagonal, find the square root of 164, in this case about 12.8 inches when rounded off. (Obviously this is much easier to calculate using a calculator or a spreadsheet.)
2. Calculate the diagonal of the reduction or enlargement using the same procedures used to calculate the original.
3. Calculate the percentage. If you are calculating a reduction, divide the smaller number from Steps 1 and 2 by the larger. The result will be under 100 percent. If you are calculating an enlargement, divide the larger number by the smaller. The result will be over 100 percent.

If you don't like math, you can also calculate reductions and enlargements with a **proportion scale**. By turning the dial, you can align the original width or length on one wheel with the new width or length on the other. The scale then indicates both the percentage for reduction or enlargement and the number of times it is reduced or enlarged.

Aspect Ratios

The **aspect ratio**, the ratio of horizontal dots to vertical dots, determines the shape of a graphic. The aspect ratio of the graphic in a document must match that of the original or there will be distortion of the image. If you make its width too narrow for its height, it looks flattened vertically. If you make it too tall for its width, it looks squashed horizontally. You also see this distortion when displaying images on the screen. Many screens have different aspect ratios than printers so boxes and circles look squashed on the screen even when they print correctly.

Cropping Graphics

Sometimes images are too big or you want to include only a portion of the image in a document. Then, you want to **crop**, or remove part of, an image. This often has to be done at the time the image is scanned. To plan the areas that should be cropped, use two L-shaped pieces of white cardboard. Hold them over the image and slide them in and out so the image shows through the rectangle between them. You can quickly experiment with several possible image areas and proportions.

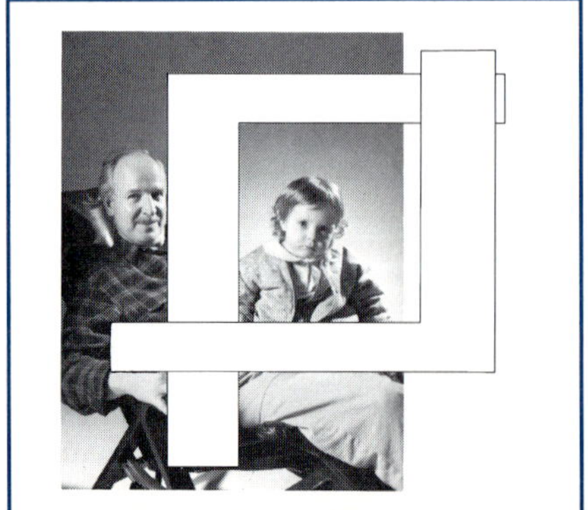

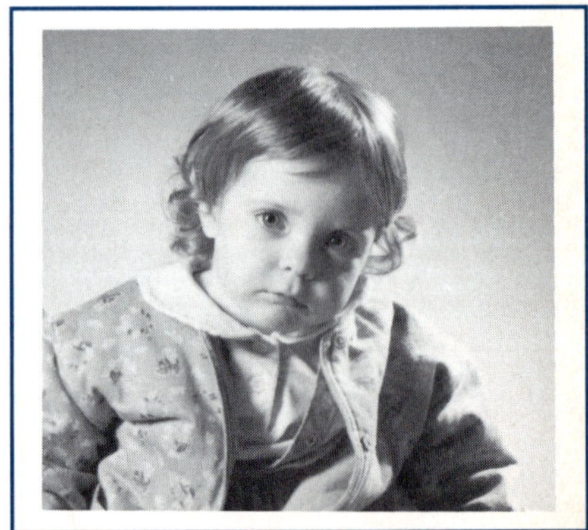

You can use WordPerfect's GRAB program, which captures any graphics image that can be displayed on the screen. (The WordPerfect Edit screen is not a graphics screen but the View Document screen is.) To capture images, load the GRAB.COM program before you load the program whose image you want to capture. (On a hard disk system, this program is in the same directory as your WordPerfect program files. On a floppy disk system, it is on the *Install/Utilities* disk.) You load the program from the command prompt by typing **GRAB** and then pressing **Enter**. You then load WordPerfect in your usual way. When the image you want to capture is displayed on the screen, press **Alt**-**Shift**-**F9**.

- If you hear a low-pitched buzz, it means you are not in graphics mode or have a system that is not supported by the program. You cannot capture images.
- If you hear a two-toned chime, a box is displayed on the screen. Press the arrow keys to move the box to the upper left-hand corner of the part of the screen you want to capture. Hold down **Shift** and press the arrow keys to resize the box. When the box encloses the area you want to capture, press **Enter**. Do not press any keys until you hear the two-toned chime again.

The first image file is stored in the current directory under the name GRAB.WPG. If you save a graphic and the file GRAB.WPG already exists, the new graphic is named GRAB1.WPG. Each subsequent graphic has a new number, up to GRAB9999.WPG. Once a graphic has been saved, you can include it in a document.

EXERCISE 1

SCALING ART

In this exercise, you change the size of a graphic and specify both its width and height.

1. Retrieve the TRACK2.WP5 document.
2. Assume the original size is 3 inches wide and 2.17 inches deep. Calculate a new depth for a 2 inch wide graphic.
3. Edit the figure to set both the new width and depth.
4. Save and print the document.

GRAPHICS TIPS

- Graphics can be incorporated without conversion if they are in a format supported by WordPerfect. WordPerfect supports many graphics formats created on other programs, including the following: Computer Graphics Metafile (CGM), Dr Halo PIC (DHP), AutoCad (DXF), Encapsulated Postscript (EPS), GEM Draw (GEM), Hewlett-Packard Graphics Language Plotter (HPGL), GEM Paint (IMG), Microsoft Windows Paint (MSP), PC Paintbrush (PCX), Lotus 1-2-3 (PIC), Macintosh Paint (PNTG), PC Paint Plus (PPIC), Tagged-Image-File-Format (TIFF), and WordPerfect Graphics format (WPG). Graphics created on other programs may have to be converted before they can be used.
- WordPerfect includes a graphics conversion program named GRAPHCNV.EXE. (On a hard disk system, this file is in the same directory as your WordPerfect program files. On a floppy disk system, it is on the *Install/Utilities* disk.) To load the program, type **GRAPHCNV** and then press **Enter**. Enter the name of the graphics file to be converted and the name of the file to store the conversion in when prompted to do so.

REVIEW

- You can insert graphics lines into a document to separate elements or highlight them. When you do so, you can specify their horizontal and vertical position, length, width, and shading.
- You can use advance up codes to print text in graphic lines.
- You can select Line Draw characters from a menu and then draw lines on the screen by pressing the cursor movement keys.
- You can create figure boxes in your document to hold graphics, tables, text, or equations. When you do so, you have default numbers, lines or boxes, and shading.
- To insert a graphic into a document, you insert a code that shows where it should be printed.
- You can change the default figure box lines, borders, shading, and so on by entering graphics option codes. The option code affects all figure boxes of the same type that follow it.
- You can superimpose a graphic over another graphic or text using advance up and down codes or by turning off the *Wrap Text Around Box* choice on the Graphics Definition menu.
- There are two basic types of graphics: line copy and continuous-tone copy. Line copy does not have a wide range of tones or gradations in tones but continuous tone copy does.
- There are four ways to create graphics images. You can buy already drawn clip-art, scan images into the computer, draw them with a paint program or create them with a program like Lotus 1-2-3, or use the GRAB program to capture what is on the screen and store it in a disk file.
- Graphics are created and stored as bit-mapped or vector files. Bit maps can be edited pixel by pixel but do not scale as well as vector images.
- To change the size of a graphic, you calculate its enlargement or reduction in inches, picas, or some other unit of measurement or as a percentage.
- You can scale images using the formula *Original height:Original width::New Height:New width*. You can also draw a diagonal line through a copy of the art then mark off and measure its new size, or you can use scaling angles.
- You crop graphics to eliminate unwanted parts.

QUESTIONS

TRUE/FALSE

T   F

❏   ❏   1. If you specify that a graphics line be full, it will adjust its length when you change margins.

❏ ❏ 2. You can print text within graphics lines.

❏ ❏ 3. The Line Drawing command works with any fonts that you choose.

❏ ❏ 4. Clip art has already been drawn and stored in files on a disk.

❏ ❏ 5. WordPerfect offers five types of figure boxes and each type can be used only to hold a specific kind of content.

❏ ❏ 6. Each figure box type has its own default settings for lines, numbers, and shading.

❏ ❏ 7. Since graphics and text are so different, you cannot superimpose them.

❏ ❏ 8. You can position a graphic between columns or specify that it span two or more of them.

❏ ❏ 9. If you enter a graphics options code, it affects only the next figure that follows.

❏ ❏ 10. Line art has a a range of tones that have gradations.

❏ ❏ 11. Photographs are continuous-tone copy.

❏ ❏ 12. Bit-mapped graphics can be scaled better than vector images can.

FILL IN THE BLANK

1. You can move the cursor around the screen and enter lines as you do so by using the ___________ commands.

2. You can position text in graphics lines using ___________ codes.

3. The text that flows around a graphics image is called a ___________ or ___________ .

4. To change the border on a graphic, you enter a ___________ code.

5. A figure that contains only solid blacks and whites is called ___________.

6. A figure that contains shades of gray is called a ___________.

7. The kind of graphic that can be edited pixel by pixel is called a ___________ image.

8. The kind of graphic that has lines connecting points is called a ___________ image.

9. The formula that you use to scale graphics is:

   ___________:___________::___________:___________

10. The formula that you use to specify a percentage for reduction is ___________.

11. If a graphic is distorted horizontally or vertically, its ___________ ratio is not correct.

12. When you remove unwanted areas from a graphic you are ___________ the image.

1. Aspect ratio
2. Bit-mapped graphic
3. Copyright
4. Cropping
5. Drop shadows
6. Dropped-out text
7. GRAB program
8. Continuous-tone copy
9. Line copy
10. Pixel
11. Proportion scale
12. Pull-quotes
13. Scaling angles
14. Sidebars
15. Vector graphic
16. Velox
17. Wrap around

___ The smallest area of a bit-mapped graphic

___ The ratio of horizontal to vertical

___ Text that is related to a section of a document but that is set off in a box

___ Text that is printed as white against a black or shaded background

___ Text that flows around a graphics image

___ Small sections excerpted from a document and set off by ruled lines

___ Eliminating distracting areas on an image

___ Borders that indicate a shadow under a box

___ Art that contains a wide range of tones and gradations in tones

___ Art without a wide range of tones and gradations in tones

___ A screened halftone that can be incorporated into a document just like line copy

___ A scale you can use to size art in inches, picas, or other units of measurement

___ A scale you can use to calculate enlargement or reduction as a percentage

___ A program you can use to capture graphics screen images

___ A law that protects a piece of art so that it cannot be copied without permission

___ A graphic made up of lines connecting nodes

___ A graphic made up of black and white pixels

WRITE OUT THE ANSWERS

1. List and describe the two ways in which you can add lines to your document.
2. List as many uses for the Line Draw feature as you can think of.
3. If the line drawings you create do not print out on your printer, what is the reason?
4. If you want a horizontal line to change when you change margin settings, what width would you specify for it?
5. List three ways in which you can store graphics images in disk files so that you can then combine them with a document.
6. Describe how graphics images can be inserted into a document.

P R O J E C T S

PROJECT 1

ADDING VERTICAL RULED LINES BETWEEN COLUMNS

In this project, you add vertical ruled lines to a document with columns. When you formatted this document in newspaper-style columns you specified that the left column end at 4 inches from the left edge of the page and the second column begin at 4½ inches. (Reveal codes to see these measurements in the column definition code.) You place a vertical ruled line at 4¼ inches to separate the columns.

Procedures Used
- Using vertical ruled lines to separate columns.

Text Files Needed
- NEWSCOL1.WP5

Formats
① Enter a graphics vertical line code that sets a full-page, vertical line 4 inches from the left edge of the paper.
② Enter the same code at the top of the second page.

Name:
Date: July 25, 1991
Filename: NEWSCOL1.WP5
Topic: Newspaper-style Columns

Newspaper-style columns (also called snaking columns) are those you see in newspapers, newsletters, and books. Text flows from column to column. As you enter text, it gradually fills the first column. When that column is full, text flows into the next column. When the last column on the page is full, text starts to fill the first column on the next page. If you add text to or delete text from any of the columns, the remaining text adjusts to keep the columns full.

Many publications are designed with text in a single column. However, double columns may accommodate more text per page. The shorter lines allow you to use a smaller type and less spacing between lines without losing readability.

Also, the type page can be wider when you use two columns. With 12-point type, the type page should be no wider than 27 picas. Printing on 8½-by 11-inch paper with 1-inch margins gives a line length of 6½ inches or about 39 picas—too long to be read comfortably. When set in two columns however, a text page can be 42 picas. Even with 2 picas separating the columns (the space between the columns is called a gutter), each column is 20 picas, giving a total type measure of 40 picas.

You should generally use no more than two columns for text because columns that are too narrow cause serious reading problems—frequent line breaks, only a few few words to the line, among other visual annoyances. In addition, if text is justified, there may be frequent large gaps between

words. If the document is hyphenated, many lines will end in hyphens. All of these detract from one's ease of reading. Also, the space between columns should be large enough to visually separate them when reading but not so great that the columns look like completely separate elements on the page.

When you are laying out columns, the first step is to calculate their width and the spaces (gutters) between them. To do so, follow these steps;

1. Determine the number of columns. Let's say you want three columns.

2. Determine the space between the columns. Let's say it is 2 picas.

3. Determine the width of the type page. Let's say it is 40 picas.

4. Calculate the total space for column gutters. The number of gutters is always 1 less than the number of columns. For example, for three columns having 2 picas between them, the total gutter space is 2 gutters times 2 picas, or 4 picas.

5. Subtract the total gutter space calculated in Step 4 from the width of the type page to calculate the space available for columns. For example, subtract 4 picas for gutters from the 40 picas for the type page width to get 36 picas available for the columns themselves.

6. Divide the total space available for columns calculated in Step 5 by the number of columns. For example, divide 36 picas by 3 for column widths of 13 picas each.

1

ADDING A SMALL GRAPHIC TO A LETTERHEAD

In this project, you retrieve the MEMO1.WP5 document. Then, delete the horizontal ruled line above the company name before proceeding. You then insert a small graphics image on the same line as the company's name.

Procedures Used
- Inserting a graphic as a character.

Text Files Needed
- MEMO1.WP5

Graphics Files Needed
- GLOBE2-M.WPG

Formats
① Enter a figure box code to retrieve the graphic. Make it a character anchor type, and set its height to 36 points.

Tips
- You should enter the graphic between the center code and the extra large code that precede the company name and enter a space to separate it from the name.
- After printing the document, you may find that your company name and the graphic are not perfectly aligned. Measure the distance the company name should be moved up to be centered on the graphic and enter an advance up code to move the company name up that distance.

①———  Global Warming Inc.

TO: Our Employees

FROM: Your Name
Director of Human Resource Development

DATE: JUNE 22, 199X

SUBJECT: Employee Benefits Update

In speaking with many of our fine associates during recent weeks, I have noticed one topic common to nearly every discussion. Many of us in The Jefferson Company seem to have developed a "healthy" enthusiasm for physical fitness, nutrition, and other health-related issues. This pleases me. The benefits of proper diet and exercise are many and often cited. For this reason I will not belabor the point by listing the numerous physical and psychological benefits of a health-conscious life-style. I will encourage you to utilize the *Free Modern Fitness* VIP membership that is now included in your employee benefit package. This no-cost membership is valid at any of the Modern Fitness locations in the metro area. Individual membership cards may be obtained from the Human Resources office.

Enjoy!

THE DTP ADVISOR NEWSLETTER

In this project, you add a graphic to the newsletter. You also add graphic lines and use advance up codes to print the newsletter title and article headlines in the lines.

Procedures Used
- Entering line art.
- Entering graphic lines.

Text Files Needed
- ADVISOR.WP5

Graphic Files Needed
- PRINTR-3.WPG

Formats

① Enter a code for the graphic, specifying that it is 2 inches wide. Make its anchor type "Page" and set its position so it prints 6 3/4 inches down from the top edge of the page and 3 inches in from the left.

② Enter a 1-inch-wide 10 percent gray line on a blank line above the newsletter's title.

③ Enter an advance up code at the beginning of the title to move it up .8 inch.

④ Enter a ½-inch-wide 10 percent gray line on a blank line above each of the four headlines and the "*Staff*" heading at the end of the document. (Be sure the first line is entered after the column definition code)

⑤ Enter an advance up code at the beginning of each of the four headlines and the "*Staff*" heading to move them up .2788 inch.

THE *dtp* ADVISOR

FaceLift For WordPerfect

Bitstream Inc. today announced version 1.5 of Bitstream® FaceLift™ for WordPerfect.® FaceLift brings enhanced font support to WordPerfect 5.0 and 5.1. The new FaceLift version 1.5 will create high-quality fonts on-the-fly for popular dot-matrix and inkjet printers—like the HP® DeskJet,® Canon BubbleJet and the IBM® ExecuJet—in addition to the existing on-the-fly support for the Hewlett-Packard LaserJet® series of printers. FaceLift 1.5 for WordPerfect will be available in the spring of 1991.

In addition to 13 typeface outlines provided in the original FaceLift package, FaceLift 1.5 for WordPerfect will also ship with three Symbol typefaces: ITC Zapf Dingbats® Symbol Proportional and Symbol Monospaced. Users will be able to access a total of 698 characters from the Bitstream International Character Set and from these three Symbols typefaces.

FaceLift 1.5 for WordPerfect is an easy-to-use utility that allows users to print high-quality fonts in any size from 2 to 500 point (in quarter point increments) without ever having to leave the application. The fonts are generated at print time, so the need for stored bit-map fonts is eliminated. Based on Bitstream Speedo™ technology, Face-Lift sends characters to printers in both graphics mode (laser, inkjet and dot-matrix printers) and as HP soft fonts (laser printers only). Users have full control over the number and size of soft fonts to be downloaded, depending on the memory available in the printer.

"We are very excited that FaceLift 1.5 for Word-Perfect will provide dot-matrix and inkjet users with the same high typographic quality and capabilities that HP LaserJet users have enjoyed with Bitstream type," stated Doug Lloyd, Executive Director at WordPerfect. "That, and the addition of the three new Symbol typefaces makes FaceLift a great companion for WordPerfect."

First-time users can purchase FaceLift 1.5 for WordPerfect for a suggested U.S. list price of $99. Current users of FaceLift 1.0 for WordPerfect can upgrade to version 1.5 for $24.95. In addition to the 16 typefaces included free with FaceLift, users can purchase add-on fonts from the Bitstream Library of 52 typeface packages. Also available is the FaceLift Companion Value Pack, a selection of 24 text and headline faces for a suggested U.S. list price $199.

FaceLift 1.5 for WordPerfect is the newest member of the Bitstream FaceLift product line. The initial product, FaceLift for Windows,™ shipped in August of 1990. All FaceLift products can share Bitstream typefaces (in Speedo format) stored in a single common subdirectory.

FaceLift for Wordperfect was developed in conjunction with LaserTools Corporation, a privately held company based in Emeryville, CA. LaserTools is a developer of innovative printing enhancement products—tools for printer sharing, printer control, printer acceleration, and font management.

An industry leader in typographic quality and innovative technology, Bitstream licenses fonts and related software to more than 420 hardware manufacturers and software developers worldwide. Its line of retail products is distributed by an extensive network of dealers in the United States and in 18 nations worldwide.

For more information, contact:
Bitstream Inc.
215 First Street
Cambridge, MA 02142-1270
(617) 497-6222

Lists, Tables, & Math

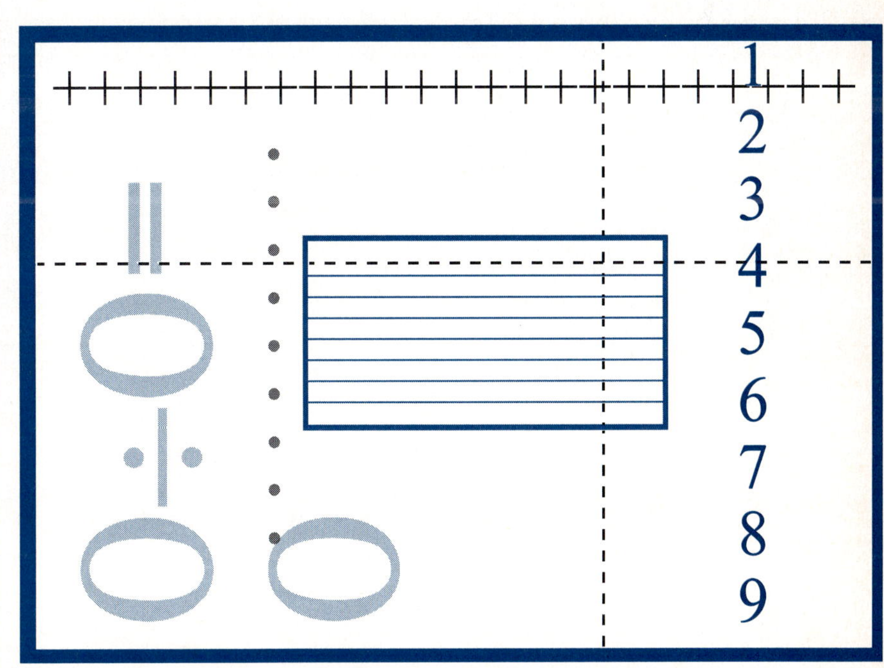

Lists and Tables

After completing this topic, you should be able to:
- Design and lay out tables and lists
- Create tables in your own documents with WordPerfect's Tables command
- Edit tables that you have created

► TUTORIAL

In this tutorial, you create a table by blocking existing tabular text.

GETTING STARTED

1. Retrieve the SPECIAL2.WP5 document.
2. Display the tab ruler so that you can get a better idea of what happens when you create a table.

CREATING A TABLE

3. Move the cursor under the "*T*" in "*TO ENTER*," and then block the entire table so the cursor blinks to the right of the section symbol (§) and not on the line below.
4. Press **Alt-F7** to display the Columns/Tables menu.
5. Press **T** for *Tables*.
6. Press **C** for *Create*.
7. Press **T** for *Tabular Column* and a table soon appears on the screen.

The SPECIAL2 Document
The new table looks like the one in this figure.

```
Name:
Date: July 26, 1991
Filename: SPECIAL2.WP5
Topic: Entering Characters with the Alt Key
```

TO ENTER	PRESS	EXAMPLE
Open quote	Alt–096	`
Close quote	Alt–039	'
Em dash	Alt–196	–
Large bullet	Alt–220	■
Small bullet	Alt–254	▪
Triangle bullet	Alt–016	▶

```
Table Edit:   Press Exit when done          Cell A1 Doc 1 Pg 1 Ln 2.31" Pos 1.12"

Ctrl–Arrows Column Widths; Ins Insert; Del Delete; Move Move/Copy;
1 Size; 2 Format; 3 Lines; 4 Header; 5 Math; 6 Options; 7 Join; 8 Split: 0
```

8. Use the arrow keys to move the cursor to the "*EXAMPLE*" column.

9. Press **Ctrl**-← repeatedly to narrow the column so it is just slightly wider than the heading. (If you narrow the column too much, you can widen it with **Ctrl**- →.)

10. With the cursor in the second column, press **Alt**-**F4** or **F12** to turn block on. Then press → to expand the highlight into the third column.

11. Press **F** for *Format.*

12. Press **1** (the letter el) for *Column.*

13. Press **J** for *Justify.*

14. Press **C** for *Center.*

15. Press **F7** to return to the Edit screen.

FINISHING UP

16. Save and print the document.

▶ D E S K T O P   P U B L I S H I N G   C O N C E P T S

When you want to itemize or rigidly organize material, you design it as a list or table. If you design it as a table, the content usually determines if you treat it as a statistical table or a text table.

Lists

A list is the most basic form a table may take. Many documents have an index, a list of tables and figures, and lists within the body text. When designing lists such as these, keep the following points in mind:

- If the list is long and narrow, you can format it into multiple columns.
- If the list has an uneven number of items for the columns, the

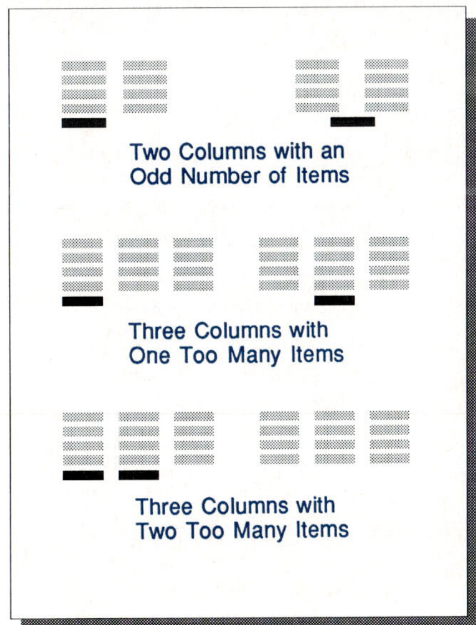

Lists
Arrangement of lists with multiple columns varies depending on the number of items in the list.

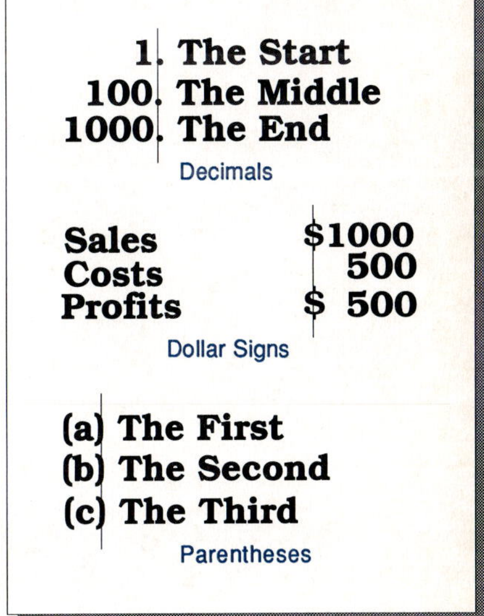

List Alignments
The items in lists should be aligned on a similar character in each entry.

leftmost column(s) should be longer or the odd item can be added to a center column.

- Items in columns should be aligned. If they are preceded by dollar signs, numbers with decimal points, or numbers or letters in parentheses, you can align them on any of those characters. Otherwise, you can align them flush left or right in the columns or, in some situations, even center them.

Statistical Tables

If the data are primarily numbers, they are best presented as a ***statistical table***. All statistical tables are constructed from a limited number of elements: the table identification, column heads, the stub, the body, and footnotes.

Statistical Tables

Statistical tables have a table ID (a), column heads (b), a body (c), and optional footnotes (d).

(a) Table 0
Major U.S. Dams and Reservoirs
(Source: Committee on Resister of Dams, Corps of Engineers, U.S. Army)

(b), (c)

Order	Dam Name	River	State	Type	Height	Year Completed
1	Oroville	Feather	California	E	754	1968
2	Hoover	Colorado	Nevada	A	725	1936
3	Dworshak	N Fork Clearwater	Idaho	G	718	1973
4	Glen Canyon	Colorado	Arizona	A	708	1966
5	New Bullards Bar	North Yuba	California	A	636	1970
6	New Melones	Stanislaus	California	R	626	1979
7	Swift	Lewis	Washington	E	610	1958
8	Mossyrock	Cowilitz	Washington	A	607	1968
9	Shasta	Sacremento	California	G	600	1945
10	Hungrey Horse	S Fork Flathead	Montana	A	564	1953
11	Grand Coulee	Columbia	Washington	G	551	1942
12	Ross	Skagit	Washington	A	541	1949

(d) E=Embankment, Earthfill; R=Embankment, Rockfill; E-R=Embankment, Earth and Rockfill; G=Gravity; A=Arch.

Table Identification
Table identification is provided by a table number and title and an optional table subhead.

- Tables should be numbered consecutively and not start over with each section. If sections are numbered, however, you can use a two-part numbering system such as 1-1, 1-2, 2-1, 2-2, and so on where the first number indicates the section and the second the table within the section. The numbers can be Roman or Arabic and on a line by themselves or run in to the title. Table numbers are usually positioned above the table.
- If the table has a caption it is usually placed below the table. Captions are formatted in headline style usually with the first letter in each word uppercased.
- If the table has a legend, it is placed on a line below the caption or run in to it. Legends are formatted sentence style unless very short, in which case they can be set headline style like the caption.

Column Heads
Column heads identify the contents of the columns in the table.

- Rules should be placed above and below column heads. The amount of ruling depends in part on the complexity of the table.
- You can capitalize the first letter in each head, or the first letter in each word.
- Tables with more than one level of head can use ***decked heads*** that have a ***spanner head*** over two or more column heads. If a spanner head is used, the rule below it should be the width of the column heads that follow.
- If the head cuts across the table and describes all of the data below it, it is called a ***cut-in head***. If a cut-in head is used, rules

should span all columns to which it applies.

- If column heads have different numbers of lines, align all of them with the bottom line of the longest head.

The Stub
The leftmost column in the table, called the **stub**, explains the con-

Decked Column Heads

You can have a heading span two related column heads as the "*Height*" heading does here.

Table 0

Major U.S. Dams and Reservoirs

(Source: Committee on Resister of Dams, Corps of Engineers, U.S. Army)

| Order | Dam Name | River | State | Type | Height | | Year |
					Feet	Meters	Completed
1	Oroville	Feather	California	E	754		1968
2	Hoover	Colorado	Nevada	A	725		1936

Cut-In Column Heads

You can have headings interrupt columns in the table body to identify the rows of data that follow.

Table 0

Major U.S. Dams and Reservoirs

(Source: Committee on Resister of Dams, Corps of Engineers, U.S. Army)

Order	Dam Name	River	State	Height	Year Completed
	Architectural Dams				
2	Hoover	Colorado	Nevada	725	1936
4	Glen Canyon	Colorado	Arizona	708	1966
5	New Bullards Bar	North Yuba	California	636	1970
8	Mossyrock	Cowilitz	Washington	607	1968
10	Hungrey Horse	S Fork Flathead	Montana	564	1953
12	Ross	Skagit	Washington	541	1949
	Embankment Dams, Earthfilled				
1	Oroville	Feather	California	754	1968
7	Swift	Lewis	Washington	610	1958
	Gravity Dams				
3	Dworshak	N Fork Clearwater	Idaho	718	1973
9	Shasta	Sacremento	California	600	1945
11	Grand Coulee	Columbia	Washington	551	1942
	Embankment Dams, Rockfilled				
6	New Melones	Stanislaus	California	626	1979

tents of the other columns on the same row.

- You can have subheads within the stub to identify the lines that follow. They can be centered in the column or flush left, with items under them indented 1 em space.
- If you have totals in the table, the "*Total*" label should be indented 2 spaces or 1 em space more than any other item above it. There should then be a rule above the line or at least a blank line.
- Leaders can be used to connect stubs with column contents, but if overused they make the table look busy.

- When stub labels are long enough so that they turn over, you can indent them using a hanging indent, or set them block style and leave space between them.

The Body
The **table body** contains the data that are identified by the labels used for stubs and column heads.

- Only significant digits should be included. If whole dollars are being presented, do not include a decimal point and two 0s after every number. You can also drop thousands (000) or millions (000,000) and note that in the table's caption or column headings.

- If dollar signs are used, they should be used only for the first number in the column and the first number that follows every break.
- Only the first letter in each label is capitalized and no punctuation is used to end a label.
- In financial tables, single and double underlines are used to indicate subtotals and totals. The underlines should be only as wide as the number, including any dollar sign and decimal point.
- If the table has totals, rules are used to set them off.
- The items in columns that should be aligned depend on the column's content. Whole numbers should be aligned on the right. Other characters that are candidates for alignment include decimal points, math symbols, dollar signs, or percent signs.
- Vertical rules are generally not used unless a table is very complicated. If you do use them, all column entries should be indented at least 2 points or 1 em space from the rules.
- One-line entries are centered if they are short and dissimilar, for example, the list of ingredients in a recipe. They are best left aligned when long.

Table Footnotes
Table footnotes provide explanations for the table's contents. They should be placed immediately below the table (not at the bottom of the page), and be separated from it by a hairline rule. Footnotes can be referenced in the table by superscripted letters, numbers, or symbols provided the item chosen will not be confused with the other elements in the table.

Text Tables
Text tables (also called **parallel columns**) are used for many text elements that need to be arranged into multiple-column formats, for example, scripts, annotated manuscripts, parts lists, and comparative text. They can also contain illustrations, perhaps with identifying or descriptive text next to them.

- If column entries are short they can be centered; otherwise, they should be flush left and perhaps indented with hanging indents.
- When a text table contains text of varying lengths, you can align all columns with the top of the stub.

Text Tables

Text tables have text arranged in parallel columns.

(Courtesy of Bitstream Inc.)

THE BREWS OF THE BOSTON BEER COMPANY	Samuel Adams Boston Lager	Samuel Adams Boston Stock Ale	Boston Lightship	Samuel Adams Double Bock	Octoberfest	Winter Lager
Malted Barley Varieties	2-row Klages/Harrington Caramel 60	2-row Klages/Harrington Caramel 60	2-row Klages/Harrington Caramel	2-row Klages/Harrington Caramel 60	2-row Klages/Harrington Caramel 60	2-row Klages Harrington Caramel 60 Malted Wheat
Hop Varieties	Hallertau Mittelfrueh Tettnang Tettnanger	Saaz, English Goldings, English Fuggles	Saaz, Hallertau Mittelfrueh Tettnang Tettnanger	Hallertau Mittelfrueh Tettnang Tettnanger	Hallertau Mittelfrueh Tettnang Tettnanger	English Goldings Hallertau Mittelfrueh Tettnang Tettnanger
Yeast Strain	Bottom Fermenting Lager Yeast	Top Fermenting Ale Yeast	Bottom Fermenting Lager Yeast	Bottom Fermenting Lager Yeast	Bottom Fermenting Lager Yeast	Bottom Fermented Lager Yeast
Availability	Year Round	Year Round	Year Round	Mid-February	Mid-September	Mid-November
Flavor Characteristics	Hoppy, floral aroma, malty, slightly sweet with a dry complex finish	Very spicy and herbal aroma balanced by malty and sweet finish	Full bodied with spicy hop note 98 calories	Heavy malt flavor, yet smooth and very full-bodied	Malty and slightly fruity aroma, extra smooth from longer aging	Hearty, spicy with a clean, crisp finish from the wheat malt
Color	Golden Amber	Rich Red-Amber	Light Golden	Dark Ruby	Reddish Amber	Deep Red Amber
Available Packages	Bottle Kegs	Bottle Kegs	Bottle Kegs	Bottle Kegs	Bottle Kegs	Bottle Keg
History of Recipe	Koch family-1870	Koch family-1930's	Patented-1987	Double first wort mash developed 1988	Traditional Brewing Style	Varies Yearly
First Brewed	1985	1988	1987	1988	1989	1989
Alcohol by Weight	3.8%	3.9%	2.2%	6.5%	5.0%	Varies Yearly
Starting Gravity	1.052	1.056	1.032	1.081	1.056	Varies Yearly
Adjuncts or Preservatives	None	None	None	None	None	None

However, if the stub is longer than the column entries, you can choose to align all column entries with the bottom of the stub.

List and Table Layout and Design
When designing lists or tables, you should keep the following points in mind:

- References to tables from within the document should be to their number, not the page on which they are located.
- If a table is too wide for the page, it may be broken up or printed in landscape mode (called **broadside**).
- If a table is narrow, indent it from both margins to set it off.
- If a table is too long and narrow, it wastes space. The best solution is to divide it into parts and run them side by side.
- All parts of a table should be set in the same typeface with space above and below the table to set it off from other parts of the text.

You can use type as small as 8 points with footnotes as small as 7 points. The table number and title are often set in the same-size font as the body, although subheadings within the table body can be smaller (or italicized).

- Titles, subheads, and other text can be set in headline style where the first letter of each word is capitalized, or in sentence style where only the first letter is capitalized. In either style you can also use small caps.
- When a table must be broken across pages, continued lines should be used to so indicate. For example, you can enter the phrase *Continued on next page* at the bottom of the first page and *Table 1—Continued* at the top of the second. You can repeat just the table number or the table number and title on the second page. You may also repeat column headings on the second page if the column content is not obvious.

Table 10 The Busiest Airports
(Based on passenger arrivals and departures in millions)

Airport	#	Airport	#
Chicago (ORD)	59	Boston	23
Dallas/Ft. Worth	48	Detroit	21
Los Angeles	45	Newark	21
Atlanta	43	Phoenix	21
New York (JFK)	30	St. Louis	20
San Francisco	30	Minneapolis/St.Paul	19
Denver	27	Orlando	17
Miami	23	Las Vegas	17
New York (LGA)	23	Houston	16
Honolulu	22		

WordPerfect's Tables feature makes it easy to create and edit organized tables. This feature automatically adds ruled lines around table entries, and you can choose to display or hide these rules.

You can define a table and then enter data into it, or you can block an existing tabular table or parallel-style columns and create your own table around it. This new feature improves on WordPerfect's parallel-style columns and math features in many respects.

Tables are made up of rows that run horizontally and columns that run vertically. The intersections of rows and columns are called **cells**. Columns are lettered from left to right: *A, B, C,* and so on. Rows are numbered from top to bottom: *1, 2, 3,* and so forth. Cell names are based on their column letter and row number. For example, the upperleft corner cell is named A1, the cell to its right is named A2, and so on. When the cursor is in a cell, the name of the cell is displayed on the status line. You can type data into a cell, and its depth adjusts automatically. You can also easily make columns wider or narrower, or add or delete new rows and columns.

There are two basic procedures when working with tables: creating and editing the table's structure, and creating and editing the table's contents. When you are editing the table's structure, you cannot enter or edit data. When you are entering or editing data, you cannot edit the table's structure. These separate modes each have their own function.

Creating and Editing a Table's Structure

To create a table, you move the cursor to the place where you want it or you block an existing tabular or parallel-column table. You then use the Table Create command.

- If you are creating a new table, you specify the number of columns and rows that you want the table to have.
- If you blocked an existing tabular table, its tab stop settings divide the new table into columns, and hard carriage returns divide it into rows.
- If you blocked parallel columns, the column definition determines the width of the columns.

→ **KEY/Strokes**

Creating a Table's Structure

1. Move the cursor to where you want a table, or block an existing tabular table or parallel-style columns.
2. Either: Press **Alt-F7** and then **T** for *Tables.*
   Or: Pull down the Layout menu and select *Tables.*
3. Press **C** for *Create.*
   - If you did not block an existing table, the prompt reads *Number of Columns: 3.* Type the number of columns (up to 32), and then press **Enter**. The prompt reads *Number of Rows: 1.* Type the number of rows (up to 32,765), and then press **Enter**.

- If you blocked a table already formatted as a tabular table or as parallel-style columns, a menu appears from which you can specify if the table is to be created from tabular columns or parallel-style columns. Make your choice based on how the block has been formatted.

The table appears on the screen, along with the Table Edit menu.

4. Edit the table's structure using any of the commands described in the table "Table Edit Menu Commands," or press **F7** to return to the Edit screen so that you can enter or edit the data in the table.

Editing a Table's Structure

1. Move the cursor anywhere in the table. (When you use the Table Edit command without the cursor in a table, and select *Tables*, then *Edit*, WordPerfect searches toward the top of the document for a table; if it doesn't find one, it then searches toward the end of the document.)

2. Either: Press **Alt-F7**.

   Or: Pull down the Layout menu and select *Tables*, then *Edit*.

3. Edit the table's structure using the commands described in the table "Table Edit Menu Commands." (If working with more than one cell, block the cells that you want to edit.)

4. Press **F7** to return to the Edit screen so that you can enter or edit the data in the table.

TABLE EDIT MENU COMMANDS

*1 **S**ize* inserts or deletes rows or columns in the table. When prompted to enter the number of rows or columns, enter the total number that you want in the table.

*2 **F**ormat* assigns formats to single cells or entire rows of columns. (See the table "Table Edit Format Menu Commands.")

*3 **L**ines* specifies line types and position and the shading of cells. This command displays two submenus, one after the other.
   - The first submenu is used to specify which lines you want to change.
   - The second submenu specifies the line style you want to use.

*4 **H**eader* specifies the rows that are to be printed at the top of the second part of a table if the table is broken by a page break. When the cursor is in a header row of a table, an asterisk appears next to the cell's name on the status line.

*5 **M**ath* allows you to calculate the numbers in a table much as if it were a spreadsheet.

*6 **O**ptions* affects all cells in the table and specifies spacing between text and lines, the way negative numbers are displayed, the alignment of the table relative to the left and right margins,

TABLE EDIT MENU COMMANDS (CONTINUED)

and gray shading for the table. If you use Full as the position for the table, its columns will automatically adjust widths if margins are changed.

7 *Join* creates one cell out of the cells that you block before you execute this command. Text in the new cell that had been in different columns will now be separated by tabs. Text that was on different rows will be separated by hard carriage returns.

8 *Split* splits a row or a column into a specified number of rows or columns.

TABLE EDIT FORMAT MENU COMMANDS

1 *Cell Formats* specifies the formats to be assigned to the selected cells.

- **1** *Type* specifies if a cell's contents are numeric (the default) or text. If numeric, they can be calculated with the Math feature.
- **2** *Attributes* changes the font size or appearance in the cell.
- **3** *Justify* aligns text horizontally in the cell.
- **4** *Vertical Alignment* aligns text in the cell.
- **5** *Lock* prevents data from being entered into a cell until it is unlocked.

2 *Column Attributes* specifies the attributes to be assigned to the selected columns.

- **1** *Width* specifies the column width. Type a width in inches, and then press **Enter**.
- **2** *Attributes* changes the font size or appearance in the column.
- **3** *Justify* aligns text horizontally in the column.
- **4** *# Digits* specifies between 0 and 15 digits following decimal points when numbers are calculated by functions or formulas. The rounded numbers, if any, are the numbers used in math calculations.

3 *Row Height* specifies the height of selected rows.

- **1** *Fixed (Single-line)* specifies that there can be no more than one line of text in the cell (no word wrap) and that the cell height does not change when the font size changes.
- **2** *Auto (Single-line)* is the same as *Fixed*, but the height changes if font sizes change.
- **3** *Fixed (Multi-line)* turns word wrap on so you can enter paragraphs in cells, but cell height does not change with font size changes.
- **4** *Auto (Multi-line)* is the same as *Fixed (Multi-line)* but cell height varies with font sizes.

Working with the Table's Structure

When you first create a table, it uses the following default settings:

- Outside lines are double lines and inside lines are single.
- Cells adjust their size based on the amount and format of the text in them, and text is aligned flush-left.

You can use these default settings, or revise them using the Table Edit menu commands. You can also use other commands to change column widths, insert or delete rows and columns, and delete text.

Moving the Cursor
To work on a table in Table Edit mode, you first move the cursor to the cell you want affected. (Press **Alt-F7** if you are not already in Table Edit mode.) In Table Edit mode, the cursor occupies the entire cell. You move it with the commands described in the table "Keys That Move the Cursor in a Table." If you want to affect several cells at the same time, block them first.

KEYS THAT MOVE THE CURSOR IN A TABLE*

To Move the Cursor	Press
One cell down	$\downarrow$
One cell up	$\uparrow$
One cell left	$\leftarrow$
One cell right	$\rightarrow$
First cell in column	**Home**, $\uparrow$
Last cell in column	**Home**, $\downarrow$
First cell in row	**Home**, $\leftarrow$
Last cell in row	**Home**, $\rightarrow$
First cell in table	**Home** (twice) $\uparrow$
Last cell in table	**Home** (twice) $\downarrow$
Specific cell	**Ctrl-Home**, cell location, **Enter**

* The **Home** and arrow keys are not the ones on the numeric keypad.

Changing Column Widths
To change a column's width, position the cursor in the column, hold down **Ctrl**, and press the left and right arrow keys to scroll it wider or narrower.

Deleting Rows and Columns
To delete rows or columns, position the cursor in the topmost row or leftmost column to be deleted. Press **Del** to display the Delete menu; then press **R** for *Rows* or **C** for *Columns*, and the prompt asks for the number to be deleted. Type the number, and then press **Enter**.

   If you block rows or columns before pressing **Del**, the blocked rows or columns are deleted without your being prompted to specify the number of rows.

Inserting Rows and Columns
To insert rows or columns, position the cursor on the row below or the column to the right of where you want them inserted. Press **Ins** to display the Insert menu, then press **R** for *Rows* or **C** for *Columns*, and the prompt asks for the number to be inserted. Type the number, and then press **Enter**.

■ Inserted rows and columns have the same attributes as the row or column in which the cursor was positioned. If cells on the same row have cells of different heights, the added row is patterned after the height of the cell that contained the cursor.

- If inserted column(s) will make the table too wide to fit within the margins, the current column will be subdivided to create the number of additional columns you specified.

If you block rows or columns before pressing **Ins** you don't have to specify the number. For example, if you block three rows or columns, three of the same type will be inserted.

Manipulating Cell Contents
Although you enter and edit cell contents in the normal Edit screen, you can delete, copy, and format it in Table Edit mode.

- To delete just the text in cells in Table Edit mode, block the text and press **Backspace**. To delete all of the text, from the cursor to the end of the row, press **Ctrl-End**.
- To copy or move text in Table Edit mode, position the cursor in any cell and use the command the same way you do on the Edit screen. The only difference is that in a table you work with all of a cell's contents. When you retrieve a block while copying or moving it, it is retrieved with its upper left corner in the cell that you position the cursor in.
- You can format text in a table's cells just like other text. You can also use the Format menu to format groups of cells (see the table "Table Edit Format Menu Commands").

Entering or Editing a Table's Contents

To enter text in a table when the normal Edit screen is displayed, position the cursor in a cell and type just as you would elsewhere in the document. If you type enough text, it wraps within the cell, and the cell expands to accommodate it.

- To move the cursor down one row in a cell, press **Enter**.
- To move the cursor to the next cell, press **Tab** or use any of the commands described in the table "Keys That Move the Cursor in a Table."
- To insert a hard tab into a cell, press **Home**, **Tab** or **Home**, **Shift-Tab**.
- To delete to the end of a line (**Ctrl-End**) and delete to the end of a page (**Ctrl-PgDn**), delete only lines and pages within a cell.
- To delete a row (if you have an enhanced keyboard), position the cursor in it and then press **Ctrl-Del**. When the prompt reads *Delete Row? No (Yes)*, press **Y**.
- To insert a row (if you have an enhanced keyboard), move to the row below where you want it inserted and then press **Ctrl-Ins**. The inserted row has the same formats as the one the cursor was in when you created it.

Copying or Moving Entire Tables

To copy or move an entire table, block it along with the table definition code that begins it and the *[Tbl Off]* code that ends it.

Deleting a Table's Structure or Contents

At times, you may want to delete an entire table, or just its structure. To delete a table but leave the text that it contains, delete the table definition code *[Tbl Def]*. The table's columns will be separated by tabs and its rows by hard carriage returns. To delete the table structure and the text it contains, block the table and both the table definition and table off codes, then press **Del**.

EXERCISE 1

EXPLORING TABLE LINES

In this exercise, you enter a table and then format it so each line has a different line pattern.

1. Retrieve the LINES.WP5 document.
2. Move the cursor below the heading and follow the instructions in the KEY/Strokes box "Creating a Table's Structure" to create a table with one column and six rows.
3. Use the Line menu choice described in the table "Table Edit Menu Commands" to remove all lines. (Be sure to block the cells first.)
4. Use the Line menu choice described in the table "Table Edit Menu Commands" to add a different line to the bottom of each cell. (Be sure to block the cells first.) The sequence offered (from top to bottom) is single, double, dashed, thick, and extra thick.
5. Exit table edit mode and add the labels in each cell that describe the line at the bottom of that cell.
6. Save and print the document.

EXERCISE 2

CHANGING TABLE LINES

In this exercise, you revise the lines used as borders on a table.

1. Retrieve the SPECIAL2.WP5 document and enter your name.
2. Move the cursor anywhere in the table and follow the instructions in the KEY/Strokes box "Editing a Table's Structure" to remove all lines. (Be sure to block the entire table first while in table edit mode.)
3. Follow the instructions in the KEY/Strokes box "Editing a Table's Structure" to add a thick line above the table column headings and a single line below them. Then, add a thick line to the bottom of the last row of the table. (Be sure to block the appropriate columns first.)
4. Save and print the document.

<hr>

EXERCISE 3

<hr>

CREATING A TABLE FROM PARALLEL COLUMNS

In this exercise, you place parallel columns into a table format.

1. Retrieve the PARCOLS1.WP5 document.
2. Move the cursor under the "*D*" in "*Dennis Hogan*" and block the columns and rows in the table (do not include the sentence that begins "*Note:*").
3. Follow the instructions in the KEY/Strokes box "Creating a Table's Structure" to create a table. Be sure to specify **P** for *Parallel Columns* when the Create Table from menu appears.
4. Use the Position command on the Table Editing Options menu to center the table on the page.
5. Save and print the document.

Math and Spreadsheets

After completing this topic, you should be able to:
- Explain the difference between importing and linking spreadsheet files
- Import and link spreadsheet files
- Make calculations in your own documents with WordPerfect's Tables command

▷ TUTORIAL

In this tutorial, you link a Lotus 1-2-3 spreadsheet with a document on the screen.

GETTING STARTED

1. Retrieve the HORIZON.WP5 document (be careful, there are three files named HORIZON, but each has a different extension) and enter your name.
2. Change the default drive/directory to the one where you save your document files.

LINKING A SPREADSHEET FILE

3. Move the cursor to the end of the document below the descriptive paragraph.
4. Press **Ctrl-F5** to display the Text In/Out menu.
5. Press **S** for **S**preadsheet.
6. Press **C** for **C**reate Link.
7. Press **F** for **F**ilename and the prompt reads *Enter filename:*.
8. Press **F5** and then **Enter** to display a list of files on the default drive/directory.
9. Highlight *HORIZON.WK1* and then press **R** for **R**etrieve.
10. Press **P** for **P**erform Link and a message reads ** Importing Spreadsheet **. In a moment the Edit screen reappears with the spreadsheet file in a table preceded and followed by comments.

FINISHING UP

11. Save and print the document. Note that the comments do not print.

▶ DESKTOP PUBLISHING CONCEPTS

Many documents contain tables of data to be calculated. For example, a sales report might include unit sales and the dollars received. The dollars received may be calculated by multiplying the units sold by their net price. Whenever calculations of this kind are required, you can perform them in a word processing program or use a separate spreadsheet program.

Math in Word Processing

You can use a word processing program's math features to calculate numbers right in a document. This is the fastest way to perform calculations if they are simple, and if the program contains the mathematical operators that you need.

Math in Spreadsheets

If calculations are complex, or if they require mathematical operations that cannot be performed within the word processing program, many people use a separate spreadsheet such as Lotus 1-2-3 or Microsoft Excel to perform the calculations. The files created with these kinds of programs can then be imported into a document file or linked to it.

- If you import the file, it is copied from the spreadsheet file into the document and no permanent connection is established.
- If you link your document to the spreadsheet file, you can automatically update the data in your document if the data in the spreadsheet file change.

▶ WORDPERFECT PROCEDURES

WordPerfect's Tables feature is ideal for making calculations in a document. After creating a table, you can enter a function or formula in any cell to make calculations for you.

- When you want to add numbers in columns, you can use of the functions described in the table "Table Editor's Math Menu Commands" to calculate subtotals, totals, and grand totals. Functions are codes that tell the program what to add and where to place the result.
- You can display the Math menu, select *Formula*, then type a formula that contains numbers or the addresses of other cells in the table. To enter formulas you use **operators** that indicate the mathematical operations to be performed. The operators that you can use to build formulas are described in the table "Math Operators." For example, a formula can be .1*11 to multiply 10% times the number 11. It can also be .1*A1 to multiply 10% times whatever number is currently entered into cell A1.

Operators are calculated from left to right when you use more than one, unless you use parentheses, in which case the numbers in the parentheses are calculated first. If you change any numbers in a table, you have to use the **Calculate** command on the Table Editor's Math menu to recalculate formulas that refer to that cell.

MATH OPERATORS

+ adds. For example, 100+200 calculates 300. A1+B1 adds the number in cell A1 to the number in cell B1.

- subtracts. For example, 200-100 calculates 100. B1-A1 subtracts the number in cell A1 from the number in cell B1.

***** multiplies. For example, 2*100 calculates 200. 2*A1 multiplies 2 times the number in cell A1.

/ divides. For example, 200/100 calculates 2. B1/A1 divides the number in cell B1 by the number in cell A1.

→ **K E Y / S t r o k e s**

Entering Formulas into a Table or Recalculating Them

1. Move the cursor into the table.
2. Press **Alt-F7** to display the Table Edit menu.
3. Move the cursor into a cell where you want to enter a formula or leave it anywhere in the table if you are recalculating a result.
4. Press **M** for *Math.*
5. Make any of the choices described in the table "Table Editor's Math Menu Commands."
6. Press **F7** to return to the Edit screen.

TABLE EDITOR'S MATH MENU COMMANDS

1 *Calculate* calculates all formulas in the table. You should always calculate a table before printing it so that the results are accurate.

2 *Formula* enables you to enter formulas into cells. These formulas can contain numbers or references to other cells.

3 *Copy Formula* copies a formula in the cell with the cursor to other cells and adjusts it using relative cell references. If the formula in its original location refers to a cell two columns over and one row up, it will refer to a cell two columns over and one row up in its new location.

- **1** *Cell* copies it to the cell whose name you type.
- **2** *Down* copies the formula down the specified number of cells.
- **3** *Right* copies the formula to the right the specified number of cells.

4 **+** (subtotal) calculates a subtotal of the numbers in the cells immediately above it in the column.

5 **=** (total) sums subtotals in the column. To calculate a total, you must first enter functions that calculate one or more subtotals.

6 ***** (grand total) sums totals in the cells above it. To calculate a grand total, you must first enter codes that calculate one or more totals.

Importing or Linking with a Spreadsheet File

WordPerfect allows you to import a spreadsheet file or link it to your document file.

Spreadsheet Link

When you establish a link with a spreadsheet file, the data in that file appear in your document, along with codes at the top and bottom of the data.

```
Link: D:\DTP\TEACHER\HORIZON.WK1  <Spreadsheet>  A1..B11
```

Altitude	Horizon
(in 1,000)	(in miles)
1	39
5	87
10	123
15	151
20	174
25	194
30	213

```
A:\HORIZON.WP5                                  Doc 1 Pg 1 Ln 4.44" Pos 1"
```

 **K E Y / S t r o k e s**

Importing or Linking with a Spreadsheet File

1. Either: Press **Ctrl-F5** and then press **S** for **S**preadsheet.
   Or: Pull down the File menu, select *Text In* and then select *S*preadsheet.
2. Make one of the menu choices described in the table "Spreadsheet Menu Options."

SPREADSHEET MENU OPTIONS

1 *Import* imports the data in the specified file but does not establish a permanent link.
- **1** *Filename* is the name of the file to be imported (you can press **F5** to display the List Files screen to locate it, and then press **R** for **R**etrieve).
- **2** *Range* is the name of the range or the cell address of the upper-left and lower-right corner cells, separated by a colon or one or two periods. If you do not specify a range, the entire file is imported.
- **3** *Type* specifies if the file is to be imported as a table or as text.
- **4** *Perform Import* imports the specified file.

2 *Create Link* establishes a permanent link with a spreadsheet file.
- **1** *Filename* is the same as on the Import menu.
- **2** *Range* is the same as on the Import menu.
- **3** *Type* is the same as on the Import menu.
- **4** *Perform Link* enters codes into your document that refer to the linked file.

3 *Edit Link* displays a menu with the same choices as **2** *Create Link*.

4 *Link Options* specifies options that define your link.
- **1** *Update on **Retrieve*** automatically updates your document whenever you retrieve it.
- **2** *Show Link Codes* displays or hides the link codes in your document.
- **3** *Update All Links* updates all tables in your document to reflect any changes in the files to which they are linked.

▶ E X E R C I S E S

EXERCISE 1

ENTERING A FORMULA IN A TABLE

In this exercise, you enter a formula in a table to multiply units sold by net price. The formula will then calculate the total revenues for the item.

1. Retrieve the REVENUES.WP5 document and enter your name.
2. Position the cursor in the cell to the right of the label "*Total Revenue*," and then press **Alt-F7** to edit the table.
3. Press **M** for *Math* and then **F** for *Formula* and the prompt reads *Enter formula:*.
4. Type **B1*B2** and then press **Enter**.
5. Exit the Table Edit mode, then save and print the document.
6. Change the net price from 10 to 20 and then follow the instruction in the KEY/Strokes box "Entering Formulas into a Table or Recalculating Them" to calculate a new total revenue.
7. Save and print the document.

EXERCISE 2

IMPORTING A SPREADSHEET FILE

In this exercise, you import a spreadsheet file into a document.

1. Retrieve the HORIZON.WP5 document.
2. Reveal codes and delete everything from the code that begins *[Link: ....]* to the end of the document.
3. Follow the instruction in the KEY/Strokes box "Importing or Linking with a Spreadsheet File" to import the HORIZON.WK1 file.
4. Save and print the document.

MATH AND SPREADSHEET TIP

When you import a spreadsheet file, column widths are based on the base font at the cursor's position. If tables are too wide, delete the file, insert a base font code for a smaller font, and then import the spreadsheet again.

REVIEW

- Tables are generally either statistical or text. Statistical tables contain numbers almost exclusively while text tables contain numbers and/or text.
- Tables are made up of rows that run horizontally and columns that run vertically. The intersections of rows and columns are called cells. Columns are lettered from left to right: *A*, *B*, *C*, and so on. Rows are numbered from top to bottom: *1*, *2*, *3*, and so forth. Cell names are based on their column letter and row number.
- There are two procedures when working with tables: creating and editing the table's structure, and creating and editing the table's contents. When you are editing the table's structure, you cannot enter or edit data. When you are entering or editing data, you cannot edit the table's structure. These separate modes each have their own function.
- You can create a table and use it to make calculations. You can enter a formula in any cell that refers to any other cells that contain numbers or other formulas.
- You can have data in a spreadsheet file appear in your document in one of two ways: you can import them or link them. Importing a file copies its data, but no permanent connection is established. Linking establishes a permanent link to the spreadsheet file, so you can automatically update the data in your document if the data in the spreadsheet file changes.
- You can make math calculations right in a document so that you don't have to leave the program to do so.

QUESTIONS

TRUE/FALSE

T   F

1. ❏ ❏ Statistical tables contain mainly numbers.
2. ❏ ❏ Decked heads are those that have more than one level.
3. ❏ ❏ Cut-in heads are those that are created manually with scissors and paste.
4. ❏ ❏ The stub in a table is its last entry.
5. ❏ ❏ WordPerfect tables contain a single large cell.
6. ❏ ❏ If you need to make calculations while working on a document, you can do so within the program.
7. ❏ ❏ If you create a link to a spreadsheet file, you can update the spreadsheet by changing numbers in the document.

❑   ❑   8. Operators are used in formulas to indicate addition,
               subtraction, multiplication, and division.

FILL IN THE BLANK

1. Tables that consist mainly of numbers are called ___________
   ___________.
2. Decked table heads are identified on the higher levels by ___________
   heads.
3. Heads within the table body that span columns are called ___________
   heads.
4. The leftmost column in a table is called the ___________ if it contains
   labels or descriptions of the row contents.
5. A table printed in landscape mode is called a ___________.
6. The smallest unit in a WordPerfect table is a ___________.
7. Connecting a document to a spreadsheet file so changes in the
   spreadsheet file can be automatically reflected in the document is
   called ___________.
8. Bringing a spreadsheet file into a document is called ___________.
9. The symbols that you enter into formulas to indicate addition,
   subtraction, multiplication, and division are called ___________.

MATCH THE COLUMNS

1. Cell

2. Cut-in heads

3. Decked heads

4. Import

5. Link

6. Operators

7. Spreadsheet

8. Statistical table

9. Structure

10. Stub

___ The overall layout of a WordPerfect table including the number of rows and columns, their widths, and borders

___ The leftmost column that identifies the contents of rows in the table body

___ The characters that specify arithmetic procedures such as addition, subtraction, multiplication, and division

___ The basic unit in a WordPerfect table

___ Tables that consist mainly of numbers

___ Heads that group related columns in the body of a table

___ Establishing a connection between a document and a spreadsheet file, so if the spreadsheet file is changed, the document can be automatically updated

___ Column heads with more than one level

___ Bringing a spreadsheet file into a document

___ A program used to calculate numbers

1. List and describe the parts of a table created with the Table Create command.
2. What two modes do you use when working with tables? Briefly describe each and its uses.
3. What command do you use to insert a row into a table when it is displayed on the regular Edit screen? To delete a row?
4. How do you enter formulas into a table?
5. What are the functions you can enter into a table? What does each do?
6. What is the difference between importing and linking a spreadsheet file?
7. What are operators? List four that you use to create formulas.
8. When you use more than one operator in a formula, in what order are the calculations made? How can you change the order?
9. If you had a table, what formula would you enter to add cells A1 and B1? To multiply them?

PROJECTS

PROJECT 1

FORMATTING A TABLE WITH CUT-IN HEADS

In this project, you change a tabbed table into a WordPerfect table and then format it with lines and cut-in heads. After creating the table, use Table Editing commands to make it look like the one in this figure.

Procedures Used
- Creating and editing tables.

Text Files Needed
- DAMS.WP5

Formats
① Enter a base font code for a 10-point type.
② Block the entire table body and create a table.

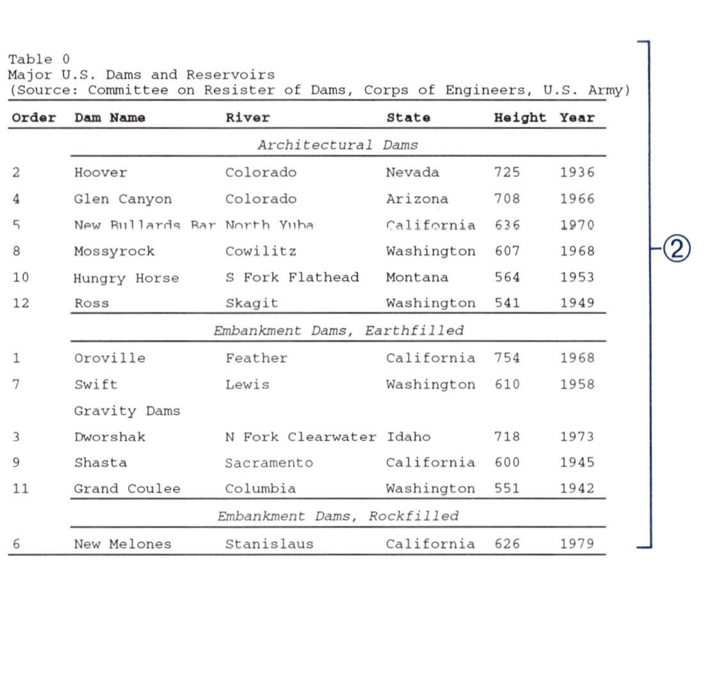

Table 0
Major U.S. Dams and Reservoirs
(Source: Committee on Resister of Dams, Corps of Engineers, U.S. Army)

Order	Dam Name	River	State	Height	Year
		Architectural Dams			
2	Hoover	Colorado	Nevada	725	1936
4	Glen Canyon	Colorado	Arizona	708	1966
5	New Bullards Bar	North Yuba	California	636	1970
8	Mossyrock	Cowilitz	Washington	607	1968
10	Hungry Horse	S Fork Flathead	Montana	564	1953
12	Ross	Skagit	Washington	541	1949
		Embankment Dams, Earthfilled			
1	Oroville	Feather	California	754	1968
7	Swift	Lewis	Washington	610	1958
	Gravity Dams				
3	Dworshak	N Fork Clearwater	Idaho	718	1973
9	Shasta	Sacramento	California	600	1945
11	Grand Coulee	Columbia	Washington	551	1942
		Embankment Dams, Rockfilled			
6	New Melones	Stanislaus	California	626	1979

Working with Long Documents

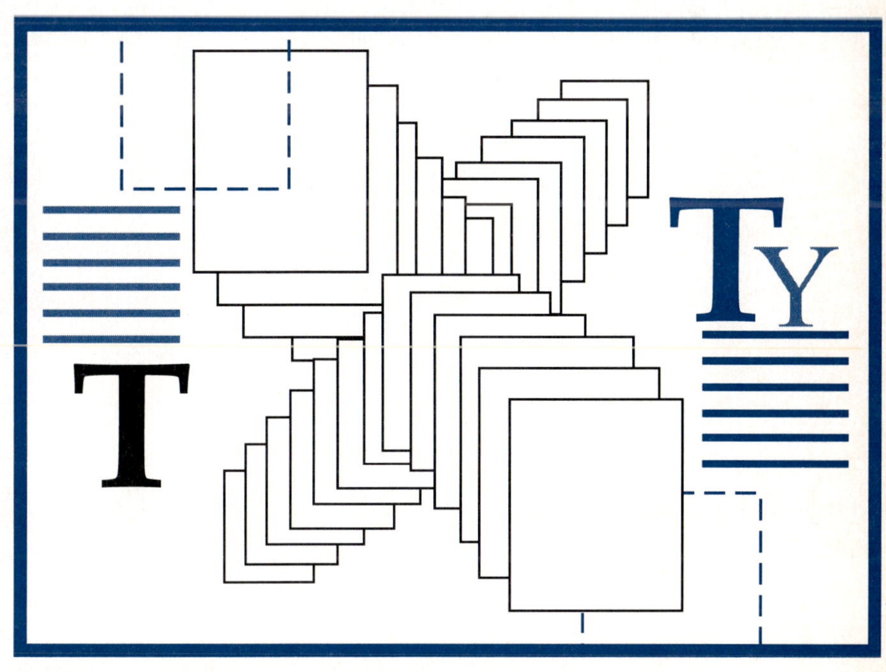

Tables of Contents and Lists

After completing this topic, you should be able to:

- Describe the format used for tables of contents
- Explain how you automatically generate tables of contents and lists
- Mark, define, and generate tables of contents and lists in your own documents

➤ T U T O R I A L

In this tutorial, you mark, define, and generate a table of contents.

GETTING STARTED

1. Retrieve the TITLEPG2.WP5 document.

MARKING A TABLE OF CONTENTS LEVEL 1 ENTRY

2. Reveal codes and block the heading "*Section Opener*," being sure you don't block the font size codes.
3. Press **Alt-F5** to display the Mark Text menu.
4. Press **C** for *ToC*, and the prompt reads *ToC Level:*
5. Type **1** and then press **Enter**.

MARKING TABLE OF CONTENTS LEVELS 2 THROUGH 5 ENTRIES

6. Block (be sure not to block advance down codes) and mark each subhead following Steps 2 through 5 assigning them the following levels:
   - *A-level subheads* should be ToC level 2.
   - *B-level subheads* should be ToC level 3.
   - *C-level subheads* should be ToC level 4.
   - *D-level subheads* should be ToC level 5.

DEFINING THE TABLE OF CONTENTS

7. Move to the blank line above the heading "*Section Opener*," press **Enter** to insert a blank line, then press **Ctrl-Enter** to enter a hard page break.
8. Move the cursor above the hard page code (*[HPg]*), press **Shift-F6** to center the cursor, type **TABLE OF CONTENTS** and then press **Enter** twice.
9. Press **Alt-F5** to display the Mark Text menu.

10. Press **D** for **D**efine.

11. Press **C** for *Define Table of* **C**ontents, and the Table of Contents Definition menu is displayed.

12. Press **N** for **N**umber of Levels, and then type **5**.

13. Press **F7** to accept the other suggested settings and return to the Edit screen.

GENERATING THE TABLE OF CONTENTS

14. Press **Alt**-**F5** to display the Mark Text menu.

15. Press **G** for **G**enerate.

16. Press **G** for **G**enerate Tables, Indexes, Automatic References, etc., and the prompt reads *Existing tables, lists, and indexes will be replaced. Continue? Yes (**N**o)*.

17. Press **Y** and the table of contents is automatically generated. All five levels are shown, each level indented from the next.

FINISHING UP

18. Save and print the document. (If a prompt appears telling you that the document may need to be generated, print it anyway.)

> **DESKTOP PUBLISHING CONCEPTS**

When working on a long document with many sections, you often need to prepare a table of contents or other types of lists to help readers find the information they need. These lists refer to headings, sub-headings, figures, tables, or other subjects in the document and provide page numbers for them. Manually preparing these references takes a great deal of time; moreover, if any revisions are made to the document, all page number references might have to be changed. Word processing and desktop publishing programs such as WordPerfect have automated the preparation of these lists.

Lists can be designed in a variety of ways. For example, tables of contents can include the preface, part and chapter titles, and subheadings down to the desired level. Lists and tables of contents can be kept relatively simple, listing just the items you want and their page numbers. You can also format the lists and tables of contents using the same procedures you use to distinguish headings in the text and place page numbers flush right.

> **WORDPERFECT PROCEDURES**

You can automatically generate a table of contents and as many as ten lists for each document.

- Tables of contents can have as many as five levels. Each level is indented 1 tab stop from the previous level. To change the indent, change the tab stops above the table of contents code.
- You can create as many as ten lists of various items in a document. When you generate the lists, entries are listed in the order in which they appear. If you want to generate a list of graphics box captions

Table of Contents

Tables of contents list chapters or other sections in a document. They can list only the major divisions or sublevels.

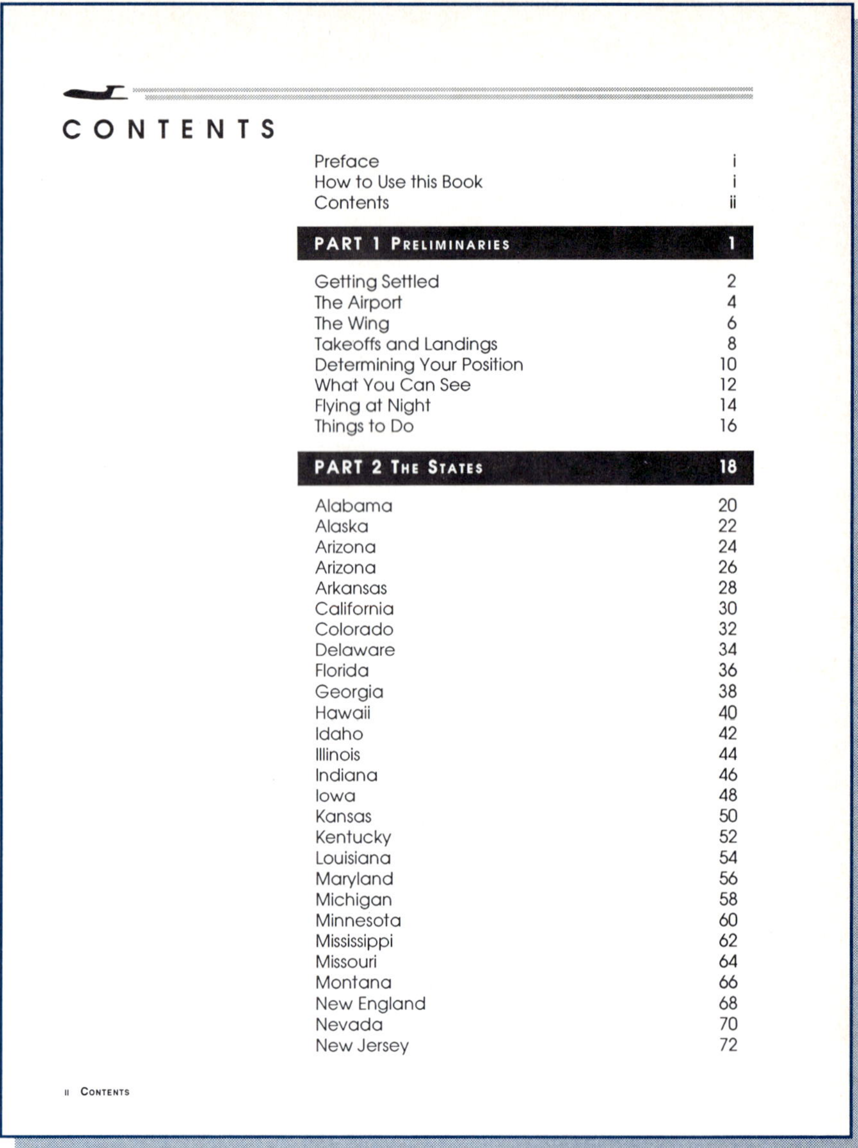

automatically, enter one of the following list definitions. (The captions themselves do not have to be marked when these lists are used to generate lists of graphics boxes.)

- Figure box captions are listed with List 6.
- Table box captions are listed with List 7.
- Text box captions are listed with List 8.
- User-defined box captions are listed with List 9.
- Equation boxes are listed with List 10.

There are three basic steps to creating automatically generated lists: marking, defining, and generating.

Marking Entries for Tables of Contents and Lists

When marking entries, you block the text that you want included in the table of contents or list and then select the type of list from a menu.

Marking Entries for a Table of Contents or a List

1. Block the text, including any format codes to be included.
2. Press **Alt-F5** to display the Mark Text menu.
3. Either: Press **C** for *ToC*, and the prompt reads *ToC Level:*. Type the level (**1** through **5**), press **Enter**, and you are returned to the Edit screen.

   Or: Press **L** for *List*, and the prompt reads *List Number:*. Type the number of the list (you can define up to ten), and you then return to the Edit screen.
4. Repeat Steps 1 through 3 for each entry.

Defining Tables of Contents or Lists

After you have marked entries for a table of contents or list, you enter a code into the document to indicate where the table of contents or list is to be generated and to specify its format. The code can be at the top of a new page if you want the table of contents or list to print by itself. You can also enter a heading for the table of contents or list if you enter the text above the definition code.

→   K E Y / S t r o k e s

Defining a Table of Contents

1. Move the cursor to where the table of contents is to begin.
2. Press **Alt-F5** to display the Mark Text menu.
3. Press **D** for *Define*.
4. Press **C** for *Define Table of Contents* to display the Table of Contents Definition menu.
5. Either: Press **Enter** to accept the suggested settings and return to the Edit screen.

   Or: Press **N**, **D**, or **P** to specify the number of levels, whether page numbers for the last level should be wrapped, and where page numbers should be printed for each level. (You cannot specify a flush-right style for the last entry if you specify that it is to wrap.) Press **F7** to return to the Edit screen.

→   K E Y / S t r o k e s

Defining a List

1. Move the cursor to where the list is to begin.
2. Press **Alt-F5** to display the Mark Text menu.
3. Press **D** for *Define*.
4. Press **L** for *Define List*, and the prompt reads *List Number (1-10):*.

5. Type a number **1** through **10** and then press **Enter** to define any one of ten lists and to display the List Definition menu for that list.
6. Make any menu choice to select the kind of numbering you want to use, and you then return to the Edit screen.

Generating Tables of Contents and Lists

Generating a table of contents or list assembles the marked entries into a list according to the definitions you entered. If you make changes in the document, you must generate the list again to update it. **Always save your file before using the command that generates tables, indexes, and lists**. Any text inadvertently entered between the codes that begin and end a list definition is automatically deleted when you generate a list the second or subsequent times.

KEY/Strokes

Generating a Table of Contents or List

1. Press **Alt-F5** to display the Mark Text menu.
2. Press **G** for *Generate*.
3. Press **G** for *Generate Tables, Indexes, Cross-References, etc.,* and the prompt reads *Existing tables, lists, and indexes will be replaced. Continue? Yes (No)*.
4. Press **Y** to continue, and the prompt reads *Generation in progress* and indicates the pass and page.

► EXERCISE

EXERCISE 1

GENERATING A LIST OF AMENDMENTS

In this exercise, you generate a list of amendments, indicating the pages that they appear on.

1. Retrieve the ALIGN2.WP5 document.
2. Follow the instructions in the KEY/Strokes box "Marking Entries for a Table of Contents or a List" to mark all of the amendment heading numbers as List 1 entries.
3. Move to the end of the document, press **Enter** twice to insert a blank line, then center a heading **LIST OF AMENDMENTS**.
4. Follow the instructions in the KEY/Strokes box "Defining a List" to enter a List 1 definition code two lines below the heading.
5. Follow the instructions in the KEY/Strokes box "Generating a Table of Contents or List" to generate the list.
6. Save and then print the document.

- If you boldface or underline entries to be included in a table of contents or a list, the placement of the marking codes is important. If the boldface and underline codes are inside the codes that mark the entries, the entries will be boldfaced or underlined when you generate the lists. If they are outside the codes, the entries will not be affected by them.
- You cannot revise definition codes, for example, to change the numbering style. To make revisions, you enter a new code. If you do so, be sure to delete the previous code, or the list will be generated twice.

Indexes

After completing this topic, you should be able to:
- Describe the format used for indexes
- Explain how you automatically generate an index
- Mark, define, and generate indexes in your own documents

▶ T U T O R I A L

In this tutorial, you mark, define, and generate an index.

GETTING STARTED

1. Retrieve the ALIGN2.WP5 document.

MARKING AN INDEX ENTRY

2. Move the cursor anywhere in the word "*Religion*" in the title for Amendment 1.
3. Press **Alt**-**F5** to display the Mark Text menu.
4. Press **I** for *Index*, and the prompt reads *Index heading: Religion*.
5. Press **Enter** and the prompt reads *Subheading:*.
6. Press **Enter** to indicate that there is no subheading for this term.

MARKING ADDITIONAL INDEX ENTRIES

7. Block and mark each of the other words or phrases in each amendment title, following Steps 2 through 6. For example, in Amendment 1, mark "*Speech,*" "*Assembly,*" and "*Politics.*" When you encounter phrases such as "*Right to Bear Arms,*" block the entry before pressing **Alt**-**F5**. Then, when the prompt reads *Index Heading*, followed by the suggested entry, change the entry to "*Arms, Right to Bear.*"

DEFINING THE INDEX

8. Move to the end of the document, then press **Enter** to insert a blank line.
9. Press **Shift**-**F6** to center the heading, type **INDEX** and then press **Enter** twice.
10. Press **Alt**-**F5** to display the Mark Text menu.
11. Press **D** for *Define*.

12. Press **I** for *Define Index*, and the prompt reads *Concordance file (Enter=none):*.
13. Press **Enter** and the Index Definition menu is displayed.
14. Press **Enter** to accept the default settings and the Edit screen appears.

GENERATING THE INDEX

15. Press **Alt**-**F5** to display the Mark Text menu.
16. Press **G** for *Generate*.
17. Press **G** for *Generate Tables, Indexes, Automatic References, etc.,* and the prompt reads *Existing tables, lists, and indexes will be replaced. Continue? Yes (No)*.
18. Press **Y** and the index is automatically generated.

FINISHING UP

19. Save and print the document. (If a prompt appears telling you that the document may need to be generated, print it anyway.)

▶ DESKTOP PUBLISHING CONCEPTS

When working on a long document, you often need to prepare an index to help readers find the information they need. This index refers to subjects in the document and provides page numbers for them. Manually preparing these references takes a great deal of time; moreover, if any revisions are made to the document, all page number references might have to be changed.

Indexes are usually set in two or more columns to save room. They can be set in smaller type (8 or 9 points) with 1 point of leading to close them up. You format the entries flush left, with a ragged right margin, and indent entries as hanging indents so the key words extend out farther than the runover lines.

▶ WORDPERFECT PROCEDURES

WordPerfect allows you to prepare indexes automatically.

■ Indexes can be generated that list words or phrases appearing in your document. You can mark the entries so that they appear as headings or subheadings.
  ● If your index is to consist of a straight listing of entries, mark each as a heading, and do not specify a subheading.
  ● If you want to group selected entries under a broader heading, specify a heading, and then mark entries as subheadings. When you generate the index, all subheadings appear under the heading you specified.

There are three basic steps to creating automatically generated indexes: marking, defining, and generating.

Marking Index Entries

When creating an index, you can mark each entry in the text or create a concordance file. A **concordance file** is a master list of words that you want listed in the index. You create this list and save it just like a normal document. When you generate the index, you can specify the name of this file, and the program searches the current document for the words listed in the concordance file and adds them to the index. When creating the concordance file, keep the following rules in mind:

- Each word or phrase can be as long as you want but must end with a hard carriage return.
- You can mark all or part of any of the entries just as you would in the document itself if you want them to appear under headings. If you do not mark an entry, the phrase appears in the index as a heading. If you do mark it, the word or phrase is listed under the heading that you specify in the index mark.
- The number of entries in the file is limited by your computer's memory. If you have too many, an error message reads *Not enough memory to use entire concordance file. Continue? Yes (No)* when you generate the index. Press **Y** to use the part of the concordance file that does fit into memory, or press **N** to exit from index generation.

→ **K E Y / S t r o k e s**

Marking Entries for an Index

1. Either: Move the cursor under any character in the word to be included in the index.

   Or: Block more than one adjacent word, including any format codes to be included.

2. Press **Alt-F5** and then press **I** for *Index*. The prompt reads *Index heading:* followed by the blocked text.

3. Either: Press **Enter** if the entry is not to appear under a heading.

   Or: Type the name of the heading that the entry is to be listed under in the index, and then press **Enter**.

   The prompt reads *Subheading:*.

4. Either: Press **Enter** to use the displayed text, if any, as the subheading.

   Or: Press **F1** if the entry is not to appear under a heading. (You can also press **Enter** if no text is displayed following the prompt.)

   Or: Type another subheading, and then press **Enter** to return to the Edit screen.

5. Repeat Steps 1 through 4 for each entry.

Defining Indexes

After you have marked entries for an index, you enter a code into the document that indicates where the index is to be generated and specifies its format. The code can be at the top of a new page if you want the index to print by itself. You can also enter a heading for the index if you enter the text above the definition code.

Defining an Index

1. Move the cursor to the end of the document. (Only words above the definition code are included in the index.)
2. Press **Alt-F5** to display the Mark Text menu.
3. Press **D** for *Define*.
4. Press **I** for *Define Index*, and the prompt reads *Concordance Filename (Enter=none):*.
5. Either: Press **Enter** to continue without a concordance file.

   Or: Type the name of the concordance file and then press **Enter**.
6. Make any menu choice to select the kind of numbering you want to use, and then return to the Edit screen.

Generating Indexes

Generating an index assembles the marked entries into an index according to the definitions you entered. If you make changes to the document, you must generate the index again to update it. **Always save your file before using the command that generates tables, indexes, and lists**. Any text inadvertently entered between the codes that begin and end an index definition is automatically deleted when you generate an index the second or subsequent times.

Generating an Index

1. Press **Alt-F5** to display the Mark Text menu.
2. Press **G** for *Generate*.
3. Press **G** for *Generate Tables, Indexes, Cross-References, etc.*, and the prompt reads *Existing tables, lists, and indexes will be replaced. Continue? Yes (No).*
4. Press **Y** to continue, and the prompt reads *Generation in progress* and indicates the pass and page.

➤ E X E R C I S E S

EXERCISE 1

GENERATING AN INDEX FROM A CONCORDANCE FILE

In this exercise, you generate an index automatically using a concordance file.

1. Create a new file with the listing of words shown in the figure "Concordance File."

altocumulus
altocumulus castellanus
altostratus
cirriform
cirrocumulus
cirrostratus
cirrus
clouds
cumulonimbus
cumulus
cumulus fractus
fractus
high clouds
low clouds
middle clouds
nimbo
nimbostratus
nimbus
standing lenticular altocumulus
stratocumulus
stratus
towering cumulus

Concordance File

2. Save the file as CLOUDS.NDX.

3. Retrieve the CLOUDS2.WP5 document.

4. If you completed the activity where you formatted this document in parallel columns, move the cursor to the end of the document, and press **Alt**-**F7** to display the Columns/Tables menu. Then press **C** for *Columns* and **f** for *Off* to turn off parallel columns.

5. Press **Ctrl**-**Enter** to insert a hard page break, then center the heading **INDEX**.

6. Follow the instructions in the KEY/Strokes box "Defining an Index" to enter an index definition code two lines below the heading and specify CLOUDS.NDX as the concordance file.

7. Follow the instructions in the KEY/Strokes box "Generating an Index" to generate the index.

8. Save and then print the page of the document that has the index on it.

✔ I N D E X   T I P S

- If you boldface or underline entries to be included in an index, the placement of the marking codes is important. If the boldface and underline codes are inside the codes that mark the entries, the entries will be boldfaced or underlined when you generate the index. If they are outside the codes, the entries will not be affected by them.

- You cannot revise definition codes, for example, to change the numbering style. To make revisions, you enter a new code. If you do so, be sure to delete the previous code, or the index will be generated twice.

Assembling Documents

After completing this topic, you should be able to:
- Assemble documents on the screen by retrieving them one after the other
- Assemble documents during printing
- Assemble documents on the screen using a master document

▶ T U T O R I A L

In this tutorial, you create a master document that automatically assembles two files on the disk into a single document.

GETTING STARTED

1. Retrieve the MASTER.WP5 document and enter your name.
2. Change the default drive/directory to the one where you store your document files.

CREATING A MASTER DOCUMENT

3. Move the cursor to the end of the document, then press **Alt-F5** to display the Mark Text menu.
4. Press **S** for **S**ubdoc, and the prompt reads *Subdoc Filename:*.
5. Type **CLOUDS1.WP5** and then press **Enter**. A box is displayed on the screen indicating the name of the first subdocument.
6. Press **Ctrl-Enter** to enter a hard page break.
7. Press **Alt-F5** to display the Mark Text menu.
8. Press **S** for **S**ubdoc, and the prompt reads *Subdoc Filename:*
9. Type **CLOUDS2.WP5** and then press **Enter**.

EXPANDING THE MASTER DOCUMENT

10. Press **Alt-F5** to display the Mark Text menu.
11. Press **G** for **G**enerate to display the Generate menu.
12. Press **E** for *Expand Master Document*, and a message reads *Expanding master document.* In a moment, boxes are displayed at the beginning and end of each subdocument, indicating where each starts and ends.
13. Print the document. The contents of the two files are printed one after the other.

SAVING AND CONDENSING THE DOCUMENT

14. Press **F10**, **Enter** to save the document and the prompt reads *Document is expanded, condense it? Yes (No)*.

15. Press **Y** and the prompt reads *Save Subdocs?*

16. Press **Y** and the prompt reads *Replace CLOUDS1.WP5?* followed by a menu with three choices.

17. Press **R** for *Replace All Remaining* and the prompt reads *Document to be saved:* followed by the path and name of the master document.

18. Press **Enter** and then **Y** to save the condensed file.

SAVING WITHOUT CONDENSING THE DOCUMENT

19. Press **Alt**-**F5** to display the Mark Text menu.

20. Press **G** for *Generate* to display the Generate menu.

21. Press **E** for *Expand Master Document* and in a moment the document is expanded again.

22. Press **F10** to save the document, and the prompt reads *Document is expanded, condense it? Yes (No)*.

23. Press **N** and the prompt reads *Document to be saved:* followed by the path and name of the master document.

24. Press **Enter** and then **Y** to save the uncondensed file.

CONDENSING THE MASTER DOCUMENT

25. Press **Alt**-**F5** to display the Mark Text menu.

26. Press **G** for *Generate* to display the Generate menu.

27. Press **o** for *Condense Master Document* and the prompt reads *Save Subdocs? Yes (No)*.

28. Press **N** for *No* and single boxes are displayed on the screen, indicating the name of each subdocument.

FINISHING UP

29. Save the condensed document.

▶ D E S K T O P   P U B L I S H I N G   C O N C E P T S

You can maintain parts of a document in separate files on a disk and assemble them into documents as needed. If you add page numbers after assembling the documents, the page numbers print consecutively for the entire document. This procedure is useful in a variety of situations. For example, you can store book-length manuscripts and reports in several files to make them easier to manage and edit. The document can then be assembled for printing.

There are three ways to assemble large documents: retrieving them onto the screen, assembling them while printing, or creating a master document.

Retrieving Documents onto the Screen

To assemble documents on the screen, you retrieve them one after the other just as you normally retrieve documents. They are retrieved beginning at the cursor's position. All text below, if any, moves down to make room for the inserted text. If you use List Files to retrieve a document into one that is already on the screen, a prompt reads *Retrieve into current document? No (Yes)*. To assemble the document, press **Y**. WordPerfect retrieves the entire file. If the file contains more text than you want, you can delete unwanted sections.

Assembling Documents While Printing

You can assemble documents while printing using the *{DOCUMENT}filename~* merge code. The filename you specify is merged into the document at the point where you enter this code when you merge-print it.

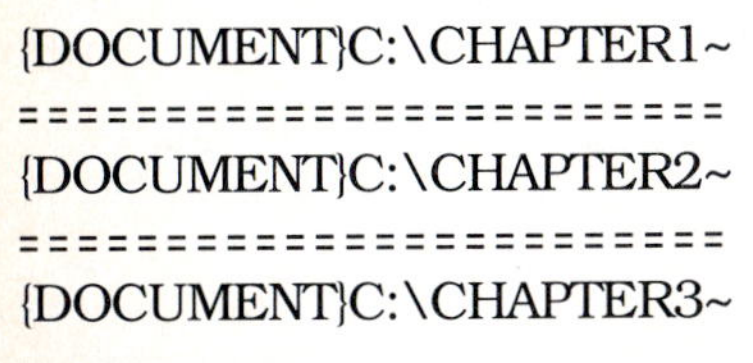

Assembling Documents While Printing
If you merge-printed this document, it would automatically print the three specified files one after the other with a hard page break between them.

→ | K E Y / S t r o k e s

Entering Codes That Merge Documents During Printing

1. Move the cursor to where you want a document inserted from the disk during printing.
2. Press **Shift-F9** to display the Merge menu.
3. Press **M** for *More* to display a pull-down menu of merge codes.
4. Use the arrow keys to move the highlight over *{DOCUMENT}filename~* and then press **Enter**. The prompt reads *Enter Filename:*.
5. Type the name of the file (precede it with a path if necessary), and then press **Enter**.
6. Repeat Steps 2 through 5 for each document to be included. Press **Ctrl-Enter** first to enter a hard page break if the next document is to begin at the top of a new page.
7. Save the document.

→ | K E Y / S t r o k e s

Merge-Printing a Document That Contains *{DOCUMENT}* Codes

1. Clear the screen of other documents.
2. Press **Ctrl-F9** to display the Merge menu.
3. Press **M** for *M*erge and the prompt reads *Primary file:*.
4. Type the name of the file that contains the *{DOCUMENT}* codes

(precede it with a path if necessary), and then press **Enter**. The prompt reads *Secondary file:*.

5. Press **Enter** without specifying a secondary file and the documents specified in the *{DOCUMENT}* codes are merged to the screen.

6. Print the merged files just as you would print a regular document.

Creating Master Documents

WordPerfect's master document feature allows you to enter codes into one document, called the ***master document***, that refer to other documents on the disk, called the ***subdocuments***. You can then expand the master document to display these subdocuments on the screen or condense the master document to remove them from the screen.

Master Documents

A master document is created by inserting subdocument codes that refer to other files on the disk. Here, subdocument codes that refer to two files on the disk have been entered into the master document below the heading. Boxes indicate the names of the subdocuments and where they will be inserted.

```
┌─────────────────────────────────────────────────────┐
│ Subdoc: CLOUDS1.WP5                                  │
└─────────────────────────────────────────────────────┘

================================================================

┌─────────────────────────────────────────────────────┐
│ Subdoc: CLOUDS2.WP5                                  │
└─────────────────────────────────────────────────────┘




A:\MASTER.WP5                          Doc 1 Pg 1 Ln 1" Pos 1"
```

Expanded Master Document

When you expand the master document, the two files appear on the screen with boxes that indicate where they begin and end.

```
┌─────────────────────────────────────────────────────┐
│ Subdoc Start: CLOUDS1.WP5                            │
└─────────────────────────────────────────────────────┘
                    Chapter
                    7
                    CLOUDS
┌─────────────────────────────────────────────────────┐
│ Subdoc End: CLOUDS1.WP5                              │
└─────────────────────────────────────────────────────┘

================================================================

┌─────────────────────────────────────────────────────┐
│ Subdoc Start: CLOUDS2.WP5                            │
└─────────────────────────────────────────────────────┘

                    TABLE OF CONTENTS

            IDENTIFICATION . . . . . . . . . . . . .  1

            HIGH CLOUDS. . . . . . . . . . . . . .  2
A:\MASTER.WP5                          Doc 1 Pg 1 Ln 1" Pos 1"
```

Subdocuments that are included in a master document can be edited as individual files, or the master document can be expanded and the subdocuments can be edited there. You can then save the expanded master file or condense it and save the subdocuments in their own individual files. But once you have saved an expanded master document, you are not prompted to condense it the next time you save it (although you can still condense it using the Generate menu).

- You can enter formatting codes into either the master document or the subdocuments, and they affect the appropriate sections. For example, a header or footer entered at the top of the master document prints on all pages of the expanded document. However, if formats have been entered into the subdocuments, those formats take precedence over formats entered into the master document. For example, if all the margins in the subdocuments are set to 1 inches and you change the margins in the master document to 2 inches, the margins in the subdocuments remain unaffected.

- To print an entire master document, you must first expand it. If you do not expand the document, only the text in the master document is printed.

- A subdocument can also include codes that refer to other subdocuments. When you expand the master document, it in turn expands all subdocuments at all levels. This is called nesting.

- If you quit or save when an expanded master document is on the screen, the prompt reads *Document is expanded, condense it? Yes (No)*. Press **N** to leave the master document expanded, or press **Y** to condense it.

- When you condense a master document, a prompt reads *Save Subdocs? Yes (No)*. Press **N** to abandon all subdocs so that the previous versions on the disk are left unchanged. Press **Y** to save the subdocs if you made any changes that you want to save. The program then gives you the option to save or not to save individual subdocs. For each file, it displays the prompt *Replace?* followed by the path and filename. Press **Y** for *Yes*, **N** for *No*, or **R** for *Replace All Remaining*.

Creating a Master Document

1. Clear the screen or retrieve an existing document that you want to make into a master document. Move the cursor to where you want to automatically insert another document from the disk.

2. Press **Alt-F5** to display the Mark Text menu.

3. Press **S** for *Subdoc*, and the prompt reads *Subdoc Filename:*.

4. Type the name of the document to be included, and then press **Enter**. A box is displayed on the screen indicating the name of the subdocument.

5. Repeat Steps 2 through 4 for each document to be included. Press **Ctrl-Enter** first to enter a hard page break if the next document is to begin at the top of a new page.

6. Save the master document.

KEY/Strokes

Expanding or Condensing a Master Document

1. Retrieve the master document if it isn't already on the screen.
2. Press **Alt-F5** to display the Mark Text menu.
3. Press **G** for *Generate* to display the Generate menu.
4. Either: Press **E** for *Expand Master Document*, and boxes are displayed at the beginning and end of each subdocument indicating where it starts and ends.

   Or: Press **o** for *Condense Master Document*, and single boxes are displayed on the screen indicating the name of each subdocument.

► EXERCISE

EXERCISE 1

ASSEMBLING A DOCUMENT DURING PRINTING

In this exercise, you assemble a document during printing.

1. Clear the screen of any other document.
2. Follow the instructions in the KEY/Strokes box "Entering Codes That Merge Documents During Printing" to specify that the documents TYPEFAC1.WP5 and TYPESTY1.WP5 are printed when you print this document.
3. Follow the instructions in the KEY/Strokes box "Merge-Printing a Document That Contains *{DOCUMENT}* Codes" to merge the documents to the screen.
4. Print the merged documents, then abandon the document on the screen without saving it.

ASSEMBLING DOCUMENTS TIP

You can use automatic references in master documents that refer to targets in other files. When you generate the references in the master document, the reference numbers are updated.

REVIEW

- You can automatically create a table of contents and up to ten lists for a document.
- To mark an entry for inclusion in a list, you block it and then use the Mark Text menu to code it. You then define the table of contents, index, or list and generate it.
- You can automatically create an index for a document.
- To mark an entry for inclusion in an index, you block it and then use the Mark Text menu to code it. You then define the index and generate it.
- A concordance file lists the words and phrases you want to appear in the index. Words in the concordance file are added to the index without marking them in the document.
- You can combine two or more files to assemble a document.
- You can assemble documents on the screen by retrieving files from the disk so that they are inserted at the cursor position.
- You can assemble a document during printing by entering *{DOCUMENT}filename~* merge codes and then printing the document that contains them.
- You can create a master document that contains text and codes that refer to other files (press **Alt-F5**). When you expand the master document, the documents it refers to are retrieved onto the screen.

QUESTIONS

TRUE/FALSE

T F

1. Tables of contents and indexes are updated automatically if you revise the document and pages are added or deleted.

2. With WordPerfect, you can create up to ten separate lists in addition to a table of contents and index.

3. Before you can generate a table of contents, the only step that you must complete is marking the entries.

4. Tables of contents can have up to five levels.

5. You save a document before generating tables of contents, lists, and indexes to protect your work.

6. You must mark all entries in a document that you want to appear in an index.

7. A concordance file is used to save a list of files that you have already indexed.

❏ ❏   8. If you retrieve a file from the disk when one is still on the screen, the one on the screen is automatically cleared.

❏ ❏   9. To merge documents during printing, you use merge codes that specify the names of the files to be merged.

❏ ❏   10. A master document contains codes that refer to other documents on the disk.

❏ ❏   11. You can expand or condense a master document.

❏ ❏   12. If you make changes to an expanded master document, you needn't save the subdocuments to save those changes.

FILL IN THE BLANK

1. To generate a table of contents, list, or index, you must first ___________ entries and then ___________ the table of contents, list, or index.

2. To eliminate the need to mark index entries in a document, you can use a ___________ file.

3. You can generate up to ___________ lists in a document, in addition to the table of contents and index.

4. Tables of contents can have up to ___________ levels.

5. The documents that a master document refers to are called ___________ .

6. The code that you enter to assemble documents during printing is ___________ .

MATCH THE COLUMNS

1. Tilde
2. Subdocs
3. Merge codes
4. Master document
5. Mark, define, generate
6. Concordance file

__ A file containing terms that you want to appear in the index

__ The documents that are referred to from a master document

__ The three steps in generating tables of contents, lists, and indexes

__ The codes used to assemble documents during printing

__ The last character in the merge code used to merge documents during printing

__ A document that refers to other documents on the disk and that can be expanded or collapsed

1. What kinds of lists can you generate automatically?
2. List the three steps you follow to generate a table of contents, list, or index automatically.
3. What kinds of lists can you generate without marking the entries in the document?
4. What is the purpose of a concordance file?
5. Describe three ways to assemble documents stored in separate files on the disk.
6. What is a master document? What are subdocuments? How are master documents and subdocuments related to each other?

PROJECTS

PROJECT 1

GENERATING A TABLE OF CONTENTS

In this project, you create a table of contents for the document on clouds. After entering a definition code and marking all of the entries, generate the table of contents.

Procedures Used
- Creating tables of contents.

Text Files Needed
- CLOUDS2.WP5

Formats
① Enter a centered heading.
② Insert a table of contents definition code above the column definition code.
③ Code all subheads within the body text as ToC level 2 entries.
④ Code all uppercase side heads as ToC level 1 entries.
⑤ Insert a hard page break between the table of contents and the text so that the table of contents prints on its own page.

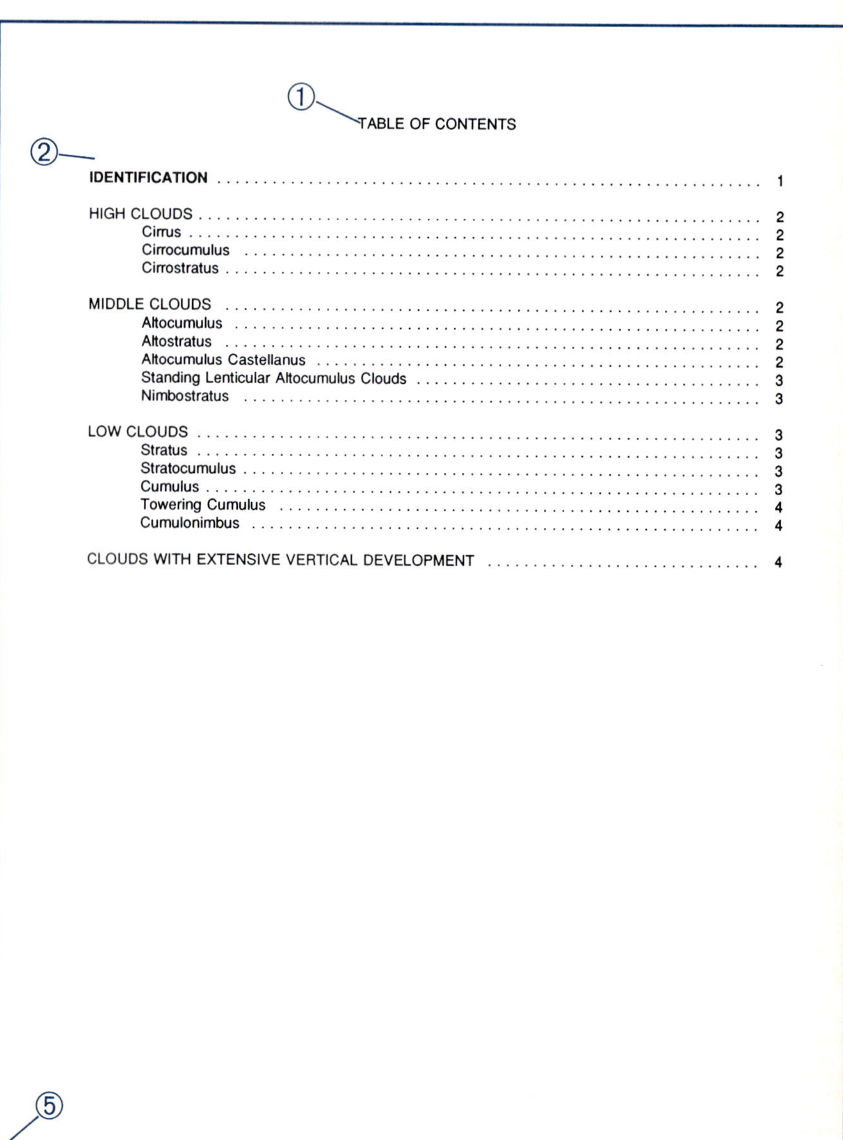

THE DTP ADVISOR NEWSLETTER

In this project, you create a table of contents for the newsletter.

Procedures Used
- Generating a table of contents.

Text Files Needed
- ADVISOR.WP5

Formats
① Enter the heading "*Contents.*" Copy a horizontal ruled line and advance up code from another headline and position them in front of the new heading. Format the heading just like the other headlines.
② Mark each of the four article headlines as table of contents level 1 entries.
③ Enter a table of contents definition code.

THE *dtp* ADVISOR

Contents

FaceLift For WordPerfect

Bitstream Inc. today announced version 1.5 of Bitstream® FaceLift™ for WordPerfect.® FaceLift brings enhanced font support to WordPerfect 5.0 and 5.1. The new FaceLift version 1.5 will create high-quality fonts on-the-fly for popular dot-matrix and inkjet printers—like the HP® DeskJet,® Canon BubbleJet and the IBM® ExecuJet—in addition to the existing on-the-fly support for the Hewlett-Packard LaserJet® series of printers. FaceLift 1.5 for Word-Perfect will be available in the spring of 1991.

In addition to 13 typeface outlines provided in the original FaceLift package, FaceLift 1.5 for WordPerfect will also ship with three Symbol typefaces: ITC Zapf Dingbats® Symbol Proportional and Symbol Monospaced. Users will be able to access a total of 698 characters from the Bitstream International Character Set and from these three Symbols typefaces.

FaceLift 1.5 for WordPerfect is an easy-to-use utility that allows users to print high-quality fonts in any size from 2 to 500 point (in quarter point increments) without ever having to leave the application. The fonts are generated at print time, so the need for stored bit-map fonts is eliminated. Based on Bitstream Speedo™ technology, FaceLift sends characters to printers in both graphics mode (laser, inkjet and dot-matrix printers) and as HP soft fonts (laser printers only). Users have full control over the number and size of soft fonts to be downloaded, depending on the memory available in the printer.

"We are very excited that FaceLift 1.5 for Word-Perfect will provide dot-matrix and inkjet users with the same high typographic quality and capabilities that HP LaserJet users have enjoyed with Bitstream type," stated Doug Lloyd, Executive Director at WordPerfect. "That, and the addition of the three new Symbol typefaces makes FaceLift a great companion for WordPerfect."

First-time users can purchase FaceLift 1.5 for WordPerfect for a suggested U.S. list price of $99. Current users of FaceLift 1.0 for WordPerfect can upgrade to version 1.5 for $24.95. In addition to the 16 typefaces included free with FaceLift, users can purchase add-on fonts from the Bitstream Library of 52 typeface packages. Also available is the FaceLift Companion Value Pack, a selection of 24 text and headline faces for a suggested U.S. list price $199.

FaceLift 1.5 for WordPerfect is the newest member of the Bitstream Face-Lift product line. The initial product, FaceLift for Windows,™ shipped in August of 1990. All FaceLift products can share Bitstream typefaces (in Speedo format) stored in a single common subdirectory.

FaceLift for Wordperfect was developed in conjunction with LaserTools Corporation, a privately held company based in Emeryville, CA. LaserTools is a developer of innovative printing enhancement products—tools for printer sharing, printer control, printer acceleration, and font management.

An industry leader in typographic quality and innovative technology, Bitstream licenses fonts and

SPRING 1993   1   VOLUME 1/NUMBER 1

Improving Productivity

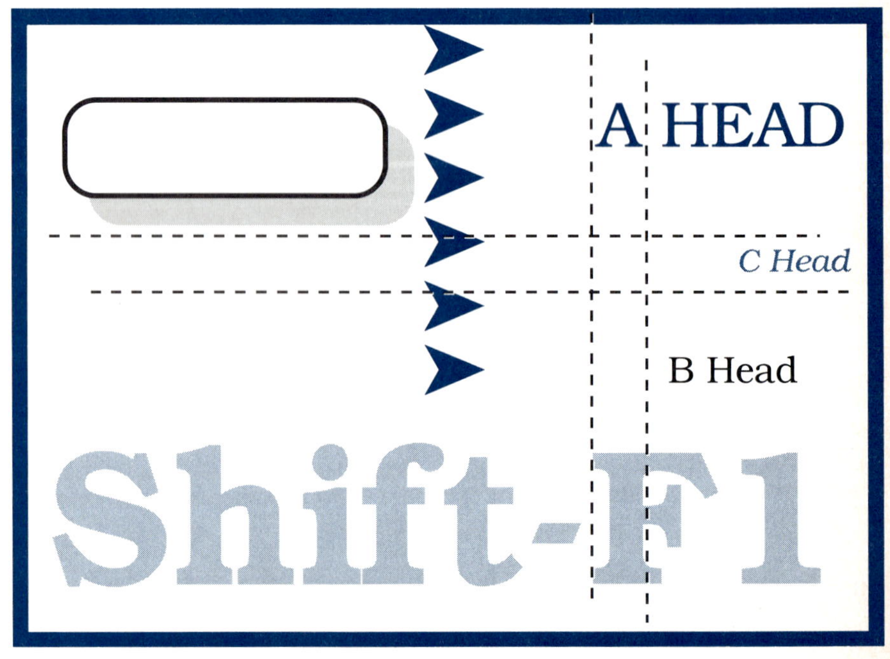

Style Sheets

After completing this topic, you should be able to:
- Explain the benefits of using style sheets to format documents
- Define styles for your own documents
- Apply styles to elements in your documents

▶ T U T O R I A L

In this tutorial, you create a style that automatically formats subheads in a document. You then revise the formats to see how all elements in the document are automatically reformatted.

GETTING STARTED

1. Retrieve the INDENTS1.WP5 document and enter your name.

DISPLAYING THE STYLE DEFINITION MENU

2. Press **Alt-F8** to display the List Styles menu. Some styles may already be listed, but ignore them for now.
3. Press **C** for *Create* to display the Edit Styles menu.
4. Press **N** for *Name*, type **SUBHEAD** and then press **Enter**.
5. Press **D** for *Description*, type **A-Level Subheads** and then press **Enter**.
6. Press **C** for *Codes* to display the definition screen containing a comment box that represents the text to be formatted in the document. The cursor should be above the box.

ADDING A RULED LINE

7. Press **Alt-F9** to display the Graphics menu.
8. Press **L** for *Line*.
9. Press **H** for *Horizontal* to display the Horizontal Line menu.
10. Press **F7** to accept the default settings and return to the style definition screen.

ADDING AN ADVANCE DOWN CODE

11. Press **Shift-F8** to display the Format menu.
12. Press **O** for *Other*.
13. Press **A** for *Advance*.
14. Press **D** for *Down* and the prompt reads *Adv. down 0"*.

15. Type **12p** and then press **Enter**.

16. Press **F7** to accept the default settings and return to the style definition screen.

CHANGING THE FONT APPEARANCE

17. Press **Alt-F4** or **F12** to turn block on, and the status line flashes *Block on.*

18. Press → to highlight the comment box (the cursor will be to the right of the *[Comment]* code displayed in the lower half of the screen).

19. Press **F6** to enter boldface codes.

20. Press **F7** three times to return to the Edit screen.

FORMATTING SUBHEADS WITH STYLES

21. Block the heading "*Indented Paragraphs.*"

22. Press **Alt-F8** to display the List Styles menu, and then highlight the style name *SUBHEAD.*

23. Press **O** for **O**n.

24. Block the headings "*II. Single and Double Indents*" and "*III. Hanging Indents*" and repeat Steps 22 and 23 to mark them with the style.

25. Save and print the document. The headings should be boldfaced with ruled lines over them.

REVISING A STYLE

26. Press **Alt-F8** to display the List Styles menu, and then highlight the style name *SUBHEAD.*

27. Press **E** for **E**dit to display the Edit Styles menu.

28. Press **C** for **C**odes to display the formatting codes.

29. Use the arrow keys to highlight the *[BOLD]* code, then press **Del** to delete it.

30. Press **Alt-F4** or **F12** to turn block on, and the status line flashes *Block on.*

31. Press → to highlight the comment box (the cursor will be to the right of the *[Comment]* code displayed in the lower half of the screen).

32. Press **Ctrl-F8** to display the Font menu.

33. Press **A** for **A**ppearance.

34. Press **I** for **I**talic.

35. Press **F7** three times to return to the Edit screen.

36. Save and print the document. Compare the two versions of the document. All the formatting changes were made by just changing the definition of the style.

FINISHING UP

37. Press **Alt-F8** to display the list of styles.

38. Press **S** for **S**ave and the prompt reads *Filename:.*

39. Type **MYSTYLES** and then press **Enter**. (The file is saved in the directory specified in the Setup menu under the Style Files section of the Location of Files menu.)

40. Press **F7** to return to the Edit screen.

You can define and save the definition of frequently used formats on **style sheets** (WordPerfect calls them lists of styles). For example, you can specify that main headings are to be uppercase and boldfaced, subheadings initial capital only and underlined, and the body of the text printed in 10-point Times Roman. When you specify these definitions on the style sheet, you define the style and add it to a menu. When assigning a style to text, you select the style from the menu.

Assume you have formatted a hundred headings and decide that you want to change the format. Without a style sheet, you have to reformat each individually. But with a style sheet, you change only the definition, and all formatted text is automatically changed. For example, you could change the definition of main headings from uppercase and boldfaced to uppercase and underlined, and every main heading is automatically reformatted. This ease of formatting makes experimentation possible. You can try different formats and print out sample pages to compare the results. You can then use only the formats you like to print the entire document quickly and easily.

You can also save the style sheet that contains these definitions so that you can use it with any document you create. When you create new documents, you use the existing style sheets to format them for printing, which saves you time and standardizes your documents.

You can create a standard style sheet for each class of documents and then use that style sheet each time one of these is created. This ensures that all versions are uniform. You can also create different style sheets for the same class of documents. For example, you can print double-spaced draft copies to make editing easier, and then you can print single-spaced final copies. This lets you print the same document in a variety of formats with little additional effort.

WordPerfect allows you to define and save the definition of frequently used formats on **lists of styles** so that you can reuse them just by selecting them from the list.

The first step in using a list of styles is to specify the name of an existing list or to create your own. There are three ways to do this.

- Specify an existing list as a style library.
- Retrieve an existing list.
- Create your own list of styles.

Specifying a Style Library

You can specify any list of styles to be the default list, called a **style library**. If you do so, and then press **Alt-F8** to display a list of files for a new document, the style library is automatically retrieved if styles do not already exist for the document. WordPerfect includes a basic list of styles in a file named LIBRARY.STY that you can use to start. (On a hard disk system, this file is in the same directory as the WordPerfect program files or in a style directory specified on the Setup menu. On a floppy disk system, it is on the disk labeled *Macros/Keyboard*.) You can also create a special directory in which to store your lists of styles and specify the name of that directory.

 **KEY/Strokes**

Specifying a Style Library

1. Either: Press **Shift-F1** to display the Setup menu.
   Or: Pull down the File menu and select *Setup*.
2. Press **L** for *Location of Files*.
3. Press **S** for *Style Files*.
4. Enter the name of the directory where you want to store style files, and then press **Enter**. The prompt reads *Library Filename*.
5. Type the path and filename for the style library, and then press **Enter**.
6. Press **F7** to return to the Edit screen.

Creating and Saving Your Own Styles

There are two ways to define styles of your own. You can enter them into the document and then copy them to the list of styles, or you can display the style list and enter them directly.

 **KEY/Strokes**

Copying a Format in a Document to the List of Styles

1. If copying a paired code, block text including both the on and off codes. If copying an open code, block just the code.
2. Either: Press **Alt-F8** to display the list of styles and the List Styles menu.
   Or: Pull down the Layout menu and select *Styles*.
   The list of styles and the List Styles menu are displayed.
3. Press **C** for *Create* to display the Edit Styles menu.
4. Enter the name and description, and then press **F7** to return to the Edit screen.

The List of Styles and List Styles Menu

When you press **Alt-F8**, the list of styles and List Styles menu are displayed. This figure shows WordPerfect's predefined styles. Your screen may not list the same styles if they have been changed or if the location of the LIBRARY.STY file has not been specified on the Location of Files setting on the Setup menu.

```
Styles

    Name            Type        Description

    Bibliogrphy    Paired      Bibliography
    Doc Init       Paired      Initialize Document Style
    Document       Outline     Document Style
    Pleading       Open        Header for numbered pleading paper
    Right Par      Outline     Right-Aligned Paragraph Numbers
    Tech Init      Open        Initialize Technical Style
    Technical      Outline     Technical Document Style












1 On; 2 Off; 3 Create; 4 Edit; 5 Delete; 6 Save; 7 Retrieve; 8 Update: 1
```

Creating, Assigning, or Modifying Styles

1. If assigning a style, move the cursor to where you want an open style to begin or end, or block text to which a paired style will be applied.
2. Either: Press **Alt-F8**.
   Or: Pull down the Layout menu and select **Styles**.
   The list of styles and the List Styles menu are displayed.
3. Select one or more of the menu items described in the table "List Styles Menu Commands."
4. If necessary, press **F7** twice to return to the Edit screen.

LIST STYLES MENU COMMANDS

1 *On* turns a style on.

2 *Off* turns a style off.

3 *Create* displays the Edit Styles menu. Select one or more of the menu items described in the table "Edit Styles Menu Choices." Press **Enter** after completing each of them to return to the *Selection:* prompt. (But press **F7** to return to the *Selection:* prompt from the *Codes* choice.)

4 *Edit* displays the Edit Styles menu for the highlighted style so that you can edit it. The choices on the menu are the same as those described for **3** *Create* (see the table "Edit Styles Menu Choices").

5 *Delete* displays a submenu.
   - **1** *Leaving Codes* deletes the style and converts all style codes of the same name in the document to the codes that the style contained.
   - **2** *Including Codes* deletes both the style code and the codes in the document.
   - **3** *Definition Only* deletes only the definition on the list of styles, but the codes remain in the document. When you scroll through the document, all codes are again listed automatically on the list of styles. This is useful when you want to list only the styles that the document actually contains.

6 *Save* saves the list so that you can use it with another document. When you select this choice, the prompt reads *Filename:.* Type the name of the file (including a path, if necessary), and then press **Enter**.

7 *Retrieve* retrieves a list of styles that has been previously saved. When you select this choice, the prompt reads *Filename:.* Type the name of the file (including a path, if necessary), and then press **Enter**. If styles have already been defined, a prompt reads *Style(s) already exist. Replace? No (Yes).*
   - Press **N** to retrieve just those styles that do not have the same name as the styles on the screen.
   - Press **Y** to retrieve all the styles.

8 *Update* updates the list of formats on the screen from the default list of styles on the disk.

The Edit Styles List and Menu
When you select Create or Edit from the List Styles menu, the Create or Edit Styles screen and menu is displayed. The screens are identical, except for their headings.

```
Styles: Edit

    1 - Name

    2 - Type            Paired

    3 - Description

    4 - Codes

    5 - Enter           HRt




Selection: 0
```

EDIT STYLES MENU CHOICES

1 *Name* is a name (up to 12 characters long) that appears in the codes when you assign styles to parts of the document.

2 *Type* refers to whether the style is an open, paired, or outline style.

- **1** *Paired* styles, like bold, insert paired codes in the document.
- **2** *Open* styles, like margins, insert open codes in the document.
- **3** *Outline* styles define outline levels.

3 *Description* describes the style so that you know what it is for. You can enter up to 54 characters.

4 *Codes* displays a screen into which you enter the codes and text that are to appear when you use the style to format the document. You enter the codes and text just as you would enter them into the document itself. Enter on codes in front of the *[Comment]* code and off codes behind it. When entering an open style, the screen does not display a *[Comment]* code.

5 *Enter* describes how the *[HRt]* code acts when you press **Enter** at the end of a section with a paired style. When you select this choice, the following menu items are displayed:

- **1** *Hrt* acts as it does normally; the off code moves down to the next line, with the cursor in front of it.
- **2** *Off* turns off a style by moving the cursor past the off code when you press **Enter**.
- **3** *Off/On* moves the cursor past the off code on the current line and inserts a new pair of codes for the style on the next line.

Assigning Styles to Text
After you have created a style, you can assign it to any text in the document.

- If entering an open style, position the cursor where the style is to begin.
- If formatting existing text with a paired style, block the text.

You then press **Alt-F8** to display the list of styles and the List Styles menu (see the table "List Styles Menu Commands"), highlight the style you want to apply, and then press **Enter** or **O** for *On* to turn the style on. If you are entering new text and have applied an open style, press → to move the cursor to the right of the off code. You can also turn the format off in other ways.

■ Press **Alt-F8** to display the list of styles and the List Styles menu, and then press **f** for *Off* to turn the style off.
■ If you defined the *Enter* choice on the Edit Styles menu (see the table "Edit Styles Menu Choices") as *Off* or *Off/On*, press **Enter** to end the style instead of using the List Styles menu to do so. If the setting for the *Enter* choice is *Off/On*, this inserts a new pair of codes, and the cursor is positioned between them.

Saving and Retrieving Lists of Styles

Styles that you create are automatically saved along with the document. You can also save a list of styles in its own file so that you can retrieve it when formatting another document.

If you edit any of the styles, add new styles, or delete styles, you have to save the list of styles again to use the updated version with other documents. When doing so, you must specify the same filename (and path) to replace the original version. When you then retrieve a previously created document where you used the previous version of the same list, you must use the Update command on the List Styles menu to update the document's list of styles to reflect the changes.

EXERCISE 1

DEFINING STYLES

In this exercise, you define a style for subheads in a document.

1. Retrieve the ALIGN2.WP5 document.
2. Follow the instructions in the KEY/Strokes box "Creating, Assigning, or Modifying Styles" to define two styles.
   • Define a style for the amendment number that boldfaces it.
   • Define a style for the amendment title that prints it italicized.
3. Follow the instructions in the KEY/Strokes box "Creating, Assigning, or Modifying Styles" to apply the styles to the first two amendments. (You will do the rest in the next topic.)
4. Save and then print the document.
5. Follow the instructions in the KEY/Strokes box "Creating, Assigning, or Modifying Styles" to revise one or both of the styles on the list of styles, and then make a new printout. Compare the two documents to see how a changed style definition changes the formats throughout the document.

STYLE TIPS

- If you are formatting text with a paired style as you enter it, enter the on code, type the text, and then either repeat the commands to turn it on, but select *Off*, or, if you defined the *Enter* choice on the Edit Styles menu as *Off* or *Off/On*, press **Enter**.
- When you reveal codes and move the cursor over a style's on or off code, the code expands to reveal the formats contained in the code.
- When you press **Alt-F8** to display a list of styles, you can use the Name Search command to locate a specific style. To do so, press **F2** and the prompt reads *(Name Search; Enter or arrows to Exit)*. Begin typing the name of the style. Each character you type moves you closer to the style until you have typed enough characters to identify it uniquely. This procedure is especially useful when you use macros to assign styles.
- When you update a style sheet, the new styles on the default style sheet are copied onto the document style sheet, and existing codes are updated. However, existing codes are not deleted from the document's list of styles, even if they were deleted from the default style sheet.
- If you move the cursor to a style in the document and then display the list of styles, the style for the highlighted element is highlighted on the list.

Automating with Macros

After completing this topic, you should be able to:
- Define macros
- Execute macros
- Edit macros

► TUTORIAL

In this tutorial, you create a macro that assigns the SUBHEAD style that you created in the last topic to the subheads in your document.

GETTING STARTED

1. Retrieve the INDENTS4.WP5 document and enter your name.

RETRIEVING STYLES

2. Press **Alt-F8** to display the List Styles menu.
3. Press **R** for **R**etrieve and the prompt reads *Filename:*.
4. Type **MYSTYLES** and then press **Enter**. If your document contains any styles with the same names as the ones being retrieved, the prompt reads *Style(s) already exist. Replace? No (Yes)*.
5. Press **Y** and in a minute you will see *SUBHEAD* appear on the list of styles.
6. Press **F7** to return to the Edit screen.

RECORDING KEYSTROKES

7. Move the cursor under the "*I*" in the subhead "*Indented Para-graphs*."
8. Press **Ctrl-F10** and the prompt reads *Define macro:*.
9. Type **SUBHEAD** and then press **Enter**. The prompt reads *Description:*.
10. Type **Assigns subhead style** and then press **Enter**. The status line flashes *Macro Def* to indicate that keystrokes are now being recorded.
11. Press **Alt-F4** or **F12** to turn block on and then press **End** to highlight the entire subhead.
12. Press **Alt-F8** to display the list of styles.
13. Press **N** and a message reads *(Name Search; Enter or arrows to Exit)*.

14. Type **SUBHEAD** (or enough letters so that style is highlighted), and then press **Enter**.

15. Press **O** for *On*.

16. Press **Ctrl-F10** and the status line no longer flashes *Macro Def.*

PLAYING BACK THE RECORDED KEYSTROKES

17. Move the cursor to the "*B*" in the subhead "*Block-Style Para-graphs.*"

18. Press **Alt-F10** and the prompt reads *Macro:.*

19. Type **SUBHEAD** and then press **Enter**. (Reveal codes and you will see that the subhead is formatted.)

20. Move the cursor to the "*S*" in the subhead "*Single and Double Indents*" and repeat Steps 18 and 19.

FINISHING UP

21. Save and print the document.

▶ DESKTOP PUBLISHING CONCEPTS

Since many of the tasks you perform during word processing are repetitive, you often find yourself pressing the same sequence of keys to save, retrieve, or print files; indent paragraphs; boldface or underline words; and so on. Programs such as WordPerfect allow you to create **macros** that automate these repetitive tasks.

There are two steps to using macros: defining them so they are saved in a file on the disk, and executing them.

Defining Macros

You can define (record) and then automatically execute (play back) any sequence of keystrokes, including text and commands. Defining and executing macros are easy and can save you a lot of time if you use the same series of keystrokes over and over again; for example:

- You can record sections of text, and then insert them into documents where needed.
- You can record and then execute a series of commands. If you have to press five or six keys to execute a command, you can store those keystrokes in a macro and execute it by pressing as few as two keys.
- You can enter a pause in a macro when you define it. When you execute the macro, it executes all keystrokes up to the pause and then waits for you to enter text or other keystrokes from the keyboard. When you do so, and then press **Enter**, the macro continues. This is useful when all but a few of the keystrokes are the same. For example, you can record all the keystrokes needed to retrieve a file from the disk but enter a pause so that you can type in the desired file's name.

▶ WORDPERFECT PROCEDURES

The first step in using macros is to define them. When defining macros you have to assign them a name so you can play them back. There are three ways to assign names.

- You can enter an eight-character name. If you do so, you then have to enter that same name to play it back.
- You can assign the macro to an **Alt**-letter key combination, so you can then execute it by holding down **Alt** and pressing the letter you assigned it to.
- You can press **Enter** to create a temporary macro that is automatically deleted when you exit WordPerfect.

If you name a macro with a name of an already existing macro, a message informs you that the macro already exists. You can use the displayed menu choices to replace the existing macro, edit it, or view its description.

When the *Macro Def* message is displayed as you define a macro, you can press **Ctrl-PgUp** to display the Macro Options menu (see the table "Macro Options Menu Commands"). You can also use a mouse to execute commands but not to move the cursor.

→   **K E Y / S t r o k e s**

Defining a Macro

1. Either: Press **Ctrl-F10**.

   Or: Pull down the Tools menu, select *Macro*, and then select *Define*.

   The prompt reads *Define macro:*.

2. Either: Type the name of the macro (up to eight characters), and then press **Enter**.

   Or: Hold down **Alt** and press a letter (**A** through **Z**) you want to assign the macro to.

   Or: Press **Enter** to create a temporary macro that is automatically deleted when you exit WordPerfect. (You cannot edit temporary macros.)

   The prompt reads *Description:*. (If you pressed **Enter**, go on to Step 4.) If a macro by the same name already exists, you are prompted to replace or edit it. Press **R** for *Replace*.

3. Type a description of the macro (up to 39 characters), and then press **Enter**. The status line flashes *Macro Def*. (When this is flashing, you are recording keystrokes.)

4. Enter the keys to be recorded in the macro. (To enter options at any point, press **Ctrl-PgUp**. See the table "Macro Options Menu Commands.")

5. Press **Ctrl-F10** to end the macro, and the status line no longer flashes *Macro Def*.

MACRO OPTIONS MENU COMMANDS

1 Pause pauses the macro during its execution when **Ctrl-PgUp** are pressed so that you can enter information from the keyboard, for example, to enter a person's name in a salutation or a filename in a file save or file retrieve macro. When you then enter text and press **Enter**, the macro resumes.

MACRO OPTIONS MENU COMMANDS (CONTINUED)

2 *Display* allows you to see the macro perform or turn off the screen update until the macro is finished.

3 *Assign* assigns values to variables. Refer to the WordPerfect manual's section on advanced macros.

4 *Comment* enters comments into the macro definition to help you understand it later when editing it. Comments that you enter are ignored when the macro is played back.

Executing Macros

When you want to replay the keystrokes that you recorded, you execute the macro. The way you do so depends on how you named it.

- If you assigned it to an **Alt**-letter key combination, you hold down **Alt** while pressing the letter key you assigned it to.
- If you assigned it a name, you press **Alt-F10**, type the name of the macro, and then press **Enter**.
- If it is a temporary macro that is automatically deleted when you exit WordPerfect, press **Alt-F10** and then **Enter**.

 **KEY/Strokes**

Executing a Macro

1. Move the cursor to where you want the macro played back.
2. Either: Press **Alt-F10** to display the prompt *Macro:*, type the name of the macro, and then press **Enter**.

   Or: Hold down **Alt** and press the letter you assigned the keystrokes to.

   Or: Press **Alt-F10** and then press **Enter** to execute a temporary macro created just for the current session.

   Or: Pull down the Tools menu, select *Macro*, and then select *Execute*. When the prompt reads *Macro:*, type the name of the macro, and then press **Enter**.

Editing Macros

WordPerfect also allows you to edit macros so that you can correct any mistakes you may have made or add additional procedures without having to redefine the keystrokes. (You cannot edit temporary macros.)

 **KEY/Strokes**

Editing a Macro

1. Either: Press **Ctrl-F10**.

   Or: Pull down the Tools menu, select *Macro*, then select *Define*.

   The prompt reads *Define macro:*.
2. Either: Type the name of the macro you want to edit, and then press **Enter**.

The Macro Edit Screen

The Macro Edit screen displays a menu and the macro. By choosing commands from the menu, you can change the macro's description or keystrokes.

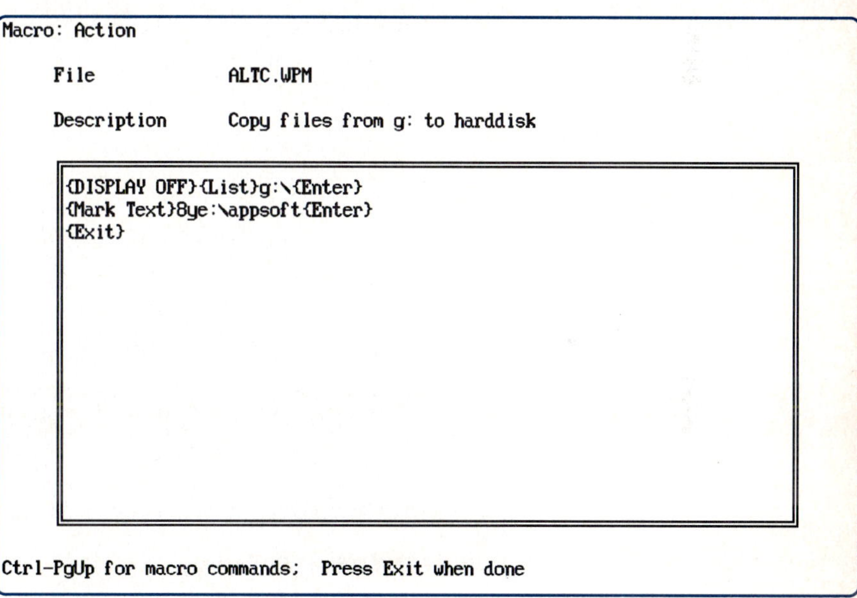

Saving and Retrieving Macros

When you save a macro, the extension .WPM is automatically assigned to it. You do not have to type this extension when defining or executing a macro, but you will see it in the List Files screen.

Macros are automatically stored in the keyboard/macro directory when they are defined. You specify this directory using the Setup menu's Location of Files command. If you do not specify a directory with this command, macros are saved on the current default directory which you can change by pressing **F5**. When defining a macro, you can also specify a path in front of the macro name to store the macro in another drive and directory. When you execute the macro, you then have to specify the same path and filename when prompted to enter the macro's name. If you have assigned a macro to a letter key and get the message

ERROR: File not found, change the default directory to the one it is stored in and try again.

To delete a macro, delete the file with the same name and the extension .WPM. (For example, a macro that you assigned to **Alt-C** is named ALTC.WPM.) Macros are stored in the directory specified in the Setup menu's Location of Files command.

➤ E X E R C I S E

EXERCISE 1

DEFINING A MACRO THAT ASSIGNS A STYLE

In this exercise, you create a macro that assigns a style to the headings in a document.

1. Retrieve the ALIGN2.WP5 document.
2. Follow the instructions in the KEY/Strokes box "Defining a Macro" to define two macros that assign the styles you created for the amendment numbers and titles in the previous topic.
3. Apply the styles to the last eight amendments. (You did the first two in the previous topic.)
4. Save and then print the document.

✔ M A C R O   T I P S

- You can see the description you entered when defining a macro with the Look command on the List Files menu.
- You can use the Repeat command to repeat a macro a specified number of times.
- To stop a macro in progress, press **F1**. (If you press **F1** while defining a macro, it just inserts the cancel code in the macro and does not cancel the macro definition process.)
- When switching between insert and typeover modes in a macro, you can use a command to force the change regardless of what the current mode is. To force typeover mode, press **Home, Ins**. To force insert mode, press **Home, Home, Ins**.

REVIEW

- If you use a variety of standard formats when formatting documents, you can save these formats as styles on a style sheet (called a list of styles by WordPerfect).
- WordPerfect provides a library of standard styles that can be used as is or modified. To use it, or to create your own library, you specify its name and path on the Setup menu.
- To define a macro, you specify a name and a description for the macro, enter the text or commands to be recorded, and then turn off definition mode.
- To execute a defined macro, you hold down **Alt** and press the letter it is assigned to or press **Alt-F10** and enter its name.

QUESTIONS

TRUE/FALSE

T F

1. A style sheet and a list of styles are two different names for the same thing.

2. The advantage of using a style to format elements is that you can change their format by just changing the style's definition.

3. You can copy a format from a document to a list of styles.

4. You can save your styles into a file and then retrieve them into another document.

5. A style library is the default list of styles.

6. Defining a macro is the process of assigning it a name and recording keystrokes.

7. You can execute a macro before you define it if you need to.

8. You can assign macros to **Alt**-letter key combinations so you can play them back by holding down the **Alt** key and a letter on the keyboard.

9. If you make a small mistake when defining a macro, you can only correct it by defining the macro all over again.

1. WordPerfect uses the phrase ___________ for what others call a style sheet.
2. The default list of styles is called the style ___________ .
3. You can assign macros names or to ___________ -letter key combinations.
4. Before you can execute a macro, you must first ___________ it.
5. To delete, copy, or move macros, you look for filenames with the extension ___________.

MATCH THE COLUMNS

1. Define
2. Execute
3. List of styles
4. Macro
5. Style library
6. Style sheet
7. WPM

__ WordPerfect's default list of styles

__ The process of recording a macro

__ The process of playing back a macro

__ The more widely used name for what WordPerfect calls a list of styles

__ The extension that WordPerfect assigns to macro files

__ Recorded keystrokes that can be played back

__ Formats that have been saved so they can be selected from a list

WRITE OUT THE ANSWERS

1. What is a list of styles?
2. What is the main advantage of using a list of styles?
3. If you want to use the same list of styles for every new document, what steps should you take?
4. Describe the purpose of macros.
5. List the steps you would follow to record a macro.
6. How do you play back a recorded macro?
7. Where are macros stored? How can you specify a different storage area?

PROJECTS

PROJECT 1

USING A MACRO TO MARK INDEX ENTRIES

Record a macro that marks the word containing the cursor as an index entry. Save it as INDEX or assign it to the **I** key so you can execute it by pressing **Alt**-**I**. Use the macro to mark the words shown in this figure and then generate an index at the end of the document.

Procedures Used
- Using a macro to mark index entries.

Text Files Needed
- ALIGN1.WP5

Formats
① Enter a centered heading at the end of the document.
② Enter an index definition code and generate the index.
③ Enter a hard page break so the index prints on a page by itself.

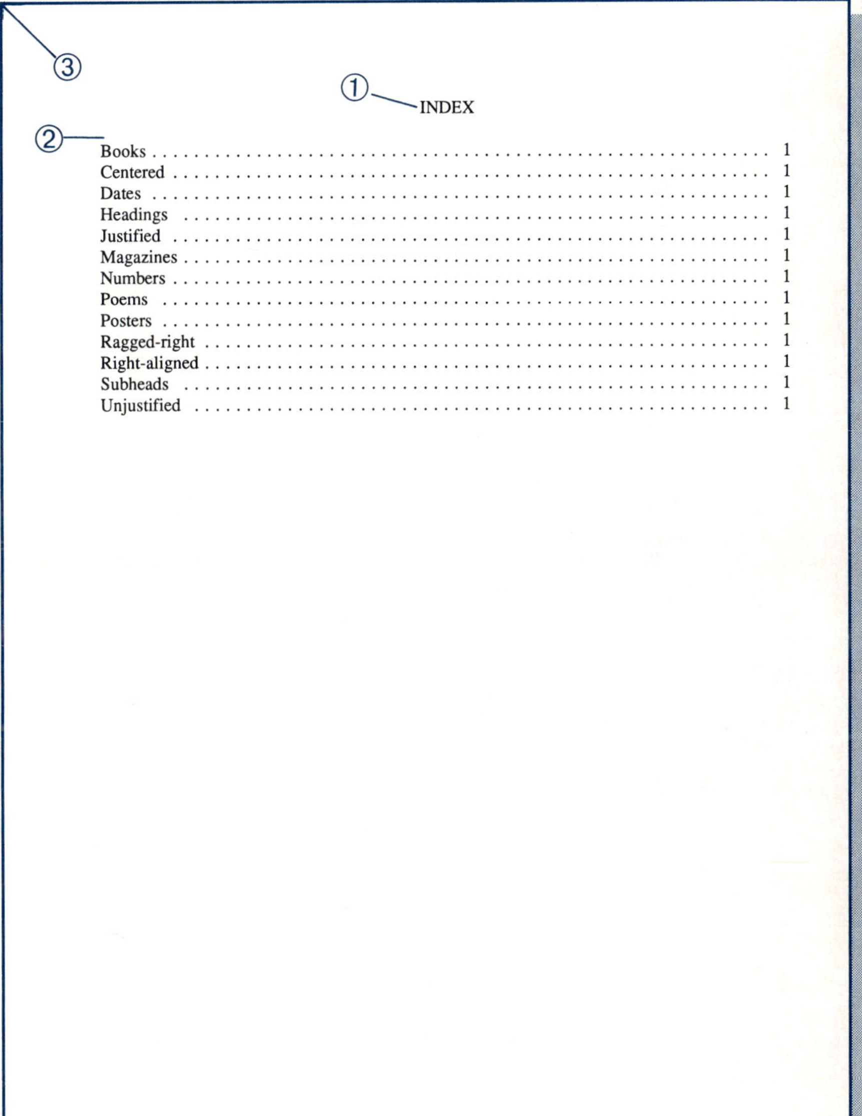

INDEX

Finishing Touches

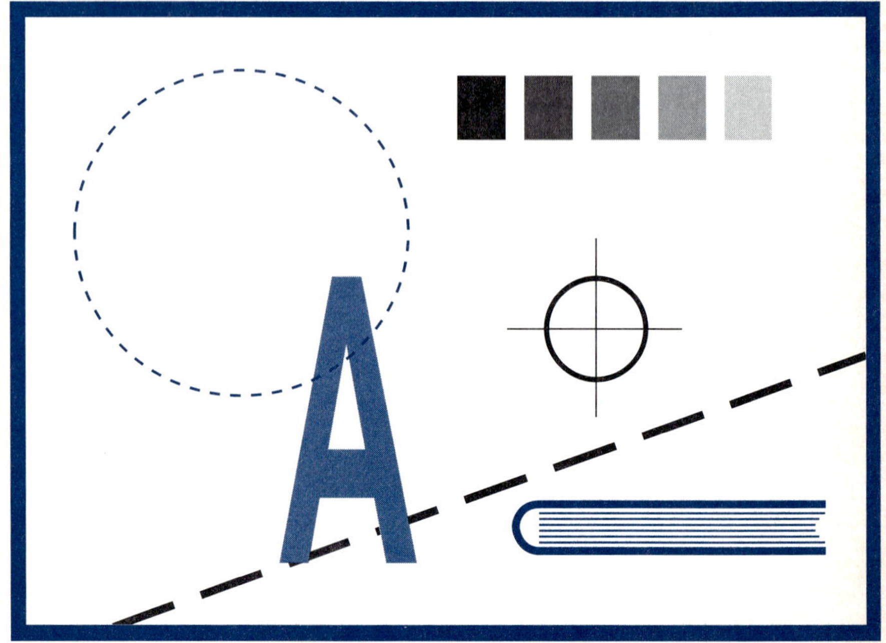

Folding, Binding, and Trimming

After completing this topic, you should be able to:
- Describe how printed sheets can be folded to create multipage documents
- Describe available binding options
- Describe how some documents are trimmed to their final size

▶ DESKTOP PUBLISHING CONCEPTS

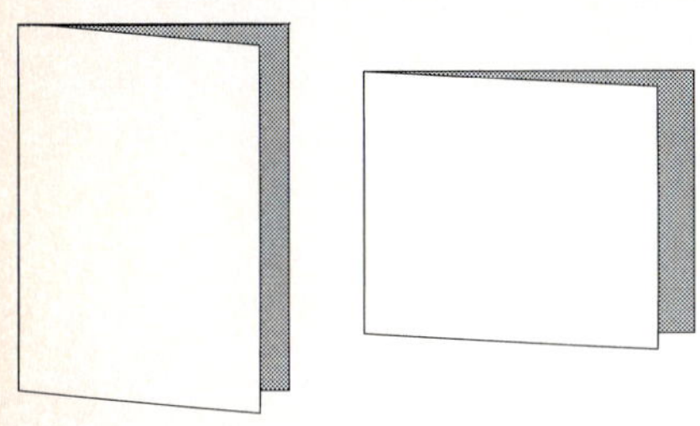

4-page Folds

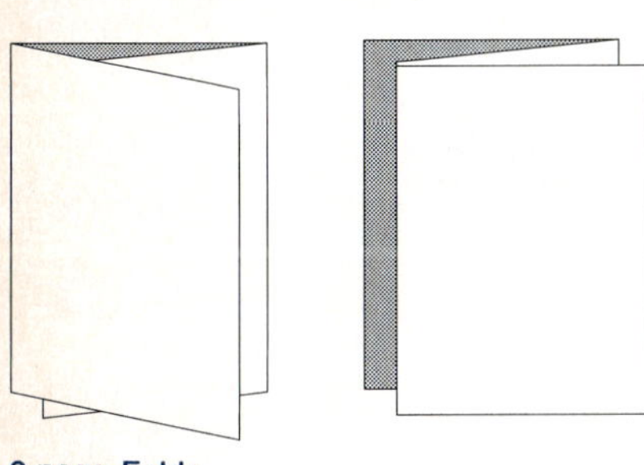

6-page Folds

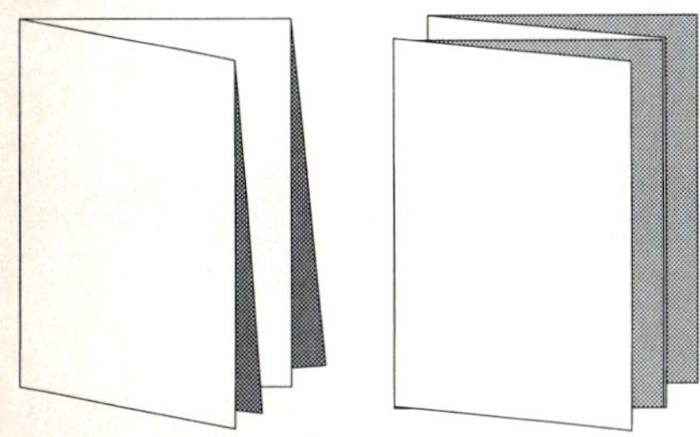

8-page Folds

Many printed documents need to be folded, bound, or trimmed. Even though these operations are the last steps in the publishing process before distribution, they must be taken into consideration when a project is designed.

Folding

Many documents are printed as many pages on a single sheet of paper. These sheets must then be folded before they can be distributed or bound. A single sheet of paper can be folded to create many pages. For example, some very small 128- (or more) page pocket guides are printed on a single sheet and then are folded, bound, and trimmed. The most common foldings, however, result in brochures or other documents ranging from 4 to 32 pages. The size of the finished publication depends on the original size of the paper and the number of folds. The combinations are almost endless. However, if you start with an 8½-by-11-inch sheet, you can easily create four- and six-page documents. Four-page documents are used for programs, small brochures, instruction booklets, and small catalogs. Six-page folders are frequently used for price lists and envelope stuffers to be mailed in regular business-size envelopes.

If the document is a book or manual, the folded sheets are called **signatures**. If the book was printed on more than one sheet, then all of the folded signatures must be collated (**gathered**). The folded and collated signatures are called **folded and gathereds** or **f&gs**.

Binding

Many documents have to be bound before they are distributed. There are a variety of bindings that can be used. Some can be finished right in the office and others can be finished only with expensive specialized equipment at commercial binderies.

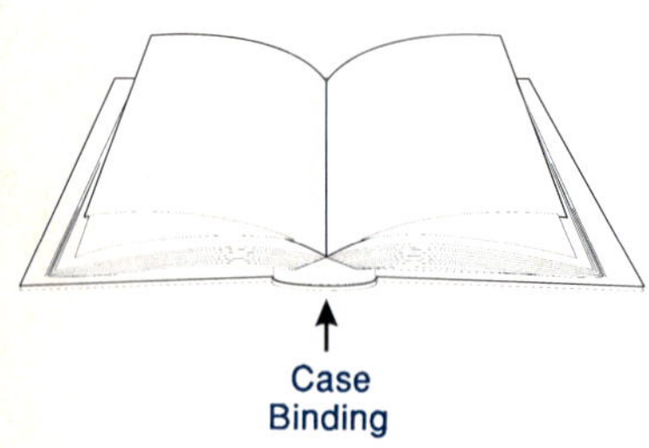

Case
Binding

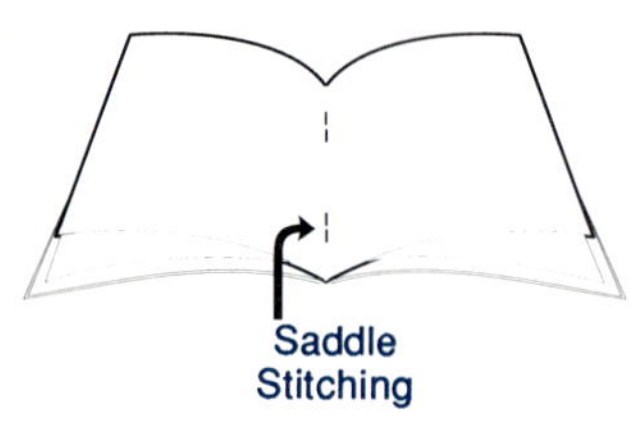

Saddle
Stitching

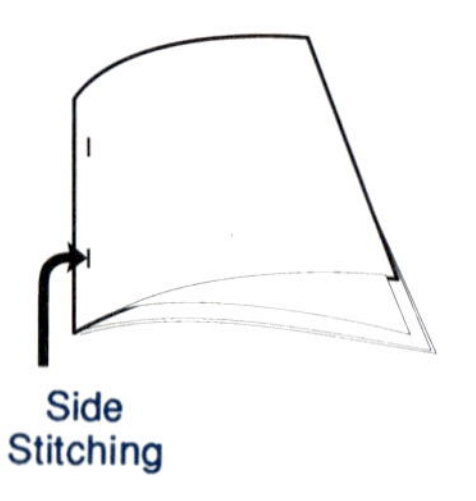

Side
Stitching

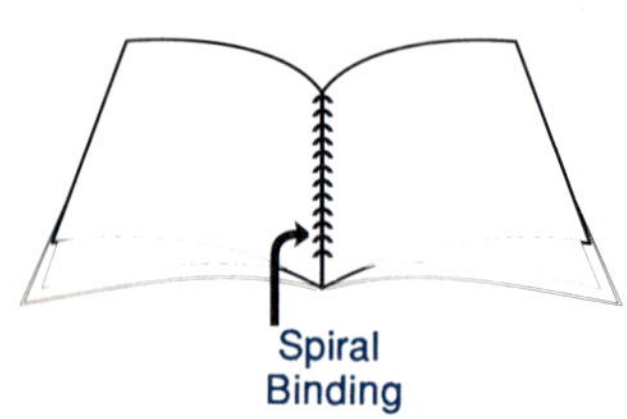

Spiral
Binding

Book Bindings

There are two basic types of book bindings: case bindings and perfect bindings (although any of the binding methods in this section can be used for books).

- **Case binding** (also called *edition binding*) is the method used for hardcover books. The signatures of the book are gathered together and then sewn or glued together at the **spine** (the spine is the back of the book, the part that shows when it is on a bookshelf). This unit is then bound to a hard cover case with endpapers and a strip of gauze that is sandwiched between the two.
- **Perfect binding** is the method used for most paperback books. After the signatures are gathered together, the binding edge is trimmed and covered with a flexible glue. A cover is then wrapped around the book and the glue holds it and the pages together.

When bound documents are thick enough, copy can be printed along the spine. This allows the book to be identified when it is on a bookshelf. The spine copy should be printed horizontally across the narrow width or vertically reading from top to bottom along the length of the spine. (In some countries, spine copy reads from bottom to top.)

Stapled Bindings

Many documents can be stapled to hold them together. There are two basic types of stapled bindings: saddle stitched and side stitched. These are the simplest and least expensive forms of binding, so they are widely used. You will frequently see them used in magazines, catalogs, brochures, and programs.

- **Saddle stitching** is stapling the document in the gutter fold. In a bindery, two-page spreads are nested inside each other and then laid across a saddle and a stapling head descends to staple them together. You can duplicate this binding method in an office using a stapler with an arm that is long enough to reach across a page.
- **Side stitching** is simply stapling the edge of the document. This method accommodates thicker documents than saddle stitching because the pages do not need to be nested. Sometimes the binding side is first covered with paper, cardboard, or a plastic strip to give it a more finished appearance, or a paper cover may be glued around the document to hide the staples. Because the staples prevent the document from being fully opened, the binding margins may have to be increased.

Mechanical Bindings

Mechanical bindings use rings of one kind or another to hold pages together. The rings are fitted into round or rectangular holes punched into the binding edge of the document. One of the major advantages of these bindings is that the bound documents lie flat when opened.

Mechanical bindings range from the familiar ring binders to spiral, wire-o, and plastic comb bindings. Documents needing ring and plastic comb bindings can frequently be bound right in the office because the binding equipment is very inexpensive and easy to use.

- **Ring binders** are those you have been familiar with since school days. The covers can be custom printed for important documents. Some versions have a clear plastic cover on the front and spine into

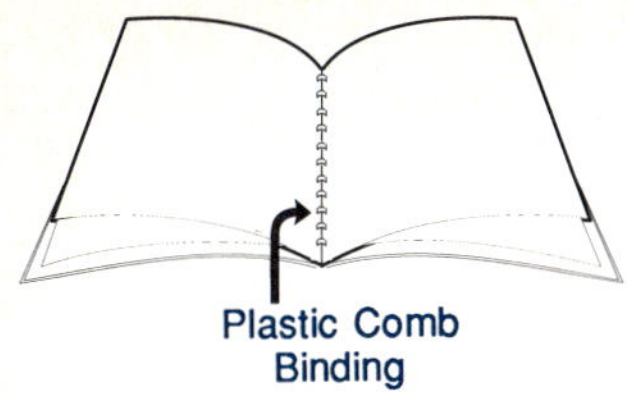

Plastic Comb
Binding

VeloBind
Binding

which you can slip printed covers. The big advantage of this kind of binding is that pages can be easily added, removed, or rearranged.

- **Spiral bindings** have a continuous wire spiral wound through small round holes punched in the edge of the document.
- **Wire-o bindings** are like spiral bindings but give a more finished look. Instead of the wire spiraling, the rings are parallel to each other so pages open more easily.
- **Plastic comb bindings** use a plastic tubular device with protruding rings to hold the pages together. The plastic comb fits through rectangular holes punched through the binding edge of the document.
- **VeloBind**®uses a simple punch and binding strips. The pins on one binding strip are fed through the punched holes and inserted into another strip with slots. A tool is then used to snap the pins into the slots, binding the document together.

Trimming

After folding or binding, a document is trimmed to its final size (although some bindings, such as case and ring, require that this be done before binding). The main purpose of trimming is to remove excess paper, but it also gives a more finished appearance to a publication. No folding process is so precise that all pages align perfectly. Trimming after they are folded makes them do so. To guide the person doing the trimming, **crop marks** are frequently printed on the pages. These marks are printed just outside of the final page area and are trimmed off after serving their purpose of helping align the trimmer.

Crop Marks

> E X E R C I S E

EXERCISE 1

CHECKING BINDINGS

Visit the library and carefully examine three magazines, three books, and three pamphlets. Note the title of each and the type of binding used.

Service Bureaus

After completing this topic, you should be able to:

- Explain the purpose of working with a service bureau
- Describe the services that service bureaus can provide
- Know how to locate service bureaus

> **D E S K T O P   P U B L I S H I N G   C O N C E P T S**

When desktop publishing documents, you are not required to perform all of the tasks that are involved. **Service bureaus** exist to provide you with help, either to make the job easier for you or to improve its quality. You can locate service bureaus in the yellow pages of the phone book under the headings "Desktop Publishing," "Typesetting," "Copying," and "Printers." Even better, you can get recommendations from designers or printers. If you are working on an important document, you should call local service bureaus and ask for a brochure and price list of their services. If you contemplate using one of their services, you should meet with them to discuss your needs as soon as possible so they can make recommendations that might speed up the job and reduce costs. These bureaus provide a variety of services, from design to printing.

Design

Service bureaus can assist with the design of your publication. In some cases they can give you a list of specifications. In other cases, they can actually create a style sheet for the program you are using. All you then have to do is attach the appropriate style to each element in the document and it will be formatted correctly.

Scanning

Service bureaus can scan graphics such as line art and photographs for you. The resulting electronic files can then be incorporated right into your document. If the document you want to work on has already been typed or printed, they can also use optical character recognition software to convert the printed pages to electronic files that you can retrieve, edit, and format with a word processing program.

Typesetting

Laser printers print documents at 300 dots per inch (dpi). This is acceptable but not fine typesetting. Many service bureaus can use the disk files that you have created and set the type using more sophisticated equipment made by firms such as Linotronic or Compugraphic.

This equipment makes it possible to increase the resolution of your document to 1500 dpi, 2400 dpi, or more. The resulting printouts are much sharper and are returned to you on reproduction paper or film that can be used to print the document. Many service bureaus accept the files on disks or you may even send the files over the phone lines if your system is equipped with a modem.

Printing
You can send out mechanicals and have them printed professionally by a commercial printer. You can also have covers printed and pamphlets, books, or manuals bound. If you plan on having the document printed by a commercial printer, you can have the pages reduced. For example, reducing 8½-by-11-inch pages just 18 percent allows them to be printed on 7-by-9-inch pages. If you plan on doing this, be sure to run a test to ensure that the text is still legible at the reduced size.

File Conversions
In addition to their other services, service bureaus may also be able to convert disk files for you. For example, your files may have been created using Word on an Apple but you need to use them with WordPerfect on an IBM PC. The files can be converted so that you can do this.

EXERCISE 1

CONTACTING A SERVICE BUREAU

Write or call a service bureau in your area to ask for a brochure on the services that it offers.

REVIEW

- A single sheet of paper can be folded in many ways to create multipage documents.
- When a job is printed by a commercial printer, it is usually printed on large sheets of paper. If the document is to be bound, and it spans more than one sheet, these sheets must be gathered.
- Books can be bound with case or perfect bindings.
- Brochures, magazines, and thin books can be bound with staples. If the pages are stapled through thc gutter fold, it is called saddle stitching. If the edges are stapled, it is called side stitching.
- Booklets, books, reports, and manuals can be bound using mechanical bindings. These include ring, spiral, wire-o, plastic comb, and VeloBind® bindings.
- If a document is printed on a sheet of paper that is larger than the printed area, it may be trimmed to give a more finished appearance.
- Service bureaus can perform many desktop publishing processes for you. These include design, scanning, typesetting, printing, and file conversion.

QUESTIONS

TRUE/FALSE

T F

1. Publications must be printed as a single page on each side of a sheet of paper.

2. If a book has many pages, each sheet that pages are printed on is folded into a signature.

3. When signatures are collated, they are called folded and gathereds.

4. Case and perfect bindings are frequently used for small brochures and pamphlets.

5. Saddle stitching and side stitching are terms that apply to stapled bindings.

6. Mechanical bindings are too rigid to allow the bound pages to lie flat when opened.

7. If you have a file that was created with a different word processing program or computer system from your own, a service bureau may be able to convert it for you.

8. If you don't have a scanner, you cannot use scanned graphics in your documents.

1. If you had a four- or eight-page pamphlet, you would consider using a ___________-stitched or ___________-stitched binding.
2. If you wanted a manual to lie flat when it was opened, the generic name for the binding style that you would use is ___________ binding.
3. Three examples of the above type of binding are ___________, ___________, and ___________ bindings.
4. To guide the person trimming a document, ___________ marks are added during printing.
5. If you needed help in the preparation of a publication, you might consider contacting a ___________ bureau.
6. You would find service bureaus to help you prepare documents listed in the Yellow Pages under the headings ___________, ___________, ___________, or ___________.

MATCH THE COLUMNS

1. Typesetting
2. Spiral binding
3. Signature
4. Side stitching
5. Service bureau
6. Saddle stitching
7. Gathered
8. Crop marks
9. Comb binding
10. Case binding

__ A group of book pages folded from the same sheet
__ A group of signatures after they have been collated
__ A binding used for hardcover books
__ A binding that uses staples through the gutter margin
__ A binding that uses staples through the edge of the pages
__ A binding that uses a spiral wire that runs through holes in the pages
__ A binding that holds a book together with a plastic tubelike device
__ The marks printed on pages to guide the person who trims them
__ A business that provides services to desktop publishers
__ One of the services provided by a service bureau

WRITE OUT THE ANSWERS

1. Describe two ways that you can fold an 8½-by-11-inch sheet of paper. List some applications for each.
2. List and describe two kinds of book bindings.
3. List and describe two kinds of stapled bindings.
4. List and describe four kinds of mechanical bindings.
5. List and briefly describe three services you might obtain from a service bureau.

Desktop Publishing Systems: A Buyer's Guide

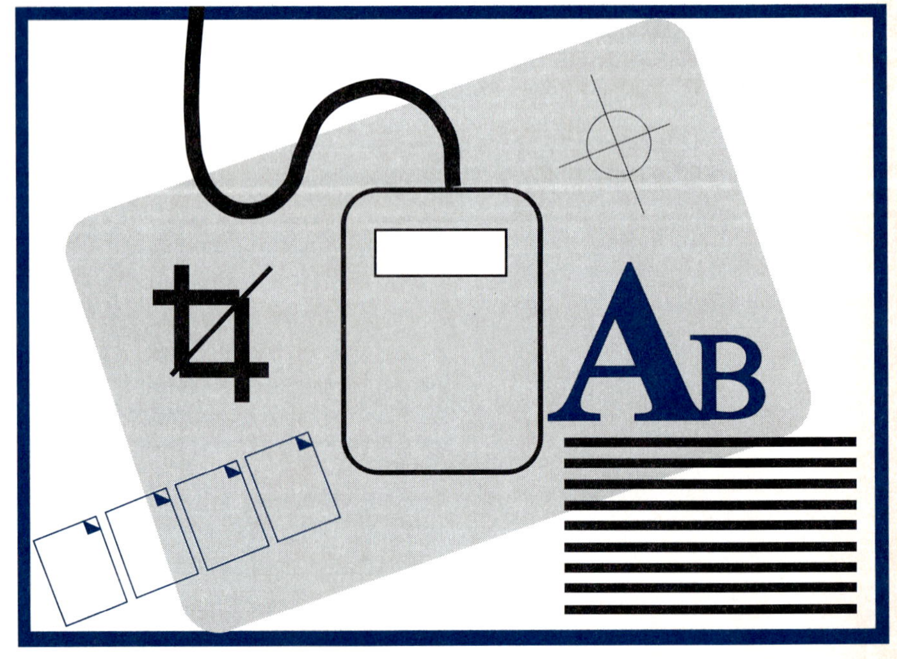

Computers

After completing this topic, you should be able to:

- Describe the three major parts of the computer and explain the function of each
- Explain the role that the microprocessor plays
- Describe what random-access memory is and what function it performs
- Explain what hard disks are and what they are used for

▶ D E S K T O P   P U B L I S H I N G   C O N C E P T S

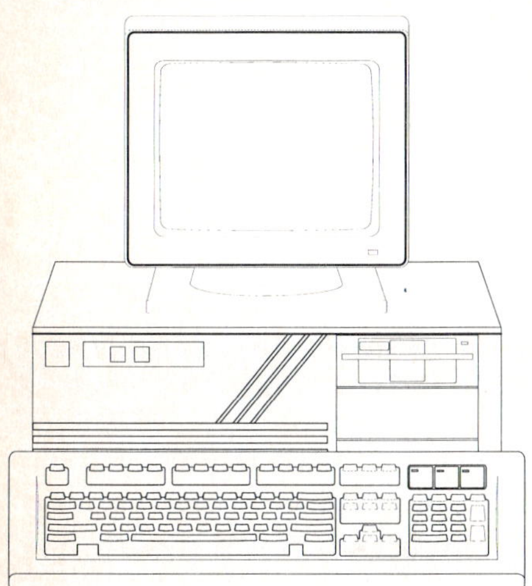

Computer

A desktop publishing system does not differ greatly from a regular microcomputer system. The basic difference is that it is easier to desktop publish documents if your system has a powerful computer with a fast hard disk drive, a good graphics display monitor, and a high-quality printer. Additional, but optional, devices such as a mouse and scanner make desktop publishing easier or more effective.

Desktop publishing frequently involves working with long documents that have complex formats and often include graphics. Working with documents of this kind requires a computer that can process information quickly so you are not subjected to long delays when scrolling the screen, making changes, or saving and retrieving document files. Many programs specify a minimum requirement for a computer but almost all programs will run better on a system with even more power than the program's publisher recommends. The components that influence how well a system runs a program are the performance of the microprocessor, the amount of memory, and the speed of the disk drive.

The Microprocessor

The speed of a computer is determined to a large extent by the **microprocessor** that is used for its **central processing unit (CPU)**. This is the device that runs all of your programs and that processes all of your data. Over the past ten years there has been a great deal of improvement in microprocessors and there are quite a few versions in use. IBM microcomputers use a variety of Intel microprocessors that are identified by numbers. The earliest IBM PCs used the Intel 8088 or 8086. The IBM AT computers introduced next used the Intel 80286 (called the "286"). Today, the most widely used chip is the Intel 80386 (called the "386") but it is slowly being replaced on newer computer models by the Intel 80486 (called the "486"), and widespread use of the 80586 is in the near future.

The most recent microprocessors are available in at least two versions. The full-featured versions are referred to by their numbers alone, for example 386 and 486, or with the suffix *-dx*, for example, 386dx and 486dx. Slightly less powerful but also less expensive versions use the suffix *-sx*, for example 386sx and 486sx.

The number of the microprocessor is not the only consideration when you are choosing a computer. Another variable is called **clock rate**, which is specified in megahertz. This is simply the speed at which the chip processes data. The higher the clock rate, the faster the computer. For example, a 33-megahertz 386 is faster than a 20-megahertz 386.

For most desktop publishing applications in a work environment where speed is essential, computers with 386sx chips are the minimum requirement. In schools, and in other environments where speed isn't as important, computers with any of the chips will suffice, provided that the programs you want to use will run well on the computer.

Random-Access Memory (RAM)

When you load a program or create a document, the data you enter through the keyboard are temporarily stored in **random-access memory** (**RAM**). Usually, if you turn off the computer, any programs or data stored in this memory are lost; thus, RAM is said to be **volatile** memory. RAM is an expensive and limited resource, but for many desktop publishing tasks, especially those involving graphics, a great deal of memory is needed. Up to 4 megabytes are useful because the computer will run faster in many situations and you can work on longer documents.

Hard Disks

When you're working on heavily formatted documents with powerful desktop publishing programs, the disk drive becomes very important. The ideal system contains a fast hard disk drive. These drives can store hundreds and even thousands of times more data than floppy disks and are ten or more times faster when saving or retrieving documents.

One of the main reasons you need a fast hard disk drive is because many applications programs store parts of their programs or data outside RAM until needed. This type of storage is called **virtual memory**. On a system that uses virtual memory, only the parts of the program or data file currently needed are stored in the computer's memory; the rest are stored on the system's hard disk drive. Although other parts of the program or data file are not actually stored in the computer's memory all of the time, they are treated as if they were. When the computer needs them, it moves something stored in memory to the disk to make memory available. It then moves the program or data from the disk into the space made available in memory. This reduces the overall cost of the system because it is cheaper to store data on a hard disk drive than it is to add additional memory chips to the computer. However, it does slow down the system because it takes more time to retrieve data from the disk than it does from memory. Since the computer is continually going to the disk drive for data, the system operates only as fast as the disk drive.

When considering a purchase, be sure to compare **access time** or *seek time* (the average time it takes for the drive to find data) and the **data transfer rate** (the rate at which data are moved from the disk into

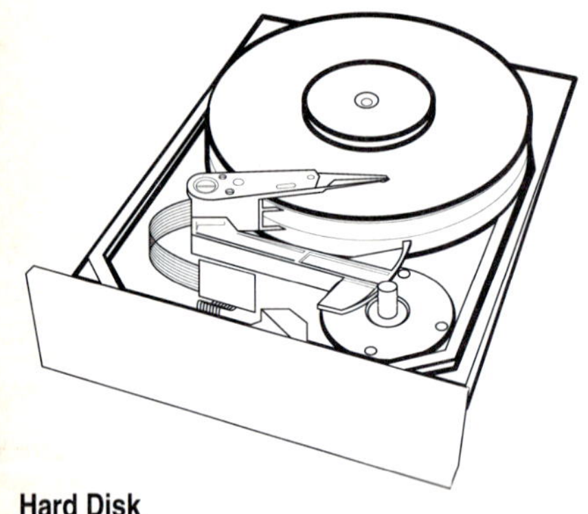

Hard Disk

memory). The faster the hard disk can find and transfer data, the faster
your program will operate.

EXERCISE 1

GETTING TO KNOW YOUR COMPUTER

The computer that you use for desktop publishing has several characteristics with which you should become familiar. Ask your instructor or
the lab assistant for help in filling out the following description of the
system.

Manufacturer	
Model	
Microprocessor	
Memory (RAM) in kilobytes or megabytes	
Disk drive capacity in megabytes	

Display Monitors

After completing this topic, you should be able to:
- Explain the difference between character and graphics displays
- Describe what resolution is and what determines it
- Explain what WYSIWYG is and why it's important

▶ D E S K T O P   P U B L I S H I N G   C O N C E P T S

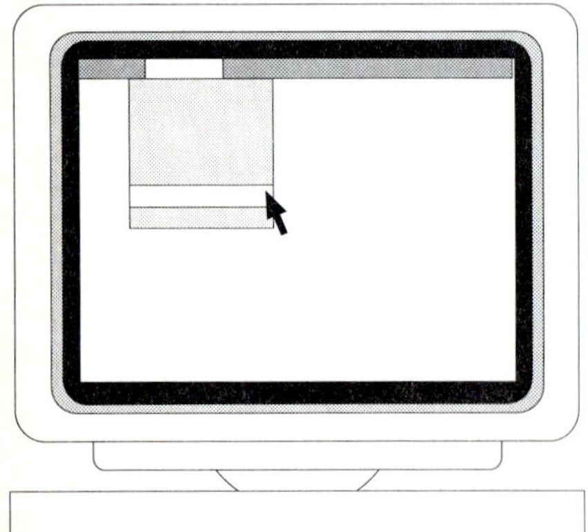

CRT Display Monitor

Computer **monitors** (also called displays) used for desktop publishing are based on a **cathode ray tube** (**CRT**) like the one used in television sets.

When you load a program, the display that you see on the screen is either a character display or a graphics display. The differences are startling, and graphics displays are increasingly becoming more common. You can see the difference on WordPerfect because the Edit screen is a character display and the View Document screen is a graphics display.

These two types of screen displays are referred to as character mode or graphics mode. Which mode you see depends both on the system you are using and the program you are running. Most computer systems today are capable of displaying graphics, but many programs do not yet take advantage of this feature and run in character mode.

Character Mode

When computers were first developed, all monitors displayed just the characters *A* through *Z*, numbers *1* through *10*, and a very limited set of other special characters (such as ■). Altogether, 256 characters, called the **character set**, could be displayed and nothing else. Because only this fixed set of characters can be displayed, this is called **character mode**. Many programs still use this mode even though monitors no longer require that they do.

Character mode has several advantages. For example, it requires little memory and operates very fast. Unfortunately, when used for desktop publishing, it also has several disadvantages. Since it can display only the characters in the computer's character set, it can display only simple graphics such as lines and boxes using the few graphics characters in the character set. Also, characters must occupy a fixed position on the screen and are all the same size. This prevents you from seeing different typefaces, typestyles and type sizes; proportional spacing; and subscripts and superscripts until you make a printout. Finally, it cannot display photographs or line drawings.

Character Mode

Until recently, character mode was the most common display. Here, WordPerfect, a typical character mode program, is shown.

```
  Curious
The Airborne Tourist
Enjoying the American Landscape from 30,000 Feet
Dennis P. Curtin, Editor

 ┌FIG 1─────────────────────────────────────────────────┐
```

Doc 1 Pg 1 Ln 1.58" Pos 2.66"

A High-Resolution Display

A Low-Resolution Display

Graphics Mode

Because of the limitations of character mode, ***graphics mode*** (also called *bit-mapped mode*) is now becoming much more popular.

On a graphics display, the screen is divided into a grid of small boxes called picture elements, or ***pixels***.

When an image is displayed on the screen, some of the pixels are illuminated, and some are left dark. On a color monitor, the colors of each pixel can also be set to one of many colors. The patterns of illuminated or colored pixels form characters and other images on the screen. This flexibility allows text and illustrations to be displayed on the screen.

The number of pixels, and hence the ***resolution*** (sharpness), of a graphics display is determined by the number of rows and columns the screen is divided into. The resolution is indicated by the number of pixels displayed horizontally on the screen by the number displayed vertically. For example, a resolution of 640 by 480 pixels indicates the screen has 640 pixels horizontally and 480 vertically.

Resolution is determined by which of the four most widely used standards, called ***display modes***, your system is using. In ascending order of sharpness:

- ***Color graphics adapters*** (**CGA**) display 320-by-200 resolution.
- ***Enhanced color graphics adapters*** (**EGA**) display 640-by-350 resolution.
- ***Video graphics array*** (**VGA**) displays 640-by-480 resolution in 16 colors and 320-by-200 resolution in 256 colors.
- ***Extended graphics array*** (**XGA**) displays 1024-by-768 resolution.

The graphics standard that your system uses is determined by the video display that is built into your computer or that was added by inserting an add-on board into a slot inside of the computer. The monitor must exactly match the mode of the board, or it must be a ***multi-sync*** monitor that can display any of the popular modes. Multi-sync monitors are initially more expensive but they allow you to upgrade to a higher resolution without buying a new monitor.

Although all of the display modes can display colors, it is not essential that the monitor also do so. Since most printers cannot print colors,

Graphics Mode

Graphics mode is becoming increasingly popular. Here, the same document as the one shown in the figure "Character Mode" is shown on a word processing program operating in graphics mode.

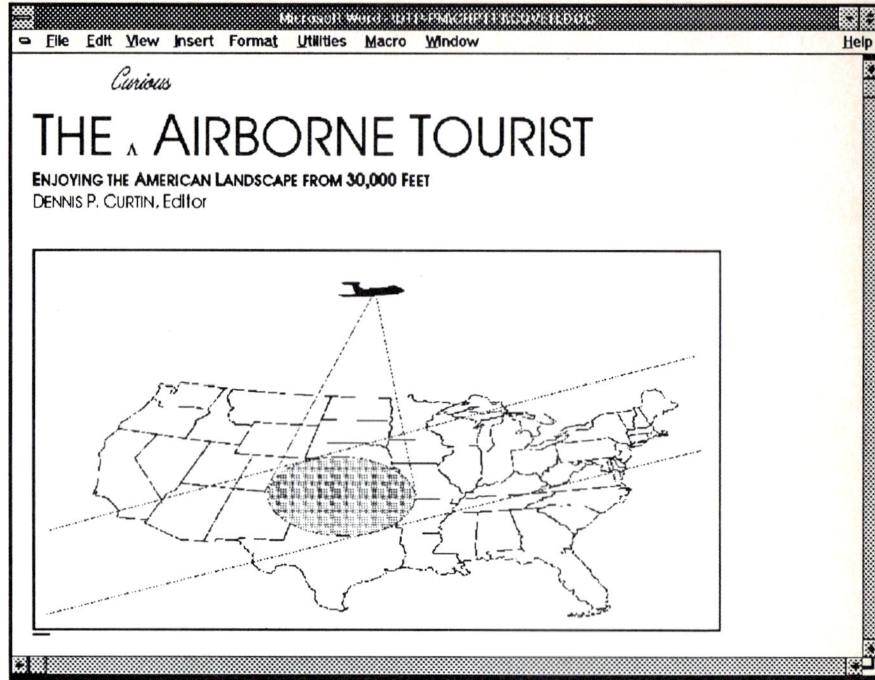

Screen Fonts

Screen fonts make a dramatic difference. Here, two examples of the letter O are displayed in 127-point Palatino type. The letter on the left is displayed with screen fonts and the one on the right is displayed without them.

formatting a document for color is not usually important. There are several ***gray-scale monitors*** that are inexpensive (about one-third the cost of a color monitor of comparable quality) and just as high quality as expensive color monitors.

Graphics displays have several advantages. They can display different fonts, type sizes, and enhancements such as italics and proportional spacing. Also, both text and graphics can be displayed on the screen at the same time, which is especially important in desktop publishing applications. But there are also disadvantages; graphics displays require a lot of memory and they operate more slowly than character displays.

The number of lines of text that you can see on a screen depends on the graphics card your system is equipped with and the choices offered by your applications program. Some of these combinations allow you to see a full page on the screen, or even two facing pages. Keep in mind, however, that to get more lines on the screen, each line must be made smaller. Smaller lines are made up of smaller, harder-to-read characters. To display a full page so you can read it easily requires a large display, perhaps 16 inches or larger. Most display screens are 14 inches, so full-page displays, although possible, can be hard to read.

WYSIWYG

The latest programs allow you to see on the screen exactly what your document will look like when you print it out. This is called ***WYSIWYG*** (pronounced "wizzy-wig") or "what you see is what you get." WYSIWYG is being incorporated into high-end word processing programs that have desktop publishing features. On programs that do not yet display a document for editing in WYSIWYG, this feature is offered as a ***document preview*** command (WordPerfect's View Document command) that lets you see how the document will look when it is printed. Although you cannot edit the document in WordPerfect when it is displayed with this command, you can see where improvements might be made before you print it out. A true WYSIWYG display has the following features:

- Characters are displayed in the actual typeface, typestyle, and type size in which they will be printed.
- Paragraphs are displayed with the same line endings and line spacings with which they will be printed.
- Line drawings or photographs that are inserted into the document are displayed on the screen.
- Pages are displayed as they will print, including headers and footers, margins, and page numbers.
- Many programs have pull-down menus, icons, and scroll bars that make the programs easy to operate. These items make up what is known as a **graphical user interface** (*GUI*).

Unfortunately, WYSIWYG displays are slow, even on the fastest computers. This is because much of the computer's processing power must be devoted to updating the screen display. For this reason, programs with a desktop publishing orientation allow you to switch back and forth between a WYSIWYG mode and a draft mode. In draft mode, graphics are not displayed and some fonts are not displayed as they will appear when printed. This reduced display allows you to scroll through the document and make corrections much faster than when in WYSIWYG mode.

For true WYSIWYG desktop publishing, your system must also be equipped with screen fonts that match your printer fonts. If your system has these, what you see on the screen is almost identical to what you will see in your printouts. If your system does not have these, at best you will get a close approximation of your printout on the screen, and sometimes your screen display gives you only a limited idea of what the printout will actually look like.

Some programs provide generic screen fonts. If the actual font is not available for display, the program picks the closest match from its library of these generic fonts. Also, if a font is too small to be displayed well, it may be **greeked**, or simulated with characters that are really just symbols to indicate where text exists on the page.

EXERCISE 1

GETTING TO KNOW YOUR MONITOR

The display monitor attached to your computer is an important component of the desktop publishing system. Ask your instructor or the lab assistant for help in filling out the following description of the monitor.

Manufacturer	
Model	
Display mode	
Color or black and white	
Resolution	

EXERCISE 2

VISITING A COMPUTER STORE

Visit a local computer store or computer department in a department store. Compare the resolution of the various monitors that are on display. Also, pick up literature for monitors and read the descriptions, paying close attention to the display modes that they are designed for.

Printers

After completing this topic, you should be able to:

- Explain how printers form characters and graphics from dots
- Describe the difference between dot-matrix and laser printers
- Explain the importance of resolution
- Explain why printer memory is required
- Briefly describe fonts and page description languages

▶ D E S K T O P   P U B L I S H I N G   C O N C E P T S

High and Low Print Quality

Printing Graphics
Here an enlargement of a small area of a photograph shows how the image is formed from dots.
(Courtesy of Richard Ashley Photography)

All printers used for desktop publishing form characters using an array of dots. These printers are called **raster printers** and there are several different types. The spacing of the dots affects the resolution, or quality, of the characters. For comparison, display monitors use about 50 to 100 dots per inch (dpi) to display text and images, dot-matrix printers 100 to 200, laser printers 300 to 600, and commercial typesetting machines 1000 to 2400. In many cases, 300 dpi is sufficient; but if it isn't, your files can be transferred to more powerful equipment that is available through many typesetting services.

Printers that print using an array of dots can also print graphics. By controlling the position dots are printed in, an illusion of brightness can be conveyed. The ability to convey brightness allows dot-matrix printers to print realistic, almost photographic, images.

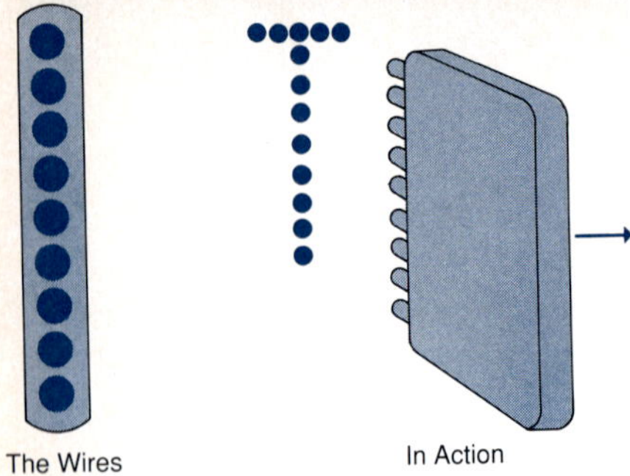

Dot-Matrix Print-head

Dot-Matrix Printers

One of the most common printers is called a ***dot-matrix printer***. This printer uses a printhead containing pins, or wires, arranged in a column to print characters. As the printhead passes across the paper, the computer tells it which pins in the printhead are to be fired to form a particular character. As the pins are fired, they strike an inked ribbon against the paper. The number of wires and dots determines the character's resolution. Less-expensive printers usually use nine pins to create characters. More expensive printers have 18 or 24 wires in their printheads.

Laser Printers

Laser printers, the most popular type of printer for desktop publishing, are very fast, usually printing eight or more pages per minute.

The resolution of laser printers is greater than dot-matrix printers because of the much higher number of dots and their greater density. Most laser printers can print 300 dpi, although printers with 400 dpi are available. Despite the great number of dots, laser printers are fast because the dots are not transferred to the paper by mechanical devices that strike a ribbon.

Laser printers provide extremely high quality. The technology used in laser printers is similar to that of office copiers. Laser printers first focus a laser beam onto a moving drum using a mirror. The moving drum is charged with electricity. As the drum revolves, it is scanned by the laser, and the image is "painted" onto the drum. The intensity of the laser beam is varied, and at selected points, it removes the electrical charge from the drum to form invisible characters with a neutral charge. Charged toner is then electrostatically attracted to these characters. This toner is transferred to the paper and fused to it by heat and pressure as it is pressed against the revolving drum.

Laser printers can print in color, but these printers are expensive. However, strides are being made in the development of lower-cost color laser printers. Moreover, laser printers are now available that print on both sides of a sheet of paper at the same time. This process is called ***duplex printing***.

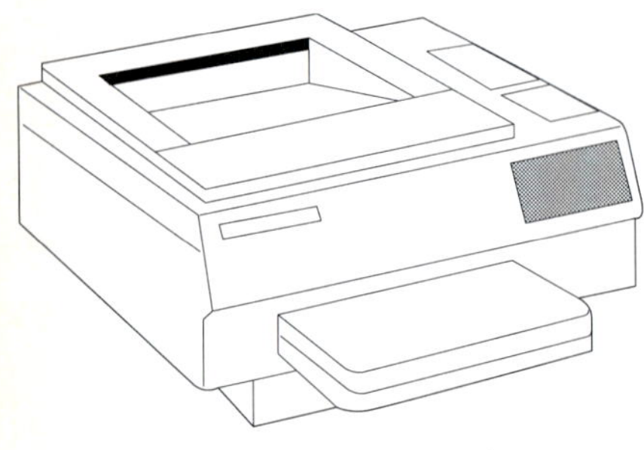

Laser Printer

Printer Features

Even with the best printers, there are significant differences that affect their use for desktop publishing applications. The most significant are their memory, their fonts, and their page description language.

Memory

Unlike dot-matrix printers where data is taken from the computer and then printed a line at a time, laser printers make up an entire page before printing it. The page is temporarily stored in the printer's memory while it is being processed and printed. If a page contains a graphics image, the memory required for it can be substantial. For example, it takes 1 megabyte to store a full-page black-and-white graphics image that is to be printed with a 300-dpi resolution. To fill the page, the printer has to address over 8 million dots. This is obviously a big chore. (If the printer matched those used by compositors and printed 1500 dots per inch, a page would require over 26 megabytes.)

If there isn't enough memory in the printer, only part of a page or image may be printed. As a rule of thumb, a printer should have at least

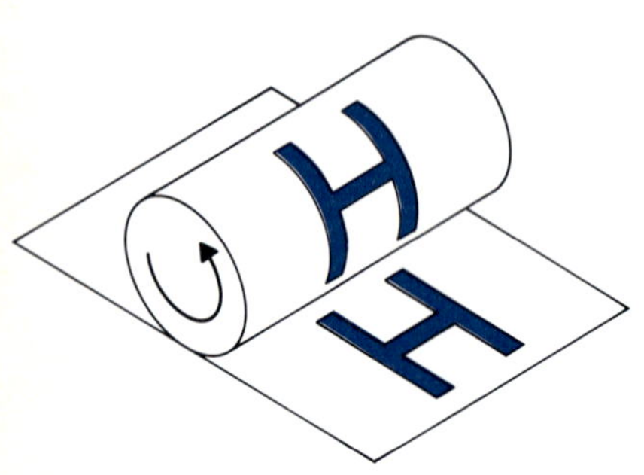

How Laser Printers Work

1 megabyte of memory, but if you are planning on printing large graphics or downloading soft fonts to the printer, you may need more.

Fonts

Many newer printers can print using fonts that are permanently stored in the printer's memory (ROM). Others are available on cartridges that are plugged into the printer when you want access to the fonts they contain. These printers can print only the fonts stored in ROM or on the cartridge plugged into the printer. These fonts are fast and do not take up room on your hard disk. However, fonts stored on disks, called **downloadable fonts**, are more flexible (if your printer will accept them). You can choose from the fonts on the disk and load them into the printer when you need them. This way, the printer has access to any fonts you want to use.

When considering fonts for purchase, consider if they are bit-mapped or scalable.

- **Bit-mapped fonts** are made up of a series of dots and can only be printed in one size, the size they come in. If you need 8, 10, 12, and 14-point versions, you must have a complete font in each size. Storage can be a problem as a result.
- **Scalable fonts** (also called *outline fonts*) are created on the fly while text is being printed by formulas stored in the computer or printer. These fonts allow a wide range of sizes while requiring very little space on the disk or in a printer's memory.

Document or Page Description Languages

Laser printers have programs built into their memory that allow them to manipulate type and graphics on the page. These programs, called document or **page description languages**, make possible many special effects.

The two most popular page description languages are Adobe's **PostScript** and Hewlett-Packard's **PCL 5**. These languages are what make sophisticated desktop publishing possible. They allow you to perform many functions that would not otherwise be possible, including:

- Scaling fonts so they print in different sizes.
- Rotating type so it can be printed at any angle.
- Printing portrait and landscape modes on the same page.
- Printing white type against a black background (dropped-out type).
- Mirroring text or graphics.

For you to use them, these features must also be supported by your applications program. If they are not supported, you can still achieve them by sending control codes to the printer, but this is an advanced approach that only very experienced users attempt.

Page Description Languages
This figure shows some of the effects made possible by Hewlett-Packard's page description language.
(Courtesy of Hewlett Packard, Inc.)

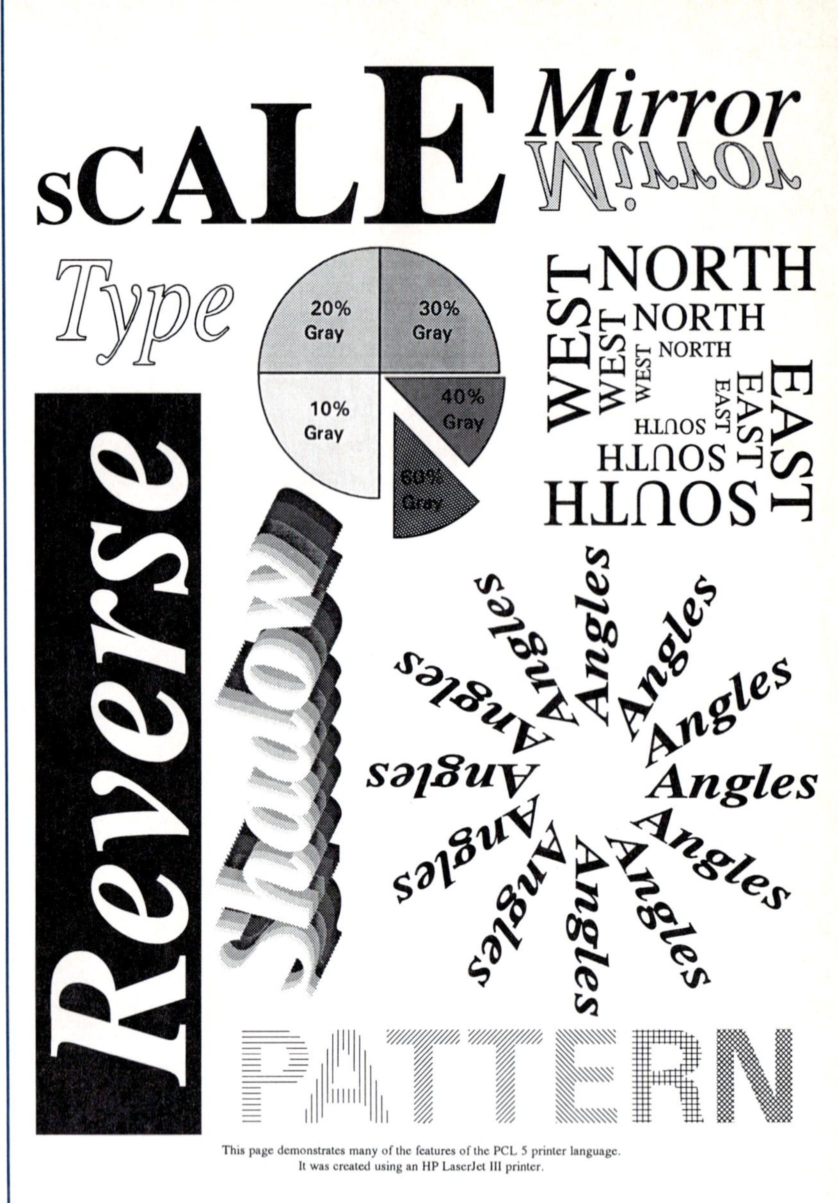

This page demonstrates many of the features of the PCL 5 printer language.
It was created using an HP LaserJet III printer.

EXERCISE 1

GETTING TO KNOW YOUR PRINTER

The printer in your system is an important component of the desktop publishing system. Ask your instructor or the lab assistant for help in filling out the following description of the printer.

Manufacturer	
Model	
Type (dot-matrix or laser)	
Memory	
Built-in fonts	

Scanners

<table>
<tr><td>

After completing this topic, you should be able to:
- Explain the purpose of text scanners
- Describe the function of a graphics scanner
- Describe some features of graphics scanners

</td></tr>
</table>

▶ D E S K T O P   P U B L I S H I N G   C O N C E P T S

You do not have to enter everything into a computer from the keyboard. *Scanners* allow you to enter text and graphics from hard copy such as printed or typed documents, photographs, or line drawings. For desktop publishing applications, there are two basic types of scanners: text scanners and graphics scanners. In many cases, the same scanner performs both functions. The hardware changes function when the software that operates it is changed. Some newer software also scans both text and graphics in one pass, and stores the information in either a text or graphics format.

Text Scanners

When you type text into a computer and then print it out on a printer, you are actually converting the text from a digital form (the form used by the computer) to a printed form. Until recently, this conversion process has been a one-way street. It was not possible to automatically convert printed copy into an electronic form that could be processed by a computer or word processing program. If a document has already been printed but has not been saved in a digital form, it is time consuming to keyboard it into the computer. To make the conversion from printed text to electronic text more efficient you can use a scanner and ***optical character recognition* (*OCR*)** software.

The scanner reads the pattern of dark characters against a light background and converts each character to its digital equivalent, which is then stored in the computer's memory or on a disk. Since the text is converted into a digital form, it can be stored, displayed, printed, and otherwise manipulated just as if it had been entered into the computer through the keyboard. Text you scan in this way can be edited by word processors and processed by other types of programs.

Graphics Scanners

To scan graphics images such as photographs, line drawings, charts, and maps into the computer, ***graphics scanners*** (also called *image digitizers*) are used to convert the printed image into digital form. Instead of converting the image into characters, graphics scanners take a digital picture of it, much as a copy machine does. The difference, of course, is that the copy is then stored in the computer in digital form. The scanner works by breaking the image up into small dots, called pixels (just like the display screen). It then assigns a numeric value to each pixel and stores it in memory or on the disk. The image can then be incorporated into a word processing or desktop publishing document or manipulated with a program designed to work with images of this kind.

Graphics scanners are available in both inexpensive 1-bit and more expensive 8-bit versions. Scanners that use 1 bit to store an image can scan only black-and-white line art that has no colors or gray tones because with 1 bit you can specify only if a pixel is black or white. Many images, such as photographs, have intermediate gray tones, and more information is needed to scan these accurately. The spectrum of tones in these images is called a ***gray scale***. Eight-bit scanners can store up to 256 tones ($2^8=256$), so they can be used to scan images of this kind. They can also scan color images and assign any one of 256 colors to each dot being scanned.

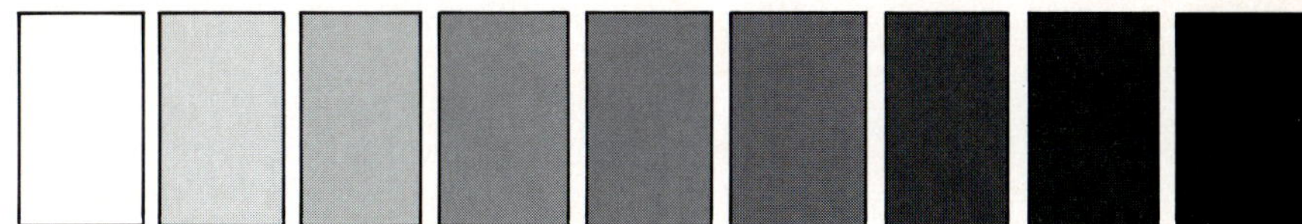

Gray Scale

Eight-bit graphics scanners can store up to 256 values to reproduce images, such as photographs, that have many tones. The arrangement of tones from light to dark is called a gray scale.

The number of bytes required to store a graphics image depends on the number of bits assigned to each pixel. For example, an 8 -by-11-inch image printed 300 dots to the inch has over 8 million pixels. To store a graphics image of this size, a 1-bit scanner requires almost 1 megabyte of memory. An 8-bit scanner requires almost 8 megabytes. Since these file sizes would create serious storage problems, scanners use a special procedure called ***file compression*** to store the files in much less space on the disk. This does not change the image at all; it stores it in less space on the disk. However, vast amounts of disk space are still required, especially when scanning photographs and other art with an 8-bit scanner.

EXERCISE 1

EXPLORING SCANNERS

Visit a computer store or look through some computer magazines for articles or reviews on scanners. Try to determine which scanners are for text, which for graphics, and which can do both.

REVIEW

- The heart of a computer is the microprocessor used for the central processing unit (CPU). Most IBM or compatible personal computers use the 286, 386, or 486 versions made by Intel.
- The suffixes *-dx* and *-sx* indicate that the microprocessor is either a full powered or a less powerful version of the microprocessor.
- Random-access memory (RAM) is the place where your current program and data are stored while you use them.
- Hard disks not only store more data than floppy disks, they also operate much faster. This is very important for programs that store parts of the current program and data file on disk until they are needed.
- Display monitors operate in character or graphics mode. Graphics mode makes WYSIWYG possible but it tends to operate more slowly.
- Screen fonts that match your printer fonts make it possible to see the document on the screen just the way it will appear in a printout.
- Laser printers are used extensively in desktop publishing. They must have sufficient memory if you plan on using downloadable fonts or printing graphics.
- Scanners allow you to convert both text and graphics into electronic form so you can manipulate them with your computer.

QUESTIONS

TRUE/FALSE

T F

1. IBM personal computers use Intel microprocessors.
2. The latest and most powerful computers use a 486 microprocessor.
3. Chips with an *-sx* suffix are faster than those with a *-dx* suffix.
4. A fast hard disk is desirable only because it stores more data.
5. Desktop publishing is best done on a character display.
6. Graphics displays are slower than character displays.
7. The sharpest display mode is XGA.
8. WYSIWYG allows you to see on the screen almost exactly what your printed document will look like.
9. Laser printers print one line at a time.
10. A duplex printer is one that is shared by two users.

❑ ❑   11. The memory in a laser printer is used to store fonts
             and your files as they are being printed.
❑ ❑   12. Some scanners can scan both text and graphics.

FILL IN THE BLANK

1. The part of the computer that processes data is called the ___________ .
2. The less-expensive version of a 386 microprocessor is referred to as
   the ___________ .
3. Two major considerations when selecting a hard disk are its
   ___________ and ___________ .
4. The four most common display modes are ___________, ___________,
   ___________, and ___________ .
5. A high-quality graphics display monitor is called a(n) ___________
   monitor.
6. WYSIWYG stands for _________________________________ .
7. Laser printers print ___________ dots per inch.
8. A printer that prints on both sides of a sheet of paper at the same time
   is called a(n) ___________ printer.
9. The process of converting printed text into electronic form is called
   ___________ .

MATCH THE COLUMNS

1. Access time   __ What you see is what you get
2. Character   __ Video graphics array display mode
   display   __ The time it takes for a drive to move data
3. Data transfer   into memory
   rate   __ The time it takes for a drive to find data
4. Duplex printer   __ The smallest element in a graphics display
5. Graphics   __ Optical character recognition
   display   __ A printer that prints on both sides of the
6. Gray-scale   paper in one pass
   monitors   __ A page description language
7. OCR   __ A display that shows all characters in the
8. Pixel   same size
9. Postscript   __ A display that allows you to see fonts in
10. VGA   different sizes
11. WYSIWYG   __ A black-and-white graphics display

1. Who makes the chips used in IBM computers? Briefly describe three of the chips used as microprocessors.
2. Explain the difference between the suffixes *-sx* and *-dx*.
3. Give three reasons why a fast hard disk drive is important.
4. Describe the difference between access time and transfer rate.
5. List and describe some differences between character and graphics displays.
6. List four display modes in descending order of resolution.
7. Explain why WYSIWYG is important.
8. Explain why scalable fonts are desirable in a printer.
9. Explain why screen fonts are desirable.
10. Describe the difference between scanning text and scanning graphics.

WordPerfect Codes

When you reveal codes (by pressing **Alt**-**F3** or **F11**), the screen divides in two and codes are revealed in the bottom half of the screen. The following table lists and describes the codes that you might see displayed in this part of the screen. In some cases, there are two codes, one to turn an attribute on and another to turn it off. In these cases, the on code is in uppercase letters and the off code is lowercased. For example, the code that shows where boldfacing has been turned on is *[BOLD]* and the one that shows where it has been turned off is *[bold]*.

WORDPERFECT CODES

Code	Description
[ ]	Hard space
_	Current position of cursor
[-]	Hyphen character
-	Soft hyphen
[/]	Hyphenation canceled
[Adv]	Printer advance
[Bline]	Baseline position
[Block]	Beginning of block
[BlockPro]	Block protection
[Bold]	Bold
[Box Num]	Graphics box caption
[Cell]	Table cell
[Center]	Center
[Center Pg]	Text centered vertically on page
[Cndl EOP]	Conditional end of page
[Cntr Tab]	Centered tab stop
[CNTR TAB]	Hard centered tab
[Col Def]	Column definition
[Col On:] [Col Off:]	Text columns begin/end
[Color]	Print color
[Comment]	Document comment
[Date]	Date/time function
[Dbl Und]	Double underline
[Dec Tab]	Decimal tab stop
[DEC TAB]	Hard decimal tab stop
[Decml/Algn Char]	Decimal character or thousands separator
[Def Mark:Index]	Index definition
[Def Mark:Listn]	List definition
[Def Mark:ToA]	Table of authorities definition
[Def Mark:ToC]	Table of contents definition
[Dorm HRt]	Dormant hard return
[DSRt]	Default soft return (entered by the program in some situations)
[End Def]	End of index, list, table of authorities, or table of contents
[End Mark]	End of marked text
[End Opt]	Endnote options

Code	Description
[Endnote]	Endnote
[Endnote Placement]	Endnote placement
[Equ Box]	Equation box
[Equ Opt]	Equation options
[Ext Large]	Extra large print
[Fig Box]	Figure box
[Fig Opt]	Figure options
[Fine]	Fine print
[Flsh Rgt]	Flush right
[Font]	Base font change
[Footer]	Footer
[Footnote]	Footnote
[Force]	Force odd/even pages
[Ftn Opt]	Footnote/endnote options
[Full Form]	Table of authorities
[Header]	Header
[Hline]	Horizontal line
[HPg]	Hard page break
[Hrd Row]	Hard row
[HRt]	Hard carriage return
[HRt-SPg]	Hard carriage return and soft page break
[Hyph Off]	Hyphenation ends
[Hyph On]	Hyphenation begins
[HZone]	Change in hyphenation zone
[→Indent]	Indent begins
[→Indent←]	Left/right indent begins
[Index]	Index mark
[Insert Pg Num]	Inserted page number
[ISRt]	Invisible soft return
[Italc]	Italics
[Just]	Right justification
[Just Lim]	Word/letter spacing justification limits
[Kern]	Kern
[L/R Mar]	Left and right margin settings
[Lang]	Language
[Large]	Large print
[Leading Adj]	Leading adjustment
[Link]	Link to spreadsheet file
[Link End]	End of link to spreadsheet
[Ln Height]	Line height
[Ln Num]	Line numbering
[Ln Spacing]	Line spacing
[←Mar Rel]	Left margin release
[Mark:List]	List entry
[Mark:ToA]	Table of authorities entry
[Mark:ToC]	Table of contents entry
[Math Def]	Math columns definition
[Math Off]	Math ends
[Math On]	Math begins
[!]	Formula calculation
[t]	Subtotal entry
[+]	Calculate subtotal
[T]	Total entry
[=]	Calculate total
[*]	Calculate grand total
[N]	Negate
[New End Num]	New endnote number
[New Equ Num]	New equation number

Code	Description
[New Fig Num]	New figure number
[New Ftn Num]	New footnote number
[New Tbl Num]	New table number
[New Txt Num]	New text box number
[New Usr Num]	New user box number
[Note Num]	Footnote/endnote reference
[Outline Lvl]	Outline style
[Outline Off]	Outline off
[Outline On]	Outline on
[Outln]	Outline attribute
[Ovrstk]	Overstrike character
[Paper Sz/Typ]	Paper size and type
[Par Num]	Paragraph number
[Par Num Def]	Paragraph numbering definition
[Pg Num]	New page number
[Pg Num Style]	Page number style
[Pg Numbering]	Page numbering
[Ptr Cmnd]	Printer command
[RedLn]	Redlining begins/ends
[Ref]	Automatic reference
[Rgt Tab]	Right-aligned tab stop
[RGT TAB]	Hard right-aligned tab stop
[Row]	Table row
[Shadw]	Shadow
[Sm Cap]	Small caps
[Small]	Small print
[SPg]	Soft page break
[SRt]	Soft carriage return
[StkOut]	Strikeout
[Style Off]	Style off
[Style On]	Style on
[Subdoc]	Subdocument
[Subdoc Start]	Subdocument begins
[Subdoc End]	Subdocument ends
[Subscpt]	Subscript
[Suppress]	Page formats suppressed
[Suprscpt]	Superscript
[T/B Mar]	Top and bottom margins
[Tab]	Left-aligned tab
[TAB]	Hard left-aligned tab
[Tab Set]	Tabs reset
[Target]	Automatic reference target
[Tbl Box]	Table box
[Tbl Def]	Table definition
[Tbl Off]	Table ends
[Tbl Opt]	Table box options
[Text Box]	Text box
[Txt Opt]	Text box options
[Und]	Underlining begins/ends
[Undrln]	Underline spaces/tabs
[Usr Box]	User-defined box
[Usr Opt]	User-defined box options
[VLine]	Vertical line
[Vry Large]	Very large print
[W/O Off]	Widow/orphan protection ends
[W/O On]	Widow/orphan protection begins
[Wrd/Ltr Spacing]	Word and letter spacing

Adding or Editing Printers

Before you can select a printer, you must first add it to the list of printers that are available for your computer. When you install WordPerfect, you specify one or more printers and the appropriate file with an .ALL extension copied from the *Printer* disks. When you then add one of the listed printers, the definition for that printer is extracted from the file and stored in a file with a .PRS extension. If you are adding a new printer, you obtain the new .ALL file from the printer manufacturer or from WordPerfect and copy it to your hard disk.

 **KEY / Strokes**

Defining Printers You Can Choose From

1. Press **Shift-F7** to display the Print menu.
2. Press **S** for *Select Printer* to display a list of printers. Press **A** for *Additional Printers* to see another list of printers. (On a floppy disk system, if your printer is not on the list, insert one of the other *Printer* disks, and then press **O** for *Other Disk*.)
3. Select any of the options described in the table "Select Printer Menu Choices."
4. Press **F7** to return to the document screen.

SELECT PRINTER MENU CHOICES

1   *Select* specifies the printer you want to print on. The currently selected printer, if any, is indicated with an asterisk (*).

2   *Additional Printers* displays a list of printers you can add. Highlight one, and then press **S** for *Select*. The prompt reads *Printer filename:*. Press **Enter** to accept the suggested filename, or enter a new eight-character filename with the extension .PRS, and then press **Enter**. Press **F7** to display the Edit menu. See the table "Printer Edit Menu Choices" for the choices you have to make to add a printer.

3   *Edit* edits the printer definition. See the table "Printer Edit Menu Choices" for the choices you can make to edit a printer definition.

4   *Copy* copies the highlighted printer definition so that you can revise it for another purpose.

5   *Delete* deletes the highlighted printer definition. The .PRS file remains in your directory.

6   *Help* displays help on the selected printer. You can press
Shift-**PrtSc** to print out a copy for reference.

7   *Update* updates printer fonts.

Printer Edit Menu

The Printer Edit menu lists choices you make to edit the definition of a printer.

```
Select Printer: Edit

      Filename                        HPLAIIPO.PRS

  1 - Name                            HP LaserJet III PostScript

  2 - Port                            LPT1:

  3 - Sheet Feeder                    None

  4 - Cartridges/Fonts/Print Wheels

  5 - Initial Base Font               Times Roman 12pt

  6 - Path for Downloadable
        Fonts and Printer
        Command Files

  7 - Print to Hardware Port          No




Selection: 0
```

PRINTER EDIT MENU CHOICES

1   *Name* identifies the printer on the Select Printer menu so that
you can recognize it later. You can enter up to 36 characters.

2   *Port* specifies the port the printer is connected to or the name
of the file when printing to the disk. Parallel printers are normally connected to LPT1 and serial printers to COM1.

3   *Sheet Feeder* displays a list of sheet feeders you can choose
from if your printer has one.

4   *Cartridges/Fonts/Print Wheels* specifies the cartridges and
fonts available to your printer.

5   *Initial Base Font* displays a list of internal printer fonts and
those you marked in **4** *Cartridges/Fonts/Print Wheels*. You
move the highlight over the name of the initial font you want
to use and then press **S** for *Select*. The font you select is the
current default font for your documents.

6   *Path for Downloadable Fonts and Printer Command Files* specifies the path to the directory you have stored soft fonts in.

7   *Print to Hardware Port* sends data directly to a serial or parallel port and speeds up printing.

Specifying Cartridges and Fonts

To use cartridges or soft fonts, you first have to select them so that the program knows they are available. You do so by displaying a list of cartridges or soft fonts and then marking them with an asterisk (*) to indicate that they are available when a print job begins or with a plus sign (+) to indicate that they should be loaded into the printer when needed. On some printers, you can also mark a font with both an asterisk and a plus sign to have a font loaded initially but removed when memory is needed to load another font. If a font is unloaded, it is automatically reloaded at the end of the print job.

- When you mark a font as being available when a print job begins, the font cartridge must be in the printer, or you must press **I** for *Initialize Printer* from the Print menu to download soft fonts before beginning a print job. If your printer cannot swap fonts, printer memory is decreased. If all memory is used, documents may not print correctly. Further, the amount of memory used for fonts decreases the amount available for graphics, so you may encounter problems when printing documents that include graphics.
- When you mark a font so that it is loaded during a print job, fonts are moved into and out of the printer as necessary. This slows the printer down but conserves printer memory so that you can use more fonts or combine fonts and graphics without running out of printer memory. Some printers cannot swap fonts during a print job.

KEY/Strokes

Specifying Cartridges and Fonts

1. Press **Shift-F7** to display the Print menu.
2. Press **S** for *Select Printer*.
3. Highlight the printer name you want to specify cartridges and fonts for.
4. Press **E** for *Edit*.
5. Press **C** for *Cartridges/Fonts/Print Wheels* to display a list of options, which vary depending on the printer you are editing. (The prompt reads *This printer has no other cartridges or fonts* if none are available.)
6. Highlight *Built-In, Cartridges* or *Soft Fonts*, and then press **S** for *Select*.

The IBM Character Set

This table illustrates all the characters in the IBM extended character set built into the computer's memory. To enter a special character, first locate the character that you want to enter. Then hold down **Alt** and type the three-digit number to the left of the desired character in the table. For example, hold down **Alt** and then type **024** to enter the up arrow, type **013** or **014** to enter the musical notes, or type **171** to enter the   character.

001	☻	051	3	101	e	151	ù	201	╔	251	√
002	●	052	4	102	f	152	ÿ	202	╩	252	ⁿ
003	♥	053	5	103	g	153	Ö	203	╦	253	²
004	♦	054	6	104	h	154	Ü	204	╠	254	■
005	♣	055	7	105	i	155	¢	205	═		
006	♠	056	8	106	j	156	£	206	╬		
007	•	057	9	107	k	157	¥	207	╧		
008	◘	058	:	108	l	158	₧	208	╨		
009	○	059	;	109	m	159	ƒ	209	╤		
010	■	060	<	110	n	160	á	210	╥		
011	♂	061	=	111	o	161	í	211	╙		
012	♀	062	>	112	p	162	ó	212	╘		
013	♪	063	?	113	q	163	ú	213	╒		
014	♫	064	@	114	r	164	ñ	214	╓		
015	☼	065	A	115	s	165	Ñ	215	╫		
016	►	066	B	116	t	166	ª	216	╪		
017	◄	067	C	117	u	167	º	217	┘		
018	↕	068	D	118	v	168	¿	218	┌		
019	‼	069	E	119	w	169	⌐	219	█		
020	¶	070	F	120	x	170	¬	220	▄		
021	§	071	G	121	y	171	½	221	▌		
022	▬	072	H	122	z	172	¼	222	▐		
023	↨	073	I	123	{	173	¡	223	▀		
024	↑	074	J	124	|	174	«	224	α		
025	↓	075	K	125	}	175	»	225	ß		
026	→	076	L	126	~	176	░	226	Γ		
027	←	077	M	127	⌂	177	▒	227	π		
028	∟	078	N	128	Ç	178	▓	228	Σ		
029	↔	079	O	129	ü	179	│	229	σ		
030	▲	080	P	130	é	180	┤	230	µ		
031	▼	081	Q	131	â	181	╡	231	τ		
032		082	R	132	ä	182	╢	232	Φ		
033	!	083	S	133	à	183	╖	233	Θ		
034	"	084	T	134	å	184	╕	234	Ω		
035	#	085	U	135	ç	185	╣	235	δ		
036	$	086	V	136	ê	186	║	236	∞		
037	%	087	W	137	ë	187	╗	237	φ		
038	&	088	X	138	è	188	╝	238	ε		
039	'	089	Y	139	ï	189	╜	239	∩		
040	(	090	Z	140	î	190	╛	240	≡		
041	)	091	[	141	ì	191	┐	241	±		
042	*	092	\	142	Ä	192	└	242	≥		
043	+	093	]	143	Å	193	┴	243	≤		
044	,	094	^	144	É	194	┬	244	⌠		
045	-	095	_	145	æ	195	├	245	⌡		
046	.	096	`	146	Æ	196	─	246	÷		
047	/	097	a	147	ô	197	┼	247	≈		
048	0	098	b	148	ö	198	╞	248	°		
049	1	099	c	149	ò	199	╟	249	·		
050	2	100	d	150	û	200	╚	250	·		

The WordPerfect Character Sets

These tables illustrate the characters in WordPerfect's character sets. To enter a special character, press **Ctrl-V**, type the number of the character set, a comma, the number of the character, and then press **Enter**.

Character Set 0

```
    0 1 2 3 4 5 6 7 8 9 0 1 2 3 4 5 6 7 8 9 0 1 2 3 4 5 6 7 8 9
                         1                   2
  0
 30       ! " ? $ % & ' ( ) ' + , - . / 0 1 2 3 4 5 6 7 8 9 : ;
 60 < = > ? @ A B C D E F G H I J K L M N O P Q R S T U V W X Y
 90 Z [ \ ] ^ _ ` a b c d e f g h i j k l m n o p q r s t u v w
120 x y z { | } ~
```

Character Set 1

```
    0 1 2 3 4 5 6 7 8 9 0 1 2 3 4 5 6 7 8 9 0 1 2 3 4 5 6 7 8 9
                         1                   2
  0 ` · ˜ ^ _ / ´ ¨ - , , . , ° · " ˇ / — ˘ ß ı ȷ Á á Â â
 30 Ä ä À à Å å Æ æ Ç ç É é Ê ê Ë ë È è Í í Î î Ï ï Ì ì Ñ ñ Ó ó
 60 Ô ô Ö ö Ò ò Ú ú Û û Ü ü Ù ù Ÿ ÿ Ã ã Đ đ Ø ø Õ õ Ý ý Ð ð Þ þ
 90 Ă ă Ā ā Ą ą Ć ć Č č Ĉ ĉ Ċ ċ Ď ď Ě ě Ė ė Ē ē Ę ę Ǵ ǵ Ğ ğ Ĝ ĝ
120 Ġ ġ Ĝ Ġ ġ Ĥ ĥ Ħ ħ ı İ ĩ Ī ī ĳ Ĵ ĵ Ķ ķ Ĺ ĺ Ĺ ĺ
150 Ł ł Ł ł Ń ń Ň ň Ñ ñ Ŋ ŋ Ó ó Ő ő Œ œ Ŕ ŕ Ř ř Ŗ ŗ Ś ś Š š Ş ş
180 Ŝ ŝ Ť ť Ţ ţ Ŧ ŧ Ũ ũ Ů ů Ű ű Ų ų Ú ú Û û Ŵ ŵ Ŷ ŷ Ź ź Ž ž Ż ż
210 Ŋ ŋ Ð đ Ŀ Ī Ñ ñ Ř ř Š š Ť ť Ŷ ÿ Ý ý Ď ď O' o' U' u'
```

Character Set 2

```
    0 1 2 3 4 5 6 7 8 9 0 1 2 3 4 5 6 7 8 9 0 1 2 3 4 5 6 7 8 9
                         1                   2
  0 . · · ' · = — κ · ' ' · · · ' ' ' · · ( )
```

Character Set 3

```
    0 1 2 3 4 5 6 7 8 9 0 1 2 3 4 5 6 7 8 9 0 1 2 3 4 5 6 7 8 9
                         1                   2
  0 █ ▌ ▐ ▀ ▄ ▬ ─ │ ┌ ┐ └ ┘ ├ ┤ ┬ ┴ ┼
 30 ... (box-drawing characters)
 60 ... (box-drawing characters)
```

Character Set 4

```
    0 1 2 3 4 5 6 7 8 9 0 1 2 3 4 5 6 7 8 9 0 1 2 3 4 5 6 7 8 9
                         1                   2
  0 • ○ ■ ▪ · ¶ § ¡ ¿ « » £ ¥ ₧ ƒ ª º ½ ¼ ¢ ² ⁿ ® © ¤ ¾ ³ ´ · ·
 30 " " " – — ‹ › ○ □ † ‡ ™ ℠ ℞ ● ○ ■ · □ ─ ﬀ ﬁ ﬂ ﬃ ﬄ … $ ₣ ₲
 60 ₠ £ , „ ⅓ ⅔ ⅛ ⅜ ⅝ ⅞ ⓐ ⓟ ⓒ % ‰ ‱ № ¹
```

Character Set 5

```
    0 1 2 3 4 5 6 7 8 9 0 1 2 3 4 5 6 7 8 9 0 1 2 3 4 5 6 7 8 9
                         1                   2
  0 ♥ ♦ ♣ ♠ ♂ ♀ ☺ ☻ ♪ ♫ ■ ⌂ ‼ √ ⚓ ⌐ ¬ □ ▪ ○ ↔ ✓ □ ⊠ ⊗ # ♭ ♮
 30 ♯ ☿ ☼ ⚷ _
```

Character Set 6

```
    0 1 2 3 4 5 6 7 8 9 0 1 2 3 4 5 6 7 8 9 0 1 2 3 4 5 6 7 8 9
                         1                   2
  0 — ± ≤ ≥ ∝ / / \ + | ⟨ ⟩ ~ ≈ ≡ ∈ ∩ ‖ Σ ∞ → ← ↑ ↓ ↔ ↕ ▶ ◀ ▲
 30 ▼ · · ∘ · Å · μ − × ∫ ∏ ∓ ∇ ∂ ′ ″ ‾ ℮ ℓ ℏ ℜ ℘ ↤ ↦ ⇒ ⇐ ⇑ ⇓
 60 ⇔ ⇕ ↗ ↘ ↙ ↖ ∪ ⊂ ⊃ ⊇ ⊆ ∅ ⌈ ⌉ ⌊ ⌋ ≪ ≫ ∠ ⊘ ⊕ ⊖ ⊙ ⊚ ∧ ∨ ⊤ ⊥
 90 ⌢ ⊢ ⊣ ■ ◇ ◆ ⟦ ⟧ ≠ ≢ ∴ ∵ ∷ ¢ ℒ ℭ З ◊ △ ▽ ◇ ★ ″ ⨿ ≣ < ≤ >
120 ≥ ∃ ∀ ≪ ≫ ⊌ ⊑ ⊒ ∪ ∩ ⊏ ⊑ ⊏ ⊑ ∆ ∇ ∆ ∇ ⇋ ⇌ ⇄ ⇆ ⇅ ↮ ↚ ↛ × ÷
150 → ← ↔ ↕ ↑ ↓ ↑ ↓ ⇈ ⇊ ∪ ∩ ⊃ ⊚ ⊛ ⊝ ⊙ ℧ △ ◁ ▷ △ ▽ ⊣ ⊢ ≠ ≠ ⋈
180 ⊨ △ ∮ ∫ ★ ⋆ ⋖ ⋗ ⋔ ⊥ ⊤ ⋋ ⋌ ⋏ ⋎ ⋓ ⋒ ⋐ ⋑ ⊐ ⊏ ⋉ ⋊ ⋈ ⊣ ⊢ ⋇ ⋈ ∊
210 ⊕ ℰ ℱ ℂ ℑ ℕ ℝ ℨ ⌐
```

Character Set 7

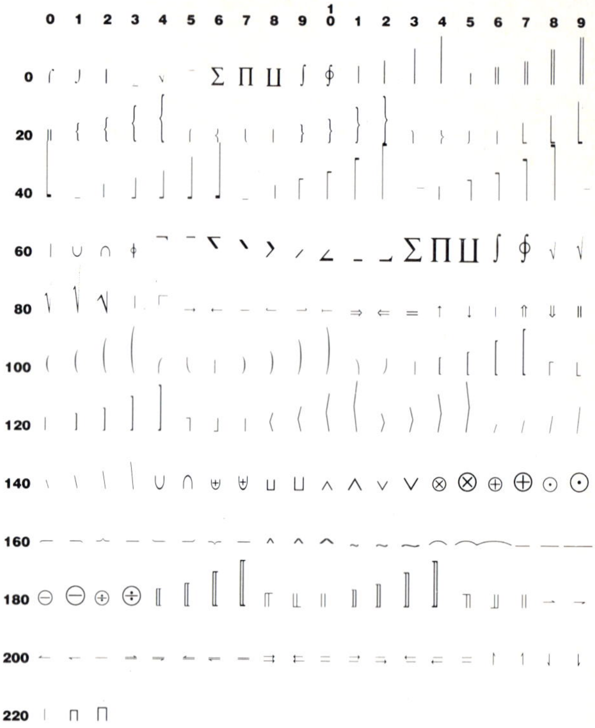

    0 1 2 3 4 5 6 7 8 9 **1**0 1 2 3 4 5 6 7 8 9

(Rows 0, 20, 40, 60, 80, 100, 120, 140, 160, 180, 200, 220 — special line-drawing, mathematical, and bracket symbols.)

Character Set 8

    0 1 2 3 4 5 6 7 8 9 **1**0 1 2 3 4 5 6 7 8 9 **2**0 1 2 3 4 5 6 7 8 9

0   Α α Β β Β в Γ γ Δ δ Ε ε Ζ ζ Η η Θ θ Ι ι Κ κ Λ λ Μ μ Ν ν Ξ ξ
30 Ο ο Π π Ρ ρ Σ σ Σ ς Τ τ Υ υ Φ φ Χ χ Ψ ψ Ω ω ά ΄ ή ί ϊ ö ύ ϋ
60 ω ε ϑ ϰ ϖ ρ Υ φ ω ; ;
90 à â ą ά ᾷ ᾁ ᾰ ᾶ ᾳ ᾴ ᾲ ᾱ ᾆ ᾳ ᾄ ᾀ ᾈ ᾃ έ έ έ έ
120 έ έ έ ή ῆ ῃ ῄ ῂ ῇ ή ή ῆ ῂ ῄ ῃ ῇ ή ή ῆ ῂ ῄ ῃ ῇ ὶ î î ï î î
150 î ῑ ῒ ῗ ῖ ὸ ὁ ὃ ö ό ὅ ö ù ῦ ῧ ü ὺ ὕ ῧ ü ῦ ü ό ῦ ö ὼ ῶ φ φ ὦ ᾦ
180 ὦ ᾧ ὦ ᾦ ᾠ φ φ ᾠ ᾤ ᾤ ᾤ ᾠ φ φ φ ΄ ΄ , ς F ϙ ϡ

Character Set 9

    0 1 2 3 4 5 6 7 8 9 **1**0 1 2 3 4 5 6 7 8 9 **2**0 1 2 3 4 5 6 7 8 9

0 א ב ג ד ה ו ז ח ט י כ ך ל מ ם נ ן ס ע פ ף צ ץ ק ר ש ת ב כ
30 פ

Character Set 10

    0 1 2 3 4 5 6 7 8 9 **1**0 1 2 3 4 5 6 7 8 9 **2**0 1 2 3 4 5 6 7 8 9

0 А а Б б В в Г г Д Д Е е Ё ё Ж ж З з И и Й й К к Л л М м Н н
30 О о П п Р р С с Т т У у Ф Х х Ц ц Ч ч Ш ш Щ щ Ъ ъ Ы ы Ь ь
60 Э э Ю ю Я я Ґ ґ Ђ ђ Ѓ ѓ Є є Ѕ ѕ І і Ї ї Ј ј Љ љ Њ њ Ћ ћ Ќ ќ
90 Ў ў Џ џ Ъ ъ Ѳ ѳ Ѵ ѵ Ѫ ѫ

Character Set 11 (Hiragana)

    0 1 2 3 4 5 6 7 8 9 **1**0 1 2 3 4 5 6 7 8 9 **2**0 1 2 3 4 5 6 7 8 9

0 ぁ ぃ ぅ ぇ ぉ っ ゃ ゅ ょ か け あ い う え お か き く け こ が ぎ ぐ げ ご さ し す
30 せ そ ざ じ ず ぜ ぞ た ち っ つ て と だ ぢ づ で ど な に ぬ ね の は ひ ふ へ ほ ば び ぶ
60 べ ぼ ぱ ぴ ぷ ぺ ぽ ま み む め も や ゆ よ ら り る れ ろ わ を ん 〔 〕 ［ ］ 「 」
90 」 。 。 、 ゛ ゜ ‐ ー ゛ ゜

Character Set 11 (Katakana)

    0 1 2 3 4 5 6 7 8 9 **1**0 1 2 3 4 5 6 7 8 9 **2**0 1 2 3 4 5 6 7 8 9

0 ァ イ ウ エ オ ッ ャ ュ ョ グ カ ケ ア イ ウ エ オ カ キ ク ケ コ ガ ギ グ ゲ ゴ サ シ ス
30 セ ソ ザ ジ ズ ゼ ゾ タ チ ッ テ ト ダ チ ヅ デ ド ナ ニ ヌ ネ ノ ハ ヒ フ ヘ ホ バ ビ ブ
60 ベ ボ パ ピ プ ペ ポ マ ミ ム メ モ ヤ ユ ヨ ラ リ ル レ ロ ワ ヲ ン 〔 〕 ［ ］ 「 」
90 」 。 。 、 ゛ ゜ ‐ ゛ ゜

Automatic Number References

WordPerfect allows you to reference numbers in a document so that if you change a number (or if it changes automatically), all numbers that refer to it change automatically. This is useful when you want to refer in the document to:

- Page numbers
- Paragraph and outline numbers
- Graphics box numbers
- Footnote and endnote numbers

To enter an automatic reference, you enter a code instead of a number in the document. This code, called the *reference code*, refers to a second code you enter, called the *target code*. The target code indicates the number of the item that the reference code refers to so that if the target number changes, the number displayed by the reference code changes automatically. For example, you can enter a reference code on page 1 that refers to a target code on page 2. The reference code displays the number *2*. If you then insert a new page between pages 1 and 2, so that the target code moves to page 3, the reference code displays the number *3*.

- You can enter a reference code in text, footnotes, endnotes, headers, footers, or text or caption areas of graphics boxes.
- You can enter a target code in text, footnotes, endnotes, and graphics box captions.
- Reference codes can refer to more than one target, for example, when referring to a figure number on a specific page (Figure 1, Page 3). To do this, you enter one reference code and one target code for each item.
- Reference codes can also refer to the same target in more than one place in the document, for example, pages 1, 4, and 5. To do this, you enter one reference code and then multiple target codes using the same target name.

To enter automatic references, you mark both the reference and target. When marking them, you assign names to the reference and target. The name you enter is what ties the codes together. For example, if you name two targets PAGE and refer to that name with the reference code, the reference code displays the number of both items marked with the target codes of the same name. You can usually mark both the reference and target in one operation. But sometimes you have to mark them in separate operations, for example,

- If the reference is in a graphics box caption.
- If the target has not yet been entered.

- If the target and reference are in separate documents to be combined with a master document.
- If you want to create multiple references, for example, pages 2, 3, and 4.

The numbers are displayed at the reference number position. However, if you make changes to a document that affect the numbers, or expand a master document, you have to generate the automatic references.

KEY/Strokes

Marking Both the Reference and the Target

1. Move the cursor to the place you want a number automatically generated. (If entering it in existing text, enter a space to position the number.)
2. Press **Alt-F5** to display the Mark Text menu.
3. Press **R** for *Cross-Ref.*
4. Press **B** for *Mark **B**oth Reference and Target.*
5. Either: Press **P** for *Page Number.*

    Or: Press **O** for *Paragraph/**O**utline Number.*

    Or: Press **F** for *Footnote Number.*

    Or: Press **E** for *Endnote Number.*

    Or: Press **G** for *Graphics Box Number,* and then select the type of graphics box.

    The prompt reads *Cross-Ref: Move to* followed by the type of target you are marking, and then *Press Enter.*
6. Move the cursor immediately after the target (if necessary, press **Alt-F3** or **F11** to reveal codes), and then press **Enter**. The prompt reads *Target Name:.*
7. Type a target name, and then press **Enter**.

KEY/Strokes

Marking a Reference Only

1. Move the cursor to the place you want a number automatically generated. (If entering it in existing text, enter a space to position the number.)
2. Press **Alt-F5** to display the Mark Text menu.
3. Press **R** for *Cross-Ref.*
4. Press **R** for *Mark **R**eference.*
5. Either: Press **P** for *Page Number.*

    Or: Press **O** for *Paragraph/**O**utline Number.*

    Or: Press **F** for *Footnote Number.*

    Or: Press **E** for *Endnote Number.*

    Or: Press **G** for *Graphics Box Number,* and then select the type of graphics box.

The prompt reads *Target Name:*.

6. Type a target name, and then press **Enter**. If the target has not yet been entered, a question mark is displayed. This question mark is replaced with a number when you generate automatic references.

 **KEY/Strokes**

Marking a Target Only

1. Move the cursor immediately after a target referred to by a reference number code (if necessary, press **Alt-F3** or **F11** to reveal codes), and then press **Enter**.
2. Press **Alt-F5** to display the Mark Text menu.
3. Press **R** for *Cross-**R**ef.*
4. Press **T** for *Mark **T**arget,* and the prompt reads *Target Name:*.
5. Type a target name, and then press **Enter**.

 **KEY/Strokes**

Generating Automatic References

1. Press **Alt-F5** to display the Mark Text menu.
2. Press **G** for *Generate.*
3. Press **G** for *Generate Tables, Indexes, Cross-References, etc.,* and the prompt reads *Existing tables, lists, and indexes will be replaced. Continue? Yes (No).*
4. Press **Y** to generate the references and return to the document screen.

 **AUTOMATIC REFERENCE TIPS**

- To mark a reference in a footnote or endnote, you must display the Footnote or Endnote Editing screen during the marking procedure.
- When marking graphics boxes with automatic references, you can use the Search command to move the cursor to the space following the code.

A

Absolute tab stops. Tab stops set relative to the left edge of the paper so they do not shift when you change the left margin.

Access time. The time it takes a hard disk to locate data.

Alphabet length. The length of a complete set of lowercase letters in the same typeface, typestyle, and type size.

Ascender. The part of some lowercase letters, such as b, d, and h, that extend up above the x-height. *See also* Descender.

Aspect ratio. The ratio of horizontal dots to vertical dots that determines the shape of a graphic on the screen or printout.

B

Baseline. The bottom of the x-height on a line of type.

Binding margin. The inside margin that alternates from right to left on facing pages.

Binding offset. The distance that the margin is increased by on the side of the page to be bound.

Binding offset command. WordPerfect's command that shifts the text to the right on odd-numbered right-hand pages and to the left on even-numbered left-hand pages.

Bit-mapped fonts. Fonts with characters stored as a pattern of dots which can only be printed in one size.

Bit-mapped graphics. Graphics stored as a pattern of dots, each of which is called a pixel (for picture element).

Blind folio. A page number that is counted, but that doesn't print on the page.

Block-style paragraphs. Paragraphs that are separated from those above or below by extra spacing but that don't have paragraph indents.

Board. *See* Mechanical.

Body type. Typefaces that are easy to read and that work well for large blocks of text.

Broadside. A page printed in landscape mode.

C

Camera-ready copy. *See* Mechanical.

Carding. Adding extra space between lines to lengthen short pages.

Case binding. A binding where the signatures of the book are gathered together and then sewn or glued together at the spine. This unit is then bound to a hard cover with endpapers and a strip of gauze that is sandwiched between the two.

Cathode ray tube (*CRT*). A display tube like those used in television sets.

Cells. The intersections of rows and columns in a table.

Central processing unit (*CPU*). The device in the computer that runs all of your programs and that processes all of your data.

Character mode. A display that creates images from a fixed set of characters.

Character set. The characters in a computer, program, or printer that can be displayed or printed.

Charts. Line drawings that illustrate such things as the structure of organizations.

Clock rate. The speed at which the microprocessor processes data.

Color graphics adapter (*CGA*). A mode that displays 320-by-200 resolution.

Column heads. Labels that identify the contents of the columns in a table.

Comp. *See* Layout.

Concordance file. A list of words that will be automatically listed in an index.

Continuous tone copy. Art that contains a wide range of tones and gradations in tones. These tones range from light to dark in a series of unbroken steps.

Copy. The manuscript.

Copyrighted. Protected by law so it cannot be used without written permission.

Creation phase. The phase during which a document is written.

Crop marks. Marks used to guide the person trimming pages after printing.

Crop. Remove part of an image.

Cut-in head. A head that cuts across the columns in a table and describes all of the data below it.

D

Data transfer rate. The speed at which data are moved from a disk into the computer's memory.

Decimal tab stops. Tab stops used to align columns at the decimal point (or other specified character).

Decked table heads. Column headings with more than one level.

Descender. The part of some lowercase letters, such as g, p, q, and y, that protrude down.

Design. Specifying how a finished publication will look.

Design specs. Detailed specifications for each element in the document.

Designer. The person who prepares designs for publications.

Desktop publishing. Formatting documents with a microcomputer so they look likc thcy were set in type by a commercial typesetter.

Dingbats. Special characters that do not appear on the keyboard.

Display mode. The type of display your monitor is using.

Display type. Type that is larger than the body type used in displays and advertisements, and for title pages, chapter openers, and headlines in all kinds of publications.

Document description languages. *See* Page description languages.

Dot-matrix printer. A printer that uses a printhead containing pins, or wires, arranged in a column to print characters.

Double clicking. Quickly pressing a mouse button twice to make a selection.

Double indent. Text that is indented from both the left and right margins.

Downloadable fonts. Fonts stored on disks, which you load into the printer when you need them.

Drag. To move an item on the screen to a new position my holding down a mouse button while moving the mouse.

Drop cap. When the first character in a paragraph is set in a larger type size so it extends below the line.

Drop folios. Page numbers that are printed on the bottom of the page.

Drop shadows. Darker lines on two sides of a box that look like a shadow cast by the box.

Dropped-out text. Light text printed against a dark background. Also called reverse text.

Dummy. A preliminary pasteup to find the best arrangement of the elements in a heavily illustrated publication or one with a complicated design.

Duplex printer. A printer that prints both sides of a sheet in a single pass.

E

Edition Binding. *See* Case binding.

Em. A unit of measure that is as wide as the point size of the type being used. The em's name comes from the fact that it is approximately the size of an uppercase letter *M*.

En. A unit of measure that is one-half the width of an em, or the size of an uppercase letter *N* in the font you are using.

Endnotes. Like footnotes, but instead of printing at the bottom of the page with the matching reference number, they are printed at the end of a section, or at the end of the document.

Enhanced color graphics adapters (*EGA*). A display mode that displays 640-by-350 resolution.

Enumerations. Numbered lists.

Expressed folio. When a page is counted and a page number is printed on it.

Extended graphics array (*XGA*). A display mode that displays 1024-by-768 resolution.

F

Feathering. See carding.

File compression. A procedure that stores files in much less space on the disk than they normally require.

Film. Negatives used to make printing plates.

Flush left. *See* Left aligned.

Flush right. *See* Right aligned.

Folded and gathereds. The folded and collated signatures for a publication.

Folios. Page numbers.

Font appearance. WordPerfect's term for what others call typestyle.

Footers. Text printed at the bottom of the type page. *See also* Headers.

Footnotes. Numbered text printed at the bottom of the page on which a matching reference number appears in the body text.

Full measure. When a line of text is set so that it runs the entire width of the type page.

G

Galley proofs. Printed proofs that show how each element is formatted but that have not yet been broken into final pages.

Gathered. Sequenced signatures for a publication.

Graphical user interface (*GUI*). A screen display that has pull-down menus, icons, and scroll bars that make programs easier to operate.

Graphics mode. A display that creates images using pixels.

Graphics scanners. A scanner that scans graphics images such as photographs, line drawings, charts, and maps into the computer.

Gray scale. The spectrum of gray tones in an image.

Gray-scale monitors. Monitors that simulate colors with shades of gray.

Greeked. Text on the screen that is simulated with symbols that indicate where text appears on the page.

Grid. A grid establishes those characteristics that will be the same throughout the publication and includes the paper size, orientation, margins and type page, and the number and width of columns.

Gutter. The space between columns.

Gutter Margin. The margin on the binding side of the page.

H

Halftone screen. A process used to photograph continuous tone copy to break it up into dots of varying sizes, large dots for dark areas and small dots for light ones.

Hanging indents. Paragraphs with the second and subsequent lines indented from the left margin more than the first line.

Hard hyphens. Words or phrases hyphenated with hard hyphens do not split. If the hyphenated phrase will not fit at the end of a line, the entire phrase wraps to the next line.

Hard spaces. Spaces between words that prevent them from splitting at the end of a line.

Headers. Text printed at the top of the type page. *See also* Footer.

Hyphen characters. Phrases hyphenated with hyphen characters split following the hyphen if the words fall at the end of a line but the hyphens print out regardless of where they fall on the line.

Hyphenation zone. An area to both the left and right of the right margin that determines the length of words that are candidates for hyphenation.

I

IBM character set. A set of 254 characters resident in most IBM PCs and compatibles and supported by many, but by no means all, printers and programs.

Indented paragraphs. Paragraphs that have the first line indented from the left margin more than the second and subsequent lines.

Initial base font. The default font for your documents.

Italic. A typefaces that is slanted. *See also* Oblique.)

J

Justified. Text that is aligned with both the left and right margins.

K

Kerning. Adjusting the spacing between specific pairs of letters such as *AV, AW, AY, Ta, Ky.*

L

Landscape mode. Rotating the image on a page 90 degrees so that it is printed along the length of the page.

Laser printers. A printer that uses a laser to "paint" an image unto a revolving drum. The image is then transferred to the paper with heat and pressure.

Layout (*n.*). A polished version of design sketches.

Lay out (*v.*). Arranging text and graphics on a page.

Leading. Space added between lines of type to separate them from one another. Specified in points.

Left aligned. Text aligned with the left margin but not the right.

Letterspacing. The space between letters in a word.

Lightface. The basic font in any typeface (also called a *normal* font).

Line copy. Art that contains only solids, lines, and text.

Line height. The term that WordPerfect uses for the distance from the baseline of one line to the baseline of the next.

Line spacing. WordPerfect's command to adjust the line height setting. Setting line spacing to 1 makes line spacing the same as the line height setting; setting line spacing to 2 doubles the line height; and so on.

List of styles. *See* Style sheets.

M

Macros. Stored keystrokes that you can replay to automate many repetitive commands.

Makeup. Creating a pasteup manually or electronically.

Manufacturing phase. The phase during which a document is printed for final distribution.

Margin Release command. The command that enters text to the left of the left margin.

Markup. Writing design specs on a manuscript to guide the typesetter or desktop publisher.

Master document. A document containing codes that refer to other documents on the disk so you can expand these documents onto the screen.

Measure. The width of the type page.

Mechanical. The final pasted-up document that is then photographed by a printer to create the negatives used in the plate-making process.

Microprocessor. The electronic device used as the central processing unit (CPU) in a microcomputer.

Mirrored margins. Margins widths that are the same on the inside and outside margins, not the left and right margins.

Monitors. The screen on which your computer data are displayed.

Monospaced fonts. Fonts with the same space allocated for each letter, whether a wide *w* or a narrow *i.*

Mouse. A handheld device that moves a pointer on the screen when the device is rolled across a surface such as a desktop.

Mouse pointer. An arrow or other element that moves on the screen when a mouse is rolled across a surface. It is used to point to text and menus items that you want to select.

Multi-sync monitor. A display monitor that can display any of the available display modes.

N

Newspaper-style columns. Columns where text flows from the bottom of one column to the top of the next.

O

Oblique. A variation of italic typefaces. This term is frequently used in place of the term *italic* when the typeface is sans serif.

Offset press. A printing press used by commercial printers.

On-line editing. Editing document files using microcomputers.

Open codes. Formatting codes that affect all text to the end of the document or to the next code of the same kind.

Operators. Symbols that specify mathematical operations such as addition (+) or subtraction (-).

Optical character recognition (OCR). Using software to convert printed text to electronic form.

Orphan. The first line of a paragraph that prints by itself at the bottom of a page or column.

Outline fonts. *See* Scalable fonts.

P

Page description languages. Programs built into laser printers that allow them to manipulate type and graphics on the page.

Page makeup. Creating a pasteup manually or electronically.

Paired codes. Formatting codes where one begins a format and another ends it.

Parallel columns. *See* Parallel-style columns.

Parallel-style columns. Columns that align related text side by side.

Pasteup. All elements arranged on the page before printing.

PCL 5. Hewlett-Packard's document description language.

Penalty copy. Copy that is the most difficult to set.

Perfect binding. A binding where the binding edge is trimmed and covered with a flexible glue. A cover is then wrapped around the book and the glue holds it and the pages together.

Pica em. A special type of em which is always 12 points square.

Pica rule. A ruler that gives measurements in inches, picas, and points.

Picas. Units used to specify layout measurements such as the width and depth of type pages or columns. A pica contains exactly 12 points and there are 6 picas to the inch in WordPerfect. *See also* Points.

Pixels. The dots (or picture elements) into which a graphics screen is divided.

Plastic comb bindings. Bindings that use a plastic tubular device with protruding rings to hold pages together. The plastic comb fits through rectangular holes punched through the binding edge of the document.

Point. To indicate a selection by using a mouse to move the mouse pointer on the screen.

Point system. Adopted in 1878 as a standard system for measuring type.

Points. Units used to specify measurements that relate to type sizes and spacings. A point is equal to 0.013837 inches (about 1/72 inch). There are 12 points in a pica. *See also* Picas.

Portrait mode. The orientation of a normal document, that is, text is printed across the width of the page.

PostScript. Adobe System's document description language.

Primary leading. WordPerfect's term for extra leading added to lines within paragraphs.

Production phase. The phase during which a manuscript is prepared for the printer.

Production editor. A person who performs all of the production tasks or oversees and coordinates other specialists who perform them.

Proofreader's marks. Special symbols and terms used to indicate changes on manuscripts or proofs.

Proportion scale. A device used to calculate reductions and enlargements of artwork.

Proportional spacing. The space allocated to each character depends on its width. Therefore, a *w* is given more space than an *i*.

Pull-quotes. Short extracts from the text that are repeated, frequently in larger type or boldface type, and set off from the other text with rules or a box.

R

Ragged-left margin. The left margin on text that is aligned flush with the right margin but not with the left.

Ragged-right margin. The right margin on text that is aligned flush with the left margin but not with the right.

Random-access memory (*RAM*). Where programs or data are stored in the computer while you are using them.

Raster printers. Printers that form characters using an array of dots.

Relative tab stops. Tab stops that shift if you change the left margin so they always stay the same distance from the margin.

Reproduction proofs. A set of the galleys printed on special high-quality paper that provides a very sharp image. These (called *repros*) are then used in preparing the mechanicals, with all illustrations in place and page numbers added.

Resolution. The sharpness of an image on the screen or when printed.

Right aligned. Text aligned with the right margin but not the left.

Ring binders. Binders with rings that fit through holes punched in sheets of paper.

River. Large white spaces that may appear on several adjacent lines where text is not hyphenated.

Roman. Typefaces that are upright.

Run-around. Text that flows around a graphic.

Run-in head. A subhead where the first word, phrase, or sentence in a paragraph is highlighted, usually in italics or bold followed by a period or extra space, so it stands out.

Running footers. Text printed at the bottom of two or more sequential pages.

Running headers. Text printed at the top of two or more sequential pages.

Runover lines. *See* Turnovers.

S

Saddle stitching. A binding where the document is stapled in the gutter fold.

Sans serif typefaces. Typefaces that do not have the decorative cross marks at the end of main strokes (*sans* is French for *without*). *See also* Serif typefaces.

Scalable fonts. Characters created when needed by formulas stored in the computer or printer. These fonts allow a wide range of sizes while requiring very little space on the disk or in a printer's memory.

Scaling angles. A device used to calculate enlargements and reductions of artwork.

Scaling. Specifying the size at which you want a graphic to print.

Scanners. Devices that allow you to enter text and graphics into the computer from hard copy such as printed or typed documents, photographs, or line drawings.

Secondary leading. WordPerfect's term for extra leading added to the end of paragraphs.

Serif typefaces. Typefaces with serifs that finish off the main strokes of a letter. The most common serif typeface is Times Roman. *See also* Sans serif typefaces.

Serifs. Cross marks that finish off the main strokes of a letter.

Service bureaus. Firms that provide you with help with desktop publishing, either to make the job easier for you, or to improve its quality.

Set solid. Lines set with no leading.

Set. Typesetting a manuscript.

Short pages. Pages that are shorter than called for in the design.

Side heads. Headings and subheadings in one column with body text in another.

Side stitching. A binding where the edge of the document is stapled.

Sidebars. Sections of text related to but not included in the body text that are sometimes set off by being enclosed in a box.

Signatures. The printed and folded sheets for a book or manual.

Sinkage. The distance from the top of the type page to the first line of the text.

Small caps. Uppercase letters that are approximately the size of the lowercase letters in the font that they accompany.

Snaking columns. *See* Newspaper-style columns

Soft hyphens. Phrases hyphenated with hyphen characters split following the hyphen if the words fall at the end of a line but the hyphens are displayed on the Edit screen, and print out, only when they fall in the hyphenation zone.

Solidus. The slash (/).

Spanner heads. Column headings in a table that span two or more column heads.

Spine. The back of the book, the part that shows when it is on a bookshelf.

Spiral bindings. Bindings that use a continuous wire spiral wound through small round holes punched in the edge of the document.

Statistical table. A table that contains primarily numbers.

Stickup cap. When the first character in a paragraph is set in a larger type size so it extends above the line.

Straight copy. Copy that is free of tables and other complex elements.

Stub. The leftmost column in the table that contains labels explaining the contents of the other columns on their rows.

Style library. WordPerfect's default list of styles.

Style sheets. A list of defined styles from which you can select.

Subdocuments. Documents that are referred to by codes in a master document.

Subscripts. Characters that print partially below the x-height of type.

Superscripts. Characters that print partially above the x-height of the line of type.

Symbols. Characters that do not appear on the keyboard.

T

Table body. The part of a table that contains the data that are identified by the labels used for stubs and column heads.

Table identification. The table number and title and an optional table subhead.

Text tables. *See* Parallel columns.

Thumbnails. Rough sketches used in the design process that show how various elements might be arranged on the page.

Tracking. Adjusting the space between letters and words. Tracking is different from kerning because it affects all characters.

Trim size. The size of the finished pages after folding and trimming.

Turnovers. The second and subsequent lines of type.

Two-page spreads. The visual unit in a bound publication when two pages are displayed side by side.

Type gauge. A gauge with slots for a range of point sizes. You find the slot where the markings line up with the baselines of each line of type and read off the size listed at the top of the slot. Subtract the type size to arrive at the leading used in the document.

Type page. The total area on a page that contains type, including running heads, text, drop folios. Also called type area.

Type size. The size of the printed character specified in points. The size is measured vertically, usually from the top of the type's ascenders to the bottom of descenders.

Typeface. A type's particular design, for example, distinctive proportions and thicknesses of lines that make them unique.

Typeface family. All of the styles related to a specific typeface.

Typemarking. Annotating a manuscript so a commercial typesetter or a desktop publisher knows how to format each element. *See also* Markup.

Typesetter. A person who sets type.

Typestyles. Variations in typefaces based on their case, slant, thickness, or width. Includes boldface, italics, and normal.

V

Vector graphics. Images stored as mathematical formulas.

VeloBind. Bindings with pins on a binding strip that fit through holes punched in the document and then into another strip with slots. A tool is then used to snap the pins into the slots, binding the document together.

Velox. A print made of a halftone screened piece of art.

Video graphics array (*VGA*). A display mode that displays 640-by-480 resolution in 16 colors and 320-by-200 resolution in 256 colors.

Virtual memory. Memory on a hard disk that is treated by the computer as if it were RAM.

Volatile memory. Memory that loses its programs or data when the power is turned off.

W

White space. Empty space around or within the type page.

Widow. The last line of a paragraph that prints by itself at the top of a page or column. Also, a short line (one word or one syllable) printing at the end of a paragraph.

Wire-o bindings. Bindings that use rings parallel to each other so pages open more easily.

Wrap around. *See* Run-around.

WYSIWYG. Pronounced "whizzy-wig" and stands for "what you see is what you get." You see on the screen exactly what your document will look like when you print it out.

X

X-height. The height of lowercase letters, not including their ascenders and descenders.

Now even dot matrix printer users can do amazing things with Bitstream type.

Introducing Bitstream FaceLift 1.5 for WordPerfect, the type utility for dot matrix, HP LaserJet, HP DeskJet and ink jet printer users.

Use any of the 756 ITC Zapf Dingbats, symbols and other Bitstream International Characters that come with FaceLift for WordPerfect, and you'll wonder how you ever managed without them.

The impact of your documents will take a giant leap forward when you use FaceLift for WordPerfect with 16 Bitstream scalable typefaces.

Now it's easier than ever to use top-quality type to create fabulous-looking documents.

Introducing the newest version of FaceLift™ for WordPerfect® 5.0/5.1 and LetterPerfect.® FaceLift lets you instantly get award-winning Bitstream® type in 2-500 point sizes from dot matrix,* HP LaserJet (and compatible), HP DeskJet,® Canon BubbleJet,® and IBM ExecJet® printers.

You can install FaceLift in a mere 10 minutes. Then, to use your Bitstream type, simply hit "Ctrl-F8", select the typefaces and sizes you want, and just print.

You'll get FaceLift with 16 Bitstream scalable typefaces, including popular faces to make your headings and text leap off the page. Plus you'll get ITC Zapf Dingbats and symbols to add flair and professionalism to all your documents.

And here's more good news: FaceLift and 16 Bitstream scalable typefaces will use just a fraction of your hard disk space.

Your 16 Bitstream typefaces will include:

Swiss™ 721 Roman
Swiss 721 Italic
Swiss 721 Bold
Swiss 721 Bold Italic

Dutch™ 801 Roman
Dutch 801 Italic
Dutch 801 Bold
Dutch 801 Bold Italic

Monospace 821

Bitstream Cooper Black

Formal Script 421

Park Avenue™ **Brush Script**™

ITC Zapf Dingbats®

Symbols Monospaced

Symbols Proportional

A Special Offer for Students!

Now you can get Bitstream FaceLift for WordPerfect—including 16 great typefaces—for only...

$59!

That's a $99 retail value at a price that won't fail you. For extra credit value, get the Companion Value Pack—*including 24 additional typefaces*—for only $199! That will give you the power of FaceLift plus 40 typefaces—an instant professional type collection for one great price.

These offers are good until December 31, 1992. To order, call Bitstream at

1-800-522-FONT

PICAS

0 1 2 3 4 5 6 7 8 9 10 11 12 13 14 15 16 17 18 19 20 21 22 23 24 25 26 27 28 29 30 31 32 33 34 35 36 37 38 39 40 41 42 43 44 45 46 47 48

Desktop Publishing with WordPerfect® 5.1, by Dennis P. Curtin

Prentice Hall, Inc.

Hairline
.5 point
1 point
2 point
4 point
6 point

POINTS

0 20 40 60 80 100 120 140 160 180 200 220 240 260 280 300 320 340 360 380 400 420 440 460 480 500 520 540 560 580

10 30 50 70 90 110 130 150 170 190 210 230 250 270 290 310 330 350 370 390 410 430 450 470 490 510 530 550 570